Scotlar

GW00370513

HOTELS AND GUEST HOUSES 2009

A castle hotel in the Highlands

Published by VisitScotland, 2008   Photography Paul Tomkins / VisitScotland / Scottish Viewpoint / Alistair Firth / Kelburn Castle / Joan Stewart / Iain Sarjeant / Nae Limits / Laurie Campbell / Hazel Marr

visitscotland.com 0845 22 55 121

Loch Awe and Kilchurn Castle, Argyll

WELCOME TO SCOTLAND

Once you've enjoyed a holiday in Scotland, it is easy to see why so many people from all over the world visit time and again. Scotland is a wonderful place for holidaymakers. From the briefest of breaks to annual vacations, Scotland has so much to offer that you'll never run out of options.

Flick through the pages of this guide and you'll immediately get a flavour of Scotland's diversity. You'll discover an inspiring array of fascinating places, each with its own unique attractions.

The best small country in the world

Though it's a relatively small country, Scotland is remarkably varied. You can climb mountains in the morning and still be on the beach in the afternoon. You can canoe across a remote loch and never see another soul all day long or you can sip coffee in a city centre pavement café and watch the whole world go by. You can get dressed up to the nines and go to a world premier on a balmy summer's evening or you can join in with some traditional music round a welcoming log fire in a quaint little pub on a cold winter's night.

Because of its remarkable diversity, Scotland is a world-class holiday destination all year round. There's always something on the go, and when you get to where you're going, you'll be spoiled for choice for somewhere to stay.

To find out more, call 0845 22 55 121 or go to visitscotland.com

A room with a view

From quiet country house hotels, to small family establishments to celebrated luxury resorts that are famed throughout the world, Scotland has everything the discerning traveller could ever want – and some of the most picturesque locations.

All over the country, you'll find that Scotland's hotel and guesthouse trade is booming and there will always be something to suit your taste and budget. So you can stay in a grand traditional hotel with four poster beds and every luxury you could imagine or you could select a family-friendly establishment that's as comfortable on your pocket as it is for a good night's sleep.

From five-star luxury to something a little more modest, there's loads of choice. You'll find inspirational, ultra-chic boutique hotels and cosy guesthouses where you can really get to know your hosts. There are even places where the hotel itself is an attraction with spas and leisure complexes, golf courses, swimming pools and other sporting facilities.

A warm welcome awaits

When you've found the ideal place, you can look forward to a rousing welcome in a country that is renowned for its hospitality. Nobody loves a good time like the Scots. Whether it's bringing in the New Year with a wee dram, swirling your partner at a ceilidh or enjoying a sumptuous dinner for two in an exclusive restaurant with a stunning view, unforgettable experiences are never far away.

There's always the likelihood too that you'll meet some great folk – locals and visitors alike – some of whom could well become friends for life. That's all just part of a visit to Scotland.

As they say in the Gaelic tongue, *ceud mille failte* – 'a hundred thousand welcomes'. Come and enjoy our beautiful country.

A view towards Edinburgh Castle from Holyrood Park

Join the Homecoming Scotland celebrations throughout 2009

HOMECOMING 2009

Join us in 2009 when Scotland will host its first ever Homecoming year which has been created and timed to mark the 250th anniversary of the birth of Scotland's national poet, the international cultural icon Robert Burns. From Burns Night to St Andrew's Day 2009 a country-wide programme of exciting and inspirational Homecoming events and activities will celebrate some of Scotland's great contributions to the world: Burns himself, Whisky, Golf, Great Scottish Minds and Innovations and our rich culture and heritage which lives on at home and through our global family. The best small country in the world.

From Orkney to Aberdeen, from Oban to the Scottish Borders, there will be a packed calendar of over 200 events and activities to choose from.

Here's a taste of what's on next year:

January 2009

Heralded by Scotland's internationally renowned Hogmanay Celebrations, the Homecoming Scotland 2009 programme will officially kick off on the weekend of Robert Burns' 250th anniversary (24-25 January) with a programme of high profile Burns events planned in key locations across Scotland.

To find out more, call 0845 22 55 121 or go to visitscotland.com

Spring 2009

May is Whisky Month with an invitation extended to come to the Home of Whisky to explore and appreciate the expertise of the stillsmen and master blenders whose diligence has created one of Scotland's biggest exports and extensions of its culture. Kicking off at the biggest ever Spirit of Speyside Whisky Festival (1-10 May), the distilleries open their doors to visitors and locals alike. From a tasting session at The Scotch Whisky Experience in Edinburgh to a 3 day whisky course in Fife, there are a range of ways to sample Scotland's national tipple. New for 2009, The Spirit of the West event (16-17 May) in the beautiful surroundings of Inveraray Castle will provide a showcase for the 16 distilleries that make up the Whisky Coast. The month concludes with Feis Ile, Islay's Annual Malt and Music Festival.

Summer 2009

Over the summer months, Homecoming Scotland 2009 will present some brand new and enhanced major international events: The Gathering 2009 in Edinburgh (25-26 July) has been created especially for the Homecoming year to celebrate the contribution that Scottish clans have made to the history and culture of the world, whilst some of Scotland's stellar international events including The Edinburgh International Festival, The Edinburgh Military Tattoo, The Edinburgh International Book Festival and The Open Golf Championship will be celebrating the year with special Homecoming activity.

Autumn 2009

In October the Highlands will present a fortnight long festival (15-30 October, provisional dates) celebrating the best of traditional Highland Culture. Built around a major international conference exploring Scotland's Global Impact, regional and fringe events will take place across the region.

Closing Celebrations

In November around St Andrew's Day and as a sensational finale to the year, Homecoming Scotland will present a major celebration of Scottish Music (28-30 November, across Scotland). From traditional Scottish folk heroes to the cutting edge of contemporary Scottish bands currently making their mark internationally, expect a truly unique St Andrews Day celebration.

2009 is a special year for Scots and for those who love Scotland.

Look out for Homecoming events throughout this guide.

Go to homecomingscotland2009.com to find out more about all the different events.

Enjoy a dram in May, Homecoming Scotland's Whisky month

Top left: Two Hillwalkers take in the view from Sgurr A Ghreadaidh on the Black Cuillin Ridge towards Loch Curuisk, Isle of Skye.
Top right: A puffin perches on a cliff edge, the Treshnish Isles, Inner Hebrides. Above: Sandy beach near Durness, Sutherland.

DON'T MISS

Walking

From the rolling hills in the south to the mountainous north, Scotland is perfect for walkers - whether it's a gentle stroll with the kids or a serious trek through the wilderness.

Beaches

Scotland's beaches are something special whether it's for a romantic stroll, or to try some surfing. Explore Fife's Blue Flag beaches or the breathtaking stretches of sand in the Outer Hebrides.

Wildlife

From dolphins in the Moray Firth to capercaillie in the Highlands and seals and puffins on the coastline, you never know what you might spot.

Culture & Heritage

From the mysterious standing stones in Orkney and the Outer Hebrides to Burns Cottage and Rosslyn Chapel, Scotland's fascinating history can be encountered throughout the country.

Rosslyn Chapel, Roslin, Midlothian

To find out more, call 0845 22 55 121 or go to visitscotland.com

Adventure

From rock climbing to sea kayaking, you can do it all. Try Perthshire for unusual adventure activities or the south of Scotland for some serious mountain biking.

Kayaking around the island of Vatersay, Outer Hebrides

Shopping

From designer stores to unique boutiques, from Glasgow's stylish city centre to Edinburgh's eclectic Old Town, Scotland is a shopper's paradise with lots of hidden gems to uncover.

Victoria Street, Edinburgh.

Golf

The country that gave the world the game of golf is still the best place to play it. With more than 500 courses in Scotland, take advantage of one of the regional golf passes on offer.

The Golf Course at Cruden Bay, Aberdeenshire.

Castles

Wherever you are in Scotland you are never far from a great Scottish icon, whether it's an impressive ruin or an imposing fortress, a fairytale castle or country estate.

Eilean Donan Castle, Loch Duich, Highlands.

Highland Games

From the famous Braemar Gathering in Aberdeenshire to the spectacular Cowal Highland Gathering in Argyll, hot foot it to some Highland Games action for pipe bands, dancers, and tossing the caber.

The sword dance at the Cowal Highland Gathering, Dunoon

Events & Festivals

In Scotland there's so much going on with fabulous events and festivals throughout the year, from the biggest names to the quirky and traditional.

The Royal Mile during the Festival, Edinburgh

If you love food, get a taste of Scotland. Scotland's natural larder offers some of the best produce in the world. Scotland's coastal waters are home to an abundance of lobster, prawns, oysters and more, whilst the land produces world famous beef, lamb and game.

There's high quality food and drink on menus all over the country often cooked up by award-winning chefs in restaurants where the view is second to none. You'll find home cooking, fine dining, takeaways and tearooms. Whether you're looking for a family-friendly pub or a romantic Highland restaurant there's the perfect place to dine. And there's no better time to indulge than when you're on holiday!

Traditional fare

Haggis and whisky might be recognised as traditional Scottish fare but why not add cullen skink, clapshot, cranachan, and clootie dumpling to the list…discover the tastes that match such ancient names. Sample some local hospitality along with regional specialities such as the Selkirk Bannock or Arbroath Smokies. Or experience the freedom of eating fish and chips straight from the wrapper while breathing in the clear evening air. Visit **eatscotland.com** and see our 'Food & Drink' section to find out more.

Farmers' markets

Scotland is a land renowned for producing ingredients of the highest quality. You can handpick fresh local produce at farmers' markets in towns and cities across the country. Create your own culinary delights or learn from the masters at the world famous Nick Nairn Cook School in Stirling. Savour the aroma, excite your taste buds and experience the buzz of a farmers' market. To find out more visit the Farmers Market information on the **eatscotland.com** website that can be found in the 'Food & Drink' section.

Live it. Visit Scotland.
eatscotland.com 0845 22 55 121

EATING AND DRINKING

Events

Scotland serves up a full calendar of food and drink festivals. Events like Taste of Edinburgh and Highland Feast are a must for foodies. Whisky fans can share their passion at the Islay Malt Whisky Festival, the Highland Whisky Festival, or the Spirit of Speyside Whisky Festival. Visit **eatscotland.com** to find out more about the events and festivals that are on in the 'What's on' section.

Tours and trails

If you're a lover of seafood spend some time exploring the rugged, unspoilt coastline of mid-Argyll following The Seafood Trail. Or if you fancy a wee dram visit the eight distilleries and cooperage on the world's only Malt Whisky Trail in Speyside. Visit visitscotland.com/cafedays to find out more about some great cafés that our visitors have discovered and enjoy a cup of something lovely surrounded by amazing scenery.

EatScotland Quality Assurance Scheme

EatScotland is a nationwide Quality Assurance Scheme from VisitScotland. The scheme includes all sectors of the catering industry from chip shops, pubs and takeaways to restaurants.

A trained team of assessors carry out an incognito visit to assess quality, standards and ambience. Only those operators who meet the EatScotland quality standards are accredited to the scheme so look out for the logo to ensure you visit Scotland's best quality establishments.

The newly launched EatScotland Silver and Gold Award Scheme recognises outstanding standards, reflecting that an establishment offers an excellent eating out experience in Scotland.

To find great EatScotland places to dine throughout the country visit **eatscotland.com**

Beach at Elie in Fife

GREEN TOURISM

Scotland is a stunning destination and we want to make sure it stays that way. That's why we encourage all tourism operators including accommodation providers to take part in our Green Tourism Business Scheme. It means you're assured of a great quality stay at an establishment that's trying to minimise its impact on the environment.

VisitScotland rigorously assesses accommodation providers against measures as diverse as energy use, using local produce on menus, or promoting local wildlife walks or cycle hire. Environmentally responsible businesses can achieve Bronze, Silver or Gold awards, to acknowledge how much they are doing to help conserve the quality of Scotland's beautiful environment.

Look out for the Bronze, Silver and Gold Green Tourism logos throughout this guide to help you decide where to stay and do your bit to help protect our environment.

For a quick reference see our directory at the back of the book which highlights all quality assured accommodation that has been awarded with the Gold, Silver or Bronze award.

green-business.co.uk

Bronze Green Tourism Award

SilverGreen Tourism Award

GoldGreen Tourism Award

Friendly faces... a wealth of helpful advice... loads of local knowledge... get the most out of your stay...

Visitor Information Centres are staffed by people 'in the know', offering friendly advice, helping to make your stay in Scotland the most enjoyable ever... whatever your needs!

LOCAL KNOWLEDGE • WHERE TO STAY • ACCOMMODATION BOOKING PLACES TO VISIT THINGS TO DO • MAPS AND GUIDES TRAVEL ADVICE • ROUTE PLANNING • WHERE TO SHOP AND EAT LOCAL CRAFTS AND PRODUCE • EVENT INFORMATION • TICKETS

Live it. Visit *Scotland.*
visitscotland.com/wheretofindus

To find out more, call 0845 22 55 121 or go to visitscotland.com

VisitScotland, under the Scottish Tourist Board brand, administers the 5-star grading schemes which assess the quality and standards of all types of visitor accommodation and attractions from castles and historic houses to garden centres and arts venues. We grade around 80 per cent of the accommodation in Scotland and 90 per cent of the visitor attractions – so wherever you want to stay or visit, we've got it covered. The schemes are monitored all year round each establishment is reviewed once a year. We do the hard work so you can relax and enjoy your holiday.

The promise of the stars:

★
It is clean, tidy and an acceptable, if basic, standard

★★
It is a good, all round standard

★★★
It is a very good standard, with attention to detail in every area

★★★★
It is excellent – using high quality materials, good food (except self-catering) and friendly, professional service

★★★★★
An exceptional standard where presentation, ambience, food (except self-catering) and service are hard to fault.

IT'S WRITTEN IN THE STARS...

How does the system work?

Our advisors visit and assess establishments on up to 50 areas from quality, comfort and cleanliness to welcome, ambience and service. If an establishment scores less than 60 per cent it will not be graded. The same star scheme now runs in England and Wales, so you can follow the stars wherever you go.

Graded visitor attractions

Visitor attractions from castles and museums to leisure centres and tours are graded with 1-5 stars depending on their level of customer care. The focus is on the standard of hospitality and service as well as presentation, quality of shop or café (if there is one) and toilet facilities.

We want you to feel welcome

Walkers Welcome and Cyclists Welcome. Establishments that carry the symbols below pay particular attention to the specific needs of walkers and cyclists.

 Cyclists Welcome

 Walkers Welcome

There are similar schemes for Anglers, Bikers, Classic Cars, Golfers, Children and Ancestral Tourism. Check with establishment when booking.

Access all areas

The following symbols will help visitors with physical disabilities to decide whether accommodation is suitable. The directory at the back of this book will highlight all quality assured establishments that have suitable accommodation.

 Unassisted wheelchair access

 Assisted wheelchair access

 Access for visitors with mobility difficulties

Further information:
Quality Assurance (at VisitScotland)
Tel: 01463 244111
Fax: 01463 244181
Email: qainfo@visitscotland.com

We welcome your comments on star-awarded properties
Tel: 01463 244122
Fax: 01463 244181
Email: qa@visitscotland.com

The Glenfinnan Viaduct, near Fort William, Highlands

TRAVEL TO SCOTLAND

It's really easy to get to Scotland whether you choose to travel by car, train, plane, coach or ferry. And once you get here travel is easy as Scotland is a compact country.

By Air

Flying to Scotland couldn't be simpler with flight times from London, Dublin and Belfast only around one hour. There are airports at Edinburgh, Glasgow, Glasgow Prestwick, Aberdeen, Dundee and Inverness. The following airlines operate flights to Scotland (although not all airports) from within the UK and Ireland:

bmi
Tel: 0870 60 70 555
From Ireland: 1332 64 8181
flybmi.com

bmi baby
Tel: 0871 224 0224
From Ireland: 1 890 340 122
bmibaby.com

British Airways
Tel: 0844 493 0787
From Ireland:]890 626 747
ba.com

Eastern Airways
Tel: 08703 669 100
easternairways.com

easyJet
Tel: 0905 821 0905
From Ireland: 1890 923 922
easyjet.com

Flybe
Tel: 0871 700 2000
From Ireland: 1392 268 529
flybe.com

Ryanair
Tel: 0871 246 0000
From Ireland: 0818 30 30 30
ryanair.com

Air France
Tel: 0870 142 4343
airfrance.co.uk

Aer Arann
Tel: 0870 876 76 76
From Ireland: 0818 210 210
aerarann.com

Jet2
Tel: 0871 226 1737
From Ireland: 0818 200017
jet2.com

AirBerlin
Tel: 0871 5000 737
airberlin.com

Aer Lingus
Tel: 0870 876 5000
From Ireland: 0818 365 000
aerlingus.com

By Rail
Scotland has major rail stations in Aberdeen, Edinburgh Waverley and Edinburgh Haymarket, Glasgow Queen Street and Glasgow Central, Perth, Stirling, Dundee and Inverness. There are regular cross border railway services from England and Wales, and good city links. You could even travel on the First ScotRail Caledonian Sleeper overnight train service from London and wake up to the sights and sounds of Scotland.

First ScotRail
Tel: 08457 55 00 33
scotrail.co.uk

Virgin Trains
Tel: 08457 222 333
virgintrains.co.uk

**National Express
East Coast**
Tel: 08457 225 225
nationalexpresseastcoast.com

National Rail
Tel: 08457 484950
nationalrail.co.uk

By Road
Scotland has an excellent road network from motorways and dual carriageway linking cities and major towns, to remote single-track roads with passing places to let others by. Whether you are coming in your own car from home or hiring a car once you get here, getting away from traffic jams and out onto Scotland's quiet roads can really put the fun back into driving. Branches of the following companies can be found throughout Scotland:

Arnold Clark
Tel: 0845 607 4500
arnoldclarkrental.com

easyCar
Tel: 08710 500444
easycar.com

Hertz
Tel: 08708 44 88 44
hertz.co.uk

Avis Rent A Car
Tel: 08445 818 181
avis.co.uk

Enterprise Rent-A-Car
Tel: 0870 350 3000
enterprise.co.uk

National Car Rental
Tel: 0870 400 4560
nationalcar.com

Budget
Tel: 0845 581 9998
budget.co.uk

Europcar
Tel: 0870 607 5000
europcarscotland.co.uk

Sixt rent a car
Tel: 0844 499 3399
sixt.co.uk

By Ferry
Scotland has over 130 inhabited islands so ferries are important. And whether you are coming from Ireland or trying to get to the outer islands, you might be in need of a ferry crossing. Ferries to and around the islands are regular and reliable and most carry vehicles. These companies all operate ferry services around Scotland:

Stena Line
Tel: 08705 204 204
stenaline.co.uk

Caledonian MacBrayne
Tel: 08000 665000
calmac.co.uk

Northlink Ferries
Tel: 08456 000 449
northlinkferries.co.uk

P&O Irish Sea
Tel: 0870 24 24 777
poirishsea.com

Western Ferries
Tel: 01369 704 452
western-ferries.co.uk

By Coach
Coach connections include express services to Scotland from all over the UK, and there is a good network of coach services once you get here too. You could even travel on the Postbus – a special feature of the Scottish mail service which carries fare-paying passengers along with the mail in rural areas where there is no other form of transport, bringing a new dimension to travel.

National Express
Tel: 08705 80 80 80
nationalexpress.com

City Link
Tel: 08705 50 50 50
citylink.co.uk

Postbus
Tel: 08457 740 740
royalmail.com/postbus

DRIVING DISTANCES

Driving distances chart (each cell shows miles and kilometres). Cities listed along the diagonal: ABERDEEN, BIRMINGHAM, CARDIFF, DOVER, DUMFRIES, DUNDEE, EDINBURGH, FORT WILLIAM, GLASGOW, HARWICH, HULL, INVERNESS, KYLE OF LOCHALSH, LONDON, MANCHESTER, NEWCASTLE, OBAN, PERTH, PRESTWICK, ROSYTH, STIRLING, STRANRAER, THURSO, TROON, ULLAPOOL, YORK.

Each row lists distances (M = miles, KM = kilometres) from the origin city to the cities above-left of it.

ABERDEEN

BIRMINGHAM — Aberdeen 421 687

CARDIFF — Aberdeen 529 851 · Birmingham 113 182

DOVER — Aberdeen 617 993 · Birmingham 200 322 · Cardiff 224 361

DUMFRIES — Aberdeen 214 344 · Birmingham 234 376 · Cardiff 335 539 · Dover 436 700

DUNDEE — Aberdeen 71 114 · Birmingham 357 575 · Cardiff 465 749 · Dover 553 890 · Dumfries 149 240

EDINBURGH — Aberdeen 131 210 · Birmingham 290 467 · Cardiff 398 641 · Dover 486 782 · Dumfries 80 128 · Dundee 62 99

FORT WILLIAM — Aberdeen 161 258 · Birmingham 396 637 · Cardiff 504 811 · Dover 592 952 · Dumfries 179 288 · Dundee 123 197 · Edinburgh 138 221

GLASGOW — Aberdeen 152 243 · Birmingham 286 461 · Cardiff 394 634 · Dover 482 776 · Dumfries 76 122 · Dundee 84 134 · Edinburgh 45 72 · Fort William 108 173

HARWICH — Aberdeen 604 972 · Birmingham 187 300 · Cardiff 242 390 · Dover 130 210 · Dumfries 370 595 · Dundee 540 869 · Edinburgh 473 761 · Fort William 578 931 · Glasgow 469 754

HULL — Aberdeen 345 556 · Birmingham 137 221 · Cardiff 251 405 · Dover 255 411 · Dumfries 205 330 · Dundee 318 509 · Edinburgh 255 408 · Fort William 384 614 · Glasgow 275 440 · Harwich 214 346

INVERNESS — Aberdeen 118 189 · Birmingham 446 717 · Cardiff 553 890 · Dover 641 1032 · Dumfries 239 385 · Dundee 134 214 · Edinburgh 162 259 · Fort William 69 110 · Glasgow 178 285 · Harwich 628 1011 · Hull 209 337

KYLE OF LOCHALSH — Aberdeen 200 320 · Birmingham 469 755 · Cardiff 577 929 · Dover 665 1000 · Dumfries 253 407 · Dundee 179 286 · Edinburgh 207 331 · Fort William 76 122 · Glasgow 184 294 · Harwich 652 1049 · Hull 254 408 · Inverness 82 131

LONDON — Aberdeen 549 878 · Birmingham 118 190 · Cardiff 150 242 · Dover 75 122 · Dumfries 349 561 · Dundee 281 453 · Edinburgh 252 405 · Fort William 346 573 · Glasgow 216 348 · Harwich 78 126 · Hull 201 324 · Inverness 590 944 · Kyle of Lochalsh 573 917

MANCHESTER — Aberdeen 345 556 · Birmingham 93 150 · Cardiff 201 324 · Dover 281 453 · Dumfries 157 252 · Dundee 350 563 · Edinburgh 201 324 · Fort William 322 518 · Glasgow 211 340 · Harwich 267 427 · Hull 95 154 · Inverness 393 633 · Kyle of Lochalsh 370 595 · London 201 322

NEWCASTLE — Aberdeen 244 390 · Birmingham 208 336 · Cardiff 323 519 · Dover 350 563 · Dumfries 91 147 · Dundee 175 280 · Edinburgh 112 179 · Fort William 267 427 · Glasgow 159 254 · Harwich 309 498 · Hull 64 102 · Inverness 237 438 · Kyle of Lochalsh 274 274 · London 288 461 · Manchester 147 237

OBAN — Aberdeen 190 304 · Birmingham 385 620 · Cardiff 493 794 · Dover 581 935 · Dumfries 168 270 · Dundee 121 194 · Edinburgh 125 200 · Fort William 50 80 · Glasgow 96 154 · Harwich 568 914 · Hull 175 281 · Inverness 112 180 · Kyle of Lochalsh 125 200 · London 502 803 · Manchester 309 498 · Newcastle 310 496

PERTH — Aberdeen 86 139 · Birmingham 348 560 · Cardiff 449 723 · Dover 550 884 · Dumfries 92 149 · Dundee 21 34 · Edinburgh 43 69 · Fort William 104 166 · Glasgow 64 104 · Harwich 484 778 · Hull 183 294 · Inverness 114 183 · Kyle of Lochalsh 158 254 · London 463 744 · Manchester 271 436 · Newcastle 152 245 · Oban 94 151

PRESTWICK — Aberdeen 177 285 · Birmingham 304 489 · Cardiff 411 662 · Dover 500 804 · Dumfries 61 98 · Dundee 113 182 · Edinburgh 79 127 · Fort William 131 210 · Glasgow 32 52 · Harwich 486 783 · Hull 168 279 · Inverness 201 324 · Kyle of Lochalsh 204 329 · London 418 673 · Manchester 228 366 · Newcastle 168 271 · Oban 120 193 · Perth 96 155

ROSYTH — Aberdeen 115 185 · Birmingham 324 522 · Cardiff 425 684 · Dover 477 768 · Dumfries 61 98 · Dundee 48 77 · Edinburgh 14 23 · Fort William 124 200 · Glasgow 47 76 · Harwich 430 692 · Inverness 108 145 · Inverness 265 426 · Kyle of Lochalsh 233 145 · London 398 247 · Manchester 379 247 · Newcastle 123 198 · Oban 114 183 · Perth 31 49 · Prestwick 79 127

STIRLING — Aberdeen 120 193 · Birmingham 313 503 · Cardiff 414 666 · Dover 514 823 · Dumfries 55 89 · Dundee 38 61 · Edinburgh 23 · Fort William 97 157 · Glasgow 29 47 · Harwich 448 722 · Hull 141 284 · Inverness 87 145 · Kyle of Lochalsh 172 234 · London 427 688 · Manchester 236 379 · Newcastle 143 231 · Oban 87 140 · Perth 37 60 · Prestwick 61 99 · Rosyth 26 42

STRANRAER — Aberdeen 241 386 · Birmingham 297 478 · Cardiff 404 651 · Dover 489 787 · Dumfries 72 115 · Dundee 172 275 · Edinburgh 133 213 · Fort William 196 314 · Glasgow 89 142 · Harwich 475 765 · Hull 202 284 · Inverness 254 424 · Kyle of Lochalsh 265 358 · London 415 664 · Manchester 224 358 · Newcastle 161 259 · Oban 87 140 · Perth 149 240 · Prestwick 54 87 · Rosyth 131 211 · Stirling 114 611

THURSO — Aberdeen 234 374 · Birmingham 555 893 · Cardiff 663 1066 · Dover 750 1208 · Dumfries 348 560 · Dundee 250 400 · Edinburgh 278 445 · Fort William 183 293 · Glasgow 293 469 · Harwich 737 1186 · Hull 319 513 · Inverness 112 180 · Kyle of Lochalsh 177 283 · London 690 1104 · Manchester 499 798 · Newcastle 391 626 · Oban 233 373 · Perth 221 311 · Prestwick 355 500 · Rosyth 254 409 · Stirling 252 406 · Stranraer 382 183

TROON — Aberdeen 183 295 · Birmingham 314 505 · Cardiff 415 668 · Dover 516 830 · Dumfries 63 101 · Dundee 119 191 · Edinburgh 82 132 · Fort William 126 203 · Glasgow 35 56 · Harwich 450 724 · Hull 171 285 · Inverness 209 336 · Kyle of Lochalsh 200 322 · London 429 690 · Manchester 237 381 · Newcastle 171 276 · Oban 116 186 · Perth 101 162 · Prestwick 5 8 · Rosyth 80 129 · Stirling 63 101 · Stranraer 60 96 · Thurso 316 508

ULLAPOOL — Aberdeen 179 286 · Birmingham 499 803 · Cardiff 607 976 · Dover 695 1118 · Dumfries 293 472 · Dundee 238 381 · Edinburgh 190 355 · Fort William 119 190 · Glasgow 222 355 · Harwich 681 1097 · Hull 424 504 · Inverness 504 806 · Kyle of Lochalsh 171 285 · London 459 690 · Manchester 444 710 · Newcastle 335 536 · Oban 169 270 · Perth 168 270 · Prestwick 255 411 · Rosyth 199 320 · Stirling 199 320 · Stranraer 128 205 · Thurso 205 327 · Troon 263 423

YORK — Aberdeen 343 552 · Birmingham 132 212 · Cardiff 246 396 · Dover 273 439 · Dumfries 151 243 · Dundee 279 449 · Edinburgh 191 308 · Fort William 318 511 · Glasgow 208 335 · Harwich 233 374 · Hull 41 65 · Inverness 367 591 · Kyle of Lochalsh 391 630 · London 208 335 · Manchester 70 113 · Newcastle 90 146 · Oban 307 495 · Perth 237 382 · Prestwick 226 363 · Rosyth 212 341 · Stirling 230 370 · Stranraer 477 767 · Thurso 352 231 · Troon 218 · Ullapool 421 678

M KM

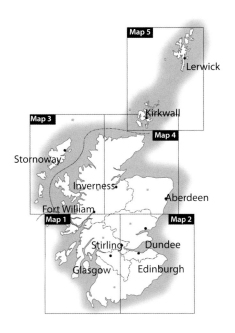

MAPS

MAP 1

A map of western Scotland and Northern Ireland showing advertised establishment locations. Labelled places include:

Row 1–2 area (Mull, Morvern): Coll, Arinagour, Calgary, Tobermory, Dervaig, Isle of Tiree, Kenovay, Scarinish, TIREE, Killiechronan, Aros, Lochaline, Salen, Fishnish, Lismore, Benderloch, North Connel, Barcaldine, Ardmaddy, Bridge of Orchy, Glencoe, Kentallen, Duror, Ballachulish, Appin, Glen Lyon, Rannoch Sta, Kinl, Rann, A828, A82

Mull / Oban area: MULL, IONA, Pennyghael, Craignure, Lochdon, Kinlochspelve, Lochbuie, Bunessan, Isle of Seil, Lerags, Oban, Kilmore, Kilninver, Kilchrenan, Inverawe, Taynuilt, Lochawe, Dalmally, Lochaweside, Kilninver, Tyndrum, Killin, Crianlarich, Lochearnhead, Balquhidder, A85, A82, A84

Row 3: Balvicar, Lochaweside, Arduaine, Kilmelford, Craobh Haven, Ardfern, Ford, Inveraray, Cairndow, St Catherines, Arrochar, Strachur, Rowardennan, Inveruglas, Brig O'Turk, Tarbet, Port of Menteith, Aberfoyle, Strathy, Trossa, Callander, Thornh, Kippe, Arnpri, A82, A83

Row 4 (Jura, Loch Fyne, Loch Lomond): COLONSAY, JURA, Crinan Loch, Minard, Carrick Castle, Inverbeg, Loch Eck, Luss, Inchmurrin, Drymen, Balfror, Fin, Scalasaig, Isle of Colonsay, Kilmartin, Crinan, Lochgilphead, Tayvallich, Achnamara, Ardrishaig, Otter Ferry, Glendaruel, Ardentinny, Blairmore, Kilmun, Clynder, Arden, Rhu, Cove, Helensburgh, Cardross, Gartocharn, Balloch, Dumbarton, Old Kilpatrick, A816, A811, Loch Lomond

Row 5: Sanaigmore, Port Askaig, Feolin, Craighouse, Tarbert, North Bute, Toward, Wemyss Bay, Skelmorlie, GLASGOW, ISLAY, Gruinart, Ballygrant, Rothesay, Ascog, Lochwinnoch, Paisley, Bruichladdich, Kennacraig, Skipness, Cumbrae, Largs, Bridgend, Bowmore, Clachan, Claonaig, Millport, Fairlie, Dalry, Barrmill, Dunlop, A8, M8, A78, A737

Row 6: Port Charlotte, Isle of Gigha, Ardminish, Lochranza, Ardrossan, Kilwinning, Kilmarnock, Galston, Portnahaven, Port Wemyss, Port Ellen, Tayinloan, Corrie, Kilnaughton Bay, BUTE, CUMBRAE, ARRAN, Carradale, Brodick, A737, A71, A76

Row 7: ATLANTIC OCEAN, Blackwaterfoot, Shiskine, Lamlash, Whiting Bay, Troon, Prestwick, Sliddery, Kilmory, Kildonan, Ayr, New Cumnoc, Machrihanish, Campbeltown, Dunure, Alloway, A70, A77, A713, Firth of Clyde, KINTYRE, A83

Row 8: Culzean, Maybole, Turnberry, Straiton, Girvan

Row 9: Ballycastle, Lendalfoot, Colmonell, Ballantrae, Glentrool, New Gallow, A26, A2

Row 10: Cairnryan, Newton Stewart, Gatehouse of Fleet, Stranraer, Glenluce, Creetown, Wigtown, Larne, Portpatrick, A75, A77, A6, A36, A8, A2

Row 11: Port Logan, Drummore, Port William, Glasserton, Whithorn, Isle of Whithorn, Borgu, Luce Bay, (P&O Irish Sea), (Stena Line)

Row 12: BELFAST, To Douglas, Isle of Man (Isle of Man Steam-Packet Company), To Birkenhead (Norfolk Line), A29, M1

Inset box: MAP 1, MAP 2

Locations shown indicate establishmnets that are advertised in our three Where to Stay guides, including Bed & Breakfast and Self Catering/Caravan & Camping. Please use a current road atlas for route planning and touring.

MAP 2

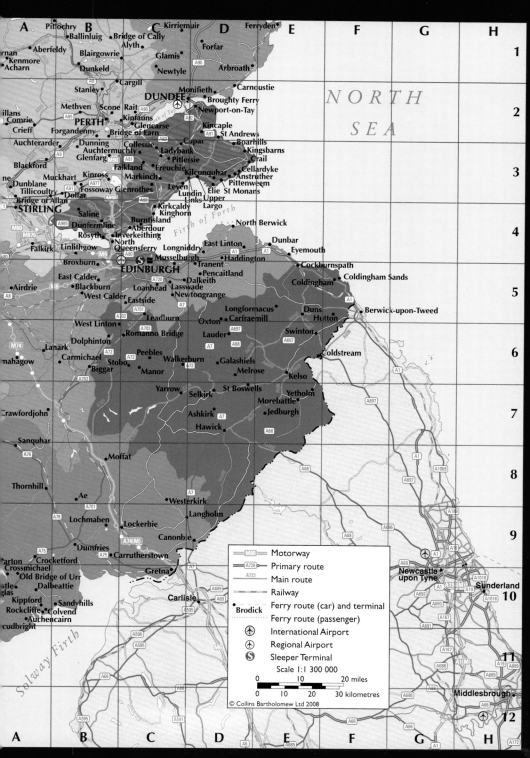

A Pitlochry · Kirriemuir · Ferryden · **NORTH SEA**

Ballinluig · Bridge of Cally · Forfar
Aberfeldy · Alyth
Kenmore · Blairgowrie · Glamis · Arbroath
Acharn · Dunkeld · Newtyle · A90
Stanley · Cargill · Carnoustie
illans · Methven · Scone · Rait · Monifieth · Broughty Ferry
Comrie · **PERTH** · Kinfauns · Newport-on-Tay
Crieff · Forgandenny · Bridge of Earn · Glencarse · Kincaple · St Andrews
Auchterarder · Dunning · Collessie · Cupar · Boarhills
Auchtermuchty · Ladybank · Kingsbarns
Blackford · Glenfarg · Pitlessie · Crail
Dunblane · Kinross · Markinch · Freuchie · Kilconquhar · Cellardyke
Muckhart · Falkland · Anstruther
Tillicoultry · Fossoway · Glenrothes · Leven · Pittenweem
Dollar · Lundin · Elie · St Monans
STIRLING · Saline · Upper · Largo
Kinghorn · Kirkcaldy
Dunfermline · Burntisland · North Berwick
Falkirk · Linlithgow · Aberdour · Inverkeithing
Rosyth · North Queensferry · Longniddry · East Linton · Dunbar
Broxburn · Musselburgh · Haddington · Eyemouth
East Calder · **EDINBURGH** · Tranent · Cockburnspath
Airdrie · Blackburn · Pencaitland · Coldingham · Coldingham Sands
West Calder · Dalkeith · Longformacus
Loanhead · Lasswade · Newtongrange · Duns · Berwick-upon-Tweed
Eastside · Leadburn · Oxton · Carfraemill · Hutton
West Linton · Swinton
Dolphinton · Romanno Bridge · Lauder · Coldstream
Lanark · Peebles · Walkerburn
Carmichael · Stobo · Manor · Galashiels · Kelso
Biggar · Yarrow · Melrose
Crawfordjohn · Selkirk · St Boswells · Yetholm
Ashkirk · Morebattle
Sanquhar · Hawick · Jedburgh
Moffat
Thornhill · Ae · Westerkirk
Lochmaben · Langholm
Dumfries · Lockerbie · Newcastle upon Tyne · Sunderland
Crocketford · Canonbie
Crossmichael · Carrutherstown
Old Bridge of Urr · Gretna
Dalbeattie · Carlisle · Middlesbrough
Kippford · Sandyhills
Rockcliffe · Colvend
Auchencairn
cudbright

Solway Firth · *Firth of Forth* · *Firth of Tay*

Legend

M80	Motorway
A726	Primary route
A723	Main route
	Railway
• Brodick	Ferry route (car) and terminal
	Ferry route (passenger)
✈	International Airport
✈	Regional Airport
Ⓢ	Sleeper Terminal

Scale 1:1 300 000

0   10   20 miles

0   10   20   30 kilometres

© Collins Bartholomew Ltd 2008

MAP 3

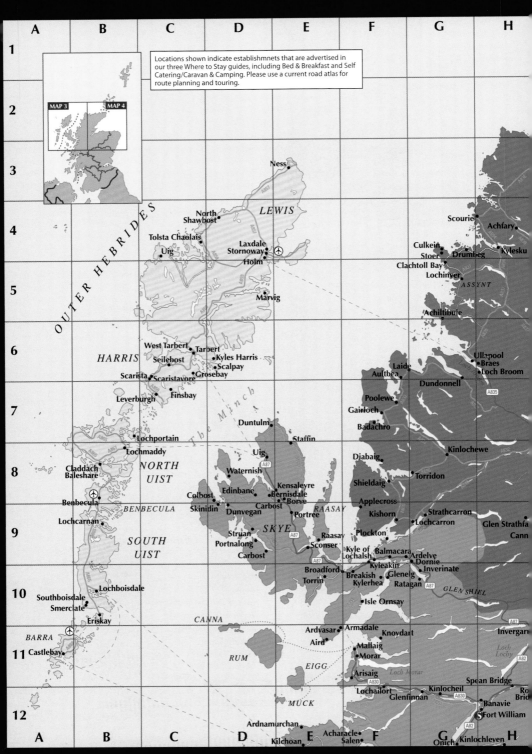

Locations shown indicate establishmnets that are advertised in our three Where to Stay guides, including Bed & Breakfast and Self Catering/Caravan & Camping. Please use a current road atlas for route planning and touring.

MAP 3 MAP 4

OUTER HEBRIDES

LEWIS
Ness
North Shawbost
Tolsta Chaolais
Uig
Laxdale
Stornoway
Holm
Marvig

HARRIS
West Tarbert
Tarbert
Seilebost
Kyles Harris
Scalpay
Scarista
Scaristavore
Grosebay
Leverburgh
Finsbay

Lochportain
Lochmaddy
NORTH UIST
Claddach
Baleshare
Benbecula
BENBECULA
Lochcarnan
SOUTH UIST

Southboisdale
Smerclate
Lochboisdale
Eriskay

BARRA
Castlebay

The Minch

Duntulm
Uig
Waternish
Staffin
Colbost
Edinbane
Kensaleyre
Bernisdale
Skinidin
Carbost
Borve
Dunvegan
Portree
RAASAY
Struan
Raasay
Portnalong
Sconser
Carbost
SKYE
Kyle of
Lochalsh
Broadford
Torrin
Breakish
Kylerhea
Isle Ornsay

CANNA

RUM

EIGG

MUCK

Ardvasar
Aird
Armadale
Knoydart
Mallaig
Morar
Arisaig
Lochailort
Glenfinnan

Ardnamurchan
Kilchoan
Acharacle
Salen

Scourie
Achfary
Culkein
Stoer
Drumbeg
Kylesku
Clachtoll Bay
Lochinver
ASSYNT
Achiltibuie

Ullapool
Braes
Loch Broom
Laide
Aultbea
Dundonnell
Poolewe
Gairloch
Badachro
Kinlochewe
Djabaig
Shieldaig
Torridon
Applecross
Kishorn
Strathcarron
Plockton
Lochcarron
Glen Strathfa
Cann
Balmacara
Ardelve
Dornie
Glenelg
Inverinate
Ratagan
GLEN SHIEL

Invergar

Loch
Lochy

Loch Morar
Kinlocheil
Spean Bridge
Ro
Brid
Banavie
Fort William
Onich
Kinlochleven

A B C D E F G H

ORKNEY

Stromness
Orphir
Hoy
Scapa Flow
Tankerness
Holm
St Mary's Holm
St Margaret's Hope
HOY
Longhope
SOUTH RONALDSAY

1

To Kirkwall
To Lerwick

Pentland Firth

2

Scarfskerry
Scrabster
Gills Bay
John o'Groats

Strathy Point
irness
Talmine
Skerray
Bettyhill
Melvich
Reay
Thurso

3

Tongue

Forsinard

Wick

Altnaharra

4

Lybster
Dunbeath

Berriedale

Helmsdale

5

Loch Shin
Loch Shin

Dornoch Firth

	Motorway
M80	
A726	Primary route
A723	Main route
	Railway
• Brodick	Ferry route (car) and terminal
	Ferry route (passenger)
✈	International Airport
✈	Regional Airport
S	Sleeper Terminal

Scale 1:1 300 000
0   10   20 miles
0 10 20 30 kilometres
© Collins Bartholomew Ltd 2008

Lairg
Rogart
Brora
Golspie

6

Bonar Bridge
Ardgay
Dornoch
Portmahomack
Tain
Inver

Moray Firth

7

Ardross
Tomich
Invergordon
Hopeman
Lossiemouth
Portknockie
Sandend
Whitehills
Crovie
Pennan
Fraserburgh
Buckie
Cullen
Portsoy
Banff
Gardenstown
Macduff

Dingwall
arve
hpeffer
aryburgh
Culbokie
Duncanston
Fortrose
Nairn
Findhorn
Forres
Elgin
Keith
Aberchirder
Peterhead

8

of Ord
Beauly
Kirkhill
Avoch
North Kessock
Ardersier
Cawdor
Auldearn
Rothiemay
Turriff

Archiestown
Aberlour

ruy
Culloden
Culloden Moor
Smithton
Daviot

INVERNESS

Ballindalloch
Glenlivet
Dufftown
Huntly
Fyvie
Rothienorman
Ellon
Cruden Bay

9

Abriachan
Brackla
Balnain
mnadrochit
h Ness

Grantown -on-Spey
Dulnain Bridge
Insch
Rhynie
Oldmeldrum
Inverurie

Carrbridge
Nethy Bridge
Tomintoul
Alford
Kintore
Potterton
Bucksburn

Errogie
Boat of Garten
Strathdon
Monymusk

Invermoriston
Aviemore
Logiecoldstone
Lumphanan
Westhill
ABERDEEN

10

t Augustus
Kincraig
Feshie Bridge
Dinnet
Aboyne
Banchory

Kingussie
Insh
Drumguish
Crathie
Ballater

Newtonmore
Braemar

Laggan

11

nlochlaggan
Stonehaven

Dalwhinnie

Glenshee
Glenesk
Fordoun

12

Spittal of Glenshee
Laurencekirk
Johnshaven

Blair Atholl
Glenisla
Dykehead
Tannadice

Killiecrankie
Kirkmichael
Memus
Brechin
Montrose

A B C D E F G H

MAP 5

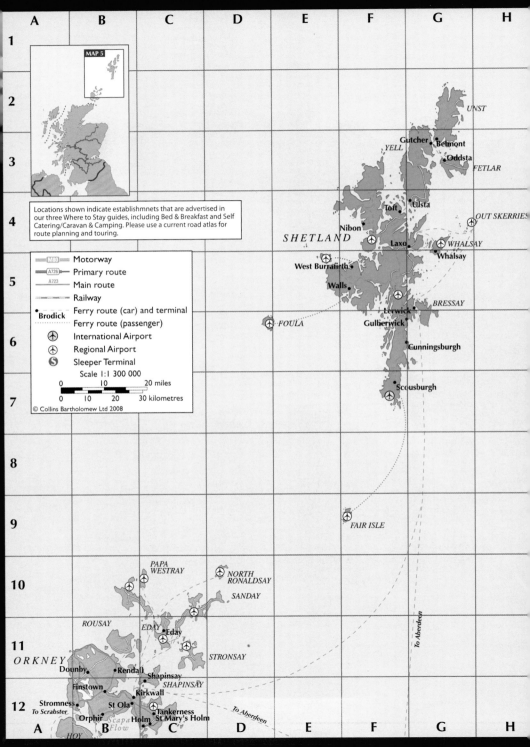

MAP 5

Locations shown indicate establishmnets that are advertised in our three Where to Stay guides, including Bed & Breakfast and Self Catering/Caravan & Camping. Please use a current road atlas for route planning and touring.

M80	Motorway
A726	Primary route
A723	Main route
	Railway
• Brodick	Ferry route (car) and terminal
	Ferry route (passenger)
✈	International Airport
✈	Regional Airport
Ⓢ	Sleeper Terminal

Scale 1:1 300 000

0   10   20 miles
0 10   20   30 kilometres

© Collins Bartholomew Ltd 2008

SHETLAND

UNST
YELL
Gutcher • Belmont
• Oddsta
FETLAR

Toft
Ulsta
OUT SKERRIES
Nibon
Laxo
✈ *WHALSAY*
Whalsay
West Burrafirth •
Walls
BRESSAY
Lerwick
Gulberwick
✈ *FOULA*

Cunningsburgh

Scousburgh

✈ *FAIR ISLE*

PAPA
WESTRAY
✈ *NORTH*
RONALDSAY
SANDAY
✈
✈
ROUSAY
EDAY
• Eday
✈
STRONSAY
ORKNEY
Dounby •
• Rendall
Shapinsay •
SHAPINSAY
Finstown •
Kirkwall
Stromness •
• St Ola
Tankerness
To Scrabster
Orphir •
Holm
St Mary's Holm
Scapa
Flow
To Aberdeen
HOY

To Aberdeen

A hotel overlooking Loch Fyne, Argyll

ACCOMMODATION LISTINGS

- Hotel & Guest House **accommodation listings** for all of Scotland.

- Establishments are listed **by location** in alphabetical order.

- At the back of this book there is a directory showing all VisitScotland quality assured **Serviced Accommodation**. This directory shows **Accessible Accommodation** for visitors with mobility difficulties and also lets you know what **Green Award** has been obtained.

- You will also find an **Index by location** which will tell you where to look if you already know where you want to go.

- Inside the back cover flap you will find a **key to the symbols**.

The town of Melrose, showing Abbey and River Tweed, Scottish Borders

SOUTH OF SCOTLAND

Ayrshire & Arran,
Dumfries & Galloway,
Scottish Borders

No matter how many times you holiday in the Scottish Borders, Ayrshire & Arran or Dumfries & Galloway, you'll always find something new and interesting to do.

The proud heritage, distinct traditions and enthralling history of Scotland's most southerly places are sure to capture your imagination.

Explore the region's imposing castles and ruined abbeys and follow the trail of an often bloody and turbulent past. It's a story of battles and skirmishes - from all out war to cattle rustling cross-border raids.

Living history

Though you'd be hard pushed to find a more peaceful part of the country these days, the legacy of these more unsettled times can still be experienced in many a Scottish Borders town during the Common Ridings. Throughout the summer months hundreds of colourful riders on horseback commemorate the days when their ancestors risked their lives patrolling town boundaries and neighbouring villages.

The South is alive with history. Traquair House, near Innerleithen, is Scotland's oldest continuously inhabited house, dating back to 1107. In Selkirk the whole town is transformed in early December as locals step back to the days when Sir Walter Scott presided over the local courtroom, by partaking in the Scott's Selkirk celebrations.

Beautiful beaches

Southern Scotland isn't just about rolling hills and lush farmland, both coasts are well worth a visit. To the east you can see the rocky cliffs and picturesque harbours at St Abbs Head and Eyemouth, while over on the west, there are the beautiful Ayrshire beaches and more than 200 miles of the lovely Solway Coast to explore.

And off the Ayrshire coast is the Isle of Arran – one of Scotland's finest islands and everything a holidaymaker could want.

Whatever your interests, you'll be spoiled for choice in southern Scotland. If you love angling, there's world-class salmon fishing on the River Tweed. If golf's your game, Turnberry, Prestwick and Royal Troon are up with the best.

If you're a mountain biker, you won't find better than Glentress or Kirroughtree, two of the 7stanes mountain bike routes. Enjoy reading? Head for Wigtown, Scotland's National Book Town and home to more than 20 bookshops. Ice cream? Who can resist Cream o' Galloway at Gatehouse of Fleet?

If you're a gardener, you'll be inspired all year round by the flourishing collection of rare plants at the Logan Botanic Garden near Stranraer and Dawyck Botanic Gardens near Peebles.

What's more, 2009 is a big year for Scotland – we're celebrating the 250th anniversary of the birth of Robert Burns. There's over 200 special events taking place throughout the year, all over Scotland. Go to homecomingscotland2009.com to find out about events in this area.

That's the South of Scotland. Bursting with brilliant places, waiting with a hearty Scottish welcome and ready to captivate you with a holiday experience you will never forget.

Enjoy an ice cream at Cream o' Galloway, Gatehouse of Fleet

What's On?

Burns Light
25 January 2009
Homecoming on your Doorstep.

Melrose 7's Rugby Tournament
11 April 2009
The Greenyards, Melrose, April 2009
Melrose is the home of rugby 7's and this popular and expanding tournament is certain to be a big crowd puller!
melrose7s.com

Spring Fling
May Bank Holiday weekend 2009
Arts and crafts open studio event.
spring-fling.co.uk

Burns an 'a' That! Festival
16 – 24 May 2009
Celebrate the 250th anniversary of Rabbie Burns' birth: more than 100 events across Ayrshire will bring together the biggest names in music, comedy and the arts.
burnsfestival.com

Ayr Flower Show
2 – 9 August 2009
Scotland's answer to the Chelsea Flower Show, the Ayr Flower Show takes place in the beautiful grounds of Rozelle Park.
ayrflowershow.org

Return To The Ridings: Border Common Ridings
7 -30 August 2009
across the Scottish Borders

Marymass
13 - 24 August 2009
A local Queen is crowned and the oldest horse racing event in the world takes place on the moor.
marymass.org

In the Footsteps of the Reivers
5 – 12 September 2009
Throughout Jedburdh and Hawick.

Wigtown Book Festival
25 September – 4 October 2009
Meet famous writers and broadcasters in the idyllic Galloway countryside.
wigtownbookfestival.com

All dates correct at time of publication. Please check before booking. VisitScotland cannot be held responsible for any inaccuracies

23

MAP

©Collins Bartholomew Ltd 2008

To find out more, call 0845 22 55 121 or go to visitscotland.com

VISITOR INFORMATION CENTRES

Visitor Information Centres are staffed by people 'in the know' offering friendly advice, helping to make your stay in Scotland the most enjoyable ever . . . whatever your needs!

Ayrshire & Arran

Ayr	22 Sandgate, Ayr, KA7 1BW	Tel: 01292 290300
Brodick	The Pier, Brodick, Isle of Arran, KA27 8AU	Tel: 01770 303774/776

Dumfries & Galloway

Dumfries	64 Whitesands, Dumfries DG1 2RS	Tel: 01387 253862
Gretna	Unit 38, Gretna Gateway Outlet Village, Glasgow Road, Gretna, DG16 5GG	Tel: 01461 337834
Kirkcudbright	Harbour Square, Kirkcudbright DG6 4HY	Tel: 01557 330494
Southwaite	M6 Service Area, Southwaite, CA4 0NS	Tel: 01697 473445
Stranraer	Burns House, 28 Harbour Street, Stranraer, Dumfries DG9 7RA	Tel: 01776 702595

Scottish Borders

Hawick	Tower Mill, Heart of Hawick Campus, Kirkstile, Hawick, TD9 0AE	Tel: 01450 373993
Jedburgh	Murray's Green, Jedburgh, TD8 6BE	Tel: 01835 863171/864099
Kelso	Town House, The Square, Kelso, TD5 7HF	Tel: 01573 228055
Melrose	Abbey House, Abbey Street, TD6 9LGR	Tel: 01896 822283
Peebles	23 High Street, Peebles, EH45 8AG	Tel: 01721 723159

LOCAL KNOWLEDGE · WHERE TO STAY · ACCOMMODATION BOOKING · PLACES TO VISIT · THINGS TO DO · MAPS AND GUIDES TRAVEL ADVICE · ROUTE PLANNING · WHERE TO SHOP AND EAT LOCAL CRAFTS AND PRODUCE · EVENT INFORMATION · TICKETS

For information and ideas about exploring Scotland in advance of your trip, call our booking and information service **0845 22 55 121** or go to **visitscotland.com**

If calling from outside the UK and Ireland **+44 1506 832 121**   From Ireland **1800 932 510**

A £4 booking fee applies for accommodation bookings made via a Visitor Information Centre and through our booking and information service.

Canyoning in North Glen Sannox on the Isle of Arran

Ayrshire & Arran

Ayrshire is home to 80 miles of unspoiled coastline and rolling green hills. Southwest of Glasgow, the area is steeped in history from Bronze Age standing stones to Medieval Viking battles and the majestic splendour of some of the best-preserved castles in the UK.

Not forgetting it is also the birthplace of world-renowned poet Robert Burns, to whom homage is paid on January 25th throughout the world. Why not experience Burns night surrounded by the scenery and culture that inspired the Bard himself.

Arran offers everything that is good about Scotland in one small and easily accessible island. It has mountains and lochs in the north, and rolling hills and meadows in the south. With fantastic walks, seven golf courses, breathtaking scenery and delicious food and drink, Arran has something for everyone.

Brodick Highland Games

To find out more, call 0845 22 55 121 or go to visitscotland.com

DON'T MISS

1 See what happens when you bring 4 of the world's best graffiti artists to Scotland and provide them with a castle as a canvas. This is exactly what the owners of Kelburn Castle did. Kelburn is the ancient home of the Earls of Glasgow and dates back to the 13th century. The graffiti project on the castle is a spectacular piece of artwork, surrounded by a beautiful country estate and wooden glen. There is plenty to interest all the family.

2 The island of Great Cumbrae, accessible via a 10-minute ferry crossing from Largs, has an undeniable charm and a fabulous setting on the Clyde with views towards Arran. The capital, Millport, is every inch the model Victorian resort, with its own museum and aquarium, as well as the Cathedral of the Isles, Europe's smallest cathedral. The sportscotland National Centre Cumbrae is perfect for thrill seekers, while Country & Western fans will enjoy the week-long festival in late summer.

3 Opened in 1995, the Isle of Arran Distillery at Lochranza enjoys a spectacular location and is among the most recent to begin production in Scotland. The distillery has a visitor centre that offers fully guided tours, and the opportunity to pour your own bottle. Peat and artificial colourings aren't used in Arran whisky, which the distillers proudly claim offers 'the true spirit of nature'.

4 Dean Castle lies in Kilmarnock, East Ayrshire. Known for its astounding collection of medieval instruments and armoury, the castle sits in a glorious country park. Dean Castle is a family favourite, with a pet corner, an adventure playground and many different woodland walks and cycle routes. Contact the castle ahead of your visit to confirm seasonal opening hours for the Castle and its facilities.

5 For some crazy outdoor fun, head to Loudoun Castle, in Galston, Ayrshire. Loudoun Castle is a terrific day out for younger kids with swashbuckling fun in the Pirates' Cove, and pony treks and tractor rides at McDougal's Farm.

6 One of the finest collections of Bronze Age standing stones in Scotland can be found at scenic Machrie Moor on Arran. Around seven separate rings of stones have been discovered on the moor, with many still laying undiscovered beneath the peat which now grows in the vicinity. Visit during the summer solstice for a truly atmospheric experience.

FOOD AND DRINK

eatscotland.com

7   With excellent local produce such as cheese, ale, honey, ice cream and chocolate made to the highest standard, the Ayrshire & Arran kitchen will delight the palate and ignite culinary creativity.

8   Being on the west coast, seafood is delicious and could not be fresher. Take advantage of the opportunity to visit an up-market fish and chip shop or order the seafood at one of the excellent restaurants.

9   With such a range of natural & local ingredients to inspire, it is no wonder that Ayrshire & Arran has such fabulous restaurants. From Michelin Star and AA rosette winning restaurants to the best that gastro pubs have to offer, Ayrshire & Arran will satisfy the biggest gourmet's appetite.

GOLF

visitscotland.com/golf

10   Scotland is not only the Home of Golf, it is the home of links golf, the original form of the game that had its beginnings in Scotland over 600 years ago. Ayrshire & Arran have some of the finest and most famous links golf courses in the world; Western Gailes, Glasgow Gailes, West Kilbride, Royal Troon, Prestwick, Prestwick St Nicholas, Turnberry Alisa (pictured) and Shiskine on the Isle of Arran are all part of the Great Scottish Links collection.

11   However, it is not just the championship courses that Ayrshire is famous for. It is the good value and spectacular play of some of the lesser renowned courses. The charm and challenge of hidden gems like Belleisle, Brodick, Prestwick St. Cuthbert, Routenburn, Lochgreen and Largs, to name just a few, offer brilliant golf at a very reasonable price.

12   Ayrshire & Arran offer 3 different golf passes which are great value for money. By spending less on the course, you will have more to spend at the 19th hole. Visit ayrshire-arran.com for more information.

13   The Open returns to Ayrshire in 2009. It will see the world's best professional golfers flock to the legendry links of Turnberry to take on the greatest challenge in professional golf. If previous years are anything to go by, the competition will be fierce and the sun will be shining.

WALKS

14   Going through forest, along the beach and across fields, the Kings Cave Forest Walk offers beautiful views across the sea to Kintyre. You also get the chance to explore the cave where reputedly Robert the Bruce hid from the English and was inspired by a spider to try, try and try again.

15   If you are looking for a short and pleasant walk with a combination of forest and open hills Dinmurchie Trail is ideal. Look out for local wildlife including deer, foxes, hares, kestrels and buzzards.

16   The Isle of Arran Coastal Way allows you to walk around the island. It is 75 miles long, but can be broken down into 7 more manageable sections. This route offers spectacular scenery and enjoyable challenges. Guide books are available at Brodick Visitor Information Centre.

17   The River Ayr Way is the first source to sea path network, which follows the river (66km) from its source at Glenbuck to the sea at Ayr. With beautiful scenery and abundant wildlife it is enjoyable to walk all or part of this route.

HISTORY

18   Robert Adam's fairytale Culzean Castle, perched on a clifftop overlooking Ailsa Craig and the Firth of Clyde, is a study in extravagance. A favourite of President Eisenhower, he was given his own apartment here by its previous owner, the Kennedy's. Fans of military history should explore the Armoury, filled with antique pistols and swords. 565 acres of country park surround the castle, with woodland walks, a walled garden and even a beach.

19   On 25th January 1759, Scotland's National Bard was born in the picturesque village of Alloway, a must for admirers of the man and his work. Here, you can visit Burns Cottage and a museum containing prized artefacts such as an original manuscript of Auld Lang Syne. Numerous surrounding sites, including the Brig O' Doon and Kirk Alloway, are familiar from Burns' epic poem Tam O'Shanter, which even has an entire visitor attraction dedicated to it.

20   The Isle of Arran Heritage Museum can be found on the main road at Rosaburn, just north of Brodick. The present group of buildings was once a working croft and smiddy, and include a farmhouse, cottage, bothy, milk house, laundry, stable, coach house and harness room. The fascinating exhibits reflect the social history, archaeology and geology of the island.

21   To visit Dalgarven Mill, and the Museum of Ayrshire Country life and Costume, is to step back in time. The comprehensive exhibition of tools, machinery, horse and harness, churns, fire irons and furnishings, evokes a powerful sense of the past, which cannot fail to leave an impression. The costume collection is constantly changing, and demonstrates how fashion has changed from 1780. The grind and splash of the wooden mill ensures the museum has an authentic ambience.

22   Dumfries House, the Georgian masterpiece designed by the renowned Scottish architect Robert Adam, opened to the public on 6th June 2008. The house, which sits in 2000 acres of East Ayrshire countryside, is opening its doors for the first time in 250 years. The former home of the Marquises of Bute, it was saved for the nation at the eleventh hour by a consortium of organisations and individuals brought together by HRH The Duke of Rothesay.

Ayrshire & Arran

Brodick, Isle of Arran
Ormidale Hotel
Map Ref: 1F6

★★ SMALL HOTEL

Open: April-October
Brodick, Isle of Arran, KA27 8BY
T: 01770 302293
E: reception@ormidale-hotel.co.uk
W: ormidale-hotel.co.uk

48704

Total number of rooms: 7

Prices from:
Single:	£39.00	Double:	£39.00
Twin:	£39.00	Family room:	£39.00

Lochranza, Isle of Arran
Apple Lodge
Map Ref: 1E6

★★★★ GUEST HOUSE

Open: All year excl Xmas and New Year
Lochranza, Isle of Arran KA27 8HJ
T: 01770 830229

12337

Total number of rooms: 4

Prices from:
Single:	£52.00	Double:	£38.00
Twin:	£38.00		

Ayr
The Richmond
Map Ref: 1G7

★★★ GUEST HOUSE

Open: All year excl Xmas and New Year
38 Park Circus, Ayr KA7 2DL
T: 01292 265153
E: richmond38@btopenworld.com
W: richmond-guest-house.co.uk

60185

Total number of rooms: 6

Prices from:
Single:	£35.00	Double:	£29.00
Twin:	£29.00	Family room:	£80.00pr

Ayr
Western House Hotel
Map Ref: 1G7

★★★★ HOTEL

Open: All year
Ayr Racecourse, 2 Craigie Road, Ayr KA8 0HA
T: 08700 55 55 10
E: pdavies@ayr-racecourse.co.uk
W: westernhousehotel.co.uk

63819

Total number of rooms: 49

Prices per room from:
Single:	£80.00	Double:	£80.00
Twin:	£80.00	Family room:	£80.00

Largs, Ayrshire
Willowbank Hotel
Map Ref: 1F5

★★★ HOTEL

Open: All year
96 Greenock Road, Largs, Ayrshire KA30 8PG
T: 01475 672311/ 675435
E: iaincsmith@btconnect.com
W: thewillowbankhotel.co.uk

64306

Total number of rooms: 30

Prices from:
Single:	£70.00	Double:	£50.00
Twin:	£50.00	Family room:	£40.00

IMPORTANT: Prices stated are estimates and may be subject to change. Prices are per person per night unless otherwise stated. Awards correct as of beginning of October 2008.

Carsphairn View, Dumfries and Galloway

Dumfries & Galloway

Dumfries & Galloway is a naturally inspiring place, where landscapes, people and atmosphere conspire to make this a holiday experience you'll never forget.

Poets and artists have found inspiration here, capturing the look and feel of this beautiful region where 200 miles of coastline meet the tide and impressive hills rise up to greet the vast clear sky.

Remember to visit Kirkcudbright Artists' Town with its thriving artistic community, studios and galleries. From the Galloway Forest Park to the Solway Coast, there are so many picturesque places to explore and an abundance of wildlife habitats.

Look out for red deer, rare red kites, wild goats and even ospreys at Wigtown, Scotland's Book Town.

For those looking for adventure, there's world class mountain biking, challenging golf courses and many activity centres waiting to offer an adrenaline rush.

Whatever you choose to do, you'll find Dumfries & Galloway the perfect setting for a great holiday adventure.

Picnic, Priorwood Gardens, Melrose

DON'T MISS

1   As you travel through Dumfries & Galloway taking in the breathtaking scenery, you will come face to face with some amazing **environmental artworks** set in the landscape: head carvings in a sheep pen in the Galloway Forest Park, sculpture within Creetown town square, Andy Goldsworthy's Striding Arches near Moniaive. You never know what intriguing works you'll discover around the next corner!

2   Set in the pretty village of New Abbey, you'll find the origin of the word sweetheart at the splendid remains of this Cistercian Abbey, **Sweetheart Abbey**, established by Lady Devorgilla in memory of her husband John Balliol. Lady Devorgilla's love for her departed husband extended to carrying his embalmed heart around with her in an ivory box. Devorgilla and the heart are now buried together before the high altar. Be sure to pop in to the welcoming Abbey Cottage tearoom after your visit.

3   **Logan Botanic Garden**, under the care of the Royal Botanic Garden, Edinburgh is Scotland's most exotic garden where a fabulous array of bizarre and exotic plants and trees flourish outdoors. Warmed by the Gulf Stream, the climate provides ideal growing conditions for many plants from the southern hemisphere including a number of palm trees, which means you may forget where you are!

4   Built in the 17th century as a home for the first Duke of Queensberry, surrounded by the 120,000 acre Queensberry Estate, Country Park and grand Victorian Gardens, **Drumlanrig Castle** houses one of the finest private art collections in the UK. Join a Castle tour, a Land Rover Tour of the Estate, stroll through beautiful gardens and woodland walks enjoying the wildlife or take to your bike on a mountain bike trail. Kids are sure to enjoy the adventure playground, and the only museum in Scotland devoted to the history of cycling.

5   Set in a beautiful woodland location at Shambellie House, New Abbey, **The National Museum of Costume** opens the door on fashion and society from the 1850s to 1950s using lifelike room settings, in conjunction with a programme of special exhibitions, workshops and children's events.

6   Painters, artists and craftsmen have flocked to this area for centuries, no place more so than **Kirkcudbright** with its pastel coloured houses and traditional working harbour, now known as the Artists' Town for its historic artistic heritage. During the summer of 2009, the annual art exhibition, in the Town Hall, provides another chance to view the successful exhibition of 2000, **'The Homecoming'**, featuring works by many of the artists who made Kirkcudbright famous as an artists' town.

HERITAGE

7   **Caerlaverock Castle** is everyone's idea of a medieval fortress, with its moat, twin towered gatehouse and imposing battlements. Britain's only triangular castle, close to Dumfries, has a turbulent history which is brought back to life with a medieval re-enactment each summer.

8   An amazing exhibition at Eastriggs tells the story of the greatest munitions factory on earth. **Devil's Porridge** was the highly explosive mixture of nitro-glycerine and nitro-cotton, hand mixed in HM Factory Gretna during World War 1. The exhibition tells the story of over 30,000 brave men and women who worked in the factory. Get an insight into their work and social life through sight and sound. Why not follow in the footsteps of runaway couples and visit nearby romantic Gretna Green?

9   **Homecoming Scotland 2009** is inspired by the 250th anniversary of the birth of Scotland's National Bard, **Robert Burns**. Pay a visit to **Ellisland Farm**, just north of Dumfries, where he wrote the famous song Auld Lang Syne, sung all over the world at New Year celebrations, **Robert Burns House**, in Dumfries where he spent the last years of his life, **The Globe Inn** his favourite "howff" (pub) and his final resting place, The Mausoleum in **St Michael's Churchyard**.

10   Dating back to about 2000 BC, the impressive remains of 2 chambered cairns at **Cairnholy** are surrounded by hills on three sides, but open to the sea to the south. With glorious views across Wigtown Bay to the Machars and the Isle of Man, just relax and enjoy the tranquillity of this historic setting.

WALKS

11   Scotland's longest waymarked walking route, the **Southern Upland Way**, runs 212 miles from Portpatrick in the west to Cockburnspath on the east coast, traversing some beautiful hill scenery. If this is too challenging, there are several sections which can be enjoyed as part of shorter walks. The coastal section from Portpatrick to Killantringan Lighthouse is a great place to start or why not try the 7½ mile section between Wanlockhead and Sanquhar for a completely different experience of the Way.

12   There are many great walks around **Moffat**, Scotland's first "Walkers are Welcome" town, where a warm welcome is guaranteed. **The Grey Mare's Tail**, in the care of the National Trust for Scotland, just a short drive from Moffat along the Selkirk Road, provides a glorious walk up the side of this impressive 61m waterfall. At the top of the falls you will reach its source, Loch Skene, whose clear waters are populated by vendace, Britain's rarest freshwater fish. Join an experienced walk leader to discover more great walks during the **Moffat Walking Festival**, held in October each year.

13   The **River Annan** walk, takes you along one side of the river from Battery Park, Annan to the village of Brydekirk, some 3 miles away, and returns along the opposite bank. This calm and peaceful walk never takes you far from the river. Should you require a shorter walk, there are 2 additional bridges over the river, allowing shorter walks of 1½ and 3 miles.

14   Enjoy a leisurely stroll along the **Jubilee Path**, linking the picturesque coastal villages of Kippford and Rockcliffe. This 2 mile walk can be made from either village as you return by the same route, although some detours can be made on other minor paths. All the walks within this section have been taken from **"Dumfries & Galloway 12 Walks"** guide which can be requested via visitdumfriesandgalloway.co.uk/walking.

WILDLIFE

visitscotland.com/wildlife

15 The graceful red kite has been successfully reintroduced to Galloway, in an area around Loch Ken. The **Galloway Red Kite Trail** takes a circular route through some impressive scenery, designed to take you closer to this elusive raptor with observation points and interpretation boards. Visit the feeding station at Bellymack Farm, near Laurieston where up to 30 have been seen at once - feeding time, 2pm.

16 **Ospreys** are back in Galloway after a break of over 100 years. Visit the County Buildings in Wigtown where you can watch live CCTV coverage of the ospreys, or edited highlights once the birds have left for Africa. Nesting ospreys can also be seen via a live video link at WWT Caerlaverock. Get an unparalleled view of ospreys sitting on their eggs and bringing up their young, the male coming back with fish to share with the female and taking over nesting duties while she eats.

17 Dumfries & Galloway is home to 20% of the Scottish population of **red squirrel**, making them easier to spot here than anywhere else. Red squirrels are well adapted to the woodland habitat in which they live, and you can even follow a waymarked Red Squirrel Walk within Dalbeattie Forest for a good chance of seeing these endearing mammals.

18 Thousands of **barnacle geese** return every year from Norway to winter on the wetlands of the Solway Firth. Dumfries & Galloway is an ornithologist's paradise, and places such as **WWT Caerlaverock** and **Mersehead Nature Reserve** make it easy to get up close. Why not join an expert on a guided walk to find out more about the birds and wildlife? Events take place from Mull of Galloway to Wanlockhead – pick up your free Countryside Events booklet at Visitor Information Centres.

ACTIVITIES

19 Scotland's Biking Heaven – world class mountain biking at the **7stanes** centres across southern Scotland offering mile upon mile of exhilarating fast flowing single track. The highlight at **Kirroughtree** is 'McMoab' with its huge slabs and ridges of exposed granite linked by boulder causeways. **Dalbeattie's** most talked about section is 'The Slab', sheer granite lying at an extreme angle. Are you brave enough to tackle 'The Dark Side', expert level northshore at **Mabie** or the 'Omega Man' descent at **Ae**, do you have the stamina to tackle the 58km 'Big Country Ride' at **Glentrool?** If this all sounds too much, don't worry, as these centres offer trails for beginners up to the most expert riders, and coupled with some stunning scenery you'll want to return again and again.

20 Explore Dumfries & Galloway using our extensive network of quiet B Roads. Take your time to discover the hidden treasures along the **Solway Coast Heritage Trail**, the **Border Reiver Trail** or **The Burns Heritage Trail**. For an extra special tour, hire a vintage car from Motorparty, near Dumfries and take to these quiet routes in style. Kirkpatrick McMillan invented the bicycle in Dumfries & Galloway and there's still no better place to travel on two wheels with over 400 miles of **signposted cycle routes**.

21 Dumfries' new state of the art leisure centre, **DG One** has a three separate swimming pool areas, one with a moveable floor, leisure water and flumes. The 80 station fitness suite is furnished with state-of-the-art equipment, and the sports hall is the biggest in Dumfries & Galloway. With a 1200 seating capacity, DG One is the ideal venue with a great programme of events and arts and entertainment performances.

22 Enjoy a fun packed break with attractions that are **great for all the family**. Show your artistic side by painting a pot at **Dalton Pottery Art Café** near Lockerbie, shoot down the astroslide at **Mabie Farm Park**, near New Abbey, take a trip on the flying fox followed by some delicious ice cream at **Cream o' Galloway**, Gatehouse of Fleet or take to the zip slide at **Dalscone Farm** on the outskirts of Dumfries. You will be spoiled for choice!

Castle Douglas, Kirkcudbrightshire
Balcary Bay Hotel
Map Ref: 2A10

★★★
COUNTRY
HOUSE
HOTEL

Open: February-November

Shore Road, Auchencairn, Castle Douglas DG7 1QZ
T: 01556 640217
E: reservations@balcary-bay-hotel.co.uk
W: balcary-bay-hotel.co.uk

13881

Balcary Bay Hotel takes its name from the beautiful bay on which it stands and is ideally suited for walking or just relaxing and enjoying the fantastic scenery. Our award-winning cuisine is guaranteed to delight, using local produce as much as possible, including Galloway beef and lamb, also Solway salmon and sea bass. We have a selection of nearly 100 wines from around the world to complement any taste. Our well-appointed bedrooms are all ensuite and are indiviually designed and well equipped. A warm welcome awaits you in Bonnie Galloway.

Total number of rooms: 20

Prices from:

Single:	£69.00	Double:	£61.00
Twin:	£61.00	Family room:	£75.00

Castle Douglas, Kirkcudbrightshire
Urr Valley Hotel
Map Ref: 2A10

★★
COUNTRY
HOUSE
HOTEL

Open: All year
Ernespie Road, Castle Douglas, DG7 3JG
T: 01556 502188
E: info@urrvalleyhotel.com
W: urrvalleyhotel.com

76361

Total number of rooms: 17

Prices from:

Single:	£40.00	Double:	£35.00
Twin:	£35.00	Family room:	£85.00pr

Colvend, nr Dalbeattie
Clonyard House Hotel
Map Ref: 2A10

★★★
COUNTRY
HOUSE
HOTEL

Open: All year

Colvend, Dalbeattie, Kirkcudbrightshire, DG5 4QW
T: 01556 630372
E: info.clonyard@virgin.net
W: clonyardhotel.co.uk

19695

Set in seven acres of wooded grounds, in national scenic area ideally situated for touring, walking, golfing, bird watching, biking. Comfortable bar and restaurant serving lunches, dinners and bar meals. All rooms centrally heated and ensuite. Most rooms on ground floor. Off street car parking, safe grounds for children.

Total number of rooms: 15

Prices from:

Single:	£50.00	Double:	£37.50
Twin:	£37.50	Family room:	£40.00

For a full listing of quality assured serviced accommodation throughout Scotland see pages 195-278.

35

Dumfries & Galloway

Dumfries
Aberdour Hotel
Map Ref: 2B9

★★ SMALL HOTEL

Open: All year excl Xmas Day and Boxing Day
16-20 Newall Terrace,
Dumfries, Dumfriesshire DG1 1LW
T: 01387 252060
E: info@aberdour-hotel.co.uk
W: aberdour-hotel.co.uk

10801

Total number of rooms: 12		
Prices from:		
Single: £40.00	Double:	£32.50
Twin: £30.00	Family room:	£80.00pr

Dumfries
Best Western Hetland Hall Hotel
Map Ref: 2B9

★★★ HOTEL

Open: All year
Carrutherstown, Dumfries, DG1 4JX
T: 01387 840201 F: 01387 840211
E: info@hetlandhallhotel.co.uk
W: hetlandhallhotel.co.uk

30173

Total number of rooms: 32		
Prices from:		
Single: £45.00	Double:	£25.00
Twin: £25.00	Family room:	£35.00

Dumfries
The Queensberry Hotel
Map Ref: 2B9

★★ SMALL HOTEL

Open: All year excl Xmas Day
12 English Street, Dumfries DG1 2BT
T: 01387 739913
E: queensberry@barracudagroup.co.uk
W: queensberryhotel.co.uk

82053

Total number of rooms: 15		
Prices from:		
Single: £45.00	Double:	£30.00
Twin: £30.00	Family room:	£30.00

Kirkcudbright
Selkirk Arms Hotel
Map Ref: 2A10

★★★ SMALL HOTEL

Open: All year except Boxing Day
High Street, Kirkcudbright DG6 4JG
T: 01557 330402
E: reception@selkirkarmshotel.co.uk
W: selkirkarmshotel.co.uk

78102

Total number of rooms: 17		
Prices per room from:		
Single: £75.00	Double:	£90.00
Twin: £90.00	Family room: £104.00	

Lockerbie, Dumfriesshire
Ravenshill House Hotel
Map Ref: 2C9

★★ SMALL HOTEL

Open: All year
12 Dumfries Road, Lockerbie,
Dumfriesshire DG11 2EF
T: 01576 202882
E: reception@ravenshillhotellockerbie.co.uk
W: ravenshillhotellockerbie.co.uk

51167

A family run hotel set in attractive gardens within
a quiet residential area ½ mile west of town centre
and M6/M74 junctions. We enjoy a reputation for
excellent food prepared using fresh local produce,
comfortable accommodation and friendly staff.
Conservatory Restaurant and Bar. Weekend, Midweek
and Golfing breaks.

Total number of rooms: 8		
Prices from:		
Single: £50.00-65.00	Double:	£37.50-42.50
Twin: £35.00-37.50	Family room:	£28.00

Moffat, Dumfriesshire
Annandale Arms Hotel

Map Ref: 2B8

Open: All year excl Xmas Day and Boxing Day
High Street, Moffat, Dumfriesshire DG10 9HF
T: 01683 220013
E: reception@annandalearmshotel.co.uk
W: annandalearmshotel.co.uk

12186

Total number of rooms: 15

Prices from:			
Single:	£55.00	Double:	£47.50
Twin:	£47.50	Family room:	£40.00

Newton Stewart, Wigtownshire
The Bruce Hotel

Map Ref: 1G10

Open: All year
88 Queen Street, Newton Stewart,
Dumfries and Galloway DG8 6JL
T: 01671 402294
E: mail@the-bruce-hotel.com
W: the-bruce-hotel.com

75976

Total number of rooms: 19

Prices from:			
Single:	£49.00	Double:	£55.00
Twin:	£55.00	Family room:	£55.00

The garden at Broughton House (NTS) in Kirkcudbright, Dumfries and Galloway

For a full listing of quality assured serviced accommodation throughout Scotland see pages 195-278.

37

St Abbs Head

Scottish Borders

The Scottish Borders stretches from rolling hills and moorland in the west, through gentler valleys to the high agricultural plains of the east, and on to the rocky Berwickshire coastline with its secluded coves and picturesque fishing villages.

In the bright spring months, fresh new growth fills the valleys and forests of the Scottish Borders. Enjoy the lure of long summer days or relax in more mellow shades of autumn when mauves and purples tint the moors. The Scottish Borders is truly 'A Destination for all seasons'.

There are many lovely towns to visit in the Scottish Borders and a huge amount to see. Take the four great Borders abbeys of Dryburgh, Kelso, Jedburgh and Melrose. They were founded by King David I

in the 12th century and though each is in ruins, a strong impression of their former glory remains.

Hawick is the centre of the local textile industry and you can still pick up bargain knitwear, tartans and tweeds at the many outlets and mills in the area.

Abbotsford, the former home of Sir Walter Scott, is now a visitor attraction just west of Melrose and you can also visit his old courtroom in Selkirk, preserved as it was in the 1800s when he presided over trials.

There's some great walking in the Scottish Borders with over 1500 miles of designated walking routes. The St Cuthbert's Way stretches 62 miles from Melrose to Lindisfarne; the Southern Upland Way is a 212 mile coast to coast trek taking in forest, farmland and hills while the Borders Abbeys Way is a very pleasant 65 mile circular route visiting all four historic abbeys.

To find out more, call 0845 22 55 121 or go to visitscotland.com

DON'T MISS

1   Take the B6404 St Boswells to Kelso road and turn onto the B6356, signposted Dryburgh Abbey. About 1 mile along this road there is a junction signposting **Scott's View** to the right. Follow this road for about 2 miles for panoramic views of the Eildon Hills and the Scottish Borders countryside stretched out before you. Great spot for a picnic.

2   **Traquair House**, near Innerleithen, dates back to the 12th century and is said to be the oldest continuously inhibited house in Scotland. Discover the Traquair Maze, one of the largest hedged mazes in Scotland. Watch out for the Medieval Fayre in May and the Summer Fair in August.

3   The **Berwickshire Coastal Path** combines great natural beauty, with magnificent birdlife. There are spectacular views with sandstone cliffs, small coves, sandy beaches and natural harbours. The 15 mile (24km) route is way-marked and strong walkers may manage it in one day. Most people prefer to break it down into shorter stretches and stop off at the pretty villages along the way. Eyemouth is the largest town on this route – enjoy fresh fish and chips from Giacopazzi's by the harbour and watch out for the family of seals in the harbour!

4   The four great **Borders Abbeys** of Kelso, Melrose, Jedburgh and Dryburgh are a must see for any visitor to the area. Melrose Abbey is said to be the resting place of the casket containing the heart of King Robert the Bruce. Dryburgh is the burial place of Field Marshall Earl Haig and Sir Walter Scott. All of the Abbeys are under the care of Historic Scotland. Kelso is the most incomplete and has free access. For access to Melrose, Jedburgh and Dryburgh an admission charge applies.

5   **Floors Castle** in Kelso is the largest inhabited castle in Scotland and home to the Roxburghe family. The house has 365 windows, one for every day of the year. The castle, grounds, gardens and restaurant are open from Easter to October with The Terrace Restaurant, walled gardens, playground and garden centre open all year. The castle hosts an extensive events calendar throughout the year.

RETAIL, CRAFTS & TEXTILES   visitscottishborders.com

6   There are still **independent artists and craftsmen** working in wool in the Borders - spinners, weavers, knitwear designers and tapestry makers - but they have also been joined by workers in other crafts, potters, glass makers, workers in stone and wood and many more, who are more than willing to welcome the visitor into their workshop and demonstrate their skills. Many sell direct to the public. A visit to the Scottish Borders will allow you to enjoy the beautiful scenery of rolling hills, meandering rivers and romantic landscapes, which provide a source of inspiration to the artists.

7   In many towns throughout the Scottish Borders, high streets are a vibrant mix of independent specialists and boutiques. Bakers carrying on the tradition of the Selkirk Bannock, a fruited tea bread; butchers winning plaudits for their haggis recipes; confectioners satisfying the Scottish sweet tooth for Soor Plooms and Hawick Balls; each add to the pleasure of shopping here. Of particular note is **Peebles**, recently voted the **'Top Independent Retailing Town in Scotland'** for its quality range of individual shops.

8   The Scottish Borders knitwear business is world famous, take a look at the catwalks each season and it is clear that top designers around the world are increasingly turning to Scotland for inspiration and materials. **Tartan, tweed, wool and cashmere**; all strut their stuff down the runway. The Scottish Borders is at the very hub of the world's woollen industry, creating colours and garments for the ever changing and exacting fashion houses. **Lochcarron of Scotland** has recently opened a new retail outlet in Selkirk and **Hawick Cashmere, Peter Scott** and **Pringle of Scotland** are all found in Hawick.

WALKS   visitscottishborders.com

9   The life and progress of St Cuthbert provided the inspiration for the **St Cuthbert's Way** walking route. Starting in Melrose and ending on Holy Island (Lindisfarne) it passes through rolling farmland, river valleys, sheltered woods, hills and moorland culminating in The Holy Island Causeway, passable only at low tide. The full route is 100km / 60 miles in length but this can be broken down into shorter stages.

10   The **Borders Abbeys Way** is a circular route linking the four great ruined Border Abbeys in Kelso, Jedburgh, Dryburgh and Melrose. The full route is 105km / 65 miles in length and can easily be broken down into stages.

11   The **Southern Upland Way** is Britain's first official coast to coast long distance footpath. It runs 212 miles (340km) from Portpatrick in the west to Cockburnspath on the Berwickshire coast. This route takes in some of the finest scenery in Southern Scotland and, of the total route, 130km / 82 miles is in the Scottish Borders. The Way goes through many remote uplands areas, providing a real challenge for the experienced walker, while some parts lie within easy reach of towns and villages and are more suitable for families and the less ambitious.

12   The **John Buchan Way** is named after the writer and diplomat who had many associations with the Scottish Borders. The 22km / 13 mile route takes you from Peebles to Broughton and ends at the John Buchan centre, which houses a collection of photographs, books and other memorabilia.

ACTIVITIES

13 **Glentress** and **Innerleithen** in the Tweed Valley and **Newcastleton** to the south have a massive reputation for some of the best **mountain biking** in the UK and beyond. Glentress is probably the best biking centre in Britain, with brilliant trails of all grades, a top-notch cafe, a bike shop with bike hire, changing and showering facilities, and a great atmosphere. Innerleithen, situated just a few miles south east of Glentress, is quite different from its better-known sister. It's a venue for the more experienced rider and home to the Traquair XC Black run – not for the faint-hearted! All three centres are part of the **7Stanes** – 7 mountain biking centres of excellence across the South of Scotland.

14 **'Freedom of the Fairways'** is Scotland's best selling **golf** pass. This pass offers access to 21 superb courses ranging from the coastal course at Eyemouth to the winner of the 'most friendly' 9-hole course, St Boswells to the championship The Roxburghe and Cardrona. The Freedom of the Fairways scheme runs between April and October and offers both senior and junior passes, available to book online at visitscottishborders.com

15 Along with mountain biking the Scottish Borders offers some superb road **cycle** routes through the peaceful Borders countryside. The **Borderloop** is a magnificent 250 mile way-marked circular route linking Peebles in the west with the Berwickshire coast at Eyemouth. The **Tweed Cycleway** starts 650 feet above sea level near Biggar and runs close by to the River Tweed through the Scottish Borders to the finish at Berwick upon Tweed. This 89 mile way-marked route can be broken down into sections and it takes in some of the key Borders towns en-route, including Peebles, Melrose, Kelso and Coldstream.

16 The Scottish Borders has everything for the angler. From the internationally famous salmon **fishing** on the **River Tweed** to the excellent sea trout fishing on its tributaries; from the rainbow trout in the local lochs to wild brown trout in the rivers; and from the course fishing of the lower Tweed to the sea fishing off the Berwickshire coast; there is plenty to choose from.

WILDLIFE   visitscotland.com/wildlife

17 The elusive, native **red squirrel** can still be found in pockets throughout the Scottish Borders. Try Paxton House, nr Berwick, Tweed Valley Forest Park and Floors Castle Estate. Anywhere with plenty of trees and peace and quiet, be sure to keep your eyes peeled!

18 The **Tweed Valley Osprey Watch** has two centres; Glentress and Kailzie Gardens. Both are open from Easter until mid-August and September respectively. Enjoy live camera action from an osprey nest within The Tweed Valley Forest Park. Follow the progress of the family, from nest building in spring to chicks hatching in May, to fledglings in August. Both centres have a variety of interpretative materials and volunteer guides. A small admission charge applies.

19 On the Berwickshire Coast, **St Abbs Head** is a National Nature Reserve. It is a landmark site for birdwatchers and wildlife enthusiasts. Thousands of breeding seabirds can be seen between April and August and migrating birds in October. The scenery is stunning with wide-sweeping views from the lighthouse on 'The Head' north towards Edinburgh and the Fife coast and south towards Holy Island, Bamburgh and the Farne Islands. There are a number of way-marked trails around the reserve which all start from the car park and information centre.

Scottish Borders

Chirnside, Berwickshire
Chirnside Hall Hotel
Map Ref: 2F5

★★★★
COUNTRY
HOUSE
HOTEL

Open: All year excl March

Chirnside, Berwickshire TD11 3LD
T: 01890 818219
E: reception@chirnsidehallhotel.com
W: chirnsidehallhotel.com

19th Century country mansion set in 5 acres of grounds, spacious ensuite bedrooms with magnificent views of the Cheviots. Open log fires. Emphasis on fine food, with innovative use of fresh Border produce.

Total number of rooms: 10

Prices per room from:
Single: £85.00   Double: £150.00
Twin: £150.00   Family room: £180.00

Lauder, Berwickshire
The Lodge, Carfraemill
Map Ref: 2D6

★★★★
RESTAURANT
WITH ROOMS

Open: All year

Carfraemill, Oxton, Lauder, Berwickshire TD2 6RA
T: 01578 750750
E: enquiries@carfraemill.co.uk
W: carfraemill.co.uk

A former coaching Inn offering friendly hospitality and bistro/restaurant meals. Situated in rural Lauderdale at the junction of the A68/A697. Ideally situated for both Edinburgh and the Borders. Experienced in weddings, business meetings and corporate hospitality.

Total number of rooms: 10

Prices from:
Single: £60.00   Double: £40.00-45.00
Twin: £45.00   Family room: £100.00pr

Peebles
Park Hotel
Map Ref: 2C6

★★★
HOTEL

Open: All year excl 1 week in January

Innerleithen Road, Peebles, EH45 8BA
T: 01721 720457
E: reserve@parkhotelpeebles.co.uk
W: parkhotelpeebles.co.uk

Relax in the friendly atmosphere of the Park Hotel. An excellent base for exploring Peebles and the Scottish Borders. All 24 bedrooms are comfortable and well equipped. Visit our beautiful oak panelled restaurant and enjoy not only delicious food but stunning views across the beautiful Tweed Valley.

Total number of rooms: 24

Prices from:
Single: £72.50   Double: £65.50
Twin: £65.50

eebles
eebles Hotel Hydro
Map Ref: 2C6

★★★
OTEL

Open: All year

Innerleithen Road, Peebles, Tweeddale EH45 8LX
T: 01721 720602
E: info@peebleshydro.co.uk
W: peebleshydro.co.uk

Peebles Hydro offers a wide range of bedrooms to suit all needs, all are ensuite, comfortable and well equipped. Set in 30 beautiful acres, there's loads of activities for young and old, both indoors and outdoors. Whilst here enjoy excellent food, treatments in the salon, swimming and so much more.

49427

Total number of rooms: 133		
Prices from:		
Single: **£99.00**	Double:	**£95.00**
Twin: **£95.00**	Family room:	**£85.00**

Boswells, Nr Melrose
hitehouse
Map Ref: 2D7

★★★
D AND
AKFAST

Open: All year

St. Boswells, Scottish Borders TD6 0ED
T: 01573 460343
E: staying@whitehousecountryhouse.com
W: whitehousecountryhouse.com

64076

Total number of rooms: 3	
Prices from:	
Single: **£70.00**	Double: **£52.00**
Twin: **£52.00**	

---

elkirk
hilipburn Country House Hotel
Map Ref: 2D7

★★★
UNTRY
OUSE
OTEL

Open: All year excl 2nd and 3rd weeks in January

Linglie Road, Selkirk, TD7 5LS
T: 01750 20747
E: info@philipburnhousehotel.co.uk
W: philipburnhousehotel.co.uk

The Philipburn Country House Hotel enjoys a tranquil setting on the outskirts of Selkirk within easy reach of the A7. With 12 individually styled bedrooms, fine dining restaurant, bistro and bar, the Philipburn is an excellent venue for any occasion. A perfect retreat to explore the Borders and local attractions.

80568

Total number of rooms: 12	
Prices from:	
Single: **£95.00**	Double: **£62.50**
Twin: **£62.50**	

For a full listing of quality assured serviced accommodation throughout Scotland see pages 195-278.

43

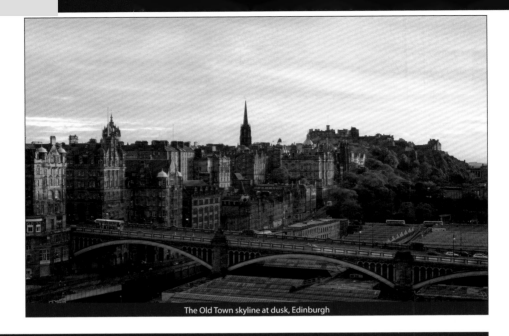

The Old Town skyline at dusk, Edinburgh

EDINBURGH AND THE LOTHIANS

Each year, more than three and a half million visitors arrive in Scotland's capital and discover one of the finest cities in the world.

Whether you're partying at the biggest Hogmanay celebrations on Earth or taking your seat in the audience at the planet's largest arts festival, Edinburgh always offers more than you could ever hope to take on in one visit.

Streets steeped in history

No trip to Edinburgh is complete without a visit to the world famous Castle. Over a million people take to its ramparts every year. Many then set off down the Esplanade and onto the Royal Mile, touching history with every step. During the Festival weeks, hundreds of performers take to the Mile in an explosion of colour and sound, creating an exciting mêlée that changes every day.

Although the trappings of modern life are never far away in the shops, cafés and bars, the Old Town's fascinating history is impossible to ignore. Edinburgh's ghosts whisper in the closes: grave robbers and thieves rubbing shoulders with poets, philosophers, kings and queens – each conjured up and colourfully interpreted in the museums, exhibitions and visitor attractions you'll pass along the way.

A city of beauty

The city's rich history is matched by its beauty. Architecturally, Edinburgh is a stunning city. That beauty extends to its parks, gardens and wild places. Don't miss the Royal Botanic Garden, the view from the top of majestic Arthur's Seat or the Water of Leith walkway, which brings a touch of the countryside right into the city.

Edinburgh is also a city by the sea with a rapidly changing seafront. The busy port of Leith has been transformed in recent years and it boasts a wonderful selection of bars and restaurants.

Get out of town

Further out of town, there's much to explore. Take a trip down the coast to places like Aberlady, Gullane, Longniddry, Dirleton, North Berwick and Dunbar. Play golf on top class courses, watch the seabirds on beautiful sandy beaches or take a boat trip around the Bass Rock.

You could cycle for miles along the Union Canal towpath, visit Roslin Glen and the mysterious Rosslyn Chapel, head for Linlithgow and its ruined Palace or enjoy a thrilling day out at the Musselburgh races.

What's more, 2009 is a big year for Scotland – we're celebrating the 250th anniversary of the birth of Robert Burns. There's over 200 special events taking place throughout the year, all over Scotland. Go to homecomingscotland2009.com to find out about events in this area.

So what is it you'd like to do on your visit to Edinburgh and the Lothians? And where would you like to stay? There's an ever expanding range to choose from. You can enjoy traditional five star luxury at the Balmoral, Sheraton or Caledonian, or enjoy the boutique version at places like the Glasshouse, the Howard or Prestonfield House. What about something simpler? Edinburgh has it all, from seaside guesthouses to family-run country houses. Just flick through the pages ahead and you'll find your ideal selection.

Ceilidh Culture

What's On?

Ceilidh Culture
27 March – 19 April 2009
A vibrant celebration of traditional Scottish arts.
ceilidhculture.co.uk

Edinburgh International Science Festival
6 – 18 April 2009
Stir the curiosity of inquiring minds.
sciencefestival.co.uk

Mary King's Ghost Fest
8 - 18 May 2009 (dates provisional)
Explore Edinburgh's haunted places.
edinburghghostfest.com

Edinburgh International Film Festival
17- 28 June 2009
The festival where the films are the stars.
edfilmfest.org.uk

The Gathering 2009
25 – 26 July 2009
Edinburgh will witness one of the largest clan gatherings in history as part of the Homecoming 2009 celebrations.
clangathering.org

Edinburgh Military Tattoo
7 – 29 August 2009
This military extravaganza is an international favourite.
edinburgh-tattoo.co.uk

Edinburgh Festival Fringe
 7 – 31 August 2009
The largest arts festival on the planet.
edfringe.com

Edinburgh International Festival
7 – 30 August 2009
The very best of opera, theatre, music and dance.
eif.org.uk

East Lothian Food & Drink Festival
25 – 27 September 2009
Food and entertainment for all ages.
foodanddrinkeastlothian.com

Edinburgh's Christmas
24 November – 25 December 2009
Edinburgh becomes a winter wonderland.
edinburghschristmas.com

Edinburgh's Hogmanay
29 December – 1 January 2010
The world's favourite place to celebrate Hogmanay.
edinburghshogmanay.com

DON'T MISS

1 Stroll down the **Royal Mile**, so-called because it boasts Edinburgh Castle at the top and the Palace of Holyroodhouse at the bottom. Browse through the wide range of quirky, independent gift shops and stop off in one of the many tea rooms or cafés along the way. Upon reaching the Canongate, you will find the new Scottish Parliament, famed for its striking contemporary architecture.

2 Never a month passes without a major event or **festival** in Edinburgh, the International Science Festival in April, the Heineken Cup, the Rugby Sevens World Series and Children's Theatre in May, International Film Festival in June, Jazz and Blues in July, Christmas or Hogmanay. And of course, there's the world's largest international arts festival in August, taking in the Fringe, the Tattoo, the Book and International Festivals.

3 **The National Galleries of Scotland** exhibit work by some of the world's most influential artists in five galleries across Edinburgh. From Rembrandt and Monet, to Picasso and Bacon, not to mention major touring exhibitions.

4 **Linlithgow Palace**, once an important royal residence and birthplace of Mary, Queen of Scots, is now a magnificent ruin. Set beside a loch, with a huge number of rooms, passages and stairways, you can imagine what life must have been like in this vast palace.

5 Within minutes of Edinburgh, you can stroll along the white sands of **East Lothian**, with only the sound of water lapping on the shore. Head for Gullane, Yellowcraig or North Berwick. The sheer expanse of each beach is truly breathtaking.

6 Set amidst the beauty of Roslin Glen, the mysterious **Rosslyn Chapel** is undoubtedly Scotland's most outstanding Gothic church. According to Dan Brown's The Da Vinci Code, this chapel is on the trail of the Holy Grail, which only adds to the intrigue.

FOOD AND DRINK

7   **Farmers' markets** are great ways to get the freshest quality, local produce. Held on every Saturday morning on Castle Terrace and the last Saturday of each month in Haddington (except December) in East Lothian, be sure to pop along early to pick up the very best supplies.

8   For the story of whisky, try either the **Scotch Whisky Experience** in Edinburgh or **Glenkinchie Distillery**, by Pencaitland. The former tells how the amber nectar is made and how best to enjoy it, while the latter is ideal for warming you up on your return from walking the East Lothian beaches.

9   For restaurants with the best views in Edinburgh, visit **Oloroso** on Castle Street or the **Forth Floor Restaurant** at Harvey Nichols in Edinburgh. Combine fine dining with panoramic cityscapes. Don't forget your camera!

10 **East Lothian** holds its annual **Food and Drink Festival** in late September each year, giving you ample opportunity to savour the best of the region's produce and hospitality.

HISTORY AND HERITAGE

11 **The Scottish Mining Museum** is located at the former Lady Victoria Colliery at Newtongrange in Midlothian. The five-star attraction has turned the story of Scotland's coal into a fascinating tour and exhibition. With every guide an ex-miner, you'll see and hear the authentic stories of a working mine.

12 **The Royal Yacht *Britannia***, former floating home of the monarchy, offers a superb visitor experience that will guide you through 40 years of royal life, including private quarters, the sick bay and the laundry!

13 Edinburgh is one of Europe's most haunted cities, surrounded by myth and legend. Take a journey back in time and experience the narrow underground closes at **Real Mary King's Close** or try one of the many walking ghost tours, if you dare!

14 With fantastic views over the Firth of Forth, the imposing 15th century **Blackness Castle** looks almost poised to set sail. Explore its darkened corridors, which still capture the atmosphere of a garrison fortress and state prison.

SHOPPING

15 **Multrees Walk** is located at the heart of the city and is headed by Scotland's flagship Harvey Nichols. Known locally as The Walk, shops include Louis Vuitton, Links of London, Azendi, Calvin Klein Underwear and Reiss. The focal point for luxury shopping, this is a must-see for all shoppers.

16 Surrounding the city centre, Edinburgh has a number of urban villages where you'll find **specialist shops**, from up-and-coming designers to crafts, jewellery, food and gifts. In the centre, try the West End, Victoria Street and Royal Mile, while Bruntsfield and Stockbridge are a little further from the city centre.

17 Only a short bus ride from the city centre, take a refreshing stroll along the waterfront in **Leith**, where you'll find independent shops and galleries, alongside contemporary bars and cafes.

ACTIVITIES AND ATTRACTIONS

18 Edinburgh and the Lothians is a superb base for **golf**, whether you choose to play some of the city's fine courses or go east to the coast. Stay in the city for the challenges of Bruntsfield Links, Prestonfield or Duddingston. Or head to the Lothians for the perfect mixture of parkland and links courses. You can enjoy inspirational views across to Fife from some courses in East Lothian.

19 There is a fantastic range of **walks and trails** throughout the scenic and historic countryside of Edinburgh and the Lothians. Through the heart of the city runs the Water of Leith where a peaceful path offers a handy escape from the vibrant centre. In East Lothian the stretch of beach from Gullane to Yellowcraig is perfect for a walk or a picnic, whilst Roslin Glen in Midlothian and Avon River in West Lothian are exhilarating walks to make best use of an afternoon.

20 The area is home to some of Scotland's most impressive visitor attractions. From interactive exhibits to wonders of the natural world, there is something for everyone. Head to the **Scottish Seabird Centre** in North Berwick or **Edinburgh Zoo** to see wildlife up close, travel back in time at **Our Dynamic Earth** or try rock climbing at the **Edinburgh International Climbing Arena**.

21 With free entry to over 30 top attractions, free return airport and city centre bus transport, a free comprehensive guidebook as well as many exclusive offers, the **Edinburgh Pass** is the best way to discover all that Edinburgh has to offer. Buy a 1, 2 or 3 day Pass from edinburghpass.com or from one of the Visitor Information Centres in Edinburgh (see next page).

MAP

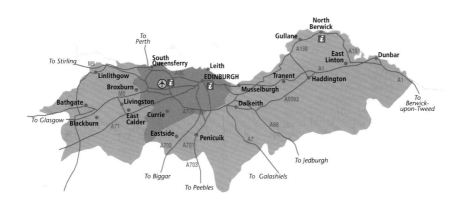

©Collins Bartholomew Ltd 2008

 VISITOR INFORMATION CENTRES

Visitor Information Centres are staffed by people 'in the know' offering friendly advice, helping to make your stay in Scotland the most enjoyable ever . . . whatever your needs!

Edinburgh and Lothians *i*		
Edinburgh	3 Princes Street, Edinburgh, EH2 2QP	Tel: 0131 473 3820
Edinburgh Airport	Main Concourse, Edinburgh International Airport, EH12 9DN	Tel: 0131 344 3120
North Berwick	1 Quality Street, North Berwick, EH39 4HJ	Tel: 01620 892197

LOCAL KNOWLEDGE • WHERE TO STAY • ACCOMMODATION BOOKING • PLACES TO VISIT • THINGS TO DO • MAPS AND GUIDES TRAVEL ADVICE • ROUTE PLANNING • WHERE TO SHOP AND EAT LOCAL CRAFTS AND PRODUCE • EVENT INFORMATION • TICKETS

For information and ideas about exploring Scotland in advance of your trip, call our booking and information service **0845 22 55 121** or go to **visitscotland.com**

If calling from outside the UK and Ireland **+44 1506 832 121**   From Ireland **1800 932 510**

A £4 booking fee applies for accommodation bookings made via a Visitor Information Centre and through our booking and information service.

Edinburgh and the Lothians

Broxburn, West Lothian
Bankhead Farm
Map Ref: 2B5

★★★★
GUEST
HOUSE

Open: All year excl Xmas
Dechmont, Broxburn, West Lothian EH52 6NB
T: 01506 811209
E: bankheadbb@aol.com
W: bankheadfarm.com

14205

Total number of rooms: 7

Prices from:

Single:	£40.00	Double:	£35.00
Twin:	£35.00	Family room:	£35.00

Dunbar, East Lothian
Springfield Guest House
Map Ref: 2E4

★★★
GUEST
HOUSE

Open: January-November
Belhaven Road, Dunbar, East Lothian EH42 1NH
T: 01368 862502
E: smeed@tesco.net

55620

Total number of rooms: 5

Prices per room from:

Single:	£30.00	Double:	£50.00
Twin:	£50.00	Family room:	£60.00

Edinburgh
Aaron Lodge
Map Ref: 2C5

★★★★
GUEST
HOUSE

Open: All year
128 Old Dalkeith Road, Edinburgh EH16 4SD
T: 0131 664 2755
E: dot@baigan.freeserve.co.uk
W: aaronlodgeedinburgh.co.uk

34321

Aaron Lodge is a luxurious 4 star guest house situated on the south side of Edinburgh. Aaron Lodge is the ideal location to make the most of Edinburgh and it's many attractions. Ideally situated, Aaron Lodge neighbours world famous attractions such as Rosslyn Chapel and the Museum of Flight. Ten minutes from the centre of Edinburgh, guests are on the doorstep of an eclectic mix of historic, beautiful and entertaining attractions such as Edinburgh Castle, Royal Yacht Britannia. Aaron Lodge is the closest accommodation to Edinburgh Royal Infirmary. At Aaron Lodge what you see is what you get.

Total number of rooms: 10

Prices from:

Single:	£35.00	Double:	£25.00
Twin:	£25.00	Family room:	£25.00

bbey Hotel (formerly the Greenside Hotel) Map Ref: 2C5

★★
ETRO
OTEL

Open: All year

9 Royal Terrace, Edinburgh, Midlothian EH7 5AB

T: 0131 557 0121
E: abbeyhotel@ednet.co.uk
W: townhousehotels.co.uk

Newly refurbished traditional Georgian terraced house. This personally run hotel is situated in a quiet city centre location close to Princes Street, Playhouse Theatre and all amenities. 10 minute walk from Waverley Station and Princes Street. Excellent selection of restaurants in immediate vicinity. Building of Architectural interest. Free WI-FI internet access.

Total number of rooms: 15			
Prices from:			
Single:	**£25.00**	Double:	**£22.50**
Twin:	**£22.50**	Family room:	**£22.50**

fton Guest House Map Ref: 2C5

★★
UEST
OUSE

Open: All year

1 Hartington Gardens, Edinburgh EH10 4LD

T: 0131 229 1019
E: info@aftonguesthouse.co.uk
W: aftonguesthouse.co.uk

Total number of rooms: 7			
Prices from:			
Single:	**£30.00**	Double:	**£25.00**
Twin:	**£25.00**	Family room:	**£25.00**

lbyn Townhouse Map Ref: 2C5

★★
UEST
OUSE

Open: All year excl Xmas

16 Hartington Gardens, Edinburgh EH10 4LD

T: 0131 229 6459
E: info@albyntownhouse.co.uk
W: albyntownhouse.co.uk

Albyn is a newly decorated three star guest house, has ten ensuite beautiful and comfortable bedrooms, free Wi-Fi, Freeview TV and three free parking spaces bookable in advance only. Very quiet, 15 minutes walk from the centre, Castle and restaurants. From £30.00 to £50.00 per person per night including full Scottish breakfast.

Total number of rooms: 10			
Prices from:			
Single:	**£45.00**	Double:	**£30.00**
Twin:	**£30.00**	Family room:	**£85.00pr**

llison House Map Ref: 2C5

★★★
UEST
OUSE

Open: All year excl Xmas

17 Mayfield Gardens, Edinburgh EH9 2AX

T: 0131 667 8049
E: info@allisonhousehotel.com
W: allisonhousehotel.com

Total number of rooms: 11			
Prices from:			
Single:	**£40.00**	Double:	**£32.50**
Twin:	**£32.50**	Family room:	**£30.00**

For a full listing of quality assured serviced accommodation throughout Scotland see pages 195-278.

51

Edinburgh and the Lothians

Edinburgh
Alpha Guest House

Map Ref: 2C5

★★★
GUEST HOUSE

Open: All year

19 Old Dalkeith Road, Edinburgh EH16 4TE
T: 0131 258 0810
E: webenquiries@briggend.com
W: briggend.com

Newly refurbished family run Guest House. Minutes from city centre and city bypass. Close to Edinburgh Royal Infirmary. On the main bus route. Full Scottish breakfast. Sky TV/Wi-Fi. Private parking.

16323

Total number of rooms: 6

Prices from:

Single:	£25.00	Double:	£20.00
Twin:	£20.00	Family room:	£20.00

Edinburgh
Ardgarth Guest House

Map Ref: 2C5

★★★
GUEST HOUSE

Open: All year excl Xmas

1 St Mary's Place, Portobello, Edinburgh EH15 2QF
T: 0131-669 3021
E: stay@ardgarth.com
W: ardgarth.com

12567

Total number of rooms: 9

Prices from:

Single:	£20.00	Double:	£40.00
Twin:	£40.00	Family room:	£40.00

Edinburgh
Barrosa Guest House

Map Ref: 2C5

★★
GUEST HOUSE

Open: February-November

21, Pilrig Street, Edinburgh, EH6 5AN
T: 0131-554 3700

14395

Total number of rooms: 5

Prices from:

Double:	£29.00-45.00	Twin:	£29.00-45.00
Family room:	£29.00-45.00		

Edinburgh
Ben Craig House

Map Ref: 2C5

★★★
GUEST HOUSE

Open: All year

3 Craigmillar Park, Newington, Edinburgh EH16 5PG
T: 0131 667 2593
E: bencraighouse@hotmail.com
W: bencraig.co.uk

14914

Total number of rooms: 9

Prices from:

Single:	£25.00	Double:	£25.00
Twin:	£25.00	Family room:	£20.00

IMPORTANT: Prices stated are estimates and may be subject to change. Prices are per person per night unless otherwise stated. Awards correct as of beginning of October 2008.

Edinburgh
est Western Bruntsfield Hotel — Map Ref: 2C5

16696

Open: All year excl Xmas Day

69 Bruntsfield Place, Edinburgh EH10 4HH
T: 0131-229 1393
E: reservations@thebruntsfield.co.uk
W: thebruntsfield.co.uk

Overlooking a park, near the city centre, this is a well appointed hotel with friendly service. The 67 ensuite bedrooms have free internet access and multi channel TV. Bisque Brasserie offers modern Scottish cuisine in a comtemporary setting. A relaxing lounge and stylish bar add to the distinctive character of this hotel.

Total number of rooms: 67

Prices per room from:

Single:	£70.00	Double:	£99.00
Twin:	£99.00	Family room:	£120.00

Edinburgh
est Western Kings Manor Hotel — Map Ref: 2C5

34051

Open: All year

100 Milton Road East, Edinburgh EH15 2NP
T: 0131 468 8003
E: reservations@kingsmanor.com
W: kingsmanor.com

Total number of rooms: 95

Prices per room from:

Single:	£65.00	Double:	£85.00
Twin:	£85.00	Family room:	£95.00

Edinburgh
he Broughton Hotel — Map Ref: 2C5

77907

Open: All year

37 Broughton Place, New Town, Edinburgh Lothian, EH1 3RR
T: 0131 558 9792
E: broughton-hotel@hotmail.co.uk
W: broughton-hotel.com

Total number of rooms: 6

Prices from:

Single:	£30.00	Double:	£25.00
Twin:	£25.00	Family room:	£25.00

Edinburgh
arrington Guest House — Map Ref: 2C5

18299

Open: February-November

38 Pilrig Street, Edinburgh EH6 5AL
T: 0131 554 4769

Total number of rooms: 8

Prices from:

Double:	£29.00-45.00	Twin: £29.00-45.00
Family room: £29.00-45.00		

For a full listing of quality assured serviced accommodation throughout Scotland see pages 195-278.

53

Edinburgh
Clarendon Hotel

Map Ref: 2C5

★★★
METRO
HOTEL

Open: All year

25-33 Shandwick Place, Edinburgh EH2 4RG
T: 0131 229 1467
E: res@clarendonhoteledi.co.uk
W: clarendonhoteledi.co.uk

Situated in the heart of the city approximately 20 yards from Princes Street. Ideally situated for the city's financial district, tourist attractions, theatres, restaurants and the EICC, all within minutes walking distance. Stylish and comfortable bedrooms.

19507

Total number of rooms: 66

Prices from:			
Single: **£35.00**		Double:	**£25.00**
Twin: **£25.00**		Family room:	**£35.00**

Edinburgh
Crioch Guest House

Map Ref: 2C5

★★★
GUEST
HOUSE

Open: All year

23 East Hermitage Place, Leith Links
Edinburgh EH6 8AD
T: 0131 554 5494
E: welcome@crioch.com
W: crioch.com

Enjoy Dora's famous full cooked, continental or vegetarian breakfast. All rooms have ensuite shower or private bathroom, and are comfortable and very clean. Crioch looks on to Leith Links park, near Leith's fine cafés, bars and restaurants. Free parking and internet (WiFi). Buses every ten minutes to the city centre.

21312

Total number of rooms: 6

Prices from:			
Single: **£30.00**		Double:	**£27.00**
Twin: **£28.50**		Family room:	**£25.00**

Edinburgh
Dene Guest House

Map Ref: 2C5

★★★
GUEST
HOUSE

Open: All year

7 Eyre Place, Off Dundas Street, Edinburgh, EH3 5ES
T: 0131 556 2700
E: deneguesthouse@yahoo.co.uk
W: deneguesthouse.com

22466

Total number of rooms: 11

Prices per room from:			
Single: **£25.00**		Double:	**£49.00**
Twin: **£49.00**		Family room:	**£79.00**

IMPORTANT: Prices stated are estimates and may be subject to change. Prices are per person per night unless otherwise stated. Awards correct as of beginning of October 2008.

Edinburgh
Dunstane City Hotel
Map Ref: 2C5

Open: All year

5 Hampton Terrace, Haymarket, Edinburgh EH12 5JD

T: 0131 337 6169
E: reservations@dunstanehotels.co.uk
W: dunstanehotels.co.uk

A contemporary luxury boutique hotel, just finished major refurbishment. The 17 bedrooms are stylish and contemporary, offering a choice of standard and superior rooms. Minutes from Edinburgh business centre and city attractions. Hotel offers free wi-fi and car parking. Our friendly staff are here to help and ensure a truly memorable break.

79350

Total number of rooms: 17			
Prices from:			
Single:	**£95.00**	Double:	**£49.50**
Twin:	**£59.50**	Family room:	**POA**

Edinburgh
Dunstane House Hotel
Map Ref: 2C5

Open: All year

4 West Coates, Haymarket, Edinburgh, EH12 5JQ

T: 0131 337 6169
E: reservations@dunstanehotels.co.uk
W: dunstanehotels.co.uk

The friendliest hotel in Edinburgh, where you will enjoy country style tranquility of a small castle in a city setting. Located only a 10 minute walk to the city centre with free private parking. Hotel offers free wi-fi and a unique lounge bar and restaurant themed on the Scottish Isles.

23861

Total number of rooms: 16			
Prices from:			
Single:	**£85.00**	Double:	**£49.50**
Twin:	**£49.50**	Family room:	**POA**

Edinburgh
Falcon Crest Guest House
Map Ref: 2C4

Open: All year excl Xmas
70 South Trinity Road, Edinburgh EH5 3NX
T/F: 0131 552 5294
E: manager@falconcrest.co.uk
W: falconcrest.co.uk

25545

Total number of rooms: 5			
Prices from:			
Single:	**£20.00**	Double:	**£24.00**
Twin:	**£20.00**	Family room:	**£20.00**

Edinburgh
Fountain Court Apartments
Map Ref: 2C5

Open: All year
123 Grove Street, Fountain Bridge, Edinburgh EH3 8AA
T: 0131 622 6677
E: enq@fcapartments.com
W: fcapartments.com

26652

Total number of apartments: 122			
Prices per Apartment from:			
One Bed:	**£100.00**	Three Bed:	**£275.00**
Two Bed:	**£150.00**		

For a full listing of quality assured serviced accommodation throughout Scotland see pages 195-278.

55

Edinburgh
Frederick House Hotel

Map Ref: 2C5

★★★
LODGE

Open: All year

42 Frederick Street, Edinburgh EH2 1EX
T: 0131 226 1999
E: frederickhouse@ednet.co.uk
W: townhousehotels.co.uk

Situated in the heart of Edinburgh close to all city centre amenities. Wide variety of restaurants and bars in the immediate vicinity. Georgian building with all rooms to a high standard including ensuite facilities, fridges and modem points. Princes Street a short walk away. Breakfast at award winning Rick's Restaurant.

26805

Total number of rooms: 45

Prices from:

Single:	£35.00	Double:	£ 25.00
Twin:	£30.00	Family room:	£22.50

Edinburgh
Gifford House

Map Ref: 2C5

★★★★
GUEST
HOUSE

Open: All year excl Xmas
103 Dalkeith Road, Edinburgh EH16 5AJ
T: 0131 667 4688
E: giffordhouse@btinternet.com
W: giffordhouseedinburgh.com

27602

Total number of rooms: 6

Prices from:

Single:	£55.00	Double:	£30.00
Twin:	£30.00	Family room:	£30.00

Edinburgh
Gildun Guest House

Map Ref: 2C5

★★★★
GUEST
HOUSE

Open: All year
9 Spence Street, Edinburgh EH16 5AG
T: 0131 667 1368
E: gildun.edin@btinternet.com
W: gildun.co.uk

27612

Total number of rooms: 8

Prices from:

Single:	£30.00	Double:	£30.00
Twin:	£30.00	Family room:	£30.00

Edinburgh
The Glasshouse

Map Ref: 2C5

★★★★★
METRO
HOTEL

Open: All year
2 Greenside Place, Edinburgh, EH1 3AA
T: 0131 525 8200
E: resglasshouse@theetoncollection.com
W: theetoncollection.com/glasshouse

59071

Total number of rooms: 65

Prices per room from:

Single:	£180.00-275.00	Double:	£180.00-275.00
Twin:	£180.00-275.00		

IMPORTANT: Prices stated are estimates and may be subject to change. Prices are per person per night unless otherwise stated. Awards correct as of beginning of October 2008.

he Glenora

Map Ref: 2C5

★★★
GUEST
HOUSE

Open: All year

14 Rosebery Crescent, Edinburgh EH12 5JY
T: 0131 337 1186
E: enquiries@glenorahotel.co.uk
W: glenorahotel.co.uk

Situated in Edinburgh's West End, this beautifully refurbished Victorian townhouse is within minutes walking distance of Princes Street, the Castle, Conference Centre, Haymarket Station and Airport bus stop. All rooms are non-smoking and have shower, WC, television, telephone and internet access. Breakfast is entirely organic.

28302

Total number of rooms: 11			
Prices from:			
Single:	**£45.00**	Double:	**£35.00**
Twin:	**£40.00**	Family room:	**£35.00**

arvest Guest House

Map Ref: 2C5

★
GUEST
OUSE

Open: All year

33 Straiton Place, The Promenade, Portobello
Edinburgh EH15 2BA
T: 0131 657 3160
E: sadol@blueyonder.co.uk
W: edinburgh-bb.com

29722

Total number of rooms: 7			
Prices per room from:			
Single:	**£25.00-30.00**	Double:	**£40.00-60.00**
Twin:	**£40.00-60.00**	Family room:	**£60.00-150.00**

aymarket Hotel

Map Ref: 2C5

★★★
ETRO
IOTEL

Open: All year

1-3 Coates Gardens, Edinburgh EH12 5LG
T: 0131 337 1775/337 1045
E: reservations@haymarket-hotel.co.uk
W: haymarket-hotel.co.uk

Beautifully presented, privately owned and run city centre hotel comprising two fully modernised, charming historical "B" listed Victorian town houses, where our emphasis is quality accommodation, impeccable service, friendly attentive staff and good food.

16770

Total number of rooms:		
Prices from:		
Single: **£40.00**	Double:	**£30.00**
Twin: **£30.00**		

For a full listing of quality assured serviced accommodation throughout Scotland see pages 195-278.

57

Edinburgh
Inverleith Hotel

Map Ref: 2C5

★★★
METRO HOTEL

Open: All year

5 Inverleith Terrace, Edinburgh EH3 5NS
T: 0131 556 2745
E: info@inverleithhotel.co.uk
W: inverleithhotel.co.uk

Only 15 minutes walk from city centre, opposite Royal Botanic Gardens. First street in centre with all day parking. Licensed residents bar specialising in Malt Whisky, free WiFi access, excellent variety of local restaurants. Family run friendly hotel suitable for business or leisure guests.

32014

Total number of rooms: 10			
Prices from:			
Single:	**£55.00**	Double:	**£35.00**
Twin:	**£35.00**	Family room:	**£29.00**

Edinburgh
The Lodge Hotel

Map Ref: 2C5

★★★★
GUEST HOUSE

Open: All year

6 Hampton Terrace, Edinburgh EH12 5JD
T: 0131 337 3682
E: info@thelodgehotel.co.uk
W: thelodgehotel.co.uk

Beautifully presented West End hotel, close to city centre attractions, shops, theatres, restaurants, galleries and conference centres. Tastefully appointed bedrooms. Private car park. Small private bar. Excellent public transport. Quiet, individually styled hotel. Ideal central base for business or pleasure.

59545

Total number of rooms: 10			
Prices per room from:			
Single:	**£50.00**	Double:	**£70.00**
Twin:	**£70.00**	Family room:	**£100.00**

Edinburgh
Menzies Guest House

Map Ref: 2C5

★★
GUEST HOUSE

Open: All year

33 Leamington Terrace, Edinburgh EH10 4JS
T: 0131 229 4629
E: info@menzies-guesthouse.co.uk
W: menzies-guesthouse.co.uk

38083

Total number of rooms: 7			
Prices from:			
Single:	**£20.00**	Double:	**£18.00**
Twin:	**£20.00**	Family room:	**£18.00**

Edinburgh
Ramada Mount Royal Hotel

Map Ref: 2C5

★★★
HOTEL

Open: All year

53 Princes Street, Edinburgh EH2 2DG
T: 0844 815 9017
E: gm.mountroyal@ramadajarvis.co.uk
W: ramadajarvis.co.uk

51079

Total number of rooms: 158			
Prices per room from:			
Single:	**£69.00**	Double:	**£79.00**
Twin:	**£79.00**	Family room:	**£99.00**

IMPORTANT: Prices stated are estimates and may be subject to change. Prices are per person per night unless otherwise stated. Awards correct as of beginning of October 2008.

Edinburgh
Ravensdown Guest House
Map Ref: 2C5

★★★
GUEST
HOUSE

Open: All year
248 Ferry Road, Edinburgh EH5 3AN
T: 0131 552 5438
E: david@ravensdownhouse.com
W: ravensdownhouse.com

73495

Total number of rooms: 7

Prices per room from:

Single:	£45.00	Double:	£70.00
Twin:	£70.00	Family room:	£85.00

Edinburgh
Rosehall Hotel
Map Ref: 2C5

★★★
METRO
HOTEL

Open: All year excl Xmas
101 Dalkeith Road, Edinburgh EH16 5AJ
T: 0131 667 9372
E: info@rosehallhotel.co.uk
W: rosehallhotel.co.uk

52119

Total number of rooms: 8

Prices from:

Single:	£35.00-70.00	Double:	£30.00-55.00
Twin:	£30.00-55.00	Family room:	£30.00-50.00

Edinburgh
Salisbury Green Hotel
Map Ref: 2C5

★★★
METRO
HOTEL

Open: All year
The University of Edinburgh,
18 Holyrood Park Road, Edinburgh EH16 5AY
T: 0131 662 2000
E: salisbury.green@ed.ac.uk
W: salisburygreen.com

Salisbury Green Hotel is a refurbished 18th Century mansion house, in beautiful grounds at the University of Edinburgh's Pollock Halls campus. Salisbury Green is both stylish and comfortable. The interior, and 36 ensuite bedrooms, perfectly reflect the atmosphere and history of the building: a distinctive and elegant location for your break away.

24473

Total number of rooms: 36

Prices per room from:

Single:	£74.00	Double:	£99.00
Twin:	£99.00	Family room:	£119.00

Edinburgh
Sandaig Guest House
Map Ref: 2C5

★★★
GUEST
HOUSE

Open: All year
5 East Hermitage Place, Edinburgh, EH6 8AA
T: 0131 554 7357
E: info@sandaigguesthouse.co.uk
W: sandaigguesthouse.co.uk

52940

Total number of rooms: 9

Prices per room from:

Single:	£35.00	Double:	£65.00
Twin:	£65.00	Family room:	£75.00

Edinburgh
Sheridan Guest House
Map Ref: 2C4

★★★
GUEST
HOUSE

Open: All year
1 Bonnington Terrace, Edinburgh EH6 4BP
T: 0131 554 4107
E: info@sheridanedinburgh.co.uk
W: sheridanedinburgh.co.uk

54428

Total number of rooms: 8

Prices from:

Single:	£49.00	Double:	£35.00
Twin:	£35.00		

For a full listing of quality assured serviced accommodation throughout Scotland see pages 195-278.

Edinburgh and the Lothians

Edinburgh
Tania Guest House
Map Ref: 2C5

★★
GUEST
HOUSE

Open: All year excluding Christmas
19 Minto Street, Edinburgh, EH9 1RQ
T: 0131 667 4144
E: Taniaguesthouse@yahoo.co.uk

57628

Total number of rooms: 6		
Prices from:		
Single: **£25.00-35.00**	Double:	**£25.00-35.00**
Twin: **£25.00-35.00**	Family room:	**£25.00-35.00**

♥ 📺 🛁 Ⓟ ☕ ✕ 🍴 Ⓥ

Edinburgh
Ten Hill Place Hotel
Map Ref: 2C5

★★★
METRO
HOTEL

Open: All year excl Xmas

10 Hill Place, Edinburgh EH8 9DS
T: 0131 662 2080
E: reservations@tenhillplace.com
W: tenhillplace.com

This innovative Edinburgh Hotel is within easy
walking distance of Princes Street, the historic Old
Town and the city centre's main tourist, shopping and
business districts; yet peacefully situated away from
main thoroughfares. The best of Edinburgh opens up
before you from right outside our front door.

71550

Total number of rooms: 78		
Prices per room from:		
Double: **£80.00**	Twin:	**£80.00**

📺 📞 🛁 Ⓟ ☕ ✕ 🍴 🍷 ♿ Ⓥ

Edinburgh
Walton Hotel
Map Ref: 2C5

★★★★
GUEST
HOUSE

Open: All year

79 Dundas Street, Edinburgh EH3 6SD
T: 0131 556 1137
E: enquiries@waltonhotel.com
W: waltonhotel.com

The Walton is a small privately run Guest House in a
listed building in Edinburgh's Georgian New Town. It
is located in the heart of the city and the short walk
from Princes Street means we are convenient for
tourist attractions, city nightlife and business visitors
alike. Off-street parking available.

63311

Total number of rooms: 10		
Prices per room from:		
Single: **£48.00-78.00**	Double:	**£82.00-152.00**
Twin: **£82.00-142.00**	Family room: £102.00-153.00	

📺 📞 🛁 Ⓟ ☕ ✕ C ♿ Ⓥ

IMPORTANT: Prices stated are estimates and may be subject to change. Prices are per person per night unless otherwise stated. Awards correct as of beginning of October 2008.

Near Edinburgh
Dalhousie Castle and Aqueous Spa   Map Ref: 2C5

Open: All year

Bonnyrigg, Near Edinburgh EH19 3JB
T: 01875 820153
E: info@dalhousiecastle.co.uk
W: dalhousiecastle.co.uk

This 13th Century Castle has 36 ensuite bedrooms of which five are in the lodge. Set in beautiful grounds, the castle has a spa, falconry, archery and two excellent restaurants. Enjoy the atmospheric ambience of the Library Bar and dinner in the two rosetted Dungeon Restaurant.

Total number of rooms: 36

Prices from:		
Single: £90.00	Double:	£115.00
Twin: £115.00	Family room:	£150.00

South Queensferry, Near Edinburgh
Dakota Forth Bridge   Map Ref: 2B4

Open: All year excl Xmas Day and Boxing Day

Ferrymuir Retail Park, South Queensferry, Edinburgh EH30 9QZ
T: 0870 423 4293
E: reservations@dakotaforthbridge.co.uk
W: dakotaforthbridge.co.uk

Eat well, sleep well, feel great at Dakota Forth Bridge. Only ten minutes from Edinburgh Airport. Ideally located for Edinburgh and Fife tourist attractions. Dakota Grill, seafood specialists and awarded Scottish Restaurant of the Year 2008. 132 bedrooms, complimentary airport shuttle. Close to the city- a million miles from mediocrity.

Total number of rooms: 132

Prices per room from:	
Double: £99.00	Twin: £99.00

The Forth Rail Bridge, Edinburgh

For a full listing of quality assured serviced accommodation throughout Scotland see pages 195-278.

61

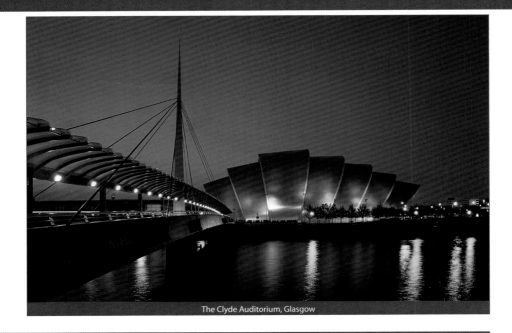

The Clyde Auditorium, Glasgow

GREATER GLASGOW AND CLYDE VALLEY

Glasgow is one of Europe's most exciting destinations, with all the energy and sophistication of a great international city.

There's so much choice it's difficult to know where to start and even harder to know when to stop.

And wherever you go in Scotland's largest city, you'll be overwhelmed by the irresistible friendliness of its inhabitants.

Shop 'til you drop

It's easy to get caught up in Glasgow's fast-moving social whirl – especially if you like shopping. Outside of London, there isn't a UK city that can touch Glasgow for quantity and quality.

If you're in need of retail therapy you'll revel in the elegance of Princes Square, the diversity of the Buchanan Galleries and the classy opulence of the Italian Centre in the chic Merchant City.

Glasgow is easily Scotland's most fashion-conscious city and its passion for all things stylish brings an exciting edge to its boutiques and malls.

That passion spills over into the cafés and bars, boutique hotels, restaurants, nightclubs, theatres and music venues. Glasgow nightlife is always exhilarating whether you're checking out the next hit band at King Tut's, watching groundbreaking theatre at Oran Mor or just sipping a pint in Ashton Lane.

The Glasgow Platter

Glasgow has one of the best restaurant scenes in the UK. From traditional afternoon tea at One Devonshire Gardens or the Willow Tearooms to every major culinary style in the world, Glasgow's restaurants have a rapidly growing international reputation.

For a selection of eating establishments available in and around Glasgow go to eatscotland.com

An Art Lover's Paradise

Glasgow is an outstanding city to step out in. The impressive legacy of its most eminent architectural sons, Charles Rennie Mackintosh and Alexander 'Greek' Thomson, can be seen in the city's streets, while its galleries and museums host one of Europe's biggest collections of civic art.

The Kelvingrove Art Gallery and Museum, restored in 2006 at a cost of £27.9 million, is a must see. This popular visitor attraction is free to enter and hosts some 8,000 exhibits.

Don't spend so long there that you miss the Burrell Collection in Pollok Country Park or the University of Glasgow's Hunterian Museum & Art Gallery.

The Great Outdoors

Despite the endless hustle and bustle, peace and tranquillity are never far away. Glasgow is known as the 'dear green place' and there are over 70 parks and gardens in the city where you can escape for a while.

Beyond the city limits, you can trace the river through the Clyde Valley all the way to the picturesque Falls of Clyde in Lanarkshire, just beside the immaculately preserved village of New Lanark which is a World Heritage Site.

On the Clyde coast you can take a trip 'doon the watter' in the P.S. Waverley, the world's last sea-going paddle steamer. At Strathclyde Country Park in Motherwell and Mugdock Country Park near Milngavie you'll enjoy a wide range of outdoor activities including walking, cycling, horse riding and much more.

Glasgow's maritime history can be explored at The Scottish Maritime Museum in Braehead and in Paisley you'll find an impressive Abbey dating back to 1163. Both places are just a short journey away from the city of Glasgow.

What's more, 2009 is a big year for Scotland – we're celebrating the 250th anniversary of the birth of Robert Burns. There's over 200 special events taking place throughout the year, all over Scotland. Go to homecomingscotland2009.com to find out about events in this area.

Whatever you choose to do, wherever you stay – either uptown in the city, in the suburbs or in the surrounding countryside – a visit to Glasgow and Clyde Valley will be a revelation and you'll be very glad you came.

What's On?

Celtic Connections
15 January – 1 February 2009
Recognised as the principal Celtic Festival in the UK, this event is a must for any traditional music lover.
celticconnections.com

Glasgow Film Festival
12 – 22 February 2009
Premiers and previews galore as Glasgow celebrates its 5th festival celebrating the city's love of the movies.
glasgowfilmfestival.org.uk

Aye Write!
The Bank of Scotland Book Festival
6 – 14 March 2009
An annual literature festival celebrating both Scottish and international writers.
ayewrite.com

Glasgow Art Fair
23 – 26 April 2009
With over 50 galleries and art organisations in one place, the 14th national fair is THE place to view, buy and sell art in Scotland.
glasgowartfair.com

Paisley Beer Festival
29 April – 2 May 2009
Scotland's largest real ale festival, with well over 100 real ales on tap.
paisleybeerfestival.org.uk

Glasgow River Festival
Mid July 2009
A weekend of land and water-based entertainment for the whole family on the banks of the River Clyde.
glasgowriverfestival.co.uk

Kirkintilloch Canal Festival
29 – 30 August 2009
Two days of fun in the 'Canal Capital of Scotland'.
kirkintillochcanalfestival.org.uk

World Pipe Band Championships
15 August 2009
Piping Live: International Piping Festival, August 10 - 16 2009
A piping spectacular, with Music of the Clans – a special series of Homecoming events dedicated to Scottish heritage and piping.
pipinglive.co.uk

Merchant City Festival, Glasgow
24 – 27 September 2009
Festival celebrating the cultural richness of the city's old commercial quarter.
merchantcityfestival.com

Glasgow's Hogmanay
31 December 2009 – 1 January 2010
Bring in the New Year with live bands.
winterfestglasgow.com

All dates correct at time of publication. Please check before booking. VisitScotland cannot be held responsible for any inaccuracies

63

DON'T MISS

1   **Kelvingrove Art Gallery and Museum** - Scotland's most visited museum re-opened in 2006 following a three-year, £27.9 million restoration project. It now has a collection of 8,000 objects on display over three floors – 4,000 more than ever before. Old favourites and exciting new arrivals are waiting to welcome you. Forget everything you think you know about museums, Kelvingrove is different.

2   Located within the World Heritage Site of **New Lanark**, the Falls of Clyde Wildlife Reserve covers 59 hectares, has woodland along the River Clyde gorge and 4 spectacular waterfalls. Breeding peregrine falcons, tawny owls and sparrowhawks rule the air while badgers, foxes and roe deer can also be seen. The river is home to otters, dippers, herons and kingfishers. The recently refurbished visitor centre includes interactive interpretation highlighting these key species.

3   It's all about fun when you're on holidays but what if at the same time you could sneak in a bit of learning? **Glasgow Science Centre** has the answer. Easily accessible from Glasgow city centre by car, subway, train or bus, the Centre stands tall and instantly recognisable on the River Clyde. The interactive exhibits can keep not only the children entertained but the adults too and that's before you hit the IMAX cinema and the ScottishPower Planetarium.

4   Glasgow University's **Hunterian Art Gallery & Museum** hosts an extensive art collection of superb quality, with outstanding works by Rembrandt, Whistler, Chardin, Stubbs, the Scottish Colourists and many more. See the most significant collection of original Charles Rennie Mackintosh works in the world and visit the Mackintosh House – his Glasgow home.

5   One of Scotland's most magnificent medieval buildings, **Glasgow Cathedral**, is one of the few Scottish medieval churches to survive the reformation of 1560 intact. The tomb of St. Mungo, Glasgow's patron saint and founder, is located within the church. Beside the Cathedral is Glasgow Necropolis, the "City of the Dead". This Victorian garden cemetery is a real hidden gem and offers a unique insight into Glasgow's social and economic heritage.

6   The **Gallery of Modern Art** opened in 1996 and is housed in an elegant, neo-classical building in the heart of the city centre. The building was refurbished to house the city's contemporary art collection, and is an appealing combination of old and new architecture. GoMA is now the second most visited contemporary gallery outside London, offering an outstanding programme of temporary exhibitions and workshops.

FOOD AND DRINK

eatscotland.com

7 In the Merchant City, **Rogano** (11 Exchange Place) is a must. Since 1935 Rogano has been preparing the finest Scottish seafood and serving it in its unique Art Deco surroundings with the wonderful flair of that bygone era. Rogano is a Glasgow institution.

8 With a motto like "Think global, eat local" it is not surprising that the menu at **Stravaigin** (28 Gibson St) has been built from diverse world influences while focusing on the best of Scottish ingredients. The result is a collection of eclectic and globe trotting dishes. Stravaigin is an excellent example of West End dining.

9 Special occasions will go off nicely at **Brian Maule at Chardon d'Or** (176 West Regent St). Brian Maul was head chef at Le Gavroche for 7 years. He combines his French culinary skill with Scottish produce to create a taste sensation! Since opening, the restaurant has been extended to include private dining rooms and a bar in the basement.

10 If Indian food is your thing, try **The Dhabba**, (44 Candleriggs) which specialises in authentic North Indian cuisine, or the Dakhin, (First Floor, 89 Candleriggs) where the focus is on South Indian cuisine. Both restaurants are situated in the fashionable Merchant City area, and both use only the freshest ingredients to create many unusual regional dishes. Perfect for the seasoned Indian food fan and novice alike.

ACTIVITIES

11 Just north of Glasgow, near Loch Lomond, is **Glengoyne Distillery**. The distillery is open all year round and offers the most in-depth range of tours in the industry, from the Masterblender Tour, where guests create their very own blended whisky, to the Cask Tasting Tour, specially designed for guests who enjoy tasting, and learning about, cask strength whisky.

12 Enjoy a seaplane flight from Glasgow to Oban Bay on Scotland's west coast with **Loch Lomond Seaplanes**. The journey, which takes approximately 25 minutes, will take you over areas of outstanding natural beauty. Once in Oban, there's time for a bite to eat and a spot of sightseeing before the return journey. Or if you prefer, extend your stay and return at a later date.

13 As you enter through the main doors of **Xscape** you can watch brave souls hanging from the ceiling as they have a go on the state of the art aerial adventure course. The Centre houses numerous outdoor shops, restaurants, bars, bowling, rock climbing, a cinema and much more. However, without a doubt the piece-de-résistance is the incredible SNO!zone which allows you to experience indoor skiing, snowboarding or sledging on the UK's biggest indoor real snow slope.

14 Charles Rennie Mackintosh is considered the father of the 'Glasgow Style', with his motifs instantly recognisable to visitors. He was a true visionary who worked almost exclusively in the city. His legacy lives on and can be enjoyed with the help of a **Mackintosh Trail** ticket giving admission to all associated attractions in and around Glasgow including the School of Art, Scotland Street School Museum, House for an Art Lover and the Mackintosh Church. The ticket can be purchased at Glasgow Visitor Information Centres, SPT Travel Centres, all participating Mackintosh venues or online at crmsociety.com.

SHOPPING

15 **Buchanan Street** is arguably one of the classiest major shopping thoroughfares in Britain. With a tempting mix of big high street names, alternative retailers and designer outlets, it's deservedly popular. **Buchanan Galleries** at the top of the street offers a choice of over 80 shops including John Lewis. A must visit.

16 The true highlight of Buchanan Street is **Princes Square**: a speciality shopping centre in a beautifully restored listed building dating from 1841. The architects have preserved many original features whilst transforming the interior to create a venue for shopping where designer boutiques and stylish eateries are linked by escalators criss-crossing over a central courtyard.

17 Visitors in search of the city's chic and modern side should head to the **Merchant City**. Originally landscaped for the homes and warehouses of 18th century tobacco barons, it is now the city's main style quarter. Wander around its innovative boutiques in search of that must-have item.

18 With strong Italian heritage, it's only fitting that there should be somewhere to purchase the latest fashions from Milan. With designer boutiques such as Versace Collections and Emporio Armani the **Italian Centre** may be easier on the eye than on the pocket, but it's ideal for a treat.

19 Glasgow is often complimented for its European flavour, and nowhere is this more in evidence than on **Byres Road**, with its fruit and veg stalls, butchers, fishmongers, flanking hip record stores and clothing retailers. Head to the West End for some wonderful eateries in the mews lanes off Byres Road.

20 Out of town there's **Braehead Shopping Centre** near Glasgow Airport, Silverburn Shopping Centre in Pollock, which opened its doors in late 2007, and Glasgow Fort located east of the city at junction 10 on the M8.

HERITAGE AND CULTURE

21 Take in a **football** match for 90 minutes you'll never forget. It would be an understatement to say that Glaswegians have a passion for the beautiful game, and Glasgow is the only city in the UK to support three 50,000+ capacity football stadiums. Situated within the national stadium of Hampden, the Scottish Football Museum is an essential attraction for all football fans.

22 From Celtic Connections each January to the Magners International Comedy Festival in March and Piping Live! in August, the Glasgow calendar is filled with live performances, **events and festivals** and entertainment throughout the year.

23 Situated within beautiful Bellahouston Park, **House for an Art Lover** was inspired by Charles Rennie Mackintosh designs from 1901. Its restaurant houses changing art exhibitions and visitors are entertained throughout the year with a programme of dinner concerts and afternoon music recitals.

24 Built in 1898 for the people of Glasgow's East End, the **People's Palace** and **Winter Gardens** tells the story of Glasgow from 1750 to the present day. Outside the museum stands the spectacular Doulton Fountain – the largest terracotta fountain in the world. Gifted to Glasgow by Henry Doulton, it has recently been restored.

MAP

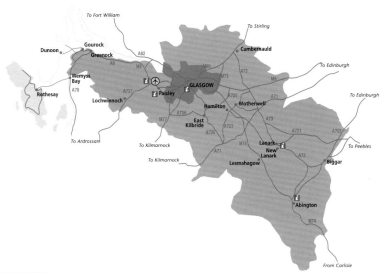

©Collins Bartholomew Ltd 2008

VISITOR INFORMATION CENTRES

Visitor Information Centres are staffed by people 'in the know' offering friendly advice, helping to make your stay in Scotland the most enjoyable ever . . . whatever your needs!

Greater Glasgow & Clyde Valley		
Abington	Welcome Break, Motorway Service Area, Junction 13, M74 Abington, ML12 6RG	Tel: 01864 502436
Glasgow	11 George Square, Glasgow G2 1DY	Tel: 0141 204 4400
Glasgow Airport	International Arrivals Hall, Glasgow International Airport, PA3 2ST	Tel: 0141 848 4440
Lanark	Horsemarket, Ladyacre Road, Lanark, ML11 7QD	Tel: 01555 661661
Paisley	9A Gilmour Street, Paisley, PA1 1DD	Tel: 0141 889 0711

LOCAL KNOWLEDGE • WHERE TO STAY • ACCOMMODATION BOOKING • PLACES TO VISIT • THINGS TO DO • MAPS AND GUIDES TRAVEL ADVICE • ROUTE PLANNING • WHERE TO SHOP AND EAT LOCAL CRAFTS AND PRODUCE • EVENT INFORMATION • TICKETS

For information and ideas about exploring Scotland in advance of your trip, call our booking and information service **0845 22 55 121** or go to **visitscotland.com**

If calling from outside the UK and Ireland **+44 1506 832 121**   From Ireland **1800 932 510**

A £4 booking fee applies for accommodation bookings made via a Visitor Information Centre and through our booking and information service.

Live it. Visit *Scotland.*
visitscotland.com/wheretofindus

Greater Glasgow and Clyde Valley

Glasgow
Acorn Hotel
Map Ref: 1H5

★★★ METRO HOTEL

Open: All year
140 Elderslie Street, Glasgow G3 7AW
T: 0141 332 6556
E: acorn@mcquadehotels.com
W: mcquadehotels.com

80387

Total number of rooms: 18

Prices from:
Single:	£55.00	Double:	£33.00
Twin:	£33.00	Family room:	£25.00

Glasgow
Adelaides Guest House
Map Ref: 1H5

★★ GUEST HOUSE

Open: All year excl between Xmas and New Year
209 Bath Street, Glasgow G2 4HZ
T: 0141 248 4970
E: reservations@adelaides.co.uk
W: adelaides.co.uk

11097

A sensitively redeveloped 1877 Baptist Church building. Modernised and upgraded with individually controllable room heating, rooms are attractively furnished. All with direct dial telephones, colour TV and complimentary tea and coffee facilities. Adelaides is central to the attractions of this revitalised city, known for its character, hospitality and friendliness.

Total number of rooms: 8

Prices from:
Single:	£30.00	Double:	£30.00
Twin:	£30.00	Family room:	£20.00

Glasgow
Albion Hotel
Map Ref: 1H5

★★★ METRO HOTEL

Open: All year
405 North Woodside Road, Glasgow G20 6NN
T: 0141 339 8620
E: info@glasgowhotelsandapartments.co.uk
W: glasgowhotelsandapartments.co.uk

11443

Total number of rooms: 17

Prices from:
Single:	£45.00	Double:	£30.00
Twin:	£30.00	Family room:	£23.00

Glasgow
Amadeus Guest House
Map Ref: 1H5

★★ GUEST HOUSE

Open: All year
411 North Woodside Road, Glasgow G20 6NN
T: 0141 339 8257
E: reservations@amadeusguesthouse.co.uk
W: amadeusguesthouse.co.uk

11842

The Amadeus Guest House is conveniently located at Kelvinbridge in the West End of Glasgow. We offer comfortable and affordable bed and continental breakfast accommodation. Our two storey Victorian townhouse has nine bedrooms mostly ensuite. Our friendly team will endeavour to make your stay enjoyable. Book early to avoid disappointment!

Total number of rooms: 9

Prices per room from:
Single:	£24.00	Double:	£58.00
Twin:	£58.00	Family room:	£70.00

IMPORTANT: Prices stated are estimates and may be subject to change. Prices are per person per night unless otherwise stated. Awards correct as of beginning of October 2008.

lasgow
mbassador Hotel

Map Ref: 1H5

★★★
METRO
HOTEL

11852

Open: All year
7 Kelvin Drive, Glasgow G20 8QG
T: 0141 946 1018
E: info@glasgowhotelsandapartments.co.uk
W: glasgowhotelsandapartments.co.uk

Total number of rooms: 17

Prices from:

Single:	£45.00	Double:	£30.00
Twin:	£30.00	Family room:	£23.00

lasgow
ampanile Hotel Glasgow

Map Ref: 1H5

★★★
HOTEL

17786

Open: All year
10 Tunnel Street, Glasgow G3 8HL
T: 0141 287 7700
E: glasgow@campanile.com
W: campanile.com

Total number of rooms: 104

Prices per room from:

Single:	£85.00	Double:	£85.00
Twin:	£85.00		

lasgow
uro Hostels

Map Ref: 1H5

★★★
OSTEL

25189

Open: All year
318 Clyde Street, Glasgow G1 4NR
T: 0141 222 2828
E: glasgow@euro-hostels.co.uk
W: euro-hostels.co.uk

At Euro Hostel you're in control. You can choose private rooms or shared dorms. The larger the room, the less each of you pay. The hostel also features our lively bar ' Osmosis,' guest kitchen and dining room, free Wi-Fi, internet access terminals, guest laundry and TV lounges.

Located in Glasgow City Centre (not nearby, but right slap in the city-centre), makes our hostel ideally suited for anyone looking for low-cost budget accommodation.

Whether your travelling alone, with a few friends or in a large group; at Euro Hostel we're 100% confident you won't find rooms like ours at a better price.

Total number of rooms: 115

Prices from:

Single:	£29.95	Double:	£18.95
Twin:	£18.95	Family room:	£16.95

For a full listing of quality assured serviced accommodation throughout Scotland see pages 195-278.

69

Glasgow
The Heritage Hotel

★★★
GUEST HOUSE

Map Ref: 1H5

66011

Open: All year excl Xmas

4-5 Alfred Terrace, Glasgow G12 8RF
T: 0141 339 6955 **F:** 0141 339 6955
E: bookings@heritagehotel.fsbusiness.co.uk
W: theheritagehotel.net

Stylish, elegant and charming - Victorian Hotel situated in the West End of Glasgow. A short stroll away from Byres Road, Kelvingrove Art Gallery, Botanic Gardens, Glasgow University and Transport Museum. Five minutes away from the underground, bus stops and restaurants. All ensuite rooms with free Wi-Fi available.

Total number of rooms: 27

Prices per room from:

Single:	£35.00	Double:	£55.00
Twin:	£60.00	Family room:	£80.00

Glasgow
The Kelvin

★★
GUEST HOUSE

Map Ref: 1H5

33519

Open: All year

15 Buckingham Terrace,
Great Western Road, Glasgow G12 8EB
T: 0141 339 7143
E: enquiries@kelvinhotel.com
W: kelvinhotel.com

Conveniently located in the heart of Glasgow's fashionable West End, close to all amenities, only 1 mile from the city centre. Quality accommodation and a warm atmosphere at this family run hotel. All rooms have Freeview TV and complimentary tea/coffee. Some rooms ensuite. Small car park and free on-street parking.

Total number of rooms: 21

Prices from:

Single:	£30.00	Double:	£25.00
Twin:	£25.00	Family room:	£22.00

Glasgow
Kelvingrove Hotel

★★★
GUEST HOUSE

Map Ref: 1H5

66030

Open: All year

944 Sauchiehall Street, Glasgow, G3 7TH
T: 0141 339 5011
E: info@kelvingrovehotel.com
W: kelvingrovehotel.com

You will always be sure of a warm welcome at the 22 room Kelvingrove which is centrally located in Glasgow's Sauchiehall Street.
Run by three generations of the same family, the hotel offers exceptional service and excellent accommodation attracting many guests back year after year.

Total number of rooms: 22

Prices from:

Single:	£50.00-70.00	Double:	£35.00-45.00
Twin:	£35.00-45.00	Family room:	£30.00-40.00

lasgow
Ialmaison Glasgow   Map Ref: 1H5

Open: All year

278 West George Street, Glasgow G2 4LL

T: 0141 572 1000
E: glasgow@malmaison.com
W: malmaison.com

37231

Total number of rooms: 72

Prices per room from:

Double: **£109.00**   Twin: **£109.00**

---

lasgow
ewton Hotel   Map Ref: 1H5

Open: All year excl Xmas

248-252 Bath Street, Glasgow G2 4JW

T: 0141 332 1666 **F:** 0141 332 7722
E: info@newtonhotel.co.uk
W: newtonhotel.co.uk

Newton Hotel is a stylish privately run hotel central to all major attractions in the vibrant and exciting city of Glasgow, with Sauchiehall Street around the corner and a variety of restaurants and bars a stones throw away. An experience too good to be missed.

67438

Total number of rooms: 19

Prices per room from:

Single: **£35.00**   Double: **£55.00**
Twin: **£65.00**   Family room: **£80.00**

---

r Glasgow
plawmoor Hotel and Restaurant Map Ref: 1G6

Open: All year excl 26th December, 1st January

Neilston Road, Uplawmoor,
Glasgow, Renfrewshire G78 4AF

T: 01505 850565
E: info@uplawmoor.co.uk
W: uplawmoor.co.uk

Located in a small picturesque village just 20 minutes from city and airport, close to Silverburn Shopping Centre, The Burrell Collection and the Ayrshire border, gateway to Burns Country. Standard and superior newly refurbished rooms, open fire, Wi-Fi, quality bar meals, real ales, 2 AA Rosette restaurant, and genuine Scottish hospitality. A warm welcome awaits.

62628

Total number of rooms: 14

Prices from:

Single: **£55.00**   Double: **£32.50**
Twin: **£32.50**

---

aisley, Renfrewshire
Dryesdale Guest House   Map Ref: 1H5

Open: All year

37 Inchinnan Road, Paisley, Renfrewshire PA3 2PR

T: 0141 889 7178
E: dd@paisley2001.freeserve.co.uk
W: ga-taxis.co.uk/dryesdale.html

23366

Total number of rooms: 6

Prices from:

Single: **£28.00**   Double: **£24.00**
Twin: **£24.00**   Family room: **£24.00**

For a full listing of quality assured serviced accommodation throughout Scotland see pages 195-278.

71

Oban waterfront at night

WEST HIGHLANDS AND ISLANDS, LOCH LOMOND, STIRLING AND TROSSACHS

Contrast is the word that best sums up an area that spans Scotland from the shores of the Forth in the east to the very tip of Tiree in the west. Here the Highlands meet the Lowlands and geography and cultures diverge.

For the visitor, the endlessly changing landscape means a rich and varied holiday experience.

There are rugged high mountains, spectacular freshwater lochs, fascinating islands and dramatic seascapes. You'll find pretty villages, mill towns, not to mention one of Scotland's newest cities, Stirling.

Discover the birthplace of the Scots nation and visit places that witnessed some of the most dramatic scenes in Scotland's history.

On the eastern side of the country the flat plain of the Forth Valley stretches up from the River Forth towards the little towns of the Hillfoots, which enjoy the spectacular backdrop of the Ochil Hills.

Elsewhere in the Forth Valley, you can visit Scotland's smallest county, Clackmannanshire, or the Wee County as it is known. Head for Dollar Glen and the magnificent Castle Campbell, once the Lowland stronghold of the Clan Campbell.

Moving to the Hillfoot towns you'll be tracing the roots of Scotland's textile industry which has thrived here for many years. Learn the history of the local woollen industry at the Mill Trail Visitor Centre in Alva.

New city, ancient history

Beyond Alva to the west lies Stirling – a city since 2002 and one of the most important places in Scottish history thanks to its strategically important location as the gateway to the Highlands.

Once, whoever controlled Stirling, controlled Scotland. Its impressive castle stands guard over all it surveys and was the capital for the Stewart Kings. It's

To find out more, call 0845 22 55 121 or go to visitscotland.com

a relatively quiet spot these days but no fewer than seven battle sites can be seen from the Castle ramparts – including Stirling Bridge, a scene of triumph for William Wallace and Bannockburn where Robert the Bruce led the Scots to victory in 1314.

A National Park on your doorstep

Scotland's first national park Loch Lomond and the Trossachs National Park, takes advantage of the natural treasures of this area and that means 20 Munros (mountains over 3,000ft) to climb, 50 rivers to fish, 22 lochs to sail and thousands of miles of road and track to cycle. When you've had your fill of activities, head for Loch Lomond Shores for a cultural and retail experience.

You can also cruise on Loch Lomond. It's Britain's biggest freshwater expanse and there's no better way to see the surrounding countryside than from the water.

Heading west the Whisky Coast round Islay and Jura are waiting to be explored – Islay alone has eight working distilleries!

A place in history

Further west still, The Cowal Peninsula with its sea lochs and deep forests is beautiful and relaxing. To get there, just jump aboard the ferry at Gourock and sail for Dunoon. While you're there, don't miss the nearby Benmore Botanic Gardens.

Explore Lochgilphead and beyond to Kilmartin where you can trace the very roots of the nation where the Scots arrived from Ireland in the 6th century.

What's more, 2009 is a big year for Scotland – we're celebrating the 250th anniversary of the birth of Robert Burns. There's over 200 special events taking place throughout the year, all over Scotland. Go to homecomingscotland2009.com to find out about events in this area.

Choosing a holiday destination in an area as diverse as this will always be difficult but the stunning array of hotels and guesthouses will help firm up your thoughts. There are historical inns, grand hotels, intimate romantic country houses, and even restaurants with rooms, so you're sure to find somewhere that will tempt you to return time and time again.

The Mishnish Hotel, Tobermory, Isle of Mull

What's On?

Big in Falkirk
2 – 3 May 2009
Scotland's largest streets arts festival features music, outdoor theatre and art in Callendar Park. A two-day extravaganza not to be missed!
biginfalkirk.co.uk

The Loch Lomond Food & Drink Festival
30 – 31 May 2009
A showcase for local food and great chefs, giving the visitor a chance to sample the delicious servings amongst the stunning backdrop of Loch Lomond.
lochlomondfoodanddrinkfestival.com

Scottish Pipe Band Championship
May 2009
For one day in May, Dumbarton will be alive to the skirl of pipes. A world-class competition with competitors from all over the globe.
rspba.org

World Fly Fishing Championships
5 – 12 June 2009
Welcoming anglers from over 25 countries over 7 days of competition, showcasing the fishing sites and surrounding landscapes of Stirling & Perthshire to an international audience.
worldflyfishingchampionships2009.com

Helensburgh and Loch Lomond Highland Games
14 June 2009
Come experience the Highland Games with traditional events such as tossing the caber, putting the stone, throwing the hammer and many more making this a fun-filled day out.
helensburghandlomondgames.co.uk

Cowal Highland Gathering
27 – 29 August 2009
Dating back to 1894, the Gathering is described as 'the largest and most spectacular Highland Games in the world'
cowalgathering.com

Connect Festival, Inveraray
28 – 30 August 2009
Pack your campervan and head for connect at Inveraray Castle. It's simply one of the best summer rock festivals in the UK.
connectmusicfestival.com

Off the Page – The Stirling Book Festival
13 – 20 September 2009
A celebration of writing in its various forms for adults, children and families. Lots of exciting events throughout the area in the library-organised festival that celebrates its fourth year.
stirling.gov.uk/offthepage

Cowalfest
9 – 18 October 2009
Scotland's largest walking festival with cycling, wildlife, the arts, film, music and drama thrown in.

All dates correct at time of publication. Please check before booking. VisitScotland cannot be held responsible for any inaccuracies

73

MAP

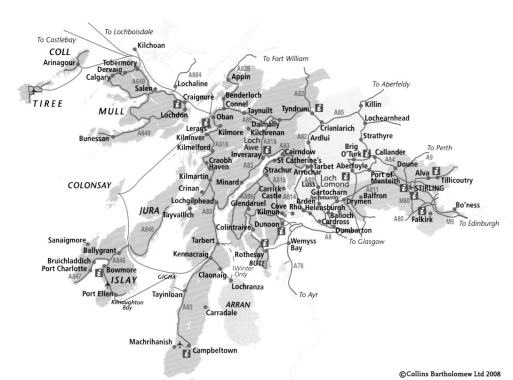

©Collins Bartholomew Ltd 2008

To find out more, call 0845 22 55 121 or go to visitscotland.com

VISITOR INFORMATION CENTRES

Visitor Information Centres are staffed by people 'in the know' offering friendly advice, helping to make your stay in Scotland the most enjoyable ever . . . whatever your needs!

West Highlands

Bowmore	The Square, Bowmore, Isle of Islay, PA43 7JP	Tel: 01496 810254
Campbeltown	Mackinnon House, The Pier, Campbeltown, PA28 6EF	Tel: 01586 552056
Craignure	The Pier, Craignure, Isle of Mull, PA65 6AY	Tel: 01680 812377
Dunoon	7 Alexander Place, Dunoon, PA23 8AB	Tel: 01369 703785
Inveraray	Front Street, Inveraray, PA32 8UY	Tel: 01499 302063
Oban	Argyll Square, Oban, PA34 4AR	Tel: 01631 563122
Rothesay	Winter Gardens, Rothesay, Isle of Bute, PA20 0AJ	Tel: 01700 502151

Loch Lomond

Aberfoyle	Trossachs Discovery Centre, Main Street, Aberfoyle, FK8 3UQ	Tel: 01877 382352
Callander	Ancaster Square, Callander, FK17 8ED	Tel: 01877 330342
Tyndrum	Main Street, Tyndrum, FK20 8RY	Tel: 01838 400324

Stirling & Trossachs

Falkirk	The Falkirk Wheel, Lime Road, Tamfourhill, Falkirk, FK1 4RS	Tel: 01324 620244
Stirling (Dumbarton Rd)	41 Dumbarton Road, Stirling, FK8 2LQ	Tel: 01786 475019
Stirling (Pirnhall)	Motorway Service Area, Junction 9, M9	Tel: 01786 814111
Tillicoultry	Unit 22, Sterling Mills Outlet Village, Devondale, Tillicoultry, Clackmannanshire, FK13 6HQ	Tel: 01259 769696

LOCAL KNOWLEDGE • WHERE TO STAY • ACCOMMODATION BOOKING • PLACES TO VISIT • THINGS TO DO • MAPS AND GUIDES TRAVEL ADVICE • ROUTE PLANNING • WHERE TO SHOP AND EAT LOCAL CRAFTS AND PRODUCE • EVENT INFORMATION • TICKETS

For information and ideas about exploring Scotland in advance of your trip, call our booking and information service **0845 22 55 121** or go to **visitscotland.com**

If calling from outside the UK and Ireland **+44 1506 832 121**   From Ireland **1800 932 510**

A £4 booking fee applies for accommodation bookings made via a Visitor Information Centre and through our booking and information service.

Island of Tiree, Inner Hebrides

West Highlands and Islands

Savour the atmosphere of the rugged west coast and take a journey around some of Scotland's most magical isles and peninsulas. The pace of island life is a powerful draw for visitors and, while there are parts of the mainland around Kintyre which feel more like island than mainland, if you're looking for the genuine island experience, you'll be spoiled for choice.

The many islands to explore include Gigha, Jura, Islay and Colonsay. And no trip to these parts would be complete without visiting Oban, the gateway to the isles, from where boats make their way to and from the likes of Mull, Coll, Tiree and Colonsay.

They all have their own special allure. Visit Islay for the whisky, deeply spiritual Iona, and Mull, where you can see colourful Tobermory (or Balamory as families with young children will recognise it). On your way to the isles stop off in Oban, its harbour is always bustling and the area around the port has a great selection of shops, bars and restaurants.

Sambayabamba at the Connect Music Festival, Inveraray

DON'T MISS

1   Wherever you travel in this area, you're never far from one of the **whisky distilleries**. Islay alone is home to eight working distilleries, producing world-famous whiskies such as Laphroaig and Bowmore, renowned for their peaty qualities. Here, you'll also find Kilchoman, a recently opened farm distillery. The neighbouring Isle of Jura manufactures its own popular malt, while Campbeltown on Kintyre now boasts two local whiskies, Springbank and Glengyle, the latter dating from only 2004. Facilities and opening hours vary.

2   **Island Exploring** is a must in the West Highlands and with such a diversity of locations all linked by ferry, it's a popular choice. Iona Abbey is considered the origin for the spread of Christianity throughout Scotland and is a must-visit on Iona. Explore Fingal's Cave on Staffa, the surfing on Tiree and the whiskies of Islay. White beaches, tasty organic food and spectacular scenery welcome you and urge your return.

3   Any trip which takes in the breathtaking Argyll coastline or Argyll's Atlantic Islands, known as **Scotland's Sea Kingdom**, promises a memorable experience. Negotiate the Gulf of Corryvreckan with its famous whirlpool and travel round Scarba while looking out for whales, dolphins, deer and eagles, or venture further to the remote Garvellachs. You can sail from Ardfern with Craignish Cruises, from Craobh Haven with Farsain Cruises, from Crinan with Gemini Cruises or from Easdale with Seafari Adventures or Sealife Adventures.

4   **Mount Stuart** on the Isle of Bute was the ancestral home of the Marquess of Bute. Today it is a high quality, award-winning, four-star attraction featuring magnificent Victorian Gothic architecture and design together with contemporary craftsmanship. Mount Stuart is surrounded by 300 acres of gloriously maintained grounds and gardens.

5   **Kilmartin Glen** is home to a myriad of Neolithic and Bronze Age monuments, coupled with early Christian carved stones and ruined castles. South of Oban, this site was capital of the ancient Celtic kingdom of Dalriada, as evidenced at Dunadd Fort, where a footprint in the stone is thought to have featured in royal inauguration ceremonies.

6   The common characteristic of the **Glorious Gardens of Argyll & Bute** is their individuality. Each garden has a variety of terrain; many are mainly level with smooth paths, while some are steep and rocky. The gardens range from informal woodland gardens to beautiful classic examples of 18th century design.

FOOD AND DRINK
eatscotland.com

7   The original **Loch Fyne Oyster Bar** and shop started in a small shed in the lay-by at the head of Loch Fyne in the early 1980s. In 1985 it moved into the old cow byre at Clachan Farm. It has been listed in the Good Food Guide every year since then.

8   Among the many fine restaurants across the West Highlands, **Coast** in Oban stands out with its clean, calming feel and contemporary approach to food. Both light bite and a la carte menus are brimming with the fresh seafood synonymous in the area. You can let your food go down while watching the sunset across Oban Bay.

9   **The Seafood Trail** takes you through some of the most spectacular coastal scenery Scotland has to offer, and enables seafood lovers to sample, share and enjoy seafood and shellfish from a wide variety of waterfront establishments.

10 The **Whisky Coast** blends incredible Scottish scenery with arguably the best sixteen single malt whiskies for a truly memorable experience. Getting to and around the Whisky Coast is surprisingly easy for the independent traveller in search of stunning landscapes and the finest whiskies, as the area is well served by road, rail, air and ferry.

WILDLIFE
visitscotland.com/wildlife

11 There are numerous operators that offer **sea trip safaris** around **Oban** and **Mull** where you can spot majestic wildlife against a backdrop of spectacular scenery. The wildlife in this area is magnificent and you may well spot the majestic sea eagle, golden eagle, or a range of seabirds along with seals, dolphins, porpoises and the occasional minke whale.

12 The extensive **Argyll Forest Park** offers a perfect introduction to Loch Lomond & The Trossachs National Park. Start at the Ardgartan Visitor Centre on the A83 at the north of Loch Long, where the Boathouse and Riverside walks provide options for pushchairs. You'll also find cycle paths, a play area and refreshments. With its spectacular mountains, glens, lochs and woodlands, many claim that Britain's first forest park is also the finest.

13 The islands of **Islay and Jura** are something of a mecca for **wildlife** lovers. With well over a hundred breeding bird species in summer, and some of Europe's largest populations of wintering wildfowl, they are a year round destination for ornithologists. Add to this some exceptional marine wildlife, including minke whales, common and bottlenose dolphins, basking sharks and literally thousands of seals, alongside some of Britain's best opportunities to spy otters, red deer and golden eagles, and you have a natural paradise. A particular highlight is the arrival of around 50,000 barnacle and white-fronted geese from the Arctic Circle each autumn.

14 **Wildlife and bird watching safaris** offer the chance to explore the remote areas of Mull with experienced guides to help you spot and learn about the wildlife which inhabits the island. This is your chance to see golden eagles, otters, harriers and merlin to name a few.

WALKS

visitscotland.com/walking

15   **Lismore** is a lovely location to get away from it all and is easy to reach by boat from Oban. The island is just 12 miles long and 1.5 miles at its widest point, and offers many interesting walks with spectacular views of the sea and mountains. Kerrera is a beautiful island where it is also possible to walk round the entire island although this walk is about 10 miles and will take some time.

16   The wonderfully unexplored Kintyre Peninsula boasts hidden coves, deserted beaches, tiny fishing communities, gentle hills, fabulous local produce and welcoming friendly people. Stretching from Tarbert to Southend, the waymarked **Kintyre Way** criss-crosses the peninsula, connecting communities and landscape, people and produce. At 89 miles long (142 kms), and with 4 to 7 days worth of walking, there's serious hiking and gentle rambles, all of which bring home the beautiful reality that is Kintyre.

17   The **West Island Way**, which opened in September 2000, is the first long distance way-marked path on a Scottish island. It encompasses some of the best walking that the Isle of Bute has to offer, runs the length of the island and embraces a variety of landscapes.

18   **The Cowal Way** follows a route running the length of Argyll's Cowal peninsula. It starts in the south-west at Portavadie beside Loch Fyne, and finishes in the north-east at Ardgartan by Loch Long, and involves walking on roads and on lochside, hill and woodland terrains. The way-marked route is 75 kms/47 miles in length and is divided into six shorter, more manageable sections.

ACTIVITIES

19   Tiny Port Askaig on Islay is something of a ferry hub, serving Colonsay, the mainland and Jura. Its proximity to the last makes it an ideal location to view the **Paps of Jura**, three rounded mountains rising out of the sea to over 730m. Relax with a drink outside the Port Askaig Hotel and soak up the view.

20   The village of Carradale on the eastern side of Kintyre makes an excellent base from which to explore the peninsula. The delightful beach and harbour area offer stunning views over the Kilbrannan Sound to the dramatic hills of **Arran**.

21   One of Scotland's most romanticised stretches of water, the narrow straits known as the **Kyles of Bute**, more than live up to their reputation. The Kyles are best admired from the viewpoint on the A886 above Colintraive, where the view to their namesake island is truly awe-inspiring. Remember to bring along your picnic so you can really make the most of this view and open space.

22   The steep 10-minute climb from the centre of Oban to **McCaig's Tower** is well worth it for the view of Oban Bay, Kerrera and the Isle of Mull. The Tower was built by a local banker in the late 19th century in an effort to replicate Rome's Colosseum. The view of the town and the islands to the west is breathtaking.

West Highlands and Islands

Rothesay, Isle of Bute
The Ardyne
Map Ref: 1F5

★★★
SMALL HOTEL

Open: All year excl Xmas

38 Mount Stuart Road, Rothesay, Isle of Bute PA20 9EB
T: 01700 502052
E: info@theardynehotel.co.uk
W: theardynehotel.co.uk

Situated on the seafront with stunning views from the lounge bar, dining room and many of the bedrooms. Excellent reputation for comfortable accommodation as well as for serving the best of Scottish Fayre.

Total number of rooms: 16

Prices from:			
Single:	**£40.00**	Double:	**£35.00**
Twin:	**£35.00**	Family room:	**£35.00**

Rothsay, Isle of Bute
Glendale Guest House
Map Ref: 1F5

★★★★
GUEST HOUSE

Open: All year excl Xmas and New Year

20 Battery Place, Rothesay, Isle of Bute PA20 9DU
T: 01700 502329
E: glendale.rothesay@btinternet.com
W: glendale-guest-house.com

Keir and Fiona welcome you to our unique Victorian house ideally situated on seafront 2 mins walk to pier and town centre. Glendale has 10 ensuite bedrooms all decorated to high standard. Relax in our beautiful residents' lounge with panoramic views of Rothesay Bay and watch the world go by. Breakfasts a speciality.

Total number of rooms: 10

Prices from:			
Single:	**£35.00**	Double:	**£30.00**
Twin:	**£30.00**	Family room:	**£75.00pr**

Rothesay Castle, Rothesay on the Isle of Bute, Argyll

IMPORTANT: Prices stated are estimates and may be subject to change. Prices are per person per night unless otherwise stated. Awards correct as of beginning of October 2008.

West Highlands and Islands

Cairndow, Argyll
Cairndow Stagecoach Inn
Map Ref: 1F3

★★
INN

Open: All year excl Xmas Day

Cairndow, Argyll & Bute PA26 8BN
T: 01499 600286
E: enq@cairndowinn.com
W: cairndowinn.com

Douglas and Catherine Fraser extend a warm welcome in the best traditions of Scottish hospitality in one of the oldest coaching inns in the Highlands. The inn has 20 en-suite rooms, six of which are deluxe lochside rooms equipped with queen-size beds, spa-baths and your own private lochside view balcony.

Total number of rooms: 19			
Prices from:			
Single:	**£50.00**	Double:	**£80.00**
Twin:	**£70.00**	Family room:	**£90.00**

Campbeltown, Argyll
Dalnaspidal Guest House
Map Ref: 1D7

★★★
GUEST
HOUSE

Open: All year excl January

Dalnaspidal, Tangy, Kilkenzie, Campbeltown PA28 6QD
T: 01586 820466
E: relax@dalnaspidal-guesthouse.com
W: dalnaspidal-guesthouse.com

Located in a spectacular rural setting just 10 minutes from Campbeltown, Dalnaspidal is a haven of peace and tranquility offering luxurious accommodation, magnificent sea and countryside views, superior service, excellent cuisine and a warm friendly welcome! Licensed Restaurant – Small Weddings – Special Occasions – Corporate Events – Gift Vouchers

Total number of rooms: 4			
Prices from:			
Single:	**£60.00**	Double:	**£42.50**
Twin:	**£42.50**	Family room:	**£36.00**

Colintraive, Argyll
Colintraive Hotel
Map Ref: 1F5

★★★
SMALL
HOTEL

Open: All year excl Xmas Day
Colintraive, Argyll and Bute, PA22 3AS
T: 01700 841207
E: colintraive@btconnect.com
W: colintraivehotel.com

Total number of rooms: 4			
Prices from:			
Single:	**£65.00**	Double:	**£45.00**
Twin:	**£45.00**	Family room:	**£100.00pr**

For a full listing of quality assured serviced accommodation throughout Scotland see pages 195-278.

81

West Highlands and Islands

Arinagour, Isle of Coll
Coll Hotel
Map Ref: 1B1

★★★
INN

Open: All year, conditions apply Xmas and New Year
Arinagour, Isle of Coll, Argyll PA78 6SZ
T: 01879 230334
E: info@collhotel.com
W: collhotel.com

20003

Total number of rooms: 6

Prices from:

| Single: | £50.00 | Double: | £45.00 |
| Twin: | £45.00 | Family room: | £45.00 |

Connel, Oban
Ronebhal Guest House
Map Ref: 1E2

★★★★
GUEST
HOUSE

Open: April-October
Connel, Oban, Argyll PA37 1PJ
T: 01631 710310
E: info@ronebhal.co.uk
W: ronebhal.co.uk

52032

Total number of rooms: 5

Prices from:

| Single: | £30.00-60.00 | Double: | £30.00-38.00 |
| Twin: | £30.00-38.00 | Family room: | £28.00-35.00 |

Dunoon, Argyll
Abbot's Brae Hotel
Map Ref: 1F5

★★★★
SMALL
HOTEL

Open: All year

West Bay, Dunoon, Argyll and Bute PA23 7QJ
T: 01369 705021
E: info@abbotsbrae.co.uk
W: abbotsbrae.co.uk

Abbot's Brae is a lovely small family-run hotel situated in it's own woodland garden. Guests always comment on the stunning views and it's peaceful secluded setting, yet it is only a mile from Dunoon, one hour from Glasgow and situated at the western gateway to the Loch Lomond National Park.

75260

Total number of rooms: 8

Prices per room from:

| Single: | £60.00 | Double: | £88.00 |
| Twin: | £98.00 | Family room: | £120.00 |

Dunoon, Argyll
Argyll Hotel
Map Ref: 1F5

★★★
HOTEL

Open: All year
Argyll Street, Dunoon PA23 7NE
T: 01369 702059
E: info@argyll-hotel.co.uk
W: argyll-hotel.co.uk

12779

Total number of rooms: 32

Prices per room from:

| Single: | £58.00 | Double: | £82.00 |
| Twin: | £82.00 | Family room: | £105.00 |

Dunoon, Argyll
Esplanade Hotel
Map Ref: 1F5

★★★
HOTEL

Open: April-October
West Bay Promenade, Dunoon PA23 7HU
T: 01369 704070
E: relax@ehd.co.uk
W: ehd.co.uk

25123

Total number of rooms: 65

Prices per room from:

| Single: | £58.00 | Double: | £82.00 |
| Twin: | £82.00 | Family room: | £105.00 |

IMPORTANT: Prices stated are estimates and may be subject to change. Prices are per person per night unless otherwise stated. Awards correct as of beginning of October 2008.

Dunoon, Argyll
The Mayfair

Map Ref: 1F5

★★
GUEST
HOUSE

Open: All year

7 Clyde Street, Kirn, Dunoon, Argyll and Bute, PA23 8DX
T: 01369 703803
E: grayson.mayfair7@fsmail.net
W: dunoonguesthouse.com

A warm and friendly welcome awaits you at The Mayfair, a beautiful Victorian Guest House with stunning views of the Firth of Clyde.
In a quiet situation, half-way between Dunoon and Hunters Quay ferry terminals and within easy walking distance of Dunoon town centre.
Discounts for 3 or more nights.

Total number of rooms: 5

Prices from:

Single:	£26.00	Double:	£26.00
Twin:	£26.00	Family room:	£30.00

Dunoon, Argyll
The Park Hotel

Map Ref: 1F5

★★
HOTEL

Open: All year

3 Glenmorag Avenue, West Bay, Dunoon PA23 7LG
T: 01369 702383
E: info@parkhoteldunoon.co.uk
W: parkhoteldunoon.co.uk

Total number of rooms: 18

Price per room from:

Single:	£40.00	Double:	£70.00
Twin:	£70.00	Family room:	POA

Dunoon, Argyll
Osborne Hotel

Map Ref: 1F5

The Osborne Hotel

Innellan · Dunoon

★★
SMALL
HOTEL

Open: All year

44 Shore Road, Innellan,
by Dunoon, Argyll and Bute PA23 7TJ
T: 01369 830445
E: osbenquiries@aol.com
W: osbornehotel.net

Stunning views await you at this delightful shoreline hotel, situated just three miles from Dunoon. Superb home cooked food served in our conservatory restaurant with fantastic panoramic scenery overlooking the islands. Forest walks, golf and pony trekking are all nearby, or enjoy a trip on the famous Waverley Paddle Steamer.

Total number of rooms: 4

Prices from:

Single:	£32.50	Double:	£32.50
Twin:	£32.50	Family room:	£75.00pr

For a full listing of quality assured serviced accommodation throughout Scotland see pages 195-278.

83

West Highlands and Islands

Inveraray, Argyll
Rudha-Na-Craige

Map Ref: 1F3

★★★★
GUEST
HOUSE

Open: All year excl Christmas

Rudha-Na-Craige, Inveraray, Argyll, PA32 8YX
T: +44 (0)1499 302668
E: enquiries@rudha-na-craige.com
W: rudha-na-craige.com

A warm welcome awaits you from your hosts, Susan and Howard Spicer at our beautiful and historical home. Overlooking Loch Fyne providing exceptional and luxurious 4★ Guest House accommodation. A short stroll (or drive) along the shore side from the centre of Inveraray with stunning loch views from every room (except single).

Total number of rooms: 6

Prices per room from:
Single: £60.00   Double: £90.00
Twin: £118.00

Calgary, Isle of Mull
Calgary Hotel

Map Ref: 1C1

★★★
RESTAURANT
WITH ROOMS

Open: March-October (weekends only November)
Calgary, By Dervaig, Isle of Mull PA75 6QW
T: 01688 400256
E: calgary.hotel@virgin.net
W: calgary.co.uk

Total number of rooms: 9

Prices from:
Single: £38.00-49.00   Double: £49.00-55.00
Twin: £38.00-49.00   Family room: £49.00-55.00

Dervaig, Isle of Mull
Druimnacroish

Map Ref: 1C1

★★★
GUEST
HOUSE

Open: March-October

Dervaig, Isle of Mull, Argyll PA75 6QW
T: 01688 400274
E: stay@druimnacroish.co.uk
W: druimnacroish.co.uk

Set on a hillside in the North West of the island, near the village of Dervaig, with superb views from every room. Spacious, relaxed atmosphere, home made bread, Wi-Fi, no TV. Private guest lounges and large conservatory. Well situated for Mull's many attractions including boat trips, walking and wildlife. Licensed.

Total number of rooms: 6

Prices from:
Double: £32.00   Twin: £32.00

IMPORTANT: Prices stated are estimates and may be subject to change. Prices are per person per night unless otherwise stated. Awards correct as of beginning of October 2008.

Tobermory, Isle of Mull
Highland Cottage
Map Ref: 1C1

Open: mid March-mid October

24 Breadalbane Street,
Tobermory, Isle of Mull PA75 6PD
T: 01688 302030
E: davidandjo@highlandcottage.co.uk
W: highlandcottage.co.uk

Family-run "Country House in the Town" small hotel in the heart of Tobermory's conservation area. Well-appointed bedrooms including 4-posters. Award-winning cuisine using local ingredients served in attractive, homely dining-room. Genuine hospitality from experienced resident owners.
AA 3 Red star/2 Rosette accolades.

30309

Total number of rooms: 6

Prices from:
Double: £75.00   Twin: £75.00

Oban, Argyll
Alltavona House
Map Ref: 1E2

Open: All year excl Xmas

Corran Esplanade, Oban, Argyll PA34 5AQ
T: 01631 565067/07771 708301
E: carol@alltavona.co.uk
W: alltavona.co.uk

67514

Total number of rooms: 10

Prices from:
Single: £35.00-80.00   Double: £30.00-45.00
Twin: £30.00-40.00

Oban, Argyll
Falls of Lora Hotel
Map Ref: 1E2

Open: February-mid December

Connel Ferry, Oban, Argyll PA37 1PB
T: 01631 710483
E: enquiries@fallsoflora.com
W: fallsoflora.com

Oban 5 miles. Overlooking Loch Etive, this fine owner-run Victorian Hotel with a modern extension has superior to inexpensive family rooms. The super cocktail bar has an open log fire and 100 brands of whisky. The attractive and comfortable bistro has an extensive menu featuring local produce.

25591

Total number of rooms: 30

Prices from:
Single: £47.50   Double: £27.50
Twin: £27.50   Family room: £31.50

For a full listing of quality assured serviced accommodation throughout Scotland see pages 195-278.

85

West Highlands and Islands

Oban, Argyll
Glenbervie Guest House
Map Ref: 1E2

★★★★
GUEST HOUSE

Open: February-November

Dalriach Road, Oban, PA34 5JD
T: 01631 564770
E: glenbervie.oban@btinternet.com
W: glenbervieoban.co.uk

Beautifully situated overlooking Oban Bay, commanding magnificent views. 2 minutes walk from town centre, promenade, harbour and amenities.

68122

Total number of rooms: 8

Prices from:

Single:	£30.00	Double:	£30.00-38.00
Twin:	£30.00-38.00		

Oban, Argyll
Kathmore Guest House
Map Ref: 1E2

★★★
GUEST HOUSE

Open: All year excl Xmas
Soroba Road, Oban, Argyll PA34 4JF
T: 01631 562104
E: wkathmore@aol.com
W: kathmore.co.uk

67995

Total number of rooms: 8

Prices from:

Single:	£30.00-60.00	Double:	£25.00-37.50
Twin:	£25.00-35.00	Family room:	£65.00-95.00pr

Oban, Argyll
Royal Hotel
Map Ref: 1E2

★★★
HOTEL

Open: All year

Argyll Square, Oban, Argyll, PA34 4BE
T: 01631 563021
E: salesroyaloban@strathmorehotels.com
W: strathmorehotels.com

Situated in the centre of Oban, the hotel is an ideal base for visiting the West Coast of Scotland and Mull and Iona. Built in 1895, the hotel offers traditional Scottish hospitality within modern surroundings. Recent improvements include refurbishment of the lounge and bar and installation of FREE Wi-Fi access.

68081

Total number of rooms: 91

Prices from:

Single:	£50.00	Double:	£45.00
Twin:	£45.00		

Oban, Argyll
Sutherland Guest House
Map Ref: 1E2

★★
GUEST HOUSE

Open: All year
Corran Esplanade, Oban, Argyll PA34 5PN
T: 01631 562539
E: suthotel@aol.com
W: sutherlandhouseoban.co.uk

79223

Total number of rooms: 12

Prices per room from:

Single:	£25.00	Double:	£25.00
Twin:	£25.00	Family room:	£25.00

IMPORTANT: Prices stated are estimates and may be subject to change. Prices are per person per night unless otherwise stated. Awards correct as of beginning of October 2008.

Strachur, Argyll
The Creggans Inn

Map Ref:1F3

★★★ SMALL HOTEL

Open: All year

Strachur, Argyll and Bute, PA27 8BX
T: 01369 860279
E: info@creggans-inn.co.uk
W: creggans-inn.co.uk

Lochside family run hotel, 1 hour from Glasgow airport. Tastefully decorated bedrooms and lounges with views over Loch Fyne and to the hills beyond. Ideal base for exploring beautiful Argyll. Award winning dining room serving the finest Scottish produce. Traditional McPhunns Bar for more casual eating and drinking.

Total number of rooms: 14

Prices from:
Single: **£65.00**   Double: **£45.00**

Strachur on the east side of Loch Fyne, Argyll

For a full listing of quality assured serviced accommodation throughout Scotland see pages 195-278.

87

Canoeing on Loch Lomond, Argyll

Loch Lomond and The Trossachs

Whatever road you take to the bonny banks of Loch Lomond, you'll arrive at one of the most picturesque places in all of Scotland. This vast National Park is, indeed, one of the most beautiful places in the world.

Towns like Callander, Balloch, Killin and Aberfoyle make a great base to explore different corners of the park. And once you're there, you'll find so much to do, from watersports to mountain climbing, angling to gentle strolls in the stunning countryside.

You can even integrate the sedate with the active – catch the SS Sir Walter Scott from the Trossachs Pier and cruise Loch Katrine to Stronachlachar, then enjoy the 12-mile shore hike back.

Falls of Dochart, Killin

To find out more, call 0845 22 55 121 or go to visitscotland.com

Loch Lomond and the Trossachs

elensburgh, Argyll
ellfield
Map Ref: 1G4

★★★
B&B

Open: All year
199 East Clyde Street, Helensburgh G84 7AJ
T: 01436 673361
E: r.callaghan@virgin.net
W: scotland2000.com/bellfield

70170

Total number of rooms: 3

Prices per room from:
Single: **£35.00**   Double: **£60.00**
Twin: **£60.00**

---

elensburgh, Argyll
he County Lodge Hotel
Map Ref: 1G4

★★
MALL
OTEL

Open: All year
Old Luss Road Craigendoran,
Helensburgh, Argyll & Bute G84 7BH
T: 01436 672034
E: sales@countylodgehotel.co.uk
W: countylodgehotel.co.uk

The County Lodge is a small friendly hotel. With home cooked fayre and only minutes from Helensburgh town centre. Local for tourists and business visitors alike . Entertainment available most nights in our lounge or public bar, you're ensured an enjoyable visit. The wee hotel with the big welcome.

79012

Total number of rooms: 8

Prices from:
Single: **£44.95**   Double: **£59.90**
Twin: **£59.90**   Family room: **£59.90**
(**£10.00 per child**)

---

elensburgh, Argyll
inclair House
Map Ref: 1G4

★★★
UEST
OUSE

Open: All year
91/93 Sinclair Street, Helensburgh G84 8TR
T: 01436 676301
E: enquiries@sinclairhouse.com
W: sinclairhouse.com

Iain and Ishbel welcome you to our superior guesthouse, located only two minutes walk to the town centre and ten minutes drive to the National Park. Immaculate rooms with many extras including memory foam matresses, fridges, laptops with free internet access, new LCD TV's and DVD players.

26217

Total number of rooms: 4

Prices per room from:
Double: **£67.00**   Twin: **£73.00**
Family room: **£73.00**

Loch Lomond and the Trossachs

Lochearnhead, Perthshire
Mansewood Country House   Map Ref: 1H2

Open: All year

Lochearnhead, Perthshire, FK19 8NS
T: 01567 830213
E: stay@mansewoodcountryhouse.co.uk
W: mansewoodcountryhouse.co.uk

Family owned guest house with a warm, relaxed, friendly atmosphere. All bedrooms ensuite, public areas include small bar, lounge, and bay window seating area. Beautiful scenery, sailing on the loch, fishing, walking, golf and cycling. Great base to tour the Trossachs and Highlands, special low season offers. Evening meals/packed lunches available.

Total number of rooms: 6

Prices from:
Single: **£43.00-45.00**   Double: **£33.00-35.00**
Twin: **£33.00-35.00**

Luss, Loch Lomond
Culag Lochside Guest House   Map Ref: 1G4

Open: All year excl Xmas and New Year

Culag Lochside Guest House,
Luss, Loch Lomond, G83 8PD
T: 01436 860248
W: culag.info

A warm welcome awaits you at this picturesque guest house on the Bonnie Banks of Loch Lomond. Ensuite accommodation. Breathtaking views from all rooms. Traditional breakfast served in conservatory. Lunch, afternoon tea and dinner all served in our newly opened licensed restaurant in Luss village. Transport provided. Small parties catered for.

Total number of rooms: 10

Prices per room from:
Single: **£45.00**   Double: **£65.00**
Twin: **£65.00**   Family room: **£80.00-90.00**

Strathyre, Perthshire
Creagan House Restaurant with Accommodation   Map Ref: 1H3

Open: March-January
excl Wednesdays, Thursdays and Xmas
Strathyre, Callander, Perthshire FK18 8ND
T: 01877 384638
E: eatandstay@creaganhouse.co.uk
W: creaganhouse.co.uk

Total number of rooms: 5

Prices from:
Single: **£70.00**   Double: **£60.00**
Twin: **£60.00**

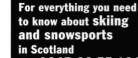

IMPORTANT: Prices stated are estimates and may be subject to change. Prices are per person per night unless otherwise stated. Awards correct as of beginning of October 2008.

Stirling Castle at Dusk

Stirling and Forth Valley

Stirling and the Forth Valley offer a huge range of visitor attractions but a recent addition to the list is proving extremely popular. Built to celebrate the new Millennium and opened in 2002, The Falkirk Wheel is a triumph of engineering. It's the world's only rotating boatlift and, standing an impressive 24 metres high, it has reconnected the Forth & Clyde Canal with the Union Canal.

Scotland's industrial heritage is well represented locally at the Bo'ness and Kinneil Steam Railway, Birkhill Fireclay Mine and Callendar House, while you can see traces of Scotland's woollen industry on the shores of the Forth in Clackmannan.

History is everywhere around Stirling. Don't miss Stirling Castle and the National Wallace Monument but remember to leave enough time to take a walk round the town and enjoy a spot of shopping too.

Port Street, Stirling

DON'T MISS

1 **Stirling Castle**, undoubtedly one of the finest in Scotland, sits high on its volcanic rock towering over the stunning countryside known as 'Braveheart Country'. A favourite royal residence over the centuries and a key military stronghold, visit the Great Hall, the Chapel Royal, and the Renaissance Palace. From the castle esplanade the sites of no less than seven historic battles can be seen, as can the majestic **National Wallace Monument** built in tribute to William Wallace.

2 The world's only rotating boatlift, **The Falkirk Wheel**, was constructed in 2002 to link the Forth & Clyde and Union canals. It is now possible for boats to traverse Central Scotland by canal for the first time in more than 40 years. Learn about Scotland's canal network in the visitor centre or board a vessel to take a trip on the mechanical marvel itself.

3 The **Antonine Wall** dates back to the 2nd century and once marked the northern frontier of the Roman Empire. Substantial lengths have been preserved and can still be seen at various sites around Falkirk. The site was awarded UNESCO World Heritage Status in July 2008. Follow the wall for a relaxed walk along the towpath on the north of the canal, taking you past the Falkirk Wheel to Bonnybridge.

4 Just a few miles north west of Stirling on the A84 you will find **Blair Drummond Safari Park**. Here you can drive through wild animal reserves and get close to lions and zebras, and a whole host of other animals. Or you can park and walk around the pet farm, see the only elephants in Scotland, watch a sea lion display, find out what it's like to hold a bird of prey and take a boat to Chimp Island. There is also an adventure play area, pedal boats for hire and for the more adventurous – the flying fox!

FOOD AND DRINK

eatscotland.com

5   The **Gargunnock Inn** is situated in the small village of Gargunnock on the A811 west of Stirling. A welcoming, friendly establishment, it serves freshly prepared, local produce in its restaurant and has a more informal bar adjoining for relaxing in after dinner.

6   **Harviestoun Country Hotel & Restaurant** in Tillicoultry is the perfect place to stop, whether it is for lunch, high tea or an evening meal. The restored 18th century steading, with the backdrop of the stunning Ochil Hills, is the ideal setting for relaxing with good food and fine wine.

7   The lovely Victorian spa town of Bridge of Allan is home to the **Bridge of Allan Brewery** where you can see how traditional Scottish handcrafted ales are produced and even have a free tasting session!

HISTORY AND HERITAGE

8   Built in tribute to Scotland's national hero Sir William Wallace, the **National Wallace Monument**, by Stirling, can be seen for miles around. The Monument exhibition tells of Sir Wallace's epic struggle for a free Scotland.

9   **Castle Campbell** is beautifully sited at the head of Dollar Glen, immediately north of Dollar. Sitting in lofty isolation and overlooked by the Ochil Hills, the castle became the chief lowland stronghold of the Campbell clan, upon whose members the successive titles of Earl, Marquis, and Duke of Argyll were bestowed. There are excellent walks through Dollar Glen to enjoy too.

10   On the site of the original battlefield, the **Bannockburn Heritage Centre** on the southern outskirts of Stirling, tells the story of the greatest victory of Scotland's favourite monarch King Robert the Bruce. Walk the battlefield and then enjoy the audio-visual presentation in the centre, recounting the battle. A re-enactment of the battle takes place over two days every September.

11   Open the door to **Callendar House** in Falkirk, and you open the door to 600 years of Scottish history. Journey through time from the days of the Jacobites to the advent of the railway, and don't forget to stop at the Georgian kitchens for some refreshments prepared using authentic Georgian recipes.

12   Discover what life was like for unfortunate inmates within the authentic Victorian **Stirling Old Town Jail**. You might well run into Jock Rankin, the notorious town hangman, and even witness an attempted jail break!

WALKS

visitscotland.com/walking

13 Walk around Muiravon Country Park along the River Avon and you'll pass the Avon Aqueduct, Scotland's longest and tallest, which carries the Union Canal above the river. Near Bo'Ness, the River Avon flows through the **Avon Gorge**, a well known local beauty spot where you can stroll through ancient woodlands, home to a variety of wildlife including deer and otters.

14 Not far from Dollar where the A823 meets the A977, it's worth stopping to explore the delightful **Rumbling Bridge**, so named because of the continuous rumbling sound of the falls and the river below. The unusual double bridge spans a narrow gorge and you'll find a network of platforms and paths that take you over the river and deep into the gorge with spectacular views of waterfalls and swirling pools.

15 The **Darn Walk** from Bridge of Allan to Dunblane is a beautiful walk which can be enjoyed at any time of the year. Highlights include a scenic stretch alongside the River Allan and the cave which was Robert Louis Stevenson's inspiration for Ben Gunn's cave in Treasure Island. The walk can be completed in 1½ to 2 hours.

16 At the heart of Clackmannanshire's 300-acre **Gartmorn Dam Country Park**, visitors can enjoy a short walk with gentle gradients suitable for wheelchairs or pushchairs. Gartmorn Dam is the oldest man-made reservoir still in use in Scotland, and is a nature reserve which is the winter home of thousands of migratory ducks.

ATTRACTIONS

17 Dating back to the 14th century, **Alloa Tower** is one of the largest surviving medieval tower houses in Scotland. The tower has been recently restored and has amazing features.

18 Situated by the banks of the River Teith, **Doune Castle** was once the ancestral home of the Earls of Moray. At one time occupied by the Jacobite troops, this castle can now be explored and makes a great picnic spot. Film lovers may also recognise the castle from scenes from 'Monty Python and the Holy Grail'.

19 Just north of Stirling, **Argaty Red Kites** is one of Scotland's red kite feeding stations. After 130 years of Scottish Natural Heritage, the RSPB has reintroduced these exciting, acrobatic birds to central Scotland. Spend a day and you can enjoy a guided walk or just watch the birds from the hide.

ridge of Allan, by Stirling

Adamo

Map Ref: 2A3

★★★ SMALL HOTEL

Open: All year
24 Henderson Street,
Bridge of Allan, Stirling FK9 4HP
T: 01786 833268
E: info@adamohotels.com
W: adamohotels.com

50773

Total number of rooms: 16

Prices per room from:

Single:	£90.00	Double:	£160.00
Twin:	£160.00	Family room:	£250.00

Stirling

King Robert Hotel

Map Ref: 2A4

★★★ HOTEL

Open: All year
Glasgow Road, Whins of Milton, Stirling FK7 0LJ
T: 01786 811666
E: info@kingroberthotel.co.uk
W: kingroberthotel.co.uk

33982

Total number of rooms: 52

Prices from:

Single:	£35.00	Double:	£25.00
Twin:	£25.00	Family room:	£35.00

Tillicoultry, by Stirling

The Harviestoun Country Hotel and Restaurant

Map Ref: 2A4

★★★ SMALL HOTEL

Open: All year
Dollar Road, Tillicoultry, Clackmannanshire FK13 6PQ
T: 01259 752522
E: info@harviestouncountryhotel.com
W: harviestouncountryhotel.com

29679

Our award winning sympathetically restored 18th century steading is centrally located at the foot of the stunning Ochil Hills. Privately owned and managed. Ten comfortable ensuite bedrooms. Lounge with open fire serving coffees, home baking, à la carte restaurant. All day dining. Function suite, conferences, weddings, bus parties. Ideal for touring, golfing, business.

Total number of rooms: 10

Prices per room from:

Single:	£65.00	Double:	£85.00
Twin:	£90.00	Family room:	£100.00

Man participating in the hammer event at the Highland Games at Callendar, Stirling

For a full listing of quality assured serviced accommodation throughout Scotland see pages 195-278.

101

Carnoustie Golf Links, Carnoustie, Angus

PERTHSHIRE, ANGUS AND DUNDEE AND THE KINGDOM OF FIFE

Scotland's heartlands are the perfect holiday destination in many ways. There's so much to discover in this part of the world that you're sure to find something that suits you perfectly. Golfing, fishing, walking, sightseeing, there's an abundance of choice and there are some wonderful places to stay.

How about one of the great international resort hotels in St Andrews or at Gleneagles where the rich and famous relax? Or you could choose a charming hotel in a holiday town like Pitlochry or a contemporary hotel on Dundee's lively quayside.

The countryside is so varied too. Fife has an enviable coastline with a number of perfect little harbour

towns, Perthshire is unspoiled and magnificent, with some of Scotland's finest woodlands and stunning lochs and hills. And then there's Dundee – the area's largest city. There's always another fascinating place waiting to be explored.

This is a holiday destination that can be as active as you want it to be. For the outdoor enthusiast, there's anything from hill walking to whitewater rafting and pretty much everything in between. Anglers love the thrill of pursuing salmon and trout on some of the country's greatest river beats or heading out to sea where the catch can be bountiful.

Golfers love this area too. Some of the world's finest courses are here, from the home of golf at St Andrews to championship quality greats Gleneagles and Carnoustie.

If wildlife's your thing, the opportunities are endless. In the countryside of Perthshire and the Angus Glens there are ospreys, eagles, otters and deer. By the sea from Fife to Angus spot a wide variety of seabirds – especially around the Montrose Basin which attracts thousands of migrant species.

You don't have to be escaping civilisation to enjoy these parts, however. There are towns and cities that you'll enjoy enormously, each with their own unique attractions. Perth has specialist shops and high street retailers. St Andrews is a fine university town with a fascinating history. Dunfermline was once the seat of Scotland's Kings while Dundee, the City of Discovery, is enjoying something of a renaissance these days and is a great place for a big day out.

What's more, 2009 is a big year for Scotland – we're celebrating the 250th anniversary of the birth of Robert Burns. There's over 200 special events taking place throughout the year, all over Scotland. Go to homecomingscotland2009.com to find out about events in this area.

Fishing village of Crail overlooking the harbour, Fife

Canadian canoeing on Loch Tay at Kenmore, Perthshire

What's On?

Snowdrop Festival 2009
February/March 2009
visitscotland.com/snowdrops

StAnza 2009
Scotland's Poetry Festival
18 - 22 March 2009
stanzapoetry.org

Angus Glens Walking Festival
28 – 31 May 2009, Angus Glens
angusanddundee.co.uk/walkingfestival

Perth Festival of the Arts
21 -31 May 2009, Perth
The Festival features world-class artists.
perthfestival.co.uk

Game Conservancy Scottish Fair
3 - 5 July 2009, Scone Palace, Perth
One of the main countryside events of the year in Scotland.
www.scottishfair.com

The 34th Scottish Transport Extravaganza
11 – 12 July 2009
Glamis Castle, Angus
svvc.co.uk

Arbroath Seafest
8 –9 August 2009
Arbroath Harbour, Arbroath
angusahead.com

Culross Music & Arts Festival
August 2009
culrossfestival.com

Blair Castle International Horse Trials & Country Fair
Blair Castle, Blair Atholl
27 – 30 August 2009
Equestrian sport on an international scale!
blairhorsetrials.co.uk

Dundee Flower and Food Festival
4 – 6 September 2009
dundeeflowerandfoodfestival.com

The Enchanted Forest
16 October – 1 November 2009
Faskally Wood, by Pitlochry
A spectacular journey of light and sound in Perthshire's Big Tree Country.
enchantedforest.org.uk

All dates correct at time of publication. Please check before booking. VisitScotland cannot be held responsible for any inaccuracies

103

MAP

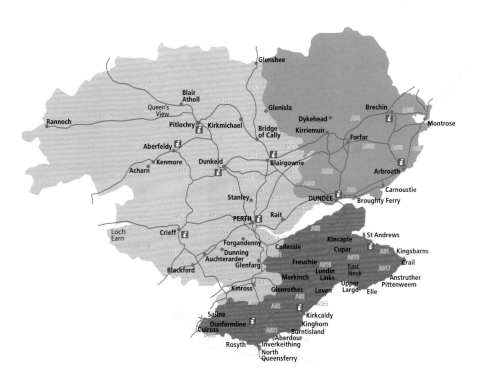

©Collins Bartholomew Ltd

VISITOR INFORMATION CENTRES

Visitor Information Centres are staffed by people 'in the know' offering friendly advice, helping to make your stay in Scotland the most enjoyable ever . . . whatever your needs!

Perthshire

Aberfeldy	The Square, Aberfeldy, PH15 2DD	Tel: 01887 820276
Blairgowrie	26 Wellmeadow, Blairgowrie PH10 6AS	Tel: 01250 872960
Crieff	High Street, Crieff, PH7 3HU	Tel: 01764 652578
Dunkeld	The Cross, Dunkeld, PH8 0AN	Tel: 01350 727688
Perth	Lower City Mills, West Mill Street, Perth, PH1 5QP	Tel: 01736 450600
Pitlochry	22 Atholl Road, Pitlochry, PH16 5BX	Tel: 01796 472215

Angus and Dundee

Arbroath	Harbour Visitor Centre, Fishmarket Quay, Arbroath, DD11 1PS	Tel: 01241 872609
Brechin	Pictavia Centre, Haughmuir, Brechin	Tel: 01356 623050
Dundee	Discovery Point, Discovery Quay, Dundee DD1 4XA	Tel: 01382 527527

Fife

Dunfermline	1 High Street, Dunfermline, KY12 7DL	Tel: 01383 720999
Kirkcaldy	The Merchant's House, 339 High Street, Kirkcaldy, KY1 1JL	Tel: 01592 267775
St Andrews	70 Market St St Andrews Fife FY16 9NU	Tel: 01334 472021

LOCAL KNOWLEDGE • WHERE TO STAY • ACCOMMODATION BOOKING • PLACES TO VISIT • THINGS TO DO • MAPS AND GUIDES TRAVEL ADVICE • ROUTE PLANNING • WHERE TO SHOP AND EAT LOCAL CRAFTS AND PRODUCE • EVENT INFORMATION • TICKETS

For information and ideas about exploring Scotland in advance of your trip, call our booking and information service **0845 22 55 121** or go to **visitscotland.com**

If calling from outside the UK and Ireland **+44 1506 832 121**   From Ireland **1800 932 510**

A £4 booking fee applies for accommodation bookings made via a Visitor Information Centre and through our booking and information service.

Schiehallion and Loch Tummel from The Queen's View, by Pitlochry

Perthshire

Perthshire is one of the most strikingly picturesque parts of Scotland. It ranges from wild and mountainous to sophisticated and cultured, from the wilderness of Rannoch Moor to the lap of luxury at the 5-star Gleneagles Hotel.

You can experience everything here, from traditional activities like golf, fishing and horse riding to more recent innovations like sphereing and white water rafting. Whatever you pursue, it will be against a backdrop of spectacular scenery; high mountains, deep forests, sparkling lochs and wide rivers.

But you don't have to spend the day pushing yourself to the limits; a walk through the forests of Big Tree Country may suffice. Take a romantic stroll through the Birks o' Aberfeldy, visit one of nine great gardens, marvel at a reconstructed Iron Age crannog on Loch Tay or simply enjoy the Queen's View near Pitlochry.

Sphereing

DON'T MISS

1 The Scottish Crannog Centre at Kenmore on Loch Tay is an authentic recreation of an ancient loch-dwelling. Imagine a round house in the middle of a loch with a thatched roof, on stilts. You can tour the Crannog to see how life used to be 2,600 years ago. Upon your return to shore, have a go at a variety of Iron Age crafts; see if you can grind the grain, drill through stone or make fire through wood friction.

2 Scone Palace, near Perth, was renowned as the traditional crowning place of Scottish kings, as the capital of the Pictish kingdom and centre of the ancient Celtic Church. Nowadays, the great house and its beautiful accompanying grounds are home to the Earls of Mansfield, and offer an ideal day out.

3 Blair Castle, the stunningly situated ancient seat of the Dukes and Earls of Atholl, is a five-star castle experience. The unmistakeable white façade is visible from the A9 just north of Blair Atholl. Dating back 740 years, the castle has played a part in some of Scotland's most tumultuous events but today it is a relaxing and fascinating place to visit.

4 The Famous Grouse Experience is housed within Glenturret Distillery, Scotland's oldest malt whisky distillery. It is an interactive attraction where visitors can familiarise themselves with this renowned tipple and the brand that accompanies it! As well as a tour of the production areas, you can enjoy a unique audio-visual presentation which gives a grouse's eye view of Scotland, and delicious food.

5 Among its many other attractions, Perthshire – known as Big Tree Country - can boast some of the most remarkable trees and woodlands anywhere in Europe. The 250 miles of way-marked paths give you an excellent opportunity to explore the area and, if you're lucky, catch a glimpse of the many different species of wildlife which make Perthshire their home. Here you'll discover Europe's oldest tree in Fortingall Churchyard, the world's highest hedge and one of Britain's tallest trees at The Hermitage by Dunkeld.

6 You'll find some of Scotland's most beautiful parks and gardens in Perthshire, ranging from small privately owned gardens to formal sumptuous gardens, containing examples of native Scottish plants and rare and exotic species from around the world. The Perthshire Gardens Collection brings together 9 spectacular examples of the gardener's art such as Kinross House, Drummond Castle and Branklyn Gardens. Heather, wild woodlands and Himalayan treasures will inspire you whether you're a horticultural enthusiast or someone who simply loves beautiful gardens.

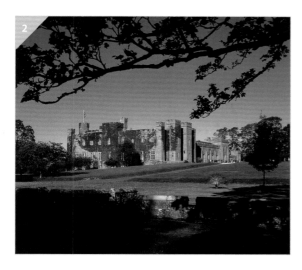

FOOD AND DRINK

eatscotland.com

7 Farmers' markets have seen a resurgence in recent years in the UK and Perth's Farmers' Market is arguably the best known in Scotland. Taking place throughout the year on the first Saturday of each month, it is something of a showcase for local producers and growers and is a rewarding visit in its own right. Look out for fish, meat and game, baked goods, fruit wines and liqueurs, honeys and preserves, fruit and vegetables, sweets and herbs. Sound tempting? Many stallholders also offer free tastings.

8 The area around Blairgowrie is Europe's centre for soft fruit production and a particular feature of the area are the signs at farms inviting you to 'pick your own' strawberries, raspberries, gooseberries, redcurrants, and tayberries. Sample the local produce of field and hedgerow at Cairn O' Mohr Wines in Errol. A family-run business it produces Scottish fruit wines made from local berries, flowers and leaves - a truly unique end product. Explore the winery through one of the on site tours before undertaking a tasting session!

9 Edradour Distillery – Scotland's smallest malt whisky distillery - can be found in the Highland foothills just to the east of Pitlochry. Built in the early 19th century Edradour is the only remaining 'farm' distillery in Perthshire and seems to have hardly changed in the 170 years of its existence. Visitors can enjoy a guided tour of the production areas, before relaxing with a wee dram of the amber nectar.

10 In addition to outstanding restaurant facilities, Baxters at Blackford offers a fantastic Scottish showcase of inspirational fine food, gifts and much, much more. Visitors are invited to taste a variety of products, from specialist chocolate in The Chocolate Parlour to tasting what Baxters is most famous for, specialty soups, in The Baxters Hub. Whether making a quick stop or for those wishing to stay a little bit longer, Baxters is ideal for the perfect day out.

WALKS

visitscotland.com/walking

11 A 63 mile (101 km) circular waymarked walking route through the scenic Perthshire and Angus Glens, The Cateran Trail follows paths used by the 15th century Caterans (cattle rustlers). Complete the whole route in a leisurely five days or enjoy a shorter section on a day's walk. Take in the soft contours of Strathardle on the Bridge of Cally to Kirkmichael section or head for the hills between Kirkmichael and the Spittal of Glenshee.

12 Revered in poetry by the national bard, Robert Burns, the Birks of Aberfeldy ('birks' being the old Scots for birch trees) line a short walk alongside the Moness Burn, reached from a car park on the Crieff Road. A circular path leads to a beautiful waterfall, where birds and flowers are abundant.

13 Lady Mary's Walk in Crieff is one of the most popular in Perthshire and provides a peaceful stroll beside the beautiful River Earn, along an avenue of mature oak, beech, lime and sweet chestnut trees. Partly accessible for wheelchairs and pushchairs, the walk is particularly photogenic in the late autumn when the beech trees are a riot of rust and gold.

14 On the A9 just north of Dunkeld, you'll find The Hermitage. A beautiful walk along the banks of the River Braan takes you to the focal point, Ossian's Hall set in a picturesque gorge and overlooking Black Linn Falls. Ask the local rangers for advice or read the display panels as you pass amidst the huge Douglas Firs en route.

WILDLIFE

visitscotland.com/wildlife

15 Glengoulandie Country Park is located in the beautiful shelter of Schiehallion, one of Scotland's best known and most popular mountains. The park is home to a beautiful herd of red deer and is a lovely escape for the whole family. It's also an ideal location for setting up camp with a site right next door.

16 Visit Loch of the Lowes between April and August and there's every chance you'll encounter its famous nesting ospreys. The Scottish Wildlife Trust's visitor centre provides interpretation on the birds, which migrate to Scotland from their winter homes in West Africa. There are also telescopes and binoculars on hand to give you a better view. Between October and March, the nature reserve is worth visiting for the sheer numbers of wildfowl which are present.

17 The Black Wood of Rannoch is one of the few remaining areas of the original Caledonian pine forest that covered the majority of Scotland. After being hunted to extinction, the capercaillie was reintroduced to Scotland at Drummond Hill, Kenmore in the 1830s. The Black Wood is an important site for capercaillie and Scottish Natural Heritage aims to extend it by removing the non-native trees to encourage a return to its natural state.

18 Each year between April and October an average of 5,400 salmon fight their way upstream from Atlantic feeding grounds to spawn in the upper reaches of the River Tummel. They must by-pass the Hydro-Electric dam at Pitlochry by travelling through the interconnected pools that form the Pitlochry 'fish ladder' – a very special attraction.

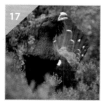

ADVENTURE

visitscotland.com/adventure

In this area you'll find over 35 different adventure activities! Here's a selection:

19 Perthshire is renowned for its stunning lochs and rivers, many of which are excellent for white water rafting. A truly unforgettable experience awaits you with a spectacular combination of rugged Highland scenery and the adrenaline rush of this activity - it's easy to understand why it's one of the most popular. Get some friends together and go for it!

20 Perthshire is the only place in Scotland where you can try sphereing. Like so many unique adventure activities, this one originated in New Zealand and is described as a 'truly amazing adrenaline buzz'. It involves a huge 12 ft inflatable ball which the willing participants strap themselves safely into and then take a wild and bouncy tumble down the hill.

21 Wet, wild and wonderful - canyoning is all this and more! Unleash your adrenaline streak as you swim through rapids, cliff jump into deep clear pools, abseil through waterfalls and slide down natural stone 'flumes'. This one is awesome and not to be missed!

22 If you enjoy wide-open spaces try a microlight flight for the nearest experience to flying like a bird. With the latest microlight technology, enjoy up to sixty miles of spectacular views and scenery in one hour. This is a great way to enjoy the Perthshire landscape as well as being the experience of a lifetime.

23 Not only can you enjoy river bugging in Perthshire but also the new innovation of Adventure Tubing at Nae Limits. The idea is simple. Take a specially designed reinforced inner tyre tube with handles and navigate your way through steep gorges, white-water runs, and jump off cliffs into deep pools below. It's truly pulse quickening stuff!

Aberfeldy, Perthshire
Fortingall Hotel   Map Ref: 2A1

★★★★
SMALL
HOTEL

Open: All year

Fortingall, Aberfeldy, Perthshire PH15 2NQ
T: 0044 (0)1887 830367
E: hotel@fortingallhotel.com
W: fortingallhotel.com

This charming eco-friendly hotel is nestled in the historic village of Fortingall at the foot of Glen Lyon. A perfect retreat, and a base for walking, cycling, golf, fishing or just relaxing. It has ten comfortable bedrooms, and the chef uses locally sourced produce in his imaginative and delicious menu. AA 4 ★★★★. AA 2 dining rosettes.

Total number of rooms: 10

Prices from:

Single:	**£99.00**	Double:	**£74.00-97.00**
Twin:	**£74.00**	Family room:	**£74.00**

Aberfeldy, Perthshire
Moness House Hotel and Country Club   Map Ref: 2A1

AWAITING
GRADING

Open: All year

Crieff Road, Aberfeldy, Perthshire, PH15 2DY
T: 0845 3302838
E: info@moness.com
W: moness.com

Set within 35 acres of woodland overlooking picturesque Aberfeldy town, Moness offers a choice of beautifully refurbished rooms, each with its own ensuite. Enjoy fine dining or relaxed meals in one of our onsite restaurants. Guests receive membership of the onsite leisure club, which includes an indoor heated pool.

Total number of rooms: 26

Prices from:

Single:	**£84.50**	Double:	**£59.50**
Twin:	**£59.50**	Family room:	**£59.50**

Auchterarder, Perthshire
The Gleneagles Hotel   Map Ref: 2B3

★★★★★
HOTEL

Open: All year

Auchterarder, Perthshire PH3 1NF
T: +44 (0)1764 662231
E: resort.sales@gleneagles.com
W: gleneagles.com

Total number of rooms: 232

Prices per room incl. breakfast from:

Double:	**£305.00**	Twin:	**£305.00**
Family room:	**£265.00**		

IMPORTANT: Prices stated are estimates and may be subject to change. Prices are per person per night unless otherwise stated. Awards correct as of beginning of October 2008.

ackford, Perthshire
lackford Hotel
Map Ref: 2A3

Open: All year

Moray Street, Blackford, Perthshire PH4 1QF

T: 01764 682497
E: info@blackfordhotel.co.uk
W: blackfordhotel.co.uk

Set in the heart of Perthshire and close to Auchterarder and the famous Scottish golf courses of Gleneagles. Wood burning stoves in our restaurant, bar and Hotel dining room together with special homemade recipes. A warm, cosy, friendly family run Hotel ideally placed only 50 minutes from Edinburgh and Glasgow. Free Wi-Fi.

Total number of rooms: 8

Prices per room from:

Single:	£40.00	Double:	£79.50
Twin:	£79.50	Family room:	£99.00

air Atholl, Perthshire
tholl Arms Hotel
Map Ref: 4C12

Open: All year excl Xmas Day

Old North Road, Blair Atholl, Pitlochry PH18 5SG

T: 01796 481205
E: info@athollarms.co.uk
W: athollarms.co.uk

Scottish Baronial style Highland Hotel, in the centre of Blair Atholl, close to castle. Offering traditional Scottish Hospitality and good base to tour the Central Highlands. Enjoy the Atholl experience all year round.

Total number of rooms: 31

Prices per room from:

Single:	£45.00	Double:	£60.00
Twin:	£60.00	Family room:	£75.00

airgowrie, Perthshire
ridge of Cally Hotel
Map Ref: 2B1

Open: All year

Bridge of Cally, Blairgowrie PH10 7JJ

T: 01250 886231   F: 01250 886793
E: enquiries@bridgeofcallyhotel.com
W: bridgeofcallyhotel.com

Our family run, riverside hotel lies in the beautiful Glen towards Royal Deeside and entrance to Scottish Highlands. Eighteen ensuite rooms of friendly, comfortable accommodation with exceptional all day dining. A unique activity planning service is available to make the most of your visit - one more reason why our guests return each year.

Total number of rooms: 18

Prices from:

Single:	£40.00	Double:	£35.00
Twin:	£35.00	Family room:	£30.00

For a full listing of quality assured serviced accommodation throughout Scotland see pages 195-278.

111

Perthshire

Blairgowrie, Perthshire
Broadmyre Motel
Map Ref: 2B1

★★
GUEST
HOUSE

Open: All year
Carsie, Blairgowrie, Perthshire PH10 6QW
T: 01250 873262
E: broadmyreroom@aol.com

16499

Total number of rooms: 5

Prices from:

Single:	£22.00-27.00	Double:	£22.00
Twin:	£22.00	Family room:	£22.00

Blairgowrie, Perthshire
The Royal Hotel
Map Ref: 2B1

AWAITING
GRADING

Open: All year
53 Allan Street, Blairgowrie, Perthshire PH10 6AB
T: 01250 872226
E: visit@theroyalhotel.org.uk
W: theroyalhotel.org.uk

52471

Total number of rooms: 29

Prices per room from:

Single:	£45.00-55.00	Double:	£65.00-89.00
Twin:	£65.00-89.00	Family room:	£100.00pr

C £ V

Dunkeld, Perthshire
Royal Dunkeld Hotel
Map Ref: 2B1

★★★
HOTEL

Open: All year

Atholl Street, Dunkeld, Perthshire PH8 0AR

T: 01350 727322 F: 01350 728989
E: reservations@royaldunkeld.co.uk
W: royaldunkeld.co.uk

Situated in the picturesque village of Dunkeld
surrounded by hills, forests and the River Tay we are
ideally located for Golfing, Fishing, Walking, Touring
and just plain relaxing. Our chefs present excellent
food using fresh local produce. A special hotel with
something for everyone.

23742

Total number of rooms: 35

Prices from:

Single:	£45.00	Double:	£34.00
Twin:	£34.00	Family room:	£34.00

Kinross, Perthshire
The Green Hotel
Map Ref: 2B3

★★★★
HOTEL

Open: All year excl 24th-26th December
2 The Muirs, Kinross KY13 8AS
T: 01577 863467
E: reservations@green-hotel.com
W: green-hotel.com

28960

Total number of rooms: 46

Prices per room from:

Single:	£67.50	Double:	£95.00
Twin:	£95.00	Family room:	£95.00

IMPORTANT: Prices stated are estimates and may be subject to change. Prices are per person per night unless otherwise stated. Awards correct as of beginning of October 2008.

tlochry, Perthshire
he Well House
Map Ref: 2A1

★★★
UEST
OUSE

63524

Open: All year excl Xmas and New Year
11 Toberargan Road, Pitlochry, Perthshire PH16 5HG
T: 01796 472239
E: enquiries@wellhouseandarrochar.co.uk
W: wellhouseandarrochar.co.uk

Total number of rooms: 7		
Prices per room from:		
Single: £35.00	Double:	**£64.00**
Twin: **£64.00**	Family room:	**£80.00**

cone. Perthshire
erth Airport Skylodge and Cottages   Map Ref: 2B2

★★★
ODGE

39042

Open: All year
Perth Airport, Scone, Perth PH2 6PL
T: 01738 555700
E: lucy.stott@morrisleslie.co.uk
W: morrisleslie.com

Beautifully placed quiet, comfortable, affordable
accommodation at Sky Lodge, Perth Airport. An ideal
place to stay whether visiting Perthshire for business
or pleasure. We have 40 ensuite rooms ranging from
spacious family rooms to compact single rooms. We
are also able to offer interconnecting rooms for larger
families.

Total number of rooms: 40		
Prices per room from:		
Single: £22.00	Double:	**£39.95**
Twin: **£39.95**	Family room:	**£49.95**

Driving near Pitlochry, Perthshire

For a full listing of quality assured serviced accommodation throughout Scotland see pages 195-278.

119

RRS Discovery at Discovery Point, Dundee

Angus and Dundee

The Angus and Dundee area boasts some of Scotland's best beaches – wonderful unspoiled stretches of sand which are at times windswept and dramatic, but more frequently warm and inviting, with the peace only occasionally shattered by the cries of the seabirds.

Dundee, you'll discover, has a proud maritime history. Captain Scott's polar research ship the RRS Discovery has returned to the city that built it and is now a top tourist attraction. The city's industrial past also features high on the tourist trail – don't miss the Verdant Works where you can learn about the jute trade that was once a mainstay of the city's economy. Today Dundee has a thriving cosmopolitan feel and dynamic cultural quarter.

For a complete contrast to city life, explore the Angus Glens. There are five: Glen Isla, Glen Prosen, Glen Lethnot, Glen Clova and Glen Esk. Each has its own unique features but all are exceptionally beautiful and wonderfully peaceful places to explore.

Lunan Bay, Angus

1. Perhaps Scotland's finest fairytale castle, **Glamis Castle** is famed for its Macbeth connections, as well as being the birthplace of the late Princess Margaret and childhood home of the late Queen Mother. Set against the backdrop of the Grampian Mountains, Glamis is an L-shaped castle built over 5-storeys in striking pink sandstone. The grounds host the Grand Scottish Proms in August each year, complete with spectacular fireworks display.

2. Little more than half an hour's drive north of the bustling city of Dundee, a series of picturesque valleys runs north into the heart of the Grampians. Collectively known as the **Angus Glens**, they offer the perfect escape for those seeking a walk, a spot of wildlife watching, a scenic picnic or a pub lunch. Ranging from gentle and wooded (Glen Isla) to the truly awe-inspiring (Glen Clova and neighbouring Glen Doll), there is more to discover here than you can fit into a single trip.

3. Discover Dundee's polar past at **Discovery Point**. Step aboard Captain Scott's famous ship that took Scott and Shackleton to Antarctica in 1901 and come face to face with the heroes of the ice in the award winning visitor centre.

4. Dundee is the perfect place for a city break, with great shopping, restaurants and nightlife. Spend a day at Dundee's vibrant and cool **Cultural Quarter** where you can indulge in speciality shopping at the Westport, visit Sensation, Dundee's Science Centre which explores the world of the senses, take in a film or an exhibition at Dundee Contemporary Arts, visit Dundee's acclaimed Rep Theatre, and round it all off with a meal at one of the many restaurants and a drink at one of the area's contemporary bars.

5. For the chance to see bottlenose dolphins at close proximity, why not book a trip on one of the **River Tay Dolphin Trips**. If you prefer to stay on dry land the dolphins can sometimes be seen from Broughty Ferry Beach. The best time to see them is from March-September.

6. Angus was the heartland of the Picts, a warrior people who lived in Scotland around 2,000 years ago and left behind many intriguing monuments. **Pictavia**, at Brechin, provides a fascinating insight including hands-on exhibits and a themed play area for all the family. The small hamlet of Aberlemno, 6 miles north-east of Forfar, is famous for its intricately sculptured Pictish cross-slab in the churchyard.

7. For an excellent view of the City and beyond, take a trip to the top of **The Law** – Dundee's highest point – an extinct volcano. Enjoy magnificent views over the River Tay, and to the hills of Angus and beyond on a clear day.

FOOD AND DRINK

eatscotland.com

8   The **But 'n Ben** in Auchmithie, just 5 miles north of Arbroath, is one of the best seafood restaurants in the area and serves as its speciality the 'smokie pancake'.

9   **Jute Café Bar** is situated on the ground floor of Dundee Contemporary Arts Centre. Its menu ranges widely, with the emphasis on informality, while the ambience goes from a relaxing morning coffee venue to a stylish evening hotspot. Eat, drink and enjoy yourself with freshly cooked contemporary dishes, everything from a light snack to a full meal.

10   **The Roundhouse Restaurant** at Lintrathen, by Kirriemuir, is an award-winning restaurant offering innovative modern menus using Angus and Perthshire produce in a peaceful rural setting. The chef is a former Master Chef of Great Britain, whose specialities include local Angus beef and game.

11   No visit to the area would be complete without stopping off to pick up some of the area's best local produce to take home. **Milton Haugh Farm Shop** specialises in the freshest seasonal potatoes, own reared beef and free range chickens. The Corn Kist Coffee Shop also serves up some delicious home made meals and tempting treats.

WALKS

visitscotland.com/walking

12   Scenic **Glen Doll** is one of the famous Angus Glens, north of Dundee. Follow one of the waymarked forest walks from the car park, or more ambitious hikers can take any of three rights of way leading over the surrounding hills into the neighbouring valleys of Glen Shee and Royal Deeside.

13   Situated five miles North West of Carnoustie, **Crombie Country Park** covers 100 hectares of mixed woodland around a picturesque reservoir. Great opportunities for wildlife watching including butterflies, water and woodland birds.

14   **Seaton Cliffs Nature Trail** is a self guided trail which goes from Arbroath into Sites of Special Scientific Interest, and the sea cliffs are spectacular. There are 15 interpretative points of interest and a wide variety of sea bird species can be seen including puffins, guillemots, razorbill and eider duck to name but a few. Allow approximately 2 hours and 30 minutes.

15   If you want to get out and about in the fresh air, see some of what Dundee has to offer, and get fit at the same time, why not try out one of the themed **Dundee city centre walks** in the Dundee Walking Guide available from the Visitor Information Centre. The trails include buildings of historical significance, examples of both 19th and 20th century architecture, plus explorations of Dundee's maritime and industrial heritage. You will also pass many of Dundee's visitor attractions where you can stop en route.

GOLF

visitscotland.com/golf

16 If you want to experience the very best in Scottish golf, a visit to the **Carnoustie Championship Course** is a must. Venue of the 2007 Open Golf Championship, the course has been deemed the 'toughest links course in the world'.

17 **Montrose Medal Golf Course**, established in 1562, is the fifth oldest golf course in the world with a traditional links layout.

18 **Downfield Golf Club** is an attractive parkland course that has played host to many golfing tournaments and has an excellent reputation as a challenging course.

19 **Kirriemuir Golf Course** is a gem of a parkland course designed by the renowned James Braid. Look out for the notorious oak tree at the 18th!

HISTORY AND HERITAGE

20 **JM Barrie's Birthplace** at Kirriemuir has been carefully restored to reflect how it might have looked in the 1860s. The exhibition next door details the life and work of this hugely talented and celebrated author, whose books include Peter Pan.

21 In 1178 William the Lion founded the now ruined Tironensian monastery that is **Arbroath Abbey**, near the harbour in Arbroath. The abbey is famously associated with the Declaration of Arbroath, signed here in 1320, which asserted Scotland's independence from England. An adjacent visitor centre tells the building's story.

22 **Edzell Castle** is an elegant 16th century residence with tower house that was home to the Lindsays. The beautiful walled garden was created by Sir David Lindsay in 1604 and features an astonishing architectural framework. The 'Pleasance' is a delightful formal garden with walls decorated with sculptured stone panels, flower boxes and niches for nesting birds.

The golf course at Aberdour, Fife

Kingdom of Fife

If you're a golfer, the ancient Kingdom of Fife will be a powerful draw. Every serious golfer wants to play the Old Course at St Andrews at least once in a lifetime and, thanks to a public allocation of rounds each day, you can. There are also 45 other fabulous courses in Fife to put your game to the test.

For keen walkers, one of the great ways to explore Fife is on foot. The Fife Coastal Path takes in some truly delightful places and you'll get to relax on some of the best beaches in the country – with five Fife beaches achieving the top standard Blue Flag status in 2008.

Fife's seaside communities have their roots in

fishing and the North Sea herring fleet used to land its catch in the East Neuk's ports. The harbour at Anstruther is still busy but the halcyon days of deep sea fishing have been consigned to the fascinating exhibitions in the Scottish Fisheries Museum in the town.

Harbour at Anstruther Fife, Fisheries Museum behind

To find out more, call 0845 22 55 121 or go to visitscotland.com

...ail, Fife
...olf Hotel
Map Ref: 2D3

28534

★★
INN

Open: All year

4 High Street, Crail, Fife KY10 3TD
T: 01333 450206
E: info@thegolfhotelcrail.com
W: thegolfhotelcrail.com

The Golf Hotel has a reputation worldwide for its excellent hospitality and outstanding value. The Garden Restaurant and famous public bar offers guests an 'Olde Worlde' Scottish experience. Fresh seafood, real ale, home-cooking and hearty breakfasts compliment our comfortable rooms, which feature Sky Sports and Setanta Golf.

Total number of rooms: 5			
Prices from:			
Single:	**£45.00**	Double:	**£30.00**
Twin:	**£30.00**	Family room:	**£30.00**

...upar, Fife
...raigsanquhar Country House Hotel
Map Ref: 2C3

21067

★★
COUNTRY
HOUSE
HOTEL

Open: All year excl 5th-31st January

Logie, Cupar, Fife KY14 4PZ
T: 01334 653426
E: info@craigsanquhar.com
W: craigsanquhar.com

Craigsanquhar is the quintessential Scottish country house hotel. Craigsanquhar provides peace and tranquility combined with international standards of comfort that the discerning guest has a right to expect. The rooms are elegant and unique. The staff are ready to serve.

Total number of rooms: 13			
Prices per room from:			
Single:	**£120.00**	Double:	**£185.00**
Twin:	**£160.00**	Suite:	**£220.00**

...unfermline, Fife
...est Western Keavil House Hotel
Map Ref: 2B4

33438

★★
COUNTRY
HOUSE
HOTEL

Open: All year excl Xmas

Crossford, Dunfermline, Fife KY12 8QW
T: 01383 736258
E: marketing@keavilhouse.co.uk
W: keavilhouse.co.uk

Historic 73 bedroom country house hotel, including extensive leisure facilities, set in 12 acres of landscaped gardens and grounds, making it an ideal location for relaxing. The hotel offers an award winning restaurant. Within easy reach of Edinburgh – 25 minutes by train and is also a central location for golfing.

Total number of rooms: 73			
Prices per room from:			
Single:	**£75.00**	Double:	**£90.00**
Twin:	**£90.00**	Family room:	**£105.00**

For a full listing of quality assured serviced accommodation throughout Scotland see pages 195-278.

129

Kingdom of Fife

Dunfermline, Fife
Clarke Cottage Guest House
Map Ref: 2B4

★★★
GUEST HOUSE

Open: All year
139 Halbeath Road, Dunfermline, Fife KY11 4LA
T: 01383 735935
E: clarkecottage@ukonline.co.uk
W: clarkecottageguesthouse.co.uk

19522

Total number of rooms: 9

Prices from:
Single: £33.00   Double: £26.00
Twin: £26.00

Dunfermline, Fife
Davaar House Hotel
Map Ref: 2B4

★★★
SMALL HOTEL

Open: All year excl December 24-26
126 Grieve Street, Dunfermline, Fife KY12 8DW
T: 01383 721886
E: enquiries@davaar-house-hotel.com
W: davaar-house-hotel.com

22219

Experience Davaar's homely atmosphere, enjoy the hospitality, comfortable rooms and excellent cooking using fresh local produce. Central location for golf in Fife. Knockhill Race Track, Edinburgh and St Andrews are within easy reach. Come and enjoy a relaxing break or business stay. We look forward to welcoming you.

Total number of rooms: 10

Prices per room from:
Single: £60.00   Double: £90.00
Twin: £90.00   Family room: £130.00

Dunfermline, Fife
Express by Holiday Inn – Dunfermline
Map Ref: 2B4

★★★
METRO HOTEL

Open: All year excl Xmas
Halbeath, Dunfermline, Fife KY11 8DY
T: 01383 748220
E: info@hiexpressdunfermline.co.uk
W: hiexpressdunfermline.co.uk

68058

Total number of rooms: 82

Prices per room from:
Single: £55.00   Double: £55.00
Twin: £55.00   Family room: £55.00

Dunfermline, Fife
Garvock House Hotel
Map Ref: 2B4

★★★★
HOTEL

Open: All year
St John's Drive, Transy, Dunfermline, Fife KY12 7TU
T: 01383 621067
E: sales@garvock.co.uk
W: garvock.co.uk

27355

Peacefully located near the heart of Dunfermline, Scotland's Ancient Capital, lies Garvock House. 26 beautifully furnished and comfortable bedrooms equipped with all the little "extras", elegant dining room with taste-tempting menus. Lunches, dinners, private parties, weddings and conferences catered for. Golf can be arranged locally.

Total number of rooms: 26

Prices per room from:
Single: £69.50   Double: £89.50
Twin: £89.50

IMPORTANT: Prices stated are estimates and may be subject to change. Prices are per person per night unless otherwise stated. Awards correct as of beginning of October 2008.

tbauchlie House Hotel

Map Ref: 2B4

★★
OTEL

Open: All year
Aberdour Road, Dunfermline, Fife KY11 4PB
T: 01383 722282
E: info@pitbauchlie.com
W: pitbauchlie.com

49892

Total number of rooms: 50		
Prices per room from:		
Single: **£90.00**	Double:	**£108.00**
Twin: **£108.00**	Family room:	**£120.00**

---

omond Hills Hotel & Leisure Centre

Map Ref: 2C3

★★
OTEL

Open: All year
High Street, Freuchie, Fife KY15 7EY
T: 01337 857329
E: reception@lomondhillshotel.com
W: lomondhillshotel.com

36274

Total number of rooms: 24		
Prices from:		
Single: **£59.95**	Double:	**£40.00**
Twin: **£40.00**	Family room:	**£29.95**

---

ilvenbank Hotel

Map Ref: 2C3

★★
OTEL

Open: All year
Huntsman's Road, Glenrothes, Fife KY7 6NT
T: 01592 742077
E: gilvenbankhotel@btconnect.com
W: gilvenbankhotel.com

73135

Total number of rooms: 19		
Prices per room from:		
Single: **£55.00**	Double:	**£55.00**
Twin: **£55.00**	Family room:	**£55.00**

---

he Bay Hotel

Map Ref: 2C4

★★
OTEL

Open: All year
Burntisland Road, Kinghorn, Fife KY3 9YE
T: 01592 892222
E: thebayhotel@pettycur.co.uk
W: thebayhotel.net

79438

Simply breathtaking. Stunning new hotel standing in an area of natural beauty with breathtaking views across River Forth to Edinburgh and beyond. The adjacent Bay Leisure centre includes a swimming pool, sauna, steam room, jacuzzi and multi gym. Soft play area for the children with bouncy castle. Our beautifully furnished restaurant offers the ultimate dining experience, from delicious snacks to fine wines and excellent service. Our popular night club, Images, for all guests who wish to enjoy a wide variety of live entertainment including cabaret, dance, traditional Scottish nights and theme nights.

Total number of rooms: 27
Prices on application

For a full listing of quality assured serviced accommodation throughout Scotland see pages 195-278.

131

Kingdom of Fife

Leven, Fife
Caledonian Hotel and Bar
Map Ref: 2C3

Open: All year
81 High Street, Leven, Fife KY8 4NG
T: 01333 424101   F: 01333 412241
E: caledonianhotel.leven@belhavenpubs.net
W: thecaledonianhotel-leven.co.uk

17588

Total number of rooms: 24

Prices per room from:

Single:	**£50.00**	Double:	**£60.00**
Twin:	**£60.00**	Family room:	**£70.00**

St Andrews, Fife
The Albany Hotel
Map Ref: 2D2

Open: All year excl Xmas and New Year
56-58 North Street, St Andrews, Fife KY16 9AH
T: 01334 477737
E: info@thealbanystandrews.co.uk
W: thealbanystandrews.co.uk

11413

Total number of rooms: 22

Prices per room from:

Single:	**£82.00**	Double:	**£133.00**
Twin:	**£133.00**	Family room:	**£205.00**

St Andrews, Fife
Craigmore Guest House
Map Ref: 2D2

Open: All year
3 Murray Park, St Andrews, Fife KY16 9AW
T: 01334 472142
E: jim.williamson@virgin.net
W: standrewscraigmore.com

21018

Total number of rooms: 7

Prices from:
Double: **£38.00-48.00**   Twin: **£38.00-48.00**
Family room: **£38.00-48.00**

St Andrews, Fife
Fairmont St Andrews, Scotland
Map Ref: 2D2

Open: All year
Crail Road, St Andrews, Fife KY16 8PN
T: 01334 837000
E: standrews.scotland@fairmont.com
W: fairmont.com/standrews

Fairmont St Andrews, Scotland, situated on a unique east coast setting commands spectacular views of the bay's golden beaches and medieval St Andrews' skyline. A luxurious five star hotel with 209 generous guest rooms, a choice of five restaurants, a revitalising new Spa, an impressive conference centre and two championship golf courses.

Total number of rooms: 209

Prices per room from:

Single:	**£159.00**	Double:	**£159.00**
Twin:	**£159.00**	Family room:	**£229.00**

St Andrews, Fife
Greyfriars Hotel
Map Ref: 2D2

Open: All year
129 North Street, St Andrews, Fife KY16 9AG
T: 01334 474906
E: stay@greyfriarshotel.co.uk
W: greyfriarshotel.co.uk

75013

Total number of rooms: 20

Prices per room from:

Single:	**£65.00**	Double:	**£100.00**
Twin:	**£100.00**	Family room:	**£150.00**

St Andrews, Fife

New Hall, University of St Andrews — Map Ref: 2D2

★★★
OTEL

ppp

Open: June-September

North Haugh, St Andrews, Fife KY16 9XW

T: 01334 467000 **F:** 01334 467001
E: new.hall@st-andrews.ac.uk
W: discoverstandrews.com

New Hall offers comfortable ensuite facilities, excellent value and a friendly service. New Hall is located within easy walking distance of the beach, golf courses and the historic town centre and is ideal for golfers, families, short breaks and holidays. All bedrooms have double beds, TVs and tea and coffee making facilities.

Total number of rooms: 100

Prices from:

Single: **£49.50**   Double: **£36.00**

St Andrews, Fife

The New Inn — Map Ref: 2D2

★★★
INN

Open: All year

21-23 St Mary's Street, St Andrews, Fife KY16 8AZ
T: 01334 461333
E: lena@grangeinn.myzen.co.uk
W: newinnstandrews.com

Total number of rooms: 4

Prices per room from:

Single: **£40.00**   Double: **£70.00**
Twin: **£70.00**   Family room: **£80.00**

St Andrews, Fife

Ogstons on North Street — Map Ref: 2D2

★★★
INN

Open: All year

127 North Street, St Andrews, Fife KY16 9AG
T: 01334 473387
E: info@ogstonsonnorthst.com
W: ogstonsonnorthst.com

Total number of rooms: 13

Prices per room from:

Single: **£72.00**   Double: **£100.00**
Twin: **£100.00**   Family room: **£125.00**

St Andrews, Fife

The Old Course Hotel, Golf Resort and Spa — Map Ref: 2D2

★★★★
OTEL

Open: All year

St Andrews, Fife KY16 9SP
T: 01334 474371
E: reservations@oldcoursehotel.co.uk
W: oldcoursehotel.co.uk

The luxurious Old Course Hotel, Golf Resort and Spa offers spectacular views across the links courses, West Sands beach, skyline of St Andrews and beautiful Scottish countryside. The sumptuous guest rooms and suites, superb dining, stunning Kohler Waters Spa and own championship golf course, The Duke's, makes this a 'must-visit' destination.

Total number of rooms: 144

Prices per room from:

Single: **£205.00**   Double: **£235.00**

For a full listing of quality assured serviced accommodation throughout Scotland see pages 195-278.

133

Kingdom of Fife

St Andrews, Fife
Yorkston Guest House
Map Ref: 2D2

★★★
GUEST HOUSE

Open: March-November

68-70 Argyle Street, St Andrews, Fife KY16 9BU
T: 01334 472019
E: yorkstonhouse@aol.com
W: yorkstonguesthouse.co.uk

Family run Guest House situated close to the West Port, town centre, shops and restaurants. Easy walking distance to the 1st tee of the Old Course. Free Wi-Fi access for guests with their own wireless enabled laptop.

64810

Total number of rooms: 10

Prices from:

Single:	£42.00	Double:	£42.00
Twin:	£42.00	Family room:	£42.00

by St Andrews, Fife
The Inn at Lathones
Map Ref: 2D2

★★★★
INN

SILVER

Open: All year excl Xmas and first 2 weeks in January
by Largoward, St Andrews, Fife KY9 1JE
T: 01334 840494
E: lathones@theinn.co.uk
W: theinn.co.uk

59338

Total number of rooms: 21

Prices from:

Single:	£120.00	Double:	£90.00
Twin:	£90.00		

Walking along the pier beside the harbour at St Andrews, Fife

The village of Dysart, near Kirkcaldy, Fife

For a full listing of quality assured serviced accommodation throughout Scotland see pages 195-278.

135

Fyvie Castle, Aberdeenshire

ABERDEEN CITY AND SHIRE

Aberdeen City and Shire is an area of contrasts. From the mountains and forests to the towering cliffs, rocky inlets, endless sandy beaches and captivating harbour towns.

Aberdeen is a thriving and cosmopolitan city with magnificent architecture and a host of cultural opportunities, from museums and art galleries to theatres and concert halls.

The 'Granite City' is also famous for its award winning floral displays. With 45 parks in the city and a celebrated Winter Garden at Duthie Park, Aberdeen is always in bloom and every season brings new floral flights of fancy.

It has a busy central shopping area yet just a short distance away there's a brilliant beach complete with an all-year funfair.

The many fascinations of the Aberdeenshire coastline extend beyond the city however. Along the coast you'll find captivating harbour towns like Stonehaven, Peterhead, Fraserburgh and Banff, as well as quaint little places like the stunning Pennan, a former smuggler's town at the foot of a cliff.

Castles and whisky galore

Aberdeen City and Shire is renowned for its castles which come in all shapes and sizes from fairytale castles to crumbling ruins and even royal holiday homes. Some great trails have been laid out for visitors to follow, including the intriguing Castle Trail.

The Deeside towns of Banchory, Ballater and Braemar have all enjoyed many decades of royal patronage, the annual highlight of which is the Braemar Gathering in September.

To find out more, call 0845 22 55 121 or go to visitscotland.com

Alongside the whisky, there are other delights that will soon have you raising your glass – music, song and, of course, fine food. Beautiful Aberdeen Angus beef, sumptuous seafood, fabulous fruit and vegetables – all come fresh to the table, prepared by the finest chefs. The Taste of Grampian, held annually in June at Inverurie, is a must for foodies.

What's more, 2009 is a big year for Scotland – we're celebrating the 250th anniversary of the birth of Robert Burns. There's over 200 special events taking place throughout the year, all over Scotland. Go to homecomingscotland2009.com to find out about events in this area.

So where would you like to stay in Aberdeen City and Shire? There's a lot of choice – from historical baronial mansions and elegant country houses to Victorian townhouses and seaside guesthouses – just take your pick!

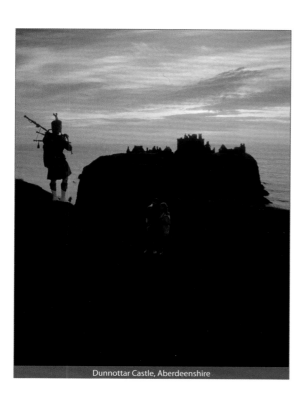

Dunnottar Castle, Aberdeenshire

What's On?

Word 09 – University of Aberdeen Writers Festival
13 – 17 May 2009
A packed programme of readings, lectures and debates as well as musical events, art exhibitions and film screenings showcasing how the Scottish word has changed the world!
abdn.ac.uk/word

Taste of Grampian, Inverurie
6 June 2009
Discover and sample a wide range of quality food and drink products.
tasteofgrampian.co.uk

The Scottish Traditional Boat Festival
2 – 5 July 2009
A colourful celebration of Scotland's great maritime heritage, with events throughout Portsoy and Banff.
stbf.bizland.com/2009

Lonach Gathering & Highland Games
22 August 2009
lonach.org

Braemar Gathering
5 September 2009
Traditional highland games.
braemargathering.org

Stonehaven Fireball Festival
31 December 2009
A spectacular winter festival to bring in the New Year.

All dates correct at time of publication. Please check before booking. VisitScotland cannot be held responsible for any inaccuracies

137

DON'T MISS

1   The restored Victorian **Old Royal Station**, Ballater now houses a museum focusing very much on Queen Victoria's journeys here, when heading to Balmoral, including a recreated waiting room and a replica of a carriage used by Queen Victoria when travelling from Windsor to Ballater. In its heyday, many famous people, including the Tsar of Russia, used Ballater Station.

2   **Balmoral Castle**, Scottish home of the Royal Family since the mid 19th century is set amid spectacular scenery. See why Queen Victoria described Balmoral as "my dear paradise in the Highlands". Visit the largest room in the castle, the ballroom, and learn the history of the castle through an audio-visual presentation.

3   From its days as a lively fishing port to its current status as Europe's North Sea oil capital, Aberdeen's historic relationship with the sea unfolds at the five-star **Aberdeen Maritime Museum** through exciting displays and exhibitions.

4   **Duff House**, a magnificent Baroque mansion designed by William Adam, is now a treasure house and cultural arts centre operated by a unique partnership of Historic Scotland, the National Galleries of Scotland and Aberdeenshire Council. Storytellers, musicians and artists are at home here and Duff House organises a regular artistic programme of exhibitions, music and lectures.

5   Held on the first Saturday of September, one of Scotland's oldest and biggest Highland Gatherings, **The Braemar Gathering** is notable not only for its size, but also for their unique chieftain, Her Majesty the Queen. Royalty is always in attendance, presiding over a programme of events that includes Highland dancing, tossing the caber, tug of war and piping.

6   Take a stroll along 2 miles of sandy beach at **Aberdeen's beachfront** and discover a range of attractions for all the family. The beach itself is famous for its golden sand and its long curved length between the harbour and the mouth of the River Don. The beach is a favourite for walkers, surfers and windsurfers and has a popular amusement area along the famous Beach Esplanade where there are restaurants, a cinema and the city's amusement park.

HERITAGE

7   Built in the 16th century, **Crathes Castle** is a splendid example of a tower house, retaining many original interior features, and a stunning walled garden complete with herbaceous borders and an array of unusual plants.

8   The charming **Braemar Castle**, now run by the community of Braemar, re-opened to the public in May 2008, and is undergoing an ambitious restoration programme to ensure a memorable experience for visitors.

9   Wander around the extensive buildings of **Dunnottar Castle**, set in a dramatic cliff top location with the sound of waves crashing on the rocks below and discover the significance of this impenetrable castle which holds many secrets of Scotland's colourful past.

10   With so many stunning castles in the region, it's no surprise that there is a **Castle Trail** taking in thirteen of the most unique examples, from fairytale castles, through rugged ruins to the elegant grandeur of country houses set in some of the most spectacular grounds.

WALKS

11   The walk around **Loch Muick**, in the shadow of Lochnagar, is mainly on fairly flat ground, following a route close to the loch side, with good views of the hills around. Look out for red deer. A short wooded section follows after reaching a Royal lodge, and then continues round the loch, passing a sandy beach, rising slightly before returning to the start point.

12   Scottish Wildlife Trust reserve at **Gight Woods**, north of Aberdeen, offers walks of up to 3 miles. The route follows the forestry track through Badiebath Woods towards the ruined Gight Castle (Byron's ancestral home) passing a number of interesting ruins, and with the opportunity to spot red squirrels.

13   The 5 mile route from **Duff House to Bridge of Alvah** is full of variety, starting through a mature deciduous wood, near the banks of the River Deveron, where you may spot kingfisher and goldeneye. The path then crosses the river, at **Bridge of Alvah**, along tracks and minor roads lined with shrubs, returning via the grounds of MacDuff Distillery back over the river, to Duff House affording great views of Banff.

14   **Ballater Royal Deeside Walking Festival** takes place each year in May, and provides a programme of walks for walkers of all capabilities from 'Munro-baggers' to those who prefer a gentle stroll, all set in magnificent walking country surrounded by breathtaking scenery.

FOOD & DRINK

15   **The Milton Restaurant & Conservatory**, situated opposite Crathes Castle on Royal Deeside, offers exquisite food in picturesque surroundings. The Milton's kitchen team of award winners, including **Grampian Chef of the Year 2008**, is renowned not only for the flavour, but also the stunning presentation of the dishes.

16   Scotch Beef can be found on the menus of top restaurants throughout Europe and the reputation of this high-class product remains undiminished. **Aberdeen Angus** is arguably the best known breed, renowned for the rich and tasty flavour of the meat.

17   On a farm near Inverurie in Aberdeenshire, **Mackie's award winning ice cream** is made using milk from their own Jersey and Holstein herds. Over 20 flavours of ice cream are created using renewable energy: the farm has three wind turbines which produce all the energy required to make this delicious ice cream.

18   **Dean's of Huntly** bake traditional Scottish all-butter shortbread, and at the visitor centre you can learn about its history and watch how the delicious shortbread is made in the viewing gallery, before visiting the café for a tasting.

ACTIVITIES

19   The fairways of Aberdeen City and Shire provide a variety of golfing experiences, from the historic links **Royal Aberdeen** with its towering dunes to the splendid inland and parkland courses which offer new challenges.

20   If you want to take part in an activity, head for **Deeside Activity Park**, where you will be amazed by the number and variety of activities on offer, from fly fishing, rock climbing, archery, kart racing, quad bike trekking to digger manoeuvres. There's a restaurant and farm shop too.

21   Aberdeen City and Shire has miles of unspoilt and often rugged coastline, so why not try **water sports** here? Yachting, canoeing, scuba diving, surfing, and water skiing are all available, but if big waves are your thing, visit Fraserburgh, former host to rounds of Scottish Wavesailing Championships. Or why not team up with Surf and Watersport Club, Banff for some expert tuition?

To find out more, call 0845 22 55 121 or go to visitscotland.com

MAP

©Collins Bartholomew Ltd 2008

 VISITOR INFORMATION CENTRES

Visitor Information Centres are staffed by people 'in the know' offering friendly advice, helping to make your stay in Scotland the most enjoyable ever . . . whatever your needs!

Aberdeen City and Shire		
Aberdeen	23 Union Street, Aberdeen, AB11 5BP	Tel: 01224 288828
Ballater	The Old Royal Station, Station Square, Ballater, AB35 5QB	Tel: 01339 755306
Braemar	Unti 3, The Mews, Mar Road, Braemar, AB35 5YL	Tel: 01339 741600

LOCAL KNOWLEDGE • WHERE TO STAY • ACCOMMODATION BOOKING • PLACES TO VISIT • THINGS TO DO • MAPS AND GUIDES TRAVEL ADVICE • ROUTE PLANNING • WHERE TO SHOP AND EAT LOCAL CRAFTS AND PRODUCE • EVENT INFORMATION • TICKETS

For information and ideas about exploring Scotland in advance of your trip, call our booking and information service **0845 22 55 121** or go to **visitscotland.com**

If calling from outside the UK and Ireland **+44 1506 832 121**   From Ireland **1800 932 510**

A £4 booking fee applies for accommodation bookings made via a Visitor Information Centre and through our booking and information service.

Live it. Visit *Scotland.*
visitscotland.com/wheretofindus

Aberdeen City and Shire

Aberdeen
Brentwood Hotel
Map Ref: 4G10

★★★
HOTEL

Open: All year excl Xmas Day and New Year's Day

101 Crown Street, Aberdeen AB11 6HH
T: 01224 595440
E: reservations@brentwood-hotel.co.uk
W: brentwood-hotel.co.uk

58314

Total number of rooms: 65

Prices from:

Single:	£43.00	Double:	£33.00
Twin:	£33.00	Family room:	£33.00

Aberdeen
Craighaar Hotel
Map Ref: 4G10

★★★
HOTEL
✉

Open: All year excl Xmas

Waterton Road, Bankhead, Aberdeen AB21 9HS
T: 01224 712275
E: info@craighaar.co.uk
W: craighaarhotel.com

20936

Total number of rooms: 55

Prices per room from:

Single:	£59.00	Double:	£65.00
Twin:	£65.00	Family room:	£75.00

Aberdeen
Furain Guest House
Map Ref: 4G10

★★★
GUEST HOUSE

Open: All year excl Xmas and New Year

92 North Deeside Road,
Peterculter, Aberdeen AB14 0QN
T: 01224 732189
E: furain@btinternet.com
W: furain.co.uk

Late Victorian house built of red granite. Family-run, convenient for town, Royal Deeside and Castle Trail. Private car parking. Close to River Dee. Well located for fishing, golf and walking.

26933

Total number of rooms: 8

Prices from:

Single:	£43.00	Double:	£28.00
Twin:	£28.00	Family room:	£74.00pr

Aberdeen
Marcliffe Hotel and Spa
Map Ref: 4G10

★★★★★
HOTEL
✉ &
SILVER

Open: All year

North Deeside Road, Cults, Aberdeen AB15 9YA
T: 01224 861000
E: info@marcliffe.com
W: marcliffe.com

The Marcliffe Hotel and Spa is set in 11 acres of wooded grounds, three miles from the centre of Aberdeen and is ideally positioned for visiting Scotland's scenic North East. The only VisitScotland 5 star hotel in Aberdeen and a member of Small Luxury Hotels of the World and Connoisseurs Scotland.

59622

Total number of rooms: 42

Prices per room from:

Single:	£150.00	Double:	£170.00
Twin:	£170.00		

IMPORTANT: Prices stated are estimates and may be subject to change. Prices are per person per night unless otherwise stated. Awards correct as of beginning of October 2008.

Aberdeen
Old Mill Inn

Map Ref: 4G10

★★★
INN

Open: All year
South Deeside Road, Maryculter, Aberdeen AB12 5FX
- **T:** 01224 733212
- **E:** info@oldmillinn.co.uk
- **W:** oldmillinn.co.uk

48319

Total number of rooms: 7		
Prices per room from:		
Single: **£69.00**	Double:	**£79.00**
Twin: **£79.00**	Family room:	**£85.00**

Aberdeen
Royal Hotel

Map Ref: 4G10

★★
HOTEL

Open: All year excl Xmas and New Year
1-3 Bath Street, Aberdeen AB11 6BJ
- **T:** 01224 585152
- **E:** info@royalhotel.uk.com
- **W:** royalhotel.uk.com

52465

Total number of rooms: 42		
Prices from:		
Single: **£55.00**	Double:	**£35.00**
Twin: **£35.00**	Family room:	**£75.00pr**

Ballater, Aberdeenshire
Cambus O'May Hotel

Map Ref: 4E11

★★★
COUNTRY
HOUSE
HOTEL

Open: All year
Cambus O'May, Ballater, Aberdeenshire AB35 5SE
- **T:** 013397 55428
- **E:** mckechnie@cambusomay.freeserve.co.uk
- **W:** cambusomayhotel.co.uk

17716

Beautiful country house hotel located in the heart of Royal Deeside with superb views over the hills. Ideally situated to explore and enjoy the many attractions and activities available in the area. The hotel offers comfortable bedrooms with modern facilities, cocktail bar and dining room providing excellent freshly prepared food.

Total number of rooms: 12		
Prices from:		
Single: **£45.00**	Double:	**£45.00**
Twin: **£45.00**	Family room:	**£45.00**

Ballater, Aberdeenshire
Deeside Hotel

Map Ref: 4E11

★★★
SMALL
HOTEL

Open: All year
Braemar Road, Ballater, Aberdeenshire AB35 5RQ
- **T:** 01339 755420
- **E:** mail@deesidehotel.co.uk
- **W:** deesidehotel.co.uk

22416

Set in lovely grounds within the village. Ensuite bedrooms have extras such as hot chocolate and home-made shortbread. The restaurant offers traditional Scottish food with a modern twist, wide-ranging wine list, real ale and malt whiskies. The sunny conservatory and log fires make this a special place in any season.

Total number of rooms: 10		
Prices from:		
£45.00		

For a full listing of quality assured serviced accommodation throughout Scotland see pages 195-278.

143

Aberdeen City and Shire

Ballater, Aberdeenshire
Glenernan Guest House
Map Ref: 4E11

★★★
GUEST
HOUSE

Open: All year
37 Braemar Road, Ballater, Aberdeenshire AB35 5RQ
T: 013397 53111
E: enquiries@glenernanguesthouse.com
W: glenernanguesthouse.com

Total number of rooms: 7

Prices from:

Single:	£38.00	Double:	£28.00
Twin:	£28.00	Family room:	£28.00

Nr Ballater, Aberdeenshire
Loch Kinord Hotel
Map Ref: 4E11

★★★
HOTEL

Open: All year
Ballater Road, Dinnet,
Aboyne, Aberdeenshire AB34 5JY
T: 013398 85229
E: stay@lochkinord.com
W: lochkinord.com

Total number of rooms: 19

Prices per room from:

Single:	£55.00	Double:	£95.00
Twin:	£95.00	Family room:	£95.00

Banchory, Aberdeenshire
The Burnett Arms Hotel
Map Ref: 4F11

★★★
SMALL
HOTEL

Open: All year
25 High Street, Banchory, Aberdeenshire AB31 5TD
T: 01330 824944
E: theburnett@btconnect.com
W: burnettarms.co.uk

Total number of rooms: 16

Prices from:

Single:	£77.00	Double:	£50.00
Twin:	£50.00	Family room:	£45.00

Banchory, Aberdeenshire
Learney Arms Hotel
Map Ref: 4F11

★★
SMALL
HOTEL

Open: All year
The Square, Torphins,
Banchory, Kincardineshire AB31 4GP
T: 01339 882202
E: sales@learneyarmshotel.com
W: learneyarmshotel.com

Total number of rooms: 12

Prices per room from:

Single:	£48.00	Double:	£78.00
Twin:	£78.00	Family room:	£85.00

Banchory, Aberdeenshire
Potarch Hotel
Map Ref: 4F11

AWAITING
GRADING

Open: All year excl 3-25 January

Potarch, Banchory AB31 4BD
T: 01339 884339
E: info@potarchhotel.co.uk
W: potarchhotel.co.uk

Set on the bank of the beautiful River Dee, a warm welcome awaits you at Potarch. With just six bedrooms, you can expect a friendly, efficient and professional service to ensure a relaxing stay. Enjoy true Scottish hospitality – complemented by good food, real ale and a wee dram!

Total number of rooms: 6

Prices from:

Single:	£45.00	Double:	£37.00
Twin:	£37.00		

Braemar, Aberdeenshire
Braemar Lodge Hotel
Map Ref: 4D11

★★ GUEST HOUSE

Open: All year
6 Glenshee Road, Braemar, Aberdeenshire AB35 5YQ
T: 013397 41627
E: mail@braemarlodge.co.uk
W: braemarlodge.co.uk

16019

Total number of rooms: 7

Prices from:
Single: **£20.00-60.00**   Double: **£20.00-60.00**

Cruden Bay, Aberdeenshire
Kilmarnock Arms Hotel
Map Ref: 4H9

★★ SMALL HOTEL

Open: All year
Bridge Street, Cruden Bay, Aberdeenshire AB42 0HD
T: 01779 812213
E: reception@kilmarnockarms.com
W: kilmarnockarms.com

The Kilmarnock Arms Hotel is a family owned and run hotel. Situated in the centre of the village of Cruden Bay, only 800m from the world renowned Cruden Bay Golf Course, the hotel offers 14 spacious ensuite rooms. You can relax and enjoy excellent cuisine and wines in our Falcon Restaurant.

33838

Total number of rooms: 14

Prices from:
Single: **£55.00**   Double: **£42.50**
Twin: **£42.50**   Family room: **£42.50**

Inverurie, Aberdeenshire
MacDonald Pittodrie House Hotel
Map Ref: 4G9

★★★ COUNTRY HOUSE HOTEL

Open: All year
Chapel of Garioch, Inverurie,
Aberdeenshire AB51 5HS
T: 08448 799066
E: pittodrie@macdonald-hotels.co.uk
W: macdonald-hotels.co.uk

Set in a 2500 acre estate, Macdonald Pittodrie House Hotel offers a unique atmosphere, nestled in the foothills of the spectacular Bennachie. The ideal leisure retreat only 25 minutes from Aberdeen airport with a reputation for producing classic Scottish cuisine using the finest local produce.

49952

Total number of rooms: 27

Prices per room from:
Single: **£96.00**   Double: **£116.00**
Twin: **£116.00**   Family room: **£136.00**

For a full listing of quality assured serviced accommodation throughout Scotland see pages 195-278.

145

Aberdeen City and Shire

Oldmeldrum, Aberdeenshire
The Redgarth
Map Ref: 4G9

★★★★
INN

✉

Open: All year excl 25-26th December and 1st-3rd January

Kirk Brae, Oldmeldrum, Aberdeenshire AB51 0DJ
T: 01651 872353
E: redgarth1@aol.com
W: redgarth.com

📺📞🛏️P🍴🍵🍽️🍷C£V

60159

Total number of rooms: 3

Prices per room from:

Single: £65.00	Double:	£85.00
Twin: £85.00		

Peterhead, Aberdeenshire
Carrick Guest House
Map Ref: 4H8

★★
GUEST
HOUSE

Open: All year

16 Merchant Street,
Peterhead, Aberdeenshire AB42 1DU
T: 01779 470610
E: carrickpeterhead@aol.com

📺🛏️P🍵🍴✕CV

18278

Total number of rooms: 6

Prices from:

Single: £30.00	Double:	£25.00
Twin: £25.00	Family room:	£70.00pr

Portsoy, Aberdeenshire
The Station Hotel
Map Ref: 4F7

★★
SMALL
HOTEL

Open: All year

Seafield Street, Portsoy, Aberdeenshire AB45 2QT
T: 01261 842327
E: enquiries@stationhotelportsoy.co.uk
W: stationhotelportsoy.co.uk

The warmest of welcomes awaits you in this small family run hotel which boasts 15 very comfortable ensuite rooms and a great restaurant. Portsoy on the Moray Coast has it all; great walking, abundant sealife, wildlife, great golf, malt whisky trail and castle trail.

📺🛏️P🍴✕🍽️🍷🍵C£🐕V

56402

Total number of rooms: 15

Prices from:

Single: £40.00	Double:	£30.00
Twin: £30.00	Family room:	£40.00

Rothienorman, Aberdeenshire
Rothie Inn
Map Ref: 4F9

★★★
INN

Open: All year excl Xmas and New Year

Main Street, Rothienorman,
Aberdeenshire AB51 8UD
T: 01651 821206
E: rothieinn@fsmail.net

📺🛏️P🍵✕🍽️C£🐕V

52263

Total number of rooms: 2

Prices from:

Single: £40.00	Twin: £30.00
Family room: £70.00pr	

IMPORTANT: Prices stated are estimates and may be subject to change. Prices are per person per night unless otherwise stated. Awards correct as of beginning of October 2008.

Stonehaven, Aberdeenshire
The Ship Inn
Map Ref: 4G11

★★
INN

Open: All year

5 Shorehead, Stonehaven, Aberdeenshire AB39 2JY
T: 01569 762617
E: enquiries@shipinnstonehaven.com
W: shipinnstonehaven.com

Inn dating back to 1771. Overlooking the local picturesque harbour of Stonehaven with open views to sea and cliffs beyond. All rooms recently refurbished. Five of which have sea views. Restaurant - The Captain's Table, serving local produce and specialising in fish.

60406

Total number of rooms: 6			
Prices per room from:			
Single:	**£55.00**	Double:	**£90.00**
Twin:	**£90.00**	Family room:	**£105.00**

New Slains Castle, on the east coast, south of Peterhead, Aberdeenshire

For a full listing of quality assured serviced accommodation throughout Scotland see pages 195-278.

147

Glen Coe, Highlands

THE HIGHLANDS AND MORAY

If you're searching for tranquillity, you'll find that life in the Highlands moves at a refreshingly relaxed pace.

Exciting, dramatic and romantic, it's hard not to be moved by the rugged majesty of the mountainous north. It's the stuff of picture postcards, with views that will be etched in your memory forever.

Unspoiled beauty

There are so many places you have to experience: the eerie silence of Glen Coe; the arctic wilderness of the Cairngorms; the deep mysteries of Loch Ness; the wild flatlands of the Flow Country; the astonishing beauty of Glen Affric; and the golden beaches of the west and north coast where you can gaze out to the Atlantic and never meet a soul all day. In this unspoiled natural environment, wildlife flourishes. You'll see red squirrels and tiny goldcrests

in the trees, otters chasing fish in fast flowing rivers, deer coming down from the hills to the forest edge, dolphins and whales off the coast, ospreys and eagles soaring overhead.

A natural playground

And this natural playground is yours to share. Climbers, walkers, mountain bikers and hunters take to the hills. Surfers, sailors, canoeists and fishermen enjoy the beaches, rivers and lochs. For the more adventurous there's skiing, canyoning and white water rafting. Whatever outdoor activity you like to pursue, you'll find experienced, professional experts on hand to ensure you enjoy it to the full.

Highland hospitality

Once you've had enough exercise and fresh air, you can be assured of some fine Highland hospitality - whether you're staying in a tiny village, a pretty

To find out more, call 0845 22 55 121 or go to visitscotland.com

town, a thriving activity centre like Aviemore or in the rapidly expanding city of Inverness. In the pubs and hotels, restaurants and other venues around the community, you'll find music and laughter. Perhaps a riotous ceilidh in full fling and unforgettable nights of eating and drinking into the wee small hours.

Back to your roots

Highlanders know how to enjoy life and they're always keen to welcome visitors – especially those who are tracing their Scottish roots. Every year people come to discover the traditional homeland of their clan, learn about their history and walk in their ancestors' footsteps over battlefields like Culloden where the Jacobite army made its last stand. You could follow Bonnie Prince Charlie over the sea to Skye, whether it's by boat or by bridge. You can even take a glass bottom boat trip around the island and watch the sea life below.

What's more, 2009 is a big year for Scotland – we're celebrating the 250th anniversary of the birth of Robert Burns. There's over 200 special events taking place throughout the year, all over Scotland. Go to homecomingscotland2009.com to find out about events in this area.

Wherever you decide to go, the Highlands, Skye and Moray will cast a spell on you and it will be a holiday you will remember for as long as you live.

Belladrum Tartan Heart Festival

What's On?

O'Neill Highland Open, Thurso
29 April – 7 May 2009
One of the most progressive events in competitive surfing.
oneilleurope.com/highlandopen

UCI Mountain Bike World Cup, Fort William
6 - 7 June 2009
Voted best event on the tour two years running.
fortwilliamworldcup.co.uk

Rock Ness, Dores, Loch Ness
13 - 14 June 2009
The only dance event with its own monster.
rockness.co.uk

Tulloch Inverness Highland Games

18 - 19 July 2009
Clan gathering and heavyweight competition in Inverness. The Highland Clans are hosting the Masters World Championships.
invernesshighlandgames.com

Inverness Highland Tattoo
21 July - 1 August 2009
Previewing artists from the Edinburgh International Tattoo.
tattooinverness.org.uk

Belladrum Tartan Heart Festival, Beauly
7 - 8 August 2009
Open air, family-friendly traditional music festival.
tartanheartfestival.co.uk

Highland Feast
September – various dates
A series of unique culinary and gastronomic events.
highlandfeast.co.uk

Blas Festival – Celebrating the Highlands

4 - 12 September 2009
A vast programme of traditional music and events, staged in some of Scotland's most spectacular and iconic landscapes.
blas-festival.com

All dates correct at time of publication. Please check before booking. VisitScotland cannot be held responsible for any inaccuracies

149

MAP

©Collins Bartholomew Ltd 2008

To find out more, call 0845 22 55 121 or go to visitscotland.com

VISITOR INFORMATION CENTRES

Visitor Information Centres are staffed by people 'in the know' offering friendly advice, helping to make your stay in Scotland the most enjoyable ever . . . whatever your needs!

Northern Highlands, Inverness, Loch Ness and Nairn

Inverness	Castle Wynd, Inverness, IV2 3BJ	Tel: 01463 252401
Drumnadrochit	The Car Park, Drumnadrochit, Inverness-shire, IV63 6TX	Tel: 01456 459086

Fort William and Lochaber, Skye and Lochalsh

Fort William	15 High Street, Fort William, PH33 6DH	Tel: 01397 701801
Portree	Bayfield Road, Portree, Isle of Skye, IV51 9EL	Tel: 01478 614906
Dunvegan	2 Lochside, Dunvegan, Isle of Skye, IV55 8WB	Tel: 01343 542666

Moray, Aviemore and the Cairngorms

Aviemore	Grampian Road, Aviemore, PH22 1PP	Tel: 01479 810930
Elgin	17 High Street, Elgin, IV30 1EG	Tel: 01343 542666

LOCAL KNOWLEDGE • WHERE TO STAY • ACCOMMODATION BOOKING • PLACES TO VISIT • THINGS TO DO • MAPS AND GUIDES TRAVEL ADVICE • ROUTE PLANNING • WHERE TO SHOP AND EAT LOCAL CRAFTS AND PRODUCE • EVENT INFORMATION • TICKETS

For information and ideas about exploring Scotland in advance of your trip, call our booking and information service **0845 22 55 121** or go to **visitscotland.com**

If calling from outside the UK and Ireland **+44 1506 832 121**   From Ireland **1800 932 510**

A £4 booking fee applies for accommodation bookings made via a Visitor Information Centre and through our booking and information service.

Looking over to the Summer Isles, Highlands

Northern Highlands, Inverness, Loch Ness and Nairn

Scotland's most northerly mainland territory is characterised by its dramatic mountains, vast wilderness and spectacular coastline.

Take in the west coast, where views of Quinag from near Kylesku are unmissable. Equally essential on the itinerary of any Highland visitor is Loch Ness, Britain's deepest and most mysterious freshwater expanse.

Don't miss the opportunity to see the Moray Firth dolphins from Chanonry Point on the Black Isle or up close from one of many wildlife cruises.

There are many fine towns and villages to visit - Ullapool, Lochcarron, Lochinver and Kinlochbervie to the west, Thurso, John O'Groats, Wick, Dornoch, Strathpeffer and Nairn on the eastern side. You should also take some time to explore the rapidly growing city of Inverness. Capital of the Highlands, it's a thriving, modern city with lots to see and do.

Fireworks set off from the Kessock Bridge, Inverness

To find out more, call 0845 22 55 121 or go to visitscotland.com

DON'T MISS

1   **Assynt** is stunningly beautiful and is home to a variety of attractions. Chief among them are; the Assynt Visitor Centre, Hydroponicum at Achiltubuie and Kerracher Gardens, Highland Stoneware, Inverpolly Nature Reserve and Ardvreck Castle.

2   **Culloden Battlefield** is the site of the last major battle fought on mainland Britain in 1746. Bonnie Prince Charlie's Jacobite troops were defeated here by the Duke of Cumberland and the Hanoverian government forces. The new visitor centre – opened in 2007 – features a battle immersion cinema and handheld multi-lingual audio devices to bring the battle to life.

3   No visit to this part of Scotland would be complete without taking time to visit **John o'Groats** and the famous signpost pointing towards Lands End – a mere 874 miles away! From here there are also regular summer sailings to Orkney so you can hop on one of the John o'Groats day tours which incorporate the ferry and a coach tour of the main island.

4   Perhaps the most spectacularly scenic of all Scottish lochs, **Loch Maree** greets unsuspecting visitors travelling north-west on the A832 between Inverness and Gairloch. Bounded by the imposing masses of Beinn Eighe to the west and Slioch to the east, the loch's shores play host to a wealth of wildlife, as well as fragments of ancient Caledonian pinewood.

5   One of the largest castles in Scotland, the ruins of **Urquhart Castle** lie on the banks of Loch Ness, near Drumnadrochit. Blown up in 1692 to prevent Jacobite occupation, this 5-star visitor attraction has a fascinating interactive visitor centre which depicts the story of the castle's turbulent history. Explore the ruins of the castle, before visiting the on-site café where you will be rewarded with breathtaking views of Loch Ness.

6   At **Golspie Highland Wildcat Trails** an adrenaline filled mix of testing uphills and challenging fast downhill sections make for an exhilarating day's mountain biking on Ben Bhraggie. After you've reached the top, views west across Sutherland and south across the Dornoch Firth make the uphill all worth it.

FOOD AND DRINK

eatscotland.com

7   Only the freshest of fish straight from the daily catch make it to the table in the **Captain's Galley**. Set in a tastefully renovated old ice house in Scrabster, near Thurso, the award winning restaurant serves up to 10 different species of fish every night. Booking is recommended.

8   **Highland Feast**, an annual food and drink festival held in September, is a celebration of the fantastic produce and culinary skills present in the local area and beyond.

9   Fresh, local ingredients are combined to make the **Falls of Shin Visitor Centre** the ultimate place to stop for lunch. See salmon leap on the magnificent waterfall as you tuck in. There is also a children's playground so you can fill up while the kids are kept entertained.

10   As with many restaurants across the Highlands, **Sutor Creek** prides itself on the use of fresh, local produce, but few produce 'real pizza' like this place. Cooked in their specially built wood-fired oven this friendly bistro in Cromarty also slow-roasts the perfect Sunday meal with local meats infused with home grown herbs and garlic.

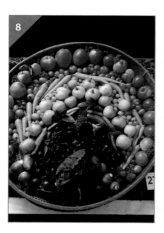

GOLF

visitscotland.com/golf

11   **Gairloch Golf Course** is superbly situated above a sandy bay beside the road into Gairloch. This 9-hole links course is one of the Highland's best kept secrets. Take your time soaking up the views towards Skye. Arrange tee times in advance to guarantee a round.

12   **Durness Golf Course**, surrounded by stunning coastal scenery, is notorious for its 9th hole, which requires players to clear the Atlantic Ocean! Check with the secretary in advance to ensure a round is possible.

13   Considered one of the finest links courses in the world, **Royal Dornoch Golf Course** is situated on public land in its namesake royal burgh, 45 miles north of Inverness. Play on the course about which Tom Watson famously remarked 'the most fun I've ever had on a golf course'.

14   A traditional Scottish links course, **Nairn West Golf Club** offers a challenge for all abilities. 20 minutes drive from Inverness, this 18-hole favourite is perfect for the discerning golfer looking to experience a course steeped in tradition.

OUTSTANDING VIEWS

15   A classic view of **Loch Ness** is to be savoured from the beach at the village of Dores (B862 from Inverness), at the quieter side of the loch to the south. Look out for Nessie, or at the very least, the resident Nessie spotter!

16   Round the bay from **Lochinver**, a minor road allows fantastic views back towards the community and the incredible sugar loaf of Suilven rising up in the background.

17   Near John o'Groats see a dramatic coastline where thousands of seabirds nest in vast colonies. A walk across the clifftop fields will reward you with a stunning view south to Thirle Door and the **Stacks of Duncansby**. The first is a rocky arch, the second a group of large jagged sea stacks. This is a spot you will want to savour, with a view that varies as you move along the clifftop path and bring into play different alignments of the stacks and arch.

18   The **Corrieshalloch Gorge** National Nature Reserve, south-east of Ullapool, comprises a box canyon dropping 200ft to the river below. Adding to the drama are the spectacular **Falls of Measach**, best seen from the viewing platform further down the footpath.

WALKS   **visitscotland.com/walking**

19   **Reelig Glen** is a short walk through spectacular old conifer and broad-leaved trees on easy paths with short gentle gradients, making it a suitable walk for almost anyone. Approximately 10 minutes from Inverness, take the A862 west towards Beauly and after 8 miles, turn left onto the minor road signposted to Reelig and Moniack and continue for 1 mile – follow the Forestry Commission of Scotland sign and look out for Britain's tallest tree named Dughall Mor.

20   Although within the city of Inverness, the **Ness Islands** walk could be a million miles from it. The islands, linked by several old bridges, offer a quiet, scenic walk through tall, native and imported trees. It offers plenty of photo opportunities and an enjoyable family walk which accommodates wheelchairs.

21   Take the minor B869 road to Stoer lighthouse, from which a 3-hour circular walk leads to a spectacular rock-stack – the **Old Man of Stoer** - surrounded by jaw-dropping cliff scenery. The path is clear throughout, and offers views to the Assynt mountains in the south, and to the islands of Lewis and Harris many miles to the west.

22   The **Caithness and Sutherland Walking Festival**, held in May, consists of themed walks led by local guides. These interesting walks explore archaeology, history and wildlife and are a great way to learn more about the surrounding area.

Brackla, (Loch Ness), Inverness-shire
Loch Ness Clansman Hotel
Map Ref: 4A9

Open: All year

Brackla, Loch Ness-side, Inverness IV3 8LA
T: 01456 450326
E: info@lochnessview.com
W: lochnessview.com

The ONLY hotel situated on the banks of Loch Ness. Fully re-furbished, facilities include beautiful bedrooms overlooking the loch, WiFi access and flat screen TVs. The Observation Lounge Bar and Cobbs Restaurant have panoramic views. Enjoy contemporary Scottish cuisine with a Mediterranean twist. Ideal touring base. 9 miles from Inverness, 4 miles from Drumnadrochit.

Total number of rooms: 26

Prices from:

Single:	£59.00	Double:	£39.50
Twin:	£39.50	Family room:	£33.00

Dornoch, Sutherland
Dornoch Castle Hotel
Map Ref: 4B6

Open: All year excl Christmas and Boxing Day

Castle Street, Dornoch, Sutherland IV25 3SD
T: 01862 810216
E: enquiries@dornochcastlehotel.com
W: dornochcastlehotel.com

Dornoch Castle is set in the beautiful, historical town of Dornoch and situated directly opposite the inspiring 12th century Dornoch Cathedral, a dramatic backdrop for an overnight stay in the quaint market square of Dornoch. This impressive Castle offers a cosy and personable stay, renowned for the best in Scottish hospitality.

Total number of rooms: 24

Prices per room from:

Single:	£54.00	Double:	£85.00
Twin:	£85.00	Family room:	£100.00

Durness, Sutherland
Wild Orchid Guest House
Map Ref: 4A3

Open: All year
Durine, Durness, Sutherland IV27 4PN
T: 01971 511280
E: wildorchidguesthouse@hotmail.co.uk
W: wildorchidguesthouse.co.uk

Total number of rooms: 8

Prices per room from:

Single:	£35.00	Double:	£56.00
Twin:	£56.00	Family room:	£75.00

Garve, Ross-shire
Inchbae Lodge Guest House
Map Ref: 4A8

Open: All year excl November
Garve, Ross-shire IV23 2PH
T: 01997 455269
E: contact@inchbae.co.uk
W: inchbae.co.uk

Total number of rooms: 7

Prices per room from:

Single:	£35.00	Double:	£59.95
Twin:	£59.95	Family room:	£59.95

Invergordon, Ross-shire
Kincraig House Hotel
Map Ref: 4B7

★★★
COUNTRY
HOUSE
HOTEL

Open: All year

Invergordon, Ross-shire IV18 0LF
T: 01349 852587
E: info@kincraig-house-hotel.co.uk
W: kincraig-house-hotel.co.uk

Kincraig House Hotel offers 15 ensuite rooms, a
number of which are newly created Premier and
Executive rooms. A refurbished à la carte Restaurant
and bar and a spacious oak panelled lounge offer
superb character and comfort.

Total number of rooms: 15	
Prices per room from:	
Single: **£70.00**	Double: **£100.00**
Twin: **£100.00**	Family room: **£125.00**

Inverness
Express by Holiday Inn
Map Ref: 4B8

★★★
METRO
HOTEL

Open: All year

Stoneyfield Business Park, Inverness IV2 7PA
T: 01463 732700
E: resinverness@expressholidayinn.co.uk
W: hiexpress.co.uk

Total number of rooms: 94	
Prices per room from:	
Double: **£50.00**	Twin: **£50.00**
Family room: **£50.00**	

Inverness
Glenmoriston Town House Hotel
Map Ref: 4B8

★★★
HOTEL

Open: All year

20 Ness Bank, Inverness IV2 4SF
T: 01463 223777
E: claire@glenmoristontownhouse.com
W: glenmoristontownhouse.com

Close to Inverness City Centre with charming views
of the River Ness. The Glenmoriston Town House
boasts two award winning restaurants; Abstract and
Contrast, luxurious bedrooms all recently renovated.
Free Wi-Fi access in all the hotel. Piano Bar with live
music every Friday and Saturday.

Total number of rooms: 30	
Prices per room from:	
Single: **£95.00**	Double: **£130.00**
Twin: **£130.00**	

For a full listing of quality assured serviced accommodation throughout Scotland see pages 195-278.

157

Inverness
Lochardil House Hotel
Map Ref: 4B8

★★★★
HOTEL

Open: All year excl Xmas and New Year
Stratherrick Road, Inverness IV2 4LF
T: 01463 235995
E: reservations@lochardil.co.uk
W: bw-lochardilhouse.co.uk

35994

Total number of rooms: 28

Prices from:

Single: **£60.00**	Double:	**£44.00**
Twin: **£44.00**	Family room:	**£84.00pr**

Inverness
MacDougall Clansman Hotel
Map Ref: 4B8

★★
METRO
HOTEL

Open: All year excl Xmas and New Year

103 Church Street, Inverness IV1 1ES
T: 01463 713702
E: info@invernesscentrehotel.co.uk
W: invernesscentrehotel.co.uk

Family-run hotel in convenient central location,
close to rail and bus stations, Tourist Information
Centre, shops and restaurants. On-street parking
and limited private parking available. Some French,
German and Spanish spoken. Please contact us to
check availability and rates. Further hotel details and
photos can be viewed on our website.

36871

Total number of rooms: 14

Prices from:

Single: **£38.00**		Double: **£29.00**
Twin: **£29.00**		

Inverness
Whinpark Guest House
Map Ref: 4B8

★★★
GUEST
HOUSE

Open: All year
17 Ardross Street, Inverness IV3 5NS
T: 01463 232549
E: info@whinparkhotel.com
W: whinparkhotel.com

63970

Total number of rooms: 13

Prices from:

Single: **£35.00**	Double:	**£25.00**
Twin: **£25.00**	Family room:	**£60.00pr**

Inverness
Winston Guest House
Map Ref: 4B8

★★★
GUEST
HOUSE

Open: All year
10 Ardross Terrace, Inverness IV3 5NQ
T: 01463 234477
E: info@winstonguesthouse.co.uk
W: winstonguesthouse.co.uk

64396

Total number of rooms: 16

Prices from:

Single: **£35.00**	Double:	**£28.00**
Twin: **£28.00**	Family room:	**£60.00pr**

Nr Inverness
North Kessock Hotel
Map Ref: 4B8

★★★
SMALL
HOTEL

Open: All year

Main Street, North Kessock, Inverness IV1 3XN
T: 01463 731208
E: northkessockhotel@btconnect.com
W: northkessockhotel.com

47694

Total number of rooms: 8

Prices per room from:

Single: **£65.00**	Double:	**£90.00-100.00**
Twin: **£90.00-100.00**	Family room:	**£105.00-150.00**

IMPORTANT: Prices stated are estimates and may be subject to change. Prices are per person per night unless otherwise stated. Awards correct as of beginning of October 2008.

John o' Groats, Caithness
Seaview Hotel

Map Ref: 4E2

54083

Open: All year
Main Street, John o' Groats, Caithness KW1 4YR
T: 01955 611220
E: seaviewhotel@btinternet.com
W: seaviewjohnogroats.co.uk

Total number of rooms: 10	
Prices per room from:	
Single: **£40.00**	Double: **£55.00**
Twin: **£55.00**	Family room: **£80.00**

Loch Shin, by Lairg
Overscaig House Hotel

Map Ref: 4A5

48851

Open: April-October
Loch Shin, Sutherland IV27 4NY
T: 01549 431203
E: visits@overscaig.com
W: overscaig.com

Spend time amidst the peace and tranquility of this wonderful location overlooking Loch Shin. Enjoy locally sourced cuisine in our loch view dining room, relax in our comfortable lounge or simply have a drink in the bar. Ideal base for birdwatching, walking, fishing, cycling or simply touring the North West Highlands.

Total number of rooms: 8	
Prices from:	
Single: **£46.00**	Double: **£46.00**
Twin: **£46.00**	Family room: **£34.00**

Lochinver, Sutherland
Inver Lodge Hotel

Map Ref: 3G5

66454

Open: Easter-October
Iolaire Road, Lochinver, Sutherland IV27 4LU
T: 01571 844496
E: stay@inverlodge.com
W: inverlodge.com

Our foreground is Lochinver Bay and the Western Sea, the back drop is the Great Peaks of Sutherland Canisp and Suillen. All bedrooms are ensuite and sea facing with wireless internet and many other facilities to make your stay comfortable and memorable.
Our restaurant offers high standards in cuisine and service which is complemented with a fine selection of wines. Come and enjoy our friendly award winning Highland hospitality.

Total number of rooms: 20	
Prices per room from:	
Single: **£135.00**	Double: **£200.00**
Twin: **£200.00**	

For a full listing of quality assured serviced accommodation throughout Scotland see pages 195-278.

159

Northern Highlands, Inverness, Loch Ness, Nairn

Lochinver, Sutherland
Polcraig
Map Ref: 3G5

★★★★
GUEST HOUSE

Open: All year
Cruamer, Lochinver, Sutherland IV27 4LD
T: 01571 844429
E: cathelmac@aol.com
W: smoothhound.co.uk/hotels/polcraig.html

50075

Total number of rooms: 6

Prices from:
Single:	£40.00	Double:	£30.00
Twin:	£30.00		

Melvich, Sutherland
Bighouse Lodge
Map Ref: 4C3

★★★★
COUNTRY HOUSE HOTEL

Open: April-December

by Melvich, Sutherland KW14 7YJ
T: 01641 531207
E: info@bighouseestate.com
W: bighouseestate.com

Stunningly located at the mouth of the Halladale River, and surrounded by water on three sides. A charming, warm and welcoming Scottish country house which is very well appointed.

15127

Total number of rooms: 11

Prices per room from:
Single:	£93.00	Double:	£140.00
Twin:	£140.00		

Muir of Ord, near Inverness
Ord House Hotel
Map Ref: 4A8

★★
COUNTRY HOUSE HOTEL

Open: April-October
Ord, Muir of Ord, Ross-shire IV6 7UH
T: 01463 870492
E: admin@ord-house.co.uk
W: ord-house.co.uk

48572

Total number of rooms: 10

Prices per room from:
Single:	£60.00	Double:	£110.00
Twin:	£110.00	Family room:	£150.00

Nairn
Invernairne Guest House
Map Ref: 4C8

★★★
GUEST HOUSE

Open: March-November, open over New Year
Thurlow Road, Nairn IV12 4EZ
T: 01667 452039
E: info@invernairne.com
W: invernairne.com

32033

Total number of rooms: 11

Prices from:
Single:	£39.50	Double:	£37.50
Twin:	£37.50	Family room:	£37.50

IMPORTANT: Prices stated are estimates and may be subject to change. Prices are per person per night unless otherwise stated. Awards correct as of beginning of October 2008.

Scourie, Sutherland
Eddrachilles Hotel
Map Ref: 3H4

Open: mid March-mid October

Badcall Bay, Scourie, Sutherland IV27 4TH
T: 01971 502080
E: info@eddrachilles.com
W: eddrachilles.com

Magnificently situated overlooking the islands of Eddrachilles Bay, this 200 year old building has been carefully refurbished, providing modern comfortable bedrooms but retaining the charm and character of older times. Fully licensed with an extensive wine list, cooking concentrates on traditional style benefiting from high quality local produce.

Total number of rooms: 11

Prices from:
Single:	**£65.00**	Double:	**£45.00**
Twin:	**£45.00**	Family room:	**£45.00**

Scourie, Sutherland
Scourie Hotel
Map Ref: 3H4

Open: April-mid October

Scourie, Sutherland IV27 4SX
T: 01971 502396   F: 01971 502423
E: patrick@scourie-hotel.co.uk
W: scourie-hotel.co.uk

Total number of rooms: 20

Prices from:
Single:	**£40.00**	Double:	**£37.00**
Twin:	**£37.00**	Family room:	**£37.00**

Strathpeffer, Ross-shire
The Garden House Guest House
Map Ref: 4A8

Open: March-November

Garden House Brae, Strathpeffer, Ross-shire IV14 9BJ
T: 01997 421242
E: garden.house.jd@btinternet.com
W: gardenhouseguesthouse.co.uk

Total number of rooms: 5

Prices from:
Single:	**£45.00**	Double:	**£30.00**
Twin:	**£30.00**		

Struy, by Beauly
The Cnoc Hotel
Map Ref: 4A9

Open: All year

Struy, by Beauly IV4 7JU
T: 01463 761264
E: cnochotel@talk21.com
W: thecnochotel.co.uk

Total number of rooms: 7

Prices from:
Single:	**£55.00**	Double:	**£45.00**
Twin:	**£45.00**	Family room:	POA

Thurso, Caithness
The Park Hotel
Map Ref: 4D3

Open: All year excl January 1, 2 and 3

Oldfield, Thurso, Caithness KW14 8RE
T: 01847 893251
E: reception@parkhotelthurso.co.uk
W: parkhotelthurso.co.uk

Total number of rooms: 21

Prices from:
Single:	**£50.00**	Double:	**£42.50**
Twin:	**£42.50**	Family room:	**£42.50**

For a full listing of quality assured serviced accommodation throughout Scotland see pages 195-278.

161

Thurso, Caithness
St Clair Hotel
Map Ref: 4D3

★★★
HOTEL

55791

Open: March-October
Sinclair Street, Thurso, Caithness KW14 7AJ
T: 01847 896481
E: stclair@northhotels.co.uk
W: northhotels.co.uk

Total number of rooms: 30

Prices per room from:
Single: **£50.00**   Double: **£70.00**
Twin: **£70.00**

Ullapool, Ross-shire
Ardvreck House
Map Ref: 3G6

★★★★
GUEST
HOUSE

12714

Open: March-November
North Road, Morefield, Ullapool, Ross-shire IV26 2TH
T: 01854 612028
E: ardvreck@btconnect.com
W: smoothhound.co.uk/hotels/ardvreck

Ardvreck House offers quality accommodation in a spectacular setting overlooking Ullapool and Loch Broom. Our rooms have ensuite shower rooms and over half have superb loch views. We provide bed and breakfast and can recommend places to eat in the village. Quiet, country location. Free wireless internet.

Total number of rooms: 10

Prices from:
Single: **£35.00**   Double: **£35.00**
Twin: **£35.00**   Family room: **£85.00pr**

Ullapool, Ross-shire
The Argyll Hotel
Map Ref: 3G6

★★
SMALL
HOTEL

83830

Open: All year
18 Argyll Street, Ullapool, IV26 2UB
T: 01854 612422
E: stay@theargyllullapool.com
W: theargyllullapool.com

Total number of rooms: 5

Prices from:
Single: **£40.00**   Double: **£30.00**
Twin: **£30.00**   Family room: **£30.00**

Ullapool, Ross-shire
Dromnan Guest House
Map Ref: 3G6

★★★★
GUEST
HOUSE

23205

Open: March-October
Garve Road, Ullapool, Ross-shire IV26 2SX
T: 01854 612333
E: info@dromnan.com
W: dromnan.co.uk

Total number of rooms: 7

Prices from:
Single: **£35.00**   Double: **£32.00**
Twin: **£33.00**   Family room: **£32.00**

Ullapool, Ross-shire
The Ferry Boat Inn
Map Ref: 3G6

AWAITING
GRADING

83431

Open: All year
Shore Street, Ullapool, Ross-shire IV26 2UJ
T: 01854 612366
E: mail@ferryboat-inn.co.uk
W: ferryboat-inn.co.uk

Total number of rooms: 9

Prices per room from:
Single: **£35.00**   Double: **£70.00**
Twin: **£70.00**   Family room: **£100.00**

IMPORTANT: Prices stated are estimates and may be subject to change. Prices are per person per night unless otherwise stated. Awards correct as of beginning of October 2008.

Elgol, Loch Scavaig, Isle of Skye

Fort William, Lochaber, Skye and Lochalsh

Fort William is known as the 'Outdoor Capital of the UK' – and little wonder. The area annually hosts the Mountain Bike World Cup and is next door to Scotland's highest mountain, Ben Nevis. The surrounding area provides a huge range of opportunities to enjoy the great outdoors.

The local scenery is quite stunning and there are hundreds of amazing places to visit. From the dramatic beauty of Glen Coe to the breathtaking views across Loch Duich, not forgetting the wild isolation of Knoydart and Ardnamurchan Point.

Take in some of the finest coastal and hill scenery on what is considered one of the great railway journeys of the world. Travel the length of the legendary Road to the Isles on the Jacobite Steam Train from Fort William to Mallaig. Take in the iconic Neptune's Staircase, Glenfinnan Viaduct and glorious coastline of Arisaig and Morar, and when you reach Mallaig you'll be able to see the jagged peaks of the Cuillin mountains on the Isle of Skye.

The turbulent history and majestic scenery of Skye and Lochalsh make the area one of Scotland's most romantic destinations. From the delightfully situated Eilean Donan Castle and the picture-postcard village of Plockton to the soaring craggy heights of the Cuillin and the eerie pinnacles of Trotternish, the area is sure to leave an imprint on your heart.

DON'T MISS

1   One of the most picturesque – and most photographed – castles in Scotland, **Eilean Donan Castle**, sits on Loch Duich, beside the tiny village of Dornie. Stroll across the causeway that links it to the shore and explore it for yourself. For a panoramic view, follow the path from the village which leads up to the Carr Brae viewpoint.

2   Take a boat trip from Elgol (B8083 from Broadford) to isolated and inspiring **Loch Coruisk**. You will get up close to Britain's most dramatic landscapes, while your local guide will make sure you don't miss out on seeing the abundant wildlife – including the famous seal colony on the banks of the loch.

3   Accessible only by boat from Mallaig or via a very long walk from Kinlochhourn, **Knoydart** is recognised as the remotest part of mainland Britain and is perfect for adventurous families. One of the best hiking spots in the country, there are also options for wildlife watching, canoeing and fishing. The scenery is outstanding and will leave a lasting impression.

4   **Camusdarach, Traigh** and the **Silver Sands of Morar** are just a selection of exquisite beaches along the shoreline between Arisaig and Mallaig. While away a few hours picnicking with the breathtaking backdrop of the Small Isles of Eigg and Rum rising sheer out of the sea in front of you and admire the changing light on the sea catching the numerous skerries that pepper the coast.

5   To travel the whole length of the Road to the Isles, hop aboard the **Jacobite Steam Train**. This steam engine runs between Fort William and Mallaig throughout the summer months and takes in some truly impressive sites such as Neptune's Staircase, the Glenfinnan Viaduct and the glorious coastline of Arisaig and Morar. Regarded as one of the Great Railway Journeys of the World, this is a must while in the area, especially for Harry Potter fans who will recognise it from the films.

6   The biggest indoor ice climbing facility in the world, **The Ice Factor**, is situated in a former aluminium works in Kinlochleven. With rock climbing walls, a gym, sauna, and plunge pool, this is a great day out for the activity enthusiast or indeed, the whole family. As the National Centre for Indoor Ice Climbing, experts can try out new techniques whilst novices can get to grips with the basics in a safe and secure environment.

To find out more, call 0845 22 55 121 or go to visitscotland.com

FOOD AND DRINK

eatscotland.com

7   The **Three Chimneys** restaurant on Skye is known far and wide as one of the most romantic eateries in the land. The candlelit crofter's cottage on the shores of Loch Dunvegan, voted 28th in Restaurant Magazine's 'definitive list' of the World's Top 50 Restaurants, is an idyllic setting for a proposal, a honeymoon or any special occasion. Book ahead to ensure your table.

8   Among the host of west coast seafood restaurants, the EatScotland approved **Holly Tree** in Kentallen stands out. The catch comes into their own pier on the shore of Loch Linnhe and is served up with magnificent views across to the Morven hills.

9   **Crannog** at the Waterfront in Fort William serves the very best in seafood. Be sure to give their speciality a try – the langoustine fresh from Loch Linnhe!

10   For an AA rosette dinner, seek out **Russell's Restaurant**, Smiddy House in Spean Bridge. Innovation and flair are deftly applied to a fine range of local produce.

WALKS

visitscotland.com/walking

11   **Glen Finnan** - From the Glenfinnan Visitor Centre car park, follow the Mallaig road across a bridge and then look out for a sign pointing towards Glenfinnan Lodge. From here continue up the glen where kids will be impressed by the famous viaduct, featured in the Harry Potter films. An easy 5½ mile route, taking in most of this scenic glen, can be completed in roughly 2 hours.

12   **Morar to Loch Morar and Mallaig** - A relatively easy walk you can enjoy without the hassle of taking the car. The starting and finishing points are both adjacent to train stations, so check out scotrail.co.uk to ensure you're onboard! Set off from Morar station and walk south, taking a left turn onto the minor road along Loch Morar's north shore. Kids should keep a look out for Nessie's cousin 'Morag' who supposedly occupies this loch. Continue along, as the road becomes a path, before arriving in Tarbet. Here, a boat departs daily at 3.30 pm throughout the summer to take you back via Loch Nevis to the connecting train at Mallaig. Allow 6 hours for the walk.

13   **Glen Coe** is one of the most popular hiking destinations in Scotland with the likes of Allt Coire for more experienced hikers and, for the less experienced walker, places like the Lost Valley to seek out. From the car parks on the A82, the path takes you across the bridge over the River Coe towards the triple buttresses known as the Three Sisters. Turn right after the bridge and follow the trail upwards. After a couple of miles you'll reach the false summit marking the edge of the hidden basin where the MacDonald clan used to hide their cattle in times of attack.

14   For a longer more challenging walk, drive 6 miles north from Portree on the Isle of Skye (A855), where you will find a car park. A path leads through woodland onto a steep climb to an area of geological formations. There are then a number of paths that can be followed to the base of the **Old Man of Storr**. Along the way you can enjoy good views across the Sound of Raasay. This walk should take in excess of 3 hours.

OUTSTANDING VIEWS

15   As you drive south on the A828, **Castle Stalker** appears before you against a beautiful backdrop. Stop at the View Café and Gift Shop for stunning vistas across Loch Linnhe to the Morvern Hills. Such a panorama has inspired many artists and here you can really appreciate their motivation.

16   From Rannoch Moor on the A82, the twin peaks of **Buachaille Etive Mor** and Buachaille Etive Beag spectacularly mark the entrance to Glen Coe. Appearing like steep-sided pyramids they stand sentinel on the moor, offering a glimpse of the wild landscape just around the corner.

17   There are many classic views of the **Cuillin Ridge**. However, for sheer drama, few views in all of Scotland compare with the sight of Sgurr Nan Gillean rearing up behind Sligachan bridge, or the full mountain range rising almost sheer from Loch Scavaig, opposite the tiny village of Elgol, west of Broadford on Skye.

18   To see the **Five Sisters of Kintail** from Ratagan Pass, take the Glenelg road from Shiel Bridge on the A87. As you rise up towards Mam Ratagan, about a mile along, take a look back over Loch Duich, framed by the majestic peaks of Kintail. Simply stunning.

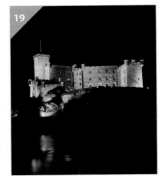

HERITAGE

19   **Dunvegan Castle** (follow the A850 from Portree), the stronghold of the MacLeod chiefs for nearly 800 years, remains their home today. Highland Cattle roam around the estate, making you feel that you've well and truly reached the Scottish Highlands!

20   Skye's only distillery, **Talisker Distillery**, is set on the shores of Loch Harport with dramatic views of the Cuillin hills. Enjoy a tipple of this alluring, sweet, full-bodied single malt on the distillery tour.

21   For a full interpretation of this amazing setting, head to the **Glencoe Visitor Centre** on the A82, 17 miles south of Fort William. Particularly eco-friendly, this centre provides a great viewing platform, as well as an interactive exhibit for kids of all ages where you can find out how it feels to climb on ice!

22   The **West Highland Museum** is to be found in Fort William and houses an historic collection that dates from Mesolithic times to the modern day. All elements of society are included, from crofters to soldiers and princes to clergy.

allachulish, Glencoe
raiglinnhe House — Map Ref: 1F1

Open: All year excl Xmas

Lettermore, Ballachulish, Argyll PH49 4JD

T: 01855 811270
E: info@craiglinnhe.co.uk
W: craiglinnhe.co.uk

Your hosts David and Beverly Hughes welcome you to Craiglinnhe House, a loch-side Victorian villa set in spectacular scenery with superb loch and mountain views. Craiglinnhe offers period charm with modern comforts, a warm friendly atmosphere, excellent food and a varied wine selection. Ideal base for exploring the Western Highlands.

Total number of rooms: 5

Prices from:
Double: £25.00-40.00   Twin: £25.00-40.00

allachulish, Glencoe
yn-Leven Guest House — Map Ref: 1F1

Open: All year excl Xmas

West Laroch, Ballachulish, Argyll PH49 4JP

T: 01855 811392
W: lynleven.co.uk

Family-run award winning guest house with the freedom and comfort of a hotel at guest house prices, situated on the shores of Loch Leven – Glencoe one mile. Magnificent scenery with spectacular views of Glencoe and Mamore Hills. All bedrooms ensuite. Colour TV, tea-making facilities. Ideal for all types of countryside activities. Restricted licence. Private parking. Satellite television. AA Selected 4 Diamonds.

Total number of rooms: 8

Prices from:
Single: £30.00-45.00   Double: £25.00-32.00
Twin: £25.00-32.00   Family room: £38.00

ornie, Ross-shire
ilean A Cheo Guest House — Map Ref: 3G9

Open: All year

Dornie, Ardelve, Kyle, Ross-shire IV40 8DY

T: 01599 555485
E: stay@scothighland.com
W: scothighland.com

Total number of rooms: 5

Prices per room from:
Single: POA   Double: POA
Twin: POA   Family room: POA

For a full listing of quality assured serviced accommodation throughout Scotland see pages 195-278.

167

Fort William, Inverness-shire
Alexandra Hotel
Map Ref: 3H12

Open: All year

The Parade, Fort William, Inverness-shire PH33 6XZ
T: 01397 702241
E: salesalexandra@strathmorehotels.com
W: strathmorehotels.com

This Victorian hotel offers a warm welcome and traditional Scottish hospitality in the heart of Fort William. Excellent service and dining goes hand in hand with a friendly atmosphere, the ideal base for your west coast break. Enjoy FREE leisure club membership at the Ben Nevis Hotel during your stay.

Total number of rooms: 94

Prices from:
Single: **£35.00**   Double: **£35.00**
Twin: **£35.00**

Fort William, Inverness-shire
Ben Nevis Hotel & Leisure Club
Map Ref: 3H12

Open: All year

North Road, Fort William, Inverness-shire PH33 6TG
T: 01397 702331
E: salesbennevis@strathmorehotels.com
W: strathmorehotels.com

Situated at the foot of Ben Nevis, the hotel is an ideal base for your Fort William holiday. Guests enjoy FREE leisure club membership for the duration of their stay. Recent refurbishments include 63 bedrooms, entire new set of gym equipment and FREE wi-fi access throughout the hotel.

Total number of rooms: 119

Prices from:
Single: **£35.00**   Double: **£35.00**
Twin: **£35.00**

The sledging area at Nevis Range Ski Centre, Fort William

ort William, Inverness-shire
lan MacDuff Hotel
Map Ref: 3H12

Open: April-October

19453

Achintore Road, Fort William,
Inverness-shire PH33 6RW
T: 01397 702341
E: reception@clanmacduff.co.uk
W: clanmacduff.co.uk

Overlooking Loch Linnhe with outstanding views of magnificent Highland scenery. Well-appointed ensuite bedrooms with colour TV, hospitality tray, telephone, hairdryer, etc. Our traditional dinner menu serves fresh produce from local beef, venison and fish suppliers. This along with freshly baked bread and desserts prepared daily form the basis of our menu. In our relaxing lounge bar delicious bar suppers are served complemented by a large selection of malt whiskies. Large car park, passenger lift, conservatory and sun patio. This family managed hotel enjoys a reputation for its friendly, helpful staff and prides itself on providing good quality and value hospitality.

Total number of rooms: 36		
Prices from:		
Single: **£40.00**	Double:	**£27.50**
Twin: **£27.50**	Family room:	**£27.50**

ort William, Inverness-shire
ochan Cottage Guest House
Map Ref: 3H12

Open: Febuary-November

35986

Lochyside, Fort William, Inverness-shire PH33 7NX
T: 01397 702695
E: lochanco@btopenworld.com
W: fortwilliam-guesthouse.co.uk

Total number of rooms: 6	
Prices from:	
Double: **£29.00**	Twin: **£29.00**

r Fort William, Inverness-shire
odge on the Loch Hotel
Map Ref: 3G12

Open: All year

59550

Onich, Near Fort William, Inverness-shire PH33 6RY
T: 01855 821238
E: info@lodgeontheloch.com
W: lodgeontheloch.com

Ideally located to explore the outdoor capital of the UK. Stunning views across Loch Linnhe. Individually designed rooms with Loch views. Lochview restaurant with great food and friendly service. Relaxing lounges for celebration drinks. Excellent place to celebrate, unwind and recharge.

Total number of rooms: 15		
Prices from:		
Single: **£86.00**	Double:	**£43.00**
Twin: **£43.00**		

For a full listing of quality assured serviced accommodation throughout Scotland see pages 195-278.

169

Glencoe, Argyll
Clachaig Inn – Glencoe   Map Ref: 1F1

★★
INN

19383

Open: All year excl Xmas Day

Glencoe, Argyll PH49 4HX
T: 01855 811252
E: inn@clachaig.com
W: clachaig.com

Situated in one of the best hill walking areas in the Highlands of Scotland, an excellent base for outdoor activities and exploring the magnificent Glens and Lochs. The Inn provides comfortable ensuite accommodation, has three lively bars where good food, cask ales and fine whiskies are served throughout the day.

Total number of rooms: 23

Prices from:
Single:	£39.00	Double:	£39.00
Twin:	£39.00	Family room:	£41.00

Glencoe, Argyll
Scorrybreac Guest House   Map Ref: 1F1

★★★★
GUEST
HOUSE

53242

Open: All year excl Xmas Day

Hospital Drive, Glencoe, Argyll PH49 4HT
T: 01855 811354
E: scorrybreac@btinternet.com
W: scorrybreac.co.uk

Set on the edge of Glencoe Village in an elevated tranquil spot. Scorrybreac has been modernised and upgraded over the years and offers six well appointed bedrooms with ensuite facilities. A spectacular view is offered from our spacious dining room and cosy lounge across Loch Leven and the mountains beyond.

Total number of rooms: 6

Prices from:
Single:	£38.00	Double:	£25.00
Twin:	£25.00		

Glencoe, Argyll
Strathassynt Guest House   Map Ref: 1F1

★★★
GUEST
HOUSE

56833

Open: All year
Loan Fern, nr Glencoe, Ballachulish, Argyll PH49 4JB
T: 01855 811261
E: info@strathassynt.com
W: strathassynt.com

Total number of rooms: 6

Prices from:
Single:	£25.00	Double:	£20.00
Twin:	£20.00	Family room:	£20.00

Glenfinnan, Near Fort William
The Prince's House Hotel   Map Ref: 3G12

★★★
SMALL
HOTEL

SILVER

50489

Open: March-December excl Xmas and 2 weeks in October
Glenfinnan, Fort William, Inverness-shire PH37 4LT
T: 01397 722246
E: princeshouse@glenfinnan.co.uk
W: glenfinnan.co.uk

Total number of rooms: 9

Prices from:
Single:	£59.00	Double:	£50.00
Twin:	£50.00		

IMPORTANT: Prices stated are estimates and may be subject to change. Prices are per person per night unless otherwise stated. Awards correct as of beginning of October 2008.

Invergarry, Inverness-shire
Glengarry Castle Hotel
Map Ref: 3H11

28180

★★★
COUNTRY
HOUSE
HOTEL

Open: 20th March-9th November

Invergarry, Inverness-shire PH35 4HW
T: 01809 501254
E: castle@glengarry.net
W: glengarry.net

Magnificently set in 60 acres of wooded grounds, this country house hotel has been privately owned and privately managed by the MacCallum family for over 40 years. Situated in the heart of the Great Glen overlooking Loch Oich this is a perfect centre for a touring holiday. To the north is Eilean Donan Castle and the Isle of Skye. Urquhart Castle, Loch Ness and Inverness can be toured to the east. Fort William, Ben Nevis and the Road to the Isles make a good trip to the west coast. We have great river, lochside and Great Glen Way walks nearby.

Total number of rooms: 26	
Prices from:	
Single: **£72.00**	Double: **£54.00**
Twin: **£54.00**	Family room: **£67.00**

Kinlochleven, Inverness-shire
Tailrace Inn
Map Ref: 3H12

66920

★★★
INN

Open: All year

Riverside Road, Kinlochleven PA40 4QH
T: 01855 831777
E: tailrace@btconnect.com
W: tailraceinn.co.uk

Total number of rooms: 6	
Prices from:	
Single: **£45.00**	Double: **£35.00**
Twin: **£35.00**	Family room: **£35.00**

Knoydart, Inverness-shire
Doune-Knoydart
Map Ref: 3F11

23031

★★★
RESTAURANT
WITH ROOMS

Open: April-September

Doune, Knoydart, Mallaig, Inverness-shire PH41 4PU
T: 01687 462667   F: 08700 940428
E: martin@doune-knoydart.co.uk
W: doune-knoydart.co.uk

SILVER

Remote and unique holiday setting on the western tip of Knoydart. Spectacular low and high level walking. Delicious home cooking, a warm welcome and total relaxation. Mountains, sea, boat trips and wildlife. Discounts for children.

Total number of rooms: 4	
Prices, full board, from:	
Single: **£72.00**	Double: **£72.00**
Twin: **£72.00**	Family room: **£72.00**

For a full listing of quality assured serviced accommodation throughout Scotland see pages 195-278.

171

Mallaig, Inverness-shire
West Highland Hotel
Map Ref: 3F11

★★★
HOTEL

63661

Open: April- October
Mallaig, Inverness-shire PH41 4QZ
T: 01687 462210
E: westhighland.hotel@virgin.net
W: westhighlandhotel.co.uk

Total number of rooms: 40

Prices from:			
Single:	£46.00	Double:	£40.00
Twin:	£40.00	Family room:	£110.00pr

Isle of Raasay, Ross-shire
Borodale House
Map Ref: 3E9

★★★
SMALL
HOTEL

50965

Open: Closed in winter except group bookings
Isle of Raasay, nr Skye, Ross-shire IV40 8PB

T: 01478 660222
E: info@isleofraasayhotel.co.uk
W: isleofraasayhotel.co.uk

Just a twenty minute ferry from Skye, Raasay's
informal family run hotel overlooks the Sound with
spectacular views to Skye's Cuillins. The restaurant
serves local produce on the casual and à la carte
menus, as well as lunch, cakes and refreshments.
A relaxing base from which to explore this beautiful
island.

Total number of rooms: 12

Prices from:			
Single:	£35.00	Double:	£35.00
Twin:	£35.00	Family room:	POA

Ardvasar, Isle of Skye
Ardvasar Hotel
Map Ref:3E11

★★★
SMALL
HOTEL

12706

Open: All year

Ardvasar, Sleat, Isle of Skye IV45 8RG

T: 01471 844223
E: richard@ardvasar-hotel.demon.co.uk
W: ardvasarhotel.com

Set in a stunning location overlooking the Sound of
Sleat and the magnificent Knoydart Mountains. Situated only 800 metres from Armadale, here the ferry
from Mallaig brings you 'over the sea to Skye'. All
rooms have been recently renovated offering a very
high standard of accommodation. Excellent local
seafood is served.

Total number of rooms: 10

Prices from:			
Single:	£80.00	Double:	£45.00
Twin:	£45.00	Family room:	£50.00

IMPORTANT: Prices stated are estimates and may be subject to change. Prices are per person per night unless otherwise stated. Awards correct as of beginning of October 2008.

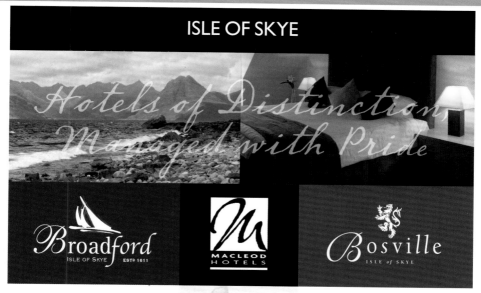

For a full listing of quality assured serviced accommodation throughout Scotland see pages 195-278.

173

Colbost, Dunvegan, Isle of Skye
The Three Chimneys & The House Overby   Map Ref: 3D8

★★★★★
RESTAURANT
WITH ROOMS

Open: All year excl three weeks in January

Colbost, Dunvegan, Isle of Skye IV55 8ZT
T: 01470 511258
E: eatandstay@threechimneys.co.uk
W: threechimneys.co.uk

Candlelit crofter's cottage restaurant in a remote and beautiful corner of Skye, with six well appointed bedroom suites adjacent. Overlooking the sea, with the misty isles of the Outer Hebrides on the horizon. Renowned worldwide for fabulous local fresh food and warm, welcoming service. A 'must' on every Scottish tour. Winter deals available.

61034

Total number of rooms: 6	
Prices per room from:	
Single: **£265.00**	Double: **£265.00**
Twin: **£265.00**	Family room: **£360.00**

Dunvegan, Isle of Skye
Dunorin House Hotel   Map Ref:3D9

★★★
SMALL
HOTEL

Open: February-October
Herebost, Dunvegan, Isle of Skye IV55 8GZ
T: 01470 521488
E: stay@dunorin.freeserve.co.uk
W: dunorinhousehotel-skye.com

23820

Total number of rooms: 10	
Prices per room from:	
Single: **£55.00**	Double: **£90.00**
Twin: **£90.00**	Family room: **£125.00**

Portree, Isle of Skye
Corran House   Map Ref:3E9

★★★★
GUEST
HOUSE

Open: All year
Eyre, Portree, Isle of Skye IV51 9XE
T: 01470 532311

20499

Total number of rooms: 5	
Prices from:	
Single: **£30.00-33.00**	Double: **£33.00-35.00**
Twin: **£33.00-35.00**	Family room: **£33.00-35.00**

Portree, Isle of Skye
Cuillin Hills Hotel   Map Ref: 3E9

★★★★
COUNTRY
HOUSE
HOTEL

Open: All year

Portree, Isle of Skye IV51 9QU
T: 01478 612003
E: info@cuillinhills-hotel-skye.co.uk
W: cuillinhills-hotel-skye.co.uk

The Cuillin Hills Hotel, Portree, enjoys some of the finest and most spectacular views in Scotland. We are famed for our Highland Hospitality, acclaimed food and drink and the relaxed comfort of our bedrooms. Traditional, relaxed friendliness is our hallmark. Welcome to Skye and experience the Cuillin Hills Hotel.

21631

Total number of rooms: 26	
Prices from:	
Single: **£85.00**	Double: **£85.00**
Twin: **£85.00**	

IMPORTANT: Prices stated are estimates and may be subject to change. Prices are per person per night unless otherwise stated. Awards correct as of beginning of October 2008.

Portree, Isle of Skye
Rosedale Hotel

Map Ref: 3E9

★★★
HOTEL

Open: March-November

Beaumont Crescent, Portree, Isle of Skye IV51 9DF

- **T:** 01478 613131
- **E:** rosedalehotelsky@aol.com
- **W:** rosedalehotelskye.co.uk

Harbour front, family run hotel with exceptional views. Created from fishermen's houses. Ideal as a base for exploring some of the most dramatic scenery imaginable. Award winning cuisine. In an outstanding waterside location.

52112

Total number of rooms: 20

Prices per room from:

Single:	£30.00-70.00	Double:	£70.00-160.00
Twin:	£70.00-140.00	Family room:	£70.00-200.00

📺📞🖥️🅿️☕🛎️✖️🍴🍷©£🐕Ⓥ

Portree, Isle of Skye
Royal Hotel

Map Ref: 3E9

★★★
HOTEL

Open: All year excl December 25th and 26th

Bank Street, Portree, Isle of Skye IV51 9BU

- **T:** 01478 612525
- **E:** info@royal-hotel-skye.com
- **W:** royal-hotel-skye.com

Family run hotel in central position overlooking Portree Bay, all rooms ensuite, leisure and fitness studio. Tianavaig restaurant overlooking the harbour serving home cooked local produce. MacNabs Inn, relaxed atmosphere where you can sample local beers and malt whiskies and live entertainment . Well Plaid, our family friendly bar diner.

52487

Total number of rooms: 23

Prices from:

Single:	£80.00	Double:	£59.00
Twin:	£59.00		

📺🛏️📞🖥️🅿️☕🛎️✖️🍴🍷©£🐕Ⓥ

The harbour's edge at Portree, Skye, Inner Hebrides

For a full listing of quality assured serviced accommodation throughout Scotland see pages 195-278.

175

Island Romance

Chic
Stylish
Dramatic

Romantic
Dream
Come true

Fantastic
Food
Fine Wine

Weddings
on land or
on board!

t: 0845 055 1117

e: info@skyehotel.co.uk

www.skyehotel.co.uk

t: 01471 833 202

e: info@duisdale.com

www.duisdale.com

Sleat, Isle of Skye, Inverness— shire IV43 8QW

Fort William and Lochaber, Skye and Lochalsh

Staffin, Isle of Skye
Flodigarry Country House Hotel — Map Ref: 3E7

82783

★★★
COUNTRY
HOUSE
HOTEL

Open: All year excl November 3rd–December 14th and January

Flodigarry, Staffin, Isle of Skye IV51 9HZ
T: 01470 552203
E: info@flodigarry.co.uk
W: flodigarry.co.uk

Flodigarry is a sheltered haven amidst the dramatic scenery of Northern Skye and is magnificently situated with panoramic views across the sea to the Torridon Mountains. The Hotel offers an excellent choice of 18 comfortable ensuite rooms both in the main house and Flora MacDonald Cottage.

Total number of rooms: 18

Prices from:

Single: **£80.00**	Double:	**£60.00**
Twin: **£50.00**	Family room:	**£80.00**

by Spean Bridge, Inverness-shire
Corriegour Lodge Hotel — Map Ref: 3H12

Open: March–October, Weekends only in February, November, December. Closed Xmas

20535

★★★
SMALL
HOTEL

SILVER

Loch Lochy, by Spean Bridge, Inverness-shire PH34 4EA
T: 01397 712685
E: info@corriegour-lodge-hotel.com
W: corriegour-lodge-hotel.com

'Better food than the top London restaurants and a view to die for' - The Mirror. This former Victorian hunting lodge enjoys the very finest setting in 'The Great Glen'. Dine in our Loch View Conservatory, enjoying the very best Scottish cuisine, fresh seafood, Aberdeen Angus, homemade breads and puddings, extensive selection of wines and malt whiskies. Our emphasis is on your total relaxation and comfort. Log fires and big comfy sofas. Come and be cushioned from the stresses of everyday life. Walking, scenery, skiing, history. Private beach and fishing school. Special Spring/Autumn breaks available.

BEST LOVED HOTELS

Total number of rooms: 10

Prices from:

Single: **£79.50**	Double:	**£79.50**
Twin: **£79.50**	Family room:	**£200.00pr**

WALKING IN SCOTLAND — visitscotland.com/walking. For everything you need to know about walking in Scotland and for a brochure Call 0845 22 55 121 Scotland. Created for Walking

For a full listing of quality assured serviced accommodation throughout Scotland see pages 195-278.

177

Loch Morlich at Glenmore

Moray, Aviemore and the Cairngorms

From the active lifestyle of Aviemore and the majestic beauty of the Caringorms; to the lure of Malt Whisky Country and the golden beaches of the Moray coast this is an area as contrasting as it is captivating.

There's inspiring landscape and diverse wildlife to spot so join ranger guided walks in the Cairngorms National Park or on the Moray Coast or spend an evening looking for pine marten and deer in a nature hide.

For watersports, including canoeing, sailing and windsurfing, head for Loch Insh or Loch Morlich. Hillwalkers will find the Cairngorm range is always a challenge while the more leisurely can wander to their heart's content in Rothiemurchus Estate, Culbin Forest, Craigellachie National Nature Reserve,

Glenlivet Estate and many other hidden gems.

For exciting mountain bike action try cycling at Moray Monster Trails or Laggan Wolftrax and ski in the winter at CairnGorm Mountain and The Lecht. There are also lots of opportunities for golfing and fishing. You can even take a steam train trip from Aviemore to Boat of Garten and Broomhill or you can ascend Cairn Gorm on the funicular railway.

Laggan Wolftrax mountain bike trails, near Laggan, Strathspey

To find out more, call 0845 22 55 121 or go to visitscotland.com

DON'T MISS

1   The **Cairngorms National Park** offers many events and activities throughout the year which are suitable for all ages and abilities. Visitor centres and ranger bases have leaflets, guides and trail maps to help you make the most of your time in the Park, and Visitor Information Centres throughout the area will be able to provide you with local information on events, attractions and activities.

2   At the heart of the beautiful Cairngorms National Park is the **CairnGorm Mountain Railway**. It takes 8 minutes from bottom to top, where an interactive exhibition tells the history and ecology of the surrounding area and you can see some stunning panoramic views of the National Park. Have a bite to eat and take in the view stretching from the Cairngorm plateau to the Monadliath Mountains and beyond.

3   **The Malt Whisky Trail** invites you to enjoy the wide-ranging flavour of eight malts as you wind your way through Speyside. Also on the trail is the family owned Speyside Cooperage where you can watch oak whisky barrels being constructed using traditional methods (see number 20).

4   Step back in time to the **Highland Folk Museum** with sites in Kingussie and Newtonmore, where you can experience over 400 years of Highland life. Re-constructions of an 18th century Highland township and 20th century working croft can be seen at Newtonmore. Both locations have programmes of live demonstrations and activities where you can see traditional skills and crafts in action.

5   **Johnstons** is the only Scottish mill to transform cashmere from fibre to garment and its story is told in their visitor centre and interactive exhibition in Elgin. They also have an engaging tour, tempting food hall and courtyard shop.

6   When **ospreys** returned to breed in Scotland the ancient Caledonian pinewood of Loch Garten was their first choice. Watch these magnificent birds bring fish to their chicks from the RSPB hide or on non-invasive CCTV. The reserve also has some excellent walks where you can spot red squirrels, crested tits and dragonflies. The ospreys are in residence from April till August but birds like capercaillie, redstart and goldeneye fill the calendar.

FOOD AND DRINK

eatscotland.com

7   At **The Old Bridge Inn**, on the outskirts of Aviemore, the staff are friendly and the service is excellent. A selection of meat, game and fish awaits and all dishes are cooked simply and with flair. The dining room adjacent to the bar area allows more formal and romantic dining with its open fire, and the puddings are all home-made and vary from day to day.

8   At the Speyside Heather Centre, near Dulnain Bridge, **The Clootie Dumpling** is the perfect opportunity to sample its namesake, a Scottish delicacy. This traditional and versatile pudding can be enjoyed in a variety of different ways from sweet to savoury. The recipe has a mixture of spices, carrots, apple, raisins and more, all mixed together in a 'cloot' (muslin cloth), steamed for hours and served with accompaniments.

9   Dine at **Craggan Mill** in the picturesque water mill near Grantown-on-Spey. Fine dining in a relaxed environment offers you the choice of bistro lunch or à la carte evening meal – all prepared from local, seasonal produce. Local artists exhibit paintings for view and sale within the restaurant and gallery.

10   **Minmore House Hotel** is an EatScotland Silver awarded restaurant set amid the spectacular scenery of the Glenlivit estate in Speyside. Their restaurant specialises in fine Scottish produce using only fresh, local ingredients, including some from their own kitchen garden.

ACTIVITIES

11   Up to 30km of fun-packed mountain biking awaits at the **Moray Monster Trails**. They work as three independent sites all linked to each other. So for those with a truly monster appetite and stamina to match, try all three sites end to end, from Fochabers to Craigellachie. For the more leisurely, the green-graded trail is at Quarrelwood, by Elgin.

12   **Inch Marshes Bird Reserve** is a birdwatching paradise! Around half of all British goldeneyes nest at Inch Marshes in spring. You're also likely to see lapwings, redshanks and curlews, as well as oystercatchers, snipe and wigeon. In winter, the marshes host flocks of whooper swans and greylag geese. Roe deer, wildcats, otters and foxes may all be seen along the edges of the marshes.

13   Enjoy year-round outdoor fun and action at the **Lecht Multi-Activity Centre**. With summer action on quad bikes, fun karts, dévalkarts and chairlift rides, winter is covered by skiing, snowboarding and tubing.

14   Take a step back in time and travel by steam engine. The **Strathspey Railway** runs from Aviemore to Broomhill (also known as Glenbogle from the TV series Monarch of the Glen) and affords beautiful views of the Cairngorms from the carriage window. To make the trip really special, you can even have afternoon tea on board.

WALKS

visitscotland.com/walking

15   **Glenmore Forest Park** has a range of walks from all-ability trails suitable for pushchairs, to longer walks through beautiful woodland which open out to give fantastic views of the Cairngorm Mountains. The Visitor Centre provides an audio-visual presentation plus café, toilets and shop.

16   Walking from **Hopeman to Lossiemouth** as part of the **Moray Coastal Trail** follows a route along the top of cliffs, giving privileged views into sandy coves and rocky headlands. There are lots of opportunities to venture onto beaches where you can relax and take in extensive views across the Moray Firth to the Black Isle and Helmsdale about 50 miles away.

17   There are a variety of waymarked trails throughout the **Rothiemurchus Estate**, with maps available from the visitor centre. The estate is teeming with Highland wildlife, including the red squirrel and the rare capercaillie, with guided tours available courtesy of Scottish Natural Heritage. Free tours on Tuesdays.

18   **Culbin Forest** meets the Moray coast between Nairn and Forres and offers cycling and walking on gentle paths with junction markers so you can make it up as you go along. Bird-watching and even the opportunity to spot otters is on offer as is a magnificent view from the 20m viewing tower at Hill 99 – a 99ft sand dune.

ATTRACTIONS

19   The **Cairngorm Reindeer Centre** is home to the only reindeer herd in the country and you can encounter the animals grazing in their natural environment. During the guided visits you can wander freely among the reindeer, stroking and feeding them. These friendly deer are a delight to all ages and, if you feel especially fond of one, you might be able to adopt it!

20   In the heart of Malt Whisky Country lies the **Speyside Cooperage**; the only working cooperage in the UK where you can experience the ancient art of producing whisky barrels.Based in Craigellachie the family owned company produces the finest casks and you can see the workers using traditional methods and tools.

Moray, Aviemore and the Cairngorms

Aviemore, Inverness-shire
Cairngorm Guest House
Map Ref: 4C10

17434

Open: All year excl Xmas
Grampian Road, Aviemore, Inverness-shire PH22 1RP

T: 01479 810630
E: enquiries@cairngormguesthouse.com
W: cairngormguesthouse.com

Total number of rooms: 12

Prices from:

Single:	£45.00	Double:	£30.00
Twin:	£30.00	Family room:	£90.00pr

Aviemore, Inverness-shire
Cairngorm Hotel
Map Ref: 4C10

17439

Open: All year
Grampian Road, Aviemore, Inverness-shire PH22 1PE

T: 01479 810233
E: reception@cairngorm.com
W: cairngorm.com

Total number of rooms: 31

Prices per room from:

Single:	£50.00	Double:	£80.00
Twin:	£80.00	Family room:	£120.00

Aviemore, Inverness-shire
Ravenscraig Guest House
Map Ref: 4C10

51158

Open: All year
141 Grampian Road, Aviemore
Inverness-shire PH22 1RP

T: 01479 810278
E: info@aviemoreonline.com
W: aviemoreonline.com

Total number of rooms: 12

Prices from:

Single:	£30.00	Double:	£30.00
Twin:	£30.00	Family room:	£30.00

Boat of Garten, Inverness-shire
The Boat Hotel
Map Ref: 4C10

78833

Open: All year
Boat of Garten, Inverness-shire PH24 3BH

T: 01479 831258
E: info@boathotel.co.uk
W: boathotel.co.uk

Located in the heart of the Cairngorms National Park, the hotel overlooks the famous Boat of Garten Golf Course. Walking, cycling, fishing, skiing . . . the hotel is perfectly located for all outdoor activities. The hotel has both a traditional bistro restaurant and a fine dining 2 AA Rosette restaurant.

Total number of rooms: 34

Prices from:

Single:	£35.00	Double:	£35.00
Twin:	£35.00	Family room:	£45.00
		Child	£15.00

Carrbridge, Inverness-shire
The Cairn Hotel
Map Ref: 4C9

17400

Open: All year excl Xmas day
Main Road, Carrbridge, Inverness-shire PH23 3AS

T: 01479 841212
E: info@cairnhotel.co.uk
W: cairnhotel.co.uk

Total number of rooms: 7

Prices from:

Single:	£26.00	Double:	£26.00
Twin:	£26.00	Family room:	£70.00pr

IMPORTANT: Prices stated are estimates and may be subject to change. Prices are per person per night unless otherwise stated. Awards correct as of beginning of October 2008.

Carrbridge, Inverness-shire
Dalrachney Lodge Hotel   Map Ref: 4C9

★★★
COUNTRY
HOUSE
HOTEL

Open: All year

Carrbridge, Inverness-shire PH23 3AT

T: 01479 841252
E: dalrachney@aol.com
W: dalrachney.co.uk

Lovingly refurbished Victorian sporting lodge in the heart of the Scottish Highlands, Dalrachney is an ideal base for a memorable holiday. Enjoy breathtaking scenery, abundant wildlife and numerous outdoor activities of Cairngorm National Park. Spacious well appointed rooms. Emphasis on good food and wine served in a relaxed and friendly setting.

22083

Total number of rooms: 10

Prices from:
Single: **£50.00**   Double: **£35.00**
Twin: **£35.00**   Family room: **£40.00**

Dulnain Bridge, by Grantown-on-Spey
Muckrach Hotel   Map Ref: 4C9

★★★
COUNTRY
HOUSE
HOTEL

Open: All year
Dulnain Bridge, Grantown-on-Spey PH26 3LY
T: 01479 851257
E: info@muckrach.com
W: muckrach.com

77411

Total number of rooms: 12

Prices per room from:
Single: **£50.00**   Double: **£100.00**
Twin: **£90.00**   Family room: **£130.00**

Forres, Moray
Cluny Bank Hotel   Map Ref: 4C8

★★★★
SMALL
HOTEL

Open: All year

69 St Leonard's Road, Forres IV36 1DW
T: 01309 674304
E: info@clunybankhotel.co.uk
W: clunybankhotel.co.uk

73753

Total number of rooms: 8

Prices per room from:
Single: **£75.00**   Double: **£110.00**
Twin: **£110.00**

Grantown-on-Spey, Moray
An Cala Guest House   Map Ref: 4C9

★★★★
GUEST
HOUSE

Open: All year excl Xmas
Woodlands Terrace, Grantown-on-Spey
Moray PH26 3JU
T: 01479 873293
E: ancala@globalnet.co.uk
W: ancala.info

11944

Total number of rooms: 4

Prices from:
Double: **£35.00-40.00**   Twin: **£35.00-40.00**
Family room: **£32.00**

Grantown-on-Spey, Moray
Ravenscourt House Hotel
Map Ref: 4C9

79435

★★★★
SMALL
HOTEL

Open: All year

Seafield Avenue, Grantown-on-Spey, PH26 3JG
T: 01479 872286
E: info@ravenscourthouse.co.uk
W: ravenscourthouse.co.uk

Friendly family run hotel offering two resident lounges, a conservatory restaurant, and a selection of twin, double and family bedrooms. Wi-fi internet access and satellite television available in bedrooms.

Total number of rooms: 8

Prices from:

Double:	£35.00	Twin:	£30.00
Family room:	£120.00pr		

Kingussie, Inverness-shire
Allt Gynack Guest House
Map Ref: 4B11

77326

★★★
GUEST
HOUSE

Open: All year
Gynack Villa, 1 High Street, Kingussie
Inverness-shire PH21 1HS
T: +44 (0) 1540 661081
E: alltgynack@tiscali.co.uk
 W: alltgynack.com

Total number of rooms: 5

Prices from:

Single:	£27.00	Double:	£25.00
Twin:	£25.00	Family room:	£25.00

Kingussie, Inverness-shire
Duke of Gordon Hotel
Map Ref: 4B11

17444

★★★
HOTEL

Open: All year

Newtonmore Road, Kingussie
Inverness-shire PH21 1HE

T: 01540 661302
E: reception@dukeofgordonhotel.co.uk
W: dukeofgordonhotel.co.uk

The Duke of Gordon Hotel is a Victorian building consisting of 65 bedrooms, three bars and à la carte carvery bar restaurants offering the best of Highland hospitality with an excellent reputation for quality food. Situated in the Cairngorms National Park in the Scottish Highlands. Extensive parking available.

Total number of rooms: 65

Prices per room from:

Single:	£69.00	Double:	£138.00
Twin:	£138.00		

IMPORTANT: Prices stated are estimates and may be subject to change. Prices are per person per night unless otherwise stated. Awards correct as of beginning of October 2008.

ngussie, Inverness-shire
cot House Hotel

Map Ref:4B11

53252

★★
MALL
OTEL

Open: All year

Newtonmore Road,
Kingussie, Inverness-shire PH21 1HE

T: 01540 661351
E: enquiries@scothouse.com
W: scothouse.com

Originally built in 1884 as a Church Manse and now a family owned Small Hotel. Popular bar for meals and drinks and restaurant has a growing good reputation. Small meetings and weddings are also accommodated.

Total number of rooms: 9

Prices per room from:

Single: **£22.00-55.00**	Double:	**£42.00-80.00**
Twin: **£42.00-80.00**	Family room:	**£62.00-118.00**

---

ssiemouth, Moray
kerry Brae Hotel

Map Ref: 4D7

54834

★★
MALL
OTEL

Open: All year excl Xmas day and New Year's day

Stotfield Road, Lossiemouth, Moray IV31 6QS

T: 01343 812040
E: info@skerrybrae.co.uk
W: skerrybrae.co.uk

Total number of rooms: 19

Prices per room from:

Single: **£55.00**	Double:	**£80.00**
Twin: **£80.00**	Family room:	**£95.00**

---

ethy Bridge, Inverness-shire
ethybridge Hotel

Map Ref: 4C10

47084

★★
OTEL

Open: All year

Nethy Bridge, Inverness-shire PH25 3DP

T: 01479 821203
E: salesnethybridge@strathmorehotels.com
W: strathmorehotels.com

The hotel offers traditional Scottish hospitality, situated amidst the beauty of the Cairngorm mountains and splendid Strathspey. The hotel's Victorian character is complemented by tasteful modern decor and fine Scottish fayre that many return to year after year. Pets welcome. Discounted children's rates. Many local attractions including Loch Garten ospreys.

Total number of rooms: 69

Prices from:

Single: **£45.00**	Double: **£45.00**
Twin: **£45.00**	

---

ewtonmore, Inverness-shire
lvey House

Map Ref: 4B11

11819

★★
UEST
OUSE

Open: All year

Golf Course Road, Newtonmore, PH20 1AT

T: 01540 673260
E: enquiries@alveyhouse.co.uk
W: alveyhouse.co.uk

Total number of rooms: 6

Prices per room from:

Single: **£24.50**	Double:	**£49.00**
Twin: **£49.00**	Family room:	**£75.00**

For a full listing of quality assured serviced accommodation throughout Scotland see pages 195-278.

Warebeth Beach, Stromness, Orkney

THE OUTER ISLANDS
Outer Hebrides, Orkney, Shetland

There's something very special about island holidays and Scotland has so many wonderful islands to explore.

On an island holiday, you can leave all the stresses of mainland life far behind. You don't have to settle for just one destination either – try a bit of island hopping, there's a lot of choice.

A different pace

At Scotland's western edge, the Outer Hebrides look out to the Atlantic swell and life moves at a relaxed pace. In this last Gaelic stronghold, a warm welcome awaits.

You can get there by ferry from Oban or from Uig on Skye – ferry prices to the Outer Hebrides have been reduced for 2009. Or travel by plane - fly to Barra and you'll land on the beach at low tide!

Lewis is the largest of the Outer Hebrides with a busy town at Stornoway and historical sites like the standing stones at Calanais stretching back over 3,000 years. It's distinctly different from the more mountainous Harris. Don't forget to visit the traditional weavers making wonderful Harris Tweed.

North and South Uist, Benbecula, Eriskay and Barra are all well worth a visit too and each has its own attractions.

Life at the crossroads

Island life can also be experienced in Scotland's two great northern archipelagos. Some 70 islands make up Orkney with 21 inhabited. Shetland, at the crossroads where the Atlantic meets the North Sea, has over 100 islands and is home to around 22,000 people and well over a million seabirds.

In Orkney, you can see the oldest houses in northern Europe at Papa Westray, dating back to 3800 BC.

To find out more, call 0845 22 55 121 or go to visitscotland.com

The influence of the Vikings in these parts is everywhere. Orcadians spoke Old Norse until the mid 1700s and the ancient Viking Parliament used to meet at Scalloway in Shetland.

These islands enjoy long summer days and at midsummer it never really gets dark. You can even play midnight golf in the 'Simmer Dim'.

In winter, the nights are long but the islanders have perfected the art of indoor life. Musicians fill the bars and community halls and there always seems to be something to celebrate.

Two great unmissable events are the winter fire festival of Up Helly Aa in Lerwick, Shetland and the Ba' in Kirkwall, Orkney, where up to 400 players take to the streets for a game of rough and tumble that is somewhere between football, rugby and all-out war.

Have a wild time

Orkney and Shetland are a joy for wildlife watchers. There are millions of birds to observe as well as otters, seals, dolphins and whales. Being surrounded by sea, angling, yachting, sea kayaking, cruising and diving are readily available.

Wherever you decide to experience island life, remember that island holidays are a popular choice and while there's a surprisingly good selection of small hotels and guest houses in the outer isles, it makes sense to book your accommodation well in advance.

The impressive cliffs of Esha Ness, north west coast of mainland, Shetland

What's On?

Orkney Jazz Weekend
24 – 26 April 2009
A weekend of jazz with local and visiting performers.
stromnesshotel.com

Shetland Folk Festival
30 April – 3 May 2009
The UK's most northerly folk festival is regarded a prestigious event for performers, locals and visitors alike.
shetlandfolkfestival.com

Orkney Folk Festival
21 – 24 May 2009
The best in modern and traditional folk music.
orkneyfolkfestival

Johnsmas Foy
18 – 28 June 2009
Recently revived festival that used to mark the arrival of the Dutch herring fleet in Shetland.
johnsmasfoy.com

St Magnus Festival
19 – 24 June 2009, Kirkwall
Midsummer celebration of the Arts.
stmagnusfestival.co.uk

Lewis Golf Week
July 2009, Stornoway
A week of golf at Stornoway Golf Club.

Taransay Fiddle Week
July 2009
Learn new skills from leading fiddlers.

Creative Connections
3 - 9 August 2009
Learn arts and crafts, traditional fiddle playing and the art of storytelling.

Harris Arts Festival
August 2009 – various dates
Celebrate arts and crafts on the island.

DON'T MISS

1   The combination of peace and tranquillity that can be found throughout the Outer Hebrides, blended with the vibrant nature of the people and their language, has been a true inspiration to many. This is demonstrated in the islands' crafts, music and culture. Arts venues such as An Lanntair in Stornoway and Taigh Chearsabhagh in Uist often attract internationally renowned performers.

2   The 5,000 year old Calanais Standing Stones on the west side of Lewis are one of the most famous landmarks in the Outer Hebrides. Second only to Stonehenge, these mystical stones are unique in their cross-shaped layout which has caused endless fascinating debate. Check out the visitor centre to form your own opinion!

3   Seallam! Visitor Centre in Northton at the southern end of the beautiful Isle of Harris provides a variety of exhibitions for both first-time and returning visitors. Browse among exhibits about the history and natural environment of the Hebrides, and find out what has influenced the development of the various island communities. Whether you wish to spend an hour or a whole day, there is plenty to occupy your attention. There is even a tea and coffee bar and a small craft-shop.

4   The area around Loch Druidibeg on South Uist is a National Nature Reserve with many different habitats including freshwater, brackish lagoon, dune, machair, peatland and scrub woodland. The loch itself is shallow but very large, with many islands: one of which is home to a resident colony of herons. The greylag geese which breed around the loch contribute to the resident population that remain in the Uists all year. Birds of prey include golden eagle, hen harriers, kestrel, peregrine and merlin.

5   Kisimul Castle is a sight to behold, situated in the bay of Castlebay Village on Barra. The stronghold of the MacNeils of Barra, this is the only surviving medieval castle in the Hebrides. Day tickets to visit the castle can be obtained at the local Visitor Information Centre.

ACTIVITIES

7   There are five official golf courses in the Hebrides: in Barra, Uist, Benbecula, Harris and Lewis. The 9-hole course at Scarista on Harris, in particular, is legendary for its stunning setting and challenging situation. You may think it's an easy option but the small greens, massive sand dunes and ever-present Atlantic winds combine for an enjoyable round!

8   The surf around the Hebrides is so good that the area is now on the map for international lovers of the sport. With over 70 beaches from white shell sands to pebble shores and almost always empty, it really is a surfer's paradise. The Isle of Lewis is positioned so it receives swells from almost every direction and is classed as having the most consistent surf in Europe.

9   With some of the most beautiful coastline in Britain and warmer water temperatures, the Hebrides is the perfect wilderness to explore by kayak. See otters, dolphins and puffins as you glide through the crystal clear waters around the islands. The coastline is a labyrinth of complex bays, inlets, dramatic cliffs, secret coves, sandy beaches and offshore islands.... a sea paddler's paradise.

10   The Outer Hebrides is a game angler's dream location and will fill you with all the emotions and pleasures associated with this wonderful and rewarding sport. Whether you are a solitary angler, form part of a larger group or simply looking for a tranquil family vacation, the Outer Hebrides has it all - namely, some of the best summer salmon and trout fishing in Europe set amidst spectacular scenery.

DON'T MISS

1 Skara Brae (B9056, 19 miles from Kirkwall) is an unrivalled example of life in Stone Age Orkney. Without doubt the best preserved village in western Europe, the houses contain stone beds, dressers, hearths and drains, giving a fantastic insight into how life was 5,000 years ago. Together with several other historical sites, it is part of a designated World Heritage Site.

2 Discovered in 1958, the Tomb of the Eagles is a 5,000 year old tomb containing ceremonial tools, beds, talons and other bones of the white-tailed eagle, pottery and working tools.

3 In the heart of Orkney's main town, Kirkwall, lies St Magnus Cathedral. It was built in 1137 by Earl Rognvald, in memory of his cousin Magnus who was earlier murdered by another cousin, Haakon, co-ruler at that time. Today the beautiful sandstone building continues to be a place of worship for the local people.

4 The Pier Arts Centre was reopened in 2007 and houses a remarkable collection of 20th century British art. The Collection charts the development of modern art in Britain and includes key work by Barbara Hepworth, Ben Nicholson and Naum Gabo amongst others.

5 Orkney is blessed with an abundance of birds and marine wildlife. Late spring sees the arrival of thousands of breeding seabirds including everybody's favourite – the colourful puffin. Grey seals breed in huge numbers around the coast in late autumn, while whales, dolphins and porpoises are regularly sighted off-shore throughout the summer. Wildlife is everywhere, and with a diverse range of professional guiding services there is something to suit everyone.

HISTORY AND HERITAGE

6 The Ring of Brodgar and the Standing Stones of Stenness (both just off the B9055) are also included within the World Heritage Site. Undeniably mystical, these spiritual places reward visitors with a real sense of ancient times.

7 Maeshowe is a central feature of the Neolithic Orkney World Heritage Site. A chambered cairn (off the A965), it is considered to be one of the finest architectural achievements of its time, around 5,000 years ago. Timed ticketing is in operation, allowing the informative guides to point out all the interesting aspects of the site, including Viking graffiti.

8 The Broch of Gurness at Aikerness (A966) is a well-organised Iron Age village, giving fascinating insight into community life 2,000 years ago.

9 Travel across the first of the Churchill Barriers to see an artistic phenomenon at the Italian Chapel. Built by Italian POWs in WWII, using only the most modest of materials, the intricate interior is all the more impressive.

DON'T MISS

1 Whatever your interests, there is something to suit every taste in Shetland. Our beautiful landscape is perfect for **walkers** – offering everything from coastal treks to energetic hikes. There are over 300 lochs holding brown trout and sea fishing is superb.

2 **Midsummer** is an especially magical time in Shetland when there are almost 19 hours of daylight to enjoy. It never really gets dark at this time of year – the other five hours between sunrise and sunset are filled with an eerie lingering twilight that's known locally as the "Simmer Dim".

3 Ever since **bird watching** became a popular British leisure pursuit in the late 19th century, Shetland's been famous, among those in the know, as the place to enjoy sensational seabird colonies and amazing rarities. If you want a close-up view of tens of thousands of breeding gannets, alongside guillemots, puffins, razorbills, kittiwakes and fulmars, then head for Sumburgh Head, Noss or Hermaness Nature Reserves.

4 Built on the historic site of Hay's Dock, is the impressive new **Shetland Museum and Archives** offers a rich insight into the development of Shetland from its geological beginnings to present day. See the museum's outstanding collection of historic boats hanging in the dramatic three-storey boat hall.

5 The accessibility of Shetland's coastline is ideal for **sea kayakers**. There are hundreds of miles of cliffs and deserted beaches as well as some of Europe's finest sea caves. Enjoy stunning cliff scenery, stack, arches and sheltered inlets. There are large colonies of seals and seabirds, most of them easily reachable by sea.

ATTRACTIONS

6 One of the best places to enjoy the cliff scenery by road is **Eshaness Lighthouse**, perched above a precipice of volcanic lava. A short walk away is an impressive collapsed cave, Da Hols o' Scraada ('the Devil's Caves'). Nearby is Da Grind o' da Navir ('Gate of the Borer'), a huge gateway in the cliffs where the sea has ripped out a huge chunk of rock and hurled it inland.

7 **Shetland Crofthouse**, Boddam, is a typical thatched crofthouse of the 19th century restored with traditional materials. The layout of the house is similar to Norse houses from 1,000 years earlier. The sweet smell of peat smoke, thick walls and cramped living space will instantly take you back to life in 1870s.

8 The broch, or fortified Iron Age tower, on the little island of Mousa is the only one in the world to have survived almost complete for more than 2,000 years. Built as a refuge against raiding local tribes, **Mousa Broch** is a wonder of archaeology, not to mention ornithology. Tiny storm petrels nest in its stone, visiting the broch only after dark – a night excursion to hear their eerie calls is an experience not to be missed.

9 A recent archaeological dig at **Old Scatness Broch**, next to Sumburgh Airport, has revealed one of Britain's most exciting Iron Age villages, with many buildings standing at or near roof height and some still even 'decorated' with yellow clay! Buried for nearly 2,000 years, the site is rich in artefacts and remarkably well preserved.

To find out more, call 0845 22 55 121 or go to visitscotland.com

MAP

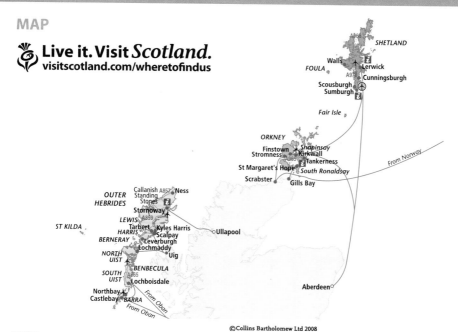

Live it. Visit *Scotland.*
visitscotland.com/wheretofindus

©Collins Bartholomew Ltd 2008

VISITOR INFORMATION CENTRES

Visitor Information Centres are staffed by people 'in the know' offering friendly advice, helping to make your stay in Scotland the most enjoyable ever . . . whatever your needs!

Outer Hebrides		
Stornoway	26 Cromwell Street, Stornoway, Isle of Lewis, HS1 2DD	Tel: 01851 703088

Orkney		
Kirkwall	The Travel Centre, West Castle Street, Kirkwall, Orkney KW15 1GU	Tel: 01856 872856

Shetland		
Lerwick	Market Cross, Lerwick, Shetland, ZE1 0LU	
Sumburgh (Airport)	Wilsness Terminal, Sumburgh Airport, Shetland ZE3 9JP	Tel: 01595 693434

LOCAL KNOWLEDGE • WHERE TO STAY • ACCOMMODATION BOOKING • PLACES TO VISIT • THINGS TO DO • MAPS AND GUIDES TRAVEL ADVICE • ROUTE PLANNING • WHERE TO SHOP AND EAT LOCAL CRAFTS AND PRODUCE • EVENT INFORMATION • TICKETS

For information and ideas about exploring Scotland in advance of your trip, call our booking and information service **0845 22 55 121** or go to **visitscotland.com**

If calling from outside the UK and Ireland **+44 1506 832 121**   From Ireland **1800 932 510**

A £4 booking fee applies for accommodation bookings made via a Visitor Information Centre and through our booking and information service.

Tarbert, Isle of Harris
Hotel Hebrides
Map Ref: 3C6

AWAITING GRADING

Open: All year

Pier Road, Tarbert, Isle of Harris
Outer Hebrides HS3 3DG
T: 01859 502364
E: stay@hotel-hebrides.com
W: hotel-hebrides.com

Boutique style hotel in the Outer Hebrides offering quality accommodation. Peace, tranquility, sublime comfort, exceptional food - and some of the most beautiful landscapes and sightseeing in Scotland.

36993

Total number of rooms: 21

Prices from:

Single: **£55.00-£60.00**	Double:	**£55.00-£65.00**
Twin: **£55.00-£65.00**	Family room:	**£130.00-£170.00**

C £ V

Ness, Isle of Lewis
Galson Farm Guest House
Map Ref: 3E3

★★★★ GUEST HOUSE

Open: All year

Galson Farm, South Galson, Isle of Lewis HS2 0SH
T: 01851 850492
E: galsonfarm@yahoo.com
W: galsonfarm.co.uk

68893

Total number of rooms: 4

Prices from:

Single: **£45.00**	Double:	**£40.00**
Twin: **£37.00**		

North east coast of the Island of Unst, Shetland

Kirkwall, Orkney
Albert Hotel
Map Ref: 5B12

★★★
SMALL
HOTEL

Open: All year
Mounthoolie Lane, Kirkwall, Orkney KW15 1JZ
T: 01856 876000
E: enquiries@alberthotel.co.uk
W: alberthotel.co.uk

11428

Total number of rooms: 18

Prices from:

Single:	£90.00	Double:	£50.00
Twin:	£55.00	Family room:	£60.00

Kirkwall, Orkney
Avalon House
Map Ref: 5B12

★★★
GUEST
HOUSE

Open: All year excl Xmas and New Year
Carness Road, Kirkwall, Orkney KW15 1UE
T: 01856 876665
E: jane@avalon-house.co.uk
W: avalon-house.co.uk

76974

Total number of rooms: 5

Prices from:

Single:	£40.00	Double:	£32.00
Twin:	£32.00	Family room:	£32.00

Kirkwall, Orkney
Kirkwall Hotel
Map Ref: 5B12

★★★
HOTEL

Open: All year excl Xmas and New Year
Harbour Street, Kirkwall, Orkney KW15 1LF
T: 01856 872232
E: enquiries@kirkwallhotel.com
W: kirkwallhotel.com

65463

Total number of rooms: 37

Prices per room from:

Single:	£60.00	Double:	£80.00
Twin:	£80.00	Family room:	£100.00

Kirkwall, Orkney
Orkney Hotel
Map Ref: 5B12

★★★
HOTEL

Open: All year
40 Victoria Street, Kirkwall, Orkney KW15 1DN
T: 01856 873477
E: info@orkneyhotel.co.uk
W: orkneyhotel.co.uk

52470

Total number of rooms: 30

Prices from:

Single:	£75.00	Double:	£49.50
Twin:	£49.50	Superior:	£59.50

Kirkwall, Orkney
Sanderlay Guest House
Map Ref: 5B12

★★★
GUEST
HOUSE

Open: All year excl Xmas
2 Viewfield Drive, Kirkwall, Orkney KW15 1RB
T: 01856 875587
E: enquiries@sanderlay.co.uk
W: sanderlay.co.uk

52953

Total number of rooms: 8

Prices from:

Single:	£35.00	Double:	£30.00
Twin:	£30.00	Family room:	£25.00

Kirkwall, Orkney
West End Hotel
Map Ref: 5B12

★★★
SMALL
HOTEL

Open: All year
14 Main Street, Kirkwall, Orkney KW15 1BU
T: 01856 872368
E: west.end@orkney.com
W: orkneyisles.co.uk/westendhotel

31611

Total number of rooms: 9

Prices per room from:

Single:	£56.00	Double:	£82.00
Twin:	£82.00	Family room:	£92.00

For a full listing of quality assured serviced accommodation throughout Scotland see pages 195-278.

193

Shetland

Scousburgh, Shetland
Spiggie Hotel
Map Ref: 5F7

★★★
SMALL
HOTEL

Open: All year

Scousburgh, Dunrossness, Shetland ZE2 9JE
T: 01950 460409
E: info@thespiggiehotel.co.uk
W: thespiggiehotel.co.uk

- Spectacular scenery
- Close to nature reserve and historical sites
- Amazing sunsets
- Peaceful and remote
- Superb locally sourced food
- Easy access to Sumburgh Airport
- White sandy beaches

68812

Total number of rooms: 6

Prices from:
Single: **£55.00-75.00**   Double: **£40.00-50.00**
Twin: **£40.00-50.00** Family room:**£40.00-50.00**

Walls, Shetland
Burrastow House
Map Ref: 5F5

★★★★
GUEST
HOUSE

Open: April-mid October

Walls, Shetland ZE2 9PD
T: 01595 809307
E: burr.hs@zetnet.co.uk
W: users.zetnet.co.uk/burrastow-house

Burrastow House – with views over Vaila Sound
is the ideal refuge for the escapist. The house
welcomes you with peat fires, a cosy library and all
the marvellous food you would want after a day's
exploring. Prepare to be astonished!

17015

Total number of rooms: 6

Prices from:
Single: **£40.00**   Double: **£40.00**
Twin: **£40.00**   Family room: **£40.00**

Stornoway, Isle of Lewis, Outer Hebrides

Directory of all VisitScotland Assured Serviced Establishments, ordered by location.
Establishments highlighted have an advertisement in this guide.

Aberdeen

Abbotswell Guest House	28 Abbotswell Crescent, Aberdeen AB12 5AR	01224 871788	★★★	Guest House	
Aberdeen Central West Premier Inn	Cocket Hat, North Anderson Drive, Aberdeen AB15 6DW	0870 9906430		Budget Hotel	
Aberdeen City Centre Premier Inn	Invelair House, West North Street, Aberdeen AB24 5AR	0870 9906300		Budget Hotel	
Aberdeen Douglas Hotel	43-45 Market Street, Aberdeen AB11 5EL	01224 582255	★★★	Hotel	
Aberdeen Guest House	218 Great Western Road, Aberdeen AB10 6PD	01224 211733	★★★	Guest House	
Aberdeen Patio Hotel	Beach Boulevard, Aberdeen AB24 5EF	01224 633339	★★★★	Hotel	♿
Adelphi Guest House	8 Whinhill Road, Aberdeen AB11 7XH	01224 583078	★★★	Guest House	
Aldersyde Guest House	138 Bon Accord Street, Aberdeen AB11 6TX	01224 580012	★★★	Guest House	
Antrim Guest House	157 Crown Street, Aberdeen AB11 6HT	01224 590987	★★	Guest House	
Arden Guest House	61 Dee Street, Aberdeen AB10 2EE	01224 580700	★★★	Guest House	
Ardoe House Hotel	South Deeside Road, Blairs, Aberdeen AB12 5YP	01224 860600	★★★★	Hotel	♿
Arkaig Guest House	43 Powis Terrace, Aberdeen AB25 3PP	01224 638872	★★★	Guest House	
Armadale Guest House	605 Holburn Street, Aberdeen AB10 7JN	01224 580636	★★★	Guest House	
Ashgrove Guest House	34 Ashgrove Road, Aberdeen AB25 3AD	01224 484861	★★★	Guest House	
Atholl Hotel	54 Kings Gate, Aberdeen AB15 4DA	01224 323505	★★★★	Hotel	
Beeches	193 Great Western Road, Aberdeen AB10 6PS	01224 586413	★★★	Guest House	
Bimini Guest House	69 Constitution Street, Aberdeen AB24 5ET	01224 646912	★★★	Guest House	
Brentwood Hotel	101 Crown Street, Aberdeen AB11 6HH	01224 595440	★★★	Hotel	
Brentwood Villa	560 King Street, Aberdeen AB24 5SR	01224 480633	★★★	Guest House	
Britannia Hotel	Malcolm Road, Aberdeen AB21 9LN	01224 409988	★★★	Hotel	♟
Burnett Guest House	75 Constitution Street, Aberdeen AB24 5ET	01224 647995	★★★	Guest House	
Butler's Islander Guest House	122 Crown Street, Aberdeen AB11 6HJ	01224 212411	★★★	Guest House	
Cedars Guest House	339 Great Western Road, Aberdeen AB10 6NW	01224 583225	★★★	Guest House	
Cloverleaf Hotel	Kepplehills Road, Bucksburn, Aberdeen AB21 9DG	01224 714294	★	Hotel	
Copthorne Hotel	122 Huntly Street, Aberdeen AB10 1SU	01224 630404	★★★★	Hotel	♿
Craighaar Hotel	Waterton Road, Aberdeen AB21 9HS	01224 712275	★★★	Hotel	
Crombie House	University of Aberdeen, Aberdeen AB24 3TS	01224 273444	★★	Campus	♿
Cults Hotel	The Square, Aberdeen AB15 9SE	01224 867632	★★★	Hotel	
Dunrovin Guest House	168 Bon-Accord Street, Aberdeen AB11 6TX	01224 586081	★★★	Guest House	

♿ Unassisted wheelchair access   ♿ Assisted wheelchair access   ♟ Access for visitors with mobility difficulties
🄟 Bronze Green Tourism Award   🄟🄟 Silver Green Tourism Award   🄟🄟🄟 Gold Green Tourism Award
For further information on our Green Tourism Business Scheme please see page 9.

Awards correct as of mid August 2008

Ellenville Guest House	50 Springbank Terrace, Aberdeen AB11 6LR	01224 213334	★★★	Guest House	
Express by Holiday Inn	Chapel Street, Aberdeen AB10 1SQ	01224 623500	★★★	Metro Hotel	♿
Furain Guest House	92 North Deeside Road, Peterculter, Aberdeen AB14 0QN	01224 732189	★★★	Guest House	
Granville Guest House	401 Great Western Road, Aberdeen AB10 6NY	01224 313043	★★★	Guest House	
Hilton Aberdeen Treetops	161 Springfield Road, Aberdeen AB15 7AQ	01224 313377	★★★★	Hotel	
Holiday Inn	Claymore Drive, Aberdeen AB23 8GP	08704 009046	★★★	Hotel	
Kildonan Guest House	410 Great Western Road, Aberdeen AB10 6NR	01224 316115	★★★	Guest House	
King's Hall	University of Aberdeen, Aberdeen AB24 3FX	01224 273444	★★	Campus	♿
Mariner Hotel	349 Great Western Road, Aberdeen AB10 6NW	01224 588901	★★★	Hotel	
Merkland Guest House	12 Merkland Road East, Aberdeen AB24 5PR	01224 634451	★★	Guest House	
Noble Guest House	376 Great Western Road, Aberdeen AB10 6PH	01224 313678	★★★	Guest House	
Northern Hotel	1 Great Northern Road, Aberdeen AB24 3PS	01224 483342	★★★	Hotel	∱
Norwood Hall Hotel	Garthdee Road, Aberdeen AB15 9NX	01224 868951	★★★★	Hotel	
Open Hearth Guest House	349 Holburn Street, Aberdeen AB10 7FQ	01224 591675	★★	Guest House	
Palm Court Hotel	81 Seafield Road, Aberdeen AB15 7YX	01224 310351	★★★★	Hotel	
Penny Meadow	189 Great Western Road, Aberdeen AB10 6PS	01224 588037	★★★★	Guest House	
Roselea House	12 Springbank Terrace, Aberdeen AB10 2LS	01224 583060	★★★	Guest House	
Royal Crown Guest House	111 Crown Street, Aberdeen AB11 2HN	01224 586461	★★★	Guest House	
Royal Hotel	Bath Street, Aberdeen AB11 6BJ	01224 585152	★★	Hotel	
Simpson's Hotel	59 Queens Road, Aberdeen AB15 4YP	01224 327777	★★★★	Hotel	
St Elmo	64 Hilton Drive, Aberdeen AB24 4NP	01224 483065	★★★★	Guest House	
The Globe Inn	13-15 North Silver Street, Aberdeen AB10 1RJ	01224 624258	★★★	Inn	
The Jays Guest House	422 King Street, Aberdeen AB24 3BR	01224 638295	★★★★	Guest House	
Thistle Aberdeen Airport Hotel	Argyll Road, Aberdeen AB21 0AF	01224 725252	★★★★	Hotel	♿
Thistle Aberdeen Caledonian	10-14 Union Terrace, Aberdeen AB10 1WE	01224 640233	★★★★	Hotel	
Travelodge Aberdeen	9 Bridge Street, Aberdeen AB11 6JL	08719 846117	AWAITING GRADING		

by Aberdeen

| Thistle Aberdeen Altens | Souterhead Road, Altens, by Aberdeen AB12 3LF | 01224 877000 | ★★★ | Hotel | ♿ |

Aberdour

| Aberdour Hotel | 38 High Street, Aberdour, Fife, KY3 0SW | 01383 860325 | ★★★ | Small Hotel | ∱ |

♿ Unassisted wheelchair access   ♿ Assisted wheelchair access   ∱ Access for visitors with mobility difficulties
🄿 Bronze Green Tourism Award   🄿🄿 Silver Green Tourism Award   🄿🄿🄿 Gold Green Tourism Award
For further information on our Green Tourism Business Scheme please see page 9.

Cairngorm Guest House	Grampian Road, Aviemore, Inverness-shire, PH22 1RP	01479 810630	★★★	Guest House		𝓟𝓟
Cairngorm Hotel	Grampian Road, Aviemore, Inverness-shire, PH22 1PE	01479 810233	★★★	Hotel		
Corrour House	Inverdruie, Aviemore, Inverness-shire, PH22 1QH	01479 810220	★★★★	Guest House		
Junipers	5 Dellmhor, Aviemore, Inverness-shire, PH22 1QW	01479 810405	★★★	Guest House		
Kinapol Guest House	Dalfaber Road, Aviemore, Inverness-shire, PH22 1PY	01479 810513	★★★	Guest House		
Macdonald Academy	Aviemore Highland Resort, Aviemore, Inverness-shire, PH22 1PF	01479 810781	★★★	Lodge	🦽	𝓟𝓟
Macdonald Highlands Hotel	Aviemore Centre, Aviemore, Inverness-shire, PH22 1PV	01479 815100	★★★★	Hotel		𝓟𝓟
MacKenzies Highland Inn	125 Grampian Road, Aviemore, Inverness-shire, PH22 1RL	01479 810672	★	Inn		
Ravenscraig Guest House	141 Grampian Road, Aviemore, Inverness-shire, PH22 1RP	01479 810278	★★★★	Guest House	🚶	𝓟𝓟
The Old Ministers House	Rothiemurchus, Aviemore, Inverness-shire, PH22 1QH	01479 812181	★★★★	Guest House		
The Rowan Tree Country Hotel	Loch Alvie, Aviemore, Inverness-shire, PH22 1QB	01479 810207	★★★	Inn		
Vermont Guest House	Grampian Road, Aviemore, Inverness-shire, PH22 1RP	01479 810470	★★★	Guest House		

by Aviemore

Hilton Coylumbridge Hotel	Coylumbridge, by Aviemore, Inverness-shire, PH22 1QN	01479 810661	AWAITING GRADING			𝓟𝓟𝓟

Ayr

Abbotsford Hotel	14 Corsehill Road, Ayr, Ayrshire, KA7 2ST	01292 261506	★★★	Small Hotel		
Ayrshire & Galloway Hotel	1 Killoch Place, Ayr, Ayrshire, KA7 2EA	01292 262626	★★	Hotel		
Belleisle Country House Hotel	Belleisle Park, Doonfoot, Ayr, Ayrshire, KA7 4DU	01292 442331	★	Country House Hotel		
Belmont	15 Park Circus, Ayr, Ayrshire, KA7 2DJ	01292 265588	★★★	Guest House		
Brig O' Doon Hotel	Alloway, Ayr, Ayrshire, KA7 4PQ	01292 442466	★★★★	Small Hotel		
Burnside Guest House	14 Queens Terrace, Ayr, Ayrshire, KA7 1DU	01292 263912	★★★★	Guest House		
bythesea Guest House	16 Queens Terrace, Ayr, Ayrshire, KA7 1DU	01292 282365	★★★★	Guest House		
Carrick Lodge Hotel	Carrick Road, Ayr, Ayrshire, KA7 2RE	01292 262846	★★★	Small Hotel		
Coila Guest House	10 Holmston Road, Ayr, Ayrshire, KA7 3BB	01292 262642	★★★★	Guest House		
Craggallan Guest House	8 Queens Terrace, Ayr, Ayrshire, KA7 1DU	01292 264998	★★★★	Guest House		
Craigholm	7 Queens Terrace, Ayr, Ayrshire, KA7 1DU	01292 261470	★★★	Guest House		
Daviot House	12 Queen's Terrace, Ayr, Ayrshire, KA7 1DU	01292 269678	★★★★	Guest House		
Dunlay House	1 Ailsa Place, Ayr, Ayrshire, KA7 1JG	01292 610230	★★★★	Guest House		
Eglinton Guest House	23 Eglinton Terrace, Ayr, Ayrshire, KA7 1JJ	01292 264623	★★	Guest House		
Ellisland	19 Racecourse Road, Ayr, Ayrshire, KA7 2TD	01292 260111	★★★★	Small Hotel		

🦽 Unassisted wheelchair access   🦽 Assisted wheelchair access   🚶 Access for visitors with mobility difficulties
𝓟 Bronze Green Tourism Award   𝓟𝓟 Silver Green Tourism Award   𝓟𝓟𝓟 Gold Green Tourism Award
For further information on our Green Tourism Business Scheme please see page 9.

Elms Court Hotel	21-23 Miller Road, Ayr, Ayrshire, KA7 2AX	01292 264191	★★★	Small Hotel		
Express by Holiday Inn Ayr	Wheatpark Place, Ayr, Ayrshire, KA8 9RT	01292 272300	AWAITING GRADING			
Fairfield House Hotel	12 Fairfield Road, Ayr, Ayrshire, KA7 2AS	01292 267461	★★★★	Hotel	⚐	
Glenpark Hotel	5 Racecourse Road, Ayr, Ayrshire, KA7 2DG	01292 263891	★★	Small Hotel		
Horizon Hotel	Esplanade, Ayr, Ayrshire, KA7 1DT	01292 264384	★★★	Hotel	⚐	
Kilkerran Guest House	15 Prestwick Road, Ayr, Ayrshire, KA8 8LD	01292 266477	★★	Guest House		
Langley Bank Guest House	39 Carrick Road, Ayr, Ayrshire, KA7 2RD	01292 264246	★★★★	Guest House		
Miller House	36 Miller Road, Ayr, Ayrshire, KA7 2AY	01292 282016	★★★	Guest House		
No. 26 The Crescent	26 Bellevue Crescent, Ayr, Ayrshire, KA7 2DR	01292 287329	★★★★★	Guest House		
Queen's Guest House	10 Queen's Terrace, Ayr, Ayrshire, KA7 1DU	01292 265618	★★★	Guest House		
Ramada Jarvis	Dalblair Road, Ayr, Ayrshire, KA7 1UG	01292 269331	★★★	Hotel	♿	🅿
Richmond Guest House	38 Park Circus, Ayr, Ayrshire, KA7 2LD	01292 265153	★★★	Guest House		
Savoy Park Hotel	16 Racecourse Road, Ayr, Ayrshire, KA7 2UT	01292 266112	★★★	Small Hotel		🅿🅿
St Andrews Hotel	7 Prestwick Road, Ayr, Ayrshire, KA8 8LD	01292 263211	★★	Inn		
The Beechwood Guest House	37/39 Prestwick Road, Ayr, Ayrshire, KA8 8LE	01292 262093	★★★	Guest House		
The Windsor	6 Alloway Place, Ayr, Ayrshire, KA7 2AA	01292 264689	★★	Guest House		
Western House Hotel	2 Whitletts Road, Ayr, Ayrshire, KA9 0JE	0870 8505666	★★★★	Hotel	⚐	

by Ayr

Enterkine Country House	Annbank, by Ayr, Ayrshire, KA6 5AL	01292 520580	★★★★	Country House Hotel		

Back, Isle of Lewis

Broad Bay House	Back, Isle of Lewis, HS2 0LQ	01851 820990	★★★★★	Guest House	♿	
Crowberry	43 Vatisker, Back, Isle of Lewis, HS2 0LF	01851 605004	★★★★	Guest House		

Ballachulish

Ballachulish House	Ballachulish, Argyll, PH49 4JX	01855 811266	★★★★★	Guest Accommodation		
Craiglinnhe House	Lettermore, Ballachulish, Argyll, PH49 4JD	01855 811270	★★★★	Guest House		
Fern Villa Guest House	Loan Fern, Ballachulish, Argyll, PH49 4JE	01855 811393	★★★	Guest House		
Isles of Glencoe Hotel & Leisure Centre	Ballachulish, Argyll, PH49 4HL	01855 811602	★★★	Hotel	♿	🅿🅿🅿
Lyn-Leven Guest House	West Laroch, Ballachulish, Argyll, PH49 4JP	01855 811392	★★★★	Guest House		
Strathassynt Guest House	Loan Fern, Ballachulish, Argyll, PH49 4JB	01855 811261	★★★	Guest House		
The Ballachulish Hotel	Ballachulish, Argyll, PH49 4JY	01855 811606	★★★	Hotel	⚐	

♿ Unassisted wheelchair access   ⚐ Assisted wheelchair access   ⚐ Access for visitors with mobility difficulties
🅿 Bronze Green Tourism Award   🅿🅿 Silver Green Tourism Award   🅿🅿🅿 Gold Green Tourism Award
For further information on our Green Tourism Business Scheme please see page 9.

Ballantrae

Glenapp Castle	Ballantrae, Ayrshire, KA26 0NZ	01465 831212	★★★★★	Hotel	休
Kings Arms Hotel	40 Main Street, Ballantrae, Ayrshire, KA26 0NB	01465 831202	★★	Inn	

Ballater

Cambus O'May Hotel	Ballater, Aberdeenshire, AB35 5SE	01339 755428	★★★	Country House Hotel	
Darroch Learg Hotel	Braemar Road, Ballater, Aberdeenshire, AB35 5UX	013397 55443	★★★★	Small Hotel	⋏
Deeside Hotel	Braemar Road, Ballater, Aberdeenshire, AB35 5RQ	013397 55420	★★★	Small Hotel	⏢
Glen Lui Hotel	14 Invercauld Road, Ballater, Aberdeenshire, AB35 5PP	01339 755402	★★★	Small Hotel	⏢⏢
Glenernan	37 Braemar Road, Ballater, Aberdeenshire, AB35 5RQ	01339 753111	★★★	Guest House	♿
Hilton Craigendarroch Hotel	Braemar Road, Ballater, Aberdeenshire, AB35 5RQ	013397 55858	★★★	Hotel	⏢
Moorside Guest House	26 Braemar Road, Ballater, Aberdeenshire, AB35 5RL	01339 755492	★★★★	Guest House	⋏
Morvada House	28 Braemar Road, Ballater, Aberdeenshire, AB35 5RL	013397 56334	★★★★	Guest House	
Netherley Guest House	2 Netherley Place, Ballater, Aberdeenshire, AB35 5QE	013397 55792	★★★★	Guest House	
The Auld Kirk	Braemar Road, Ballater, AB35 5RQ	01339 755762	★★★	Restaurant with Rooms	
The Gordon Guest House	Station Square, Ballater, Aberdeenshire, AB35 5QB	013397 55996	★★★★	Guest House	
The Green Inn	9 Victoria Road, Ballater, Aberdeenshire, AB35 5QQ	01339 755701	★★★★	Restaurant with Rooms	

by Ballater

Loch Kinord Hotel	Ballater Road, Dinnet, by Ballater, Aberdeenshire, AB34 5JY	01339 885229	★★★	Hotel	⏢⏢
The Inver Hotel	Crathie, by Ballater, Aberdeenshire, AB35 5XN	01339 742345	★★★	Inn	

Ballindalloch

Minmore House Hotel	Glenlivet, Ballindalloch, Banffshire, AB37 9DB	01807 590378	★★★	Country House Hotel	

Balloch

Norwood Guest House	60 Balloch Road, Balloch, Dunbartonshire, G83 8LE	01389 750309	★★★	Guest House	
Palombo's of Balloch	40 Balloch Road, Balloch, Dunbartonshire, G83 8LE	01389 753501	★★★	Restaurant with Rooms	
Time Out	24 Balloch Road, Balloch, Dunbartonshire, G83 8LE	07957 436731	★★★	Guest House	
Tullie Inn	Balloch Road, Balloch, Dunbartonshire, G83 8SW	01389 752052	★★★	Inn	

Ballygrant, Isle of Islay

Kilmeny	Ballygrant, Isle of Islay, PA45 7QW	01496 840668	★★★★★	Guest House	

Balquhidder

King's House Hotel	Balquhidder, Perthshire, FK19 8NY	0877 384646	★★	Small Hotel	

Banchory

Banchory Lodge Country House Hotel	Off Dee Street, Banchory, Kincardineshire, AB31 5HS	01330 822625	★★★	Country House Hotel

Banchory

Burnett Arms Hotel	25 High Street, Banchory, Kincardineshire, AB31 5TD	01330 824944	★★★	Small Hotel
Crossroads Hotel	Lumphanan, Banchory, Kincardineshire, AB31 4RH	01339 883275	★★	Inn
Raemoir Country House Hotel	Raemoir, Banchory, Kincardineshire, AB31 4ED	01330 824884	★★★	Country House Hotel

Banff

Carmelite House Hotel	Low Street, Banff, Banffshire, AB45 1AY	01261 812152	★★	Small Hotel
Fife Lodge Hotel	Sandyhill Road, Banff, Banffshire, AB45 1BE	01261 812436	★★★	Small Hotel
Gardenia House	19 Castle Street, Banff, Banffshire, AB45 1DH	01261 812675	★★★	Guest House
The Trinity and Alvah Manse	21 Castle Street, Banff, Banffshire, AB45 1DH	01261 812244	★★★	Guest House

Banknock

Glen Skirlie House & Castle	Kilsyth Road, Banknock, Stirlingshire, FK4 1UF	01324 840201	★★★★	Small Hotel

Bannockburn

King Robert Hotel	Glasgow Road, Bannockburn, Stirlingshire, FK7 OLJ	01786 811666	★★★	Hotel

Bargeddie

Auchenlea	153 Langmuir Road, Bargeddie, Lanarkshire, G69 7RT	0141 771 6870	★★★	Guest House

Barr

The King's Arms Hotel	1 Stinchar Road, Barr, Ayrshire, KA26 9TW	01465 861230	★★	Inn

Barrhead

Dalmeny Park Hotel	Lochlibo Road, Barrhead, Renfrewshire, G78 1LG	0141 881 9211	★★★★	Small Hotel

Bathgate

The Cairn Hotel	Blackburn Road, Bathgate, West Lothian, EH48 2EL	01506 633366	★★	Hotel

Bayherivagh, Isle of Barra

Heathbank Hotel	Bayherivagh, Isle of Barra, HS9 5YQ	01871 890266	★★★	Inn

Beauly

Archdale Guest House	High Street, Beauly, Inverness-shire, IV4 7BT	01463 783043	★★	Guest House
Priory Hotel	The Square, Beauly, Inverness-shire, IV4 7BX	01463 782309	★★★	Hotel

by Beauly

Tomich Hotel	Tomich, by Cannich, by Beauly, Inverness-shire, IV4 7LY	01456 415399	★★★	Small Hotel

   ♿ Unassisted wheelchair access   ♿ Assisted wheelchair access   ♿ Access for visitors with mobility difficulties
P Bronze Green Tourism Award   PP Silver Green Tourism Award   PPP Gold Green Tourism Award
For further information on our Green Tourism Business Scheme please see page 9.

| Cnoc Hotel | Struy, by Beauly, Inverness-shire, IV4 7JU | 01463 761 264 | ★★★ | Small Hotel | |

by Beith

| The Burnhouse Manor Hotel | Burnhouse, by Beith, Ayrshire, KA15 1LJ | 01560 484006 | ★★★ | Hotel | |

Benbecula, Wester Isles

Borve Guest House	5 Torlum, Benbecula, Western Isles, HS7 5PP	01870 602685	★★★★	Guest House	
Dark Island Hotel	Benbecula, Western Isles, HS7 5PJ	0870 602414	★★	Hotel	
Lionacleit Guest House	27 Liniclate, Benbecula, Western Isles, HS7 5PY	01870 602176	★★★	Guest House	
The Isle of Benbecula House Hotel	Creagorry, Benbecula, Western Isles, HS7 5PG	01870 602024	★★★	Hotel	

Benderloch

| Isle of Eriska Hotel | Benderloch, Argyll, PA37 1SD | 01631 720371 | ★★★★★ | Country House Hotel | 🦽 |

Biggar

Cornhill House	Cornhill Road, Coulter, Biggar, Lanarkshire, ML12 6QE	01899 220001	★★★	Country House Hotel	
Elphinstone Hotel	145 High Street, Biggar, Lanarkshire, ML12 6DL	01899 220044	★★	Inn	
Shieldhill Castle	Quothquan, Biggar, Lanarkshire, ML12 6NA	01899 220035	★★★★	Country House Hotel	

by Biggar

| The Glenholm Centre | Broughton, by Biggar, Lanarkshire, ML12 6JF | 01899 830408 | ★★★ | Guest House | ♿ 𝄌𝄌𝄌 |
| Skirling House | Skirling, by Biggar, Lanarkshire, ML12 6HD | 01899 860274 | ★★★★★ | Guest House | |

Birsay, Orkney

| Barony Hotel | Birsay, Orkney, KW17 2LS | 01856 721327 | ★★ | Small Hotel | |

Bishopton

| Mar Hall | Mar Estate, Bishopton, Renfrewshire, PA7 5NW | 0141 812 9999 | ★★★★★ | Hotel | |

Blackford

| Blackford Hotel | Moray Street, Blackford, Perthshire, PH4 1QF | 01764 682497 | ★★★ | Small Hotel | 🚶 |

Blackwaterfoot, Isle of Arran

| Kinloch Hotel | Blackwaterfoot, Isle of Arran, KA27 8ET | 01770 860444 | ★★★ | Hotel | 𝄌 |

Blair Atholl

Atholl Arms Hotel	Old North Road, Blair Atholl, Perthshire, PH18 5SG	01796 481205	★★★	Hotel	
Bridge of Tilt Hotel	Bridge of Tilt, Blair Atholl, Perthshire, PH18 5SU	01796 481333	★★	Hotel	
Dalgreine Guest House	Bridge of Tilt, Blair Atholl, Perthshire, PH18 5SX	01796 481276	★★★★	Guest House	
Ptarmigan House	Bridge of Tilt, Blair Atholl, Perthshire, PH18 5SZ	01796 481269	★★★	Guest House	

♿ Unassisted wheelchair access 🦽 Assisted wheelchair access 🚶 Access for visitors with mobility difficulties
𝄌 Bronze Green Tourism Award 𝄌𝄌 Silver Green Tourism Award 𝄌𝄌𝄌 Gold Green Tourism Award
For further information on our Green Tourism Business Scheme please see page 9.

| The Firs | St Andrews Crescent, Blair Atholl, Perthshire, PH18 5TA | 01796 481256 | ★★★ | Guest House | 𝒫𝒫 |

Blairgowrie

Altamount Country House Hotel	Coupar Angus Road, Blairgowrie, Perthshire, PH10 6JN	01250 873512	★★★	Country House Hotel	
Angus Hotel	Wellmeadow, Blairgowrie, Perthshire, PH10 6NQ	01250 872455	★★★	Hotel	
Bridge of Cally Hotel	Bridge of Cally, Blairgowrie, Perthshire, PH10 7JJ	01250 886231	★★★	Small Hotel	♟
Broadmyre Motel	Carsie, Blairgowrie, Perthshire, PH10 6QW	01250 873262	★★	Guest House	
Burrelton Park Inn	High Street,Burrelton, Blairgowrie, Perthshire, PH13 9NX	01828 670206	★	Inn	
Dalmunzie	Spittal of Glenshee, Blairgowrie, Perthshire, PH10 7QE	01250 885224	★★★	Country House Hotel	
Glensheiling House	Hatton Road, Blairgowrie, Perthshire, PH10 7HZ	01250 874605	★★★★	Guest House	
Ivybank Guest House	Boat Brae, Blairgowrie, Perthshire, PH10 7BH	01250 873056	★★★★	Guest House	
Kinloch House Hotel	Blairgowrie, Perthshire, PH10 6SG	01250 884237	★★★★	Country House Hotel	
Rosebank House	Balmoral Road, Blairgowrie, Perthshire, PH10 7AF	01250 872912	★★★	Guest House	
Royal Hotel	53 Allan Street, Blairgowrie, Perthshire, PH10 6AB	01250 872226	AWAITING GRADING		
The Laurels Guest House	Golf Course Road,Rosemount, Blairgowrie, Perthshire, PH10 6LH	01250 874920	★★★	Guest House	

by Blairgowrie

| Spittal of Glenshee Hotel | Glenshee, by Blairgowrie, Perthshire, PH10 7QF | 01250 885215 | AWAITING GRADING | | |
| Glenisla Hotel | Kirkton of Glenisla,Glenisla, by Blairgowrie, Perthshire, PH11 8PH | 01575 582223 | ★★ | Inn | |

Boat of Garten

Granlea House	Deshar Road, Boat of Garten, Inverness-shire, PH24 3BN	01479 831601	★★★	Guest House	
Heathbank House	Drumuillie Road, Boat of Garten, Inverness-shire, PH24 3BD	01479 831234	★★★	Guest House	𝒫𝒫
Moorfield House	Deshar Road, Boat of Garten, Inverness-shire, PH24 3BN	01479 831646	★★★★	Guest House	𝒫𝒫
The Boat Hotel	Deshar Road, Boat of Garten, Inverness-shire, PH24 3BH	01479 831258	★★★★	Hotel	
The Boat House	Deishar Road, Boat of Garten, Inverness-shire, PH24 3BN	01479 831484	★★★	Guest House	♟

Bo'ness

| Carriden House | Carriden Brae, Bo'ness, West Lothian, EH51 9SN | 01506 829811 | ★★★ | Guest House | |

Bonnyrigg

| Dalhousie Castle & Spa | Cockpen Road, Bonnyrigg, Edinburgh, Midlothian, EH19 3JB | 01875 820153 | ★★★★ | Hotel | |
| The Retreat Castle | Cockpen Road, Bonnyrigg,Edinburgh, Midlothian, EH19 3HS | 0131 6603200 | ★★★ | Small Hotel | ♿ |

Bothwell

| Bothwell Bridge Hotel | 89 Main Street, Bothwell, Lanarkshire, G71 8EU | 01698 852246 | ★★★ | Hotel | |

♿ Unassisted wheelchair access ♿ Assisted wheelchair access ♟ Access for visitors with mobility difficulties
𝒫 Bronze Green Tourism Award 𝒫𝒫 Silver Green Tourism Award 𝒫𝒫𝒫 Gold Green Tourism Award
For further information on our Green Tourism Business Scheme please see page 9.

206 To find out more, call 0845 22 55 121 or go to visitscotland.com.

Bowmore, Isle of Islay

Lambeth Guest House	Jamieson Street, Bowmore, Isle of Islay, PA43 7HL	01496 810597	★★	Guest House	
The Harbour Inn and Restaurant	The Square, Bowmore, Isle of Islay, PA43 7JR	01496 810330	★★★★	Restaurant with Rooms	

Braemar

Braemar Lodge	Glenshee Road, Braemar, Aberdeenshire, AB35 5YQ	013397 41627	★★★	Guest House	
Callater Lodge Guest House	9 Glenshee Road, Braemar, Aberdeenshire, AB35 5YQ	01339 741275	AWAITING GRADING		
Clunie Lodge Guest House	Cluniebank Road, Braemar, Aberdeenshire, AB35 5ZP	013397 41330	★★★	Guest House	
Craiglea	Hillside Road, Braemar, Aberdeenshire, AB35 5YU	013397 41641	★★★	Guest House	
Cranford Guest House	15 Glenshee Road, Braemar, Aberdeenshire, AB35 5YQ	01339 741675	★★★	Guest House	
Moorfield House	Chapel Brae, Braemar, Aberdeenshire, AB35 5YT	01339 741244	★★★	Restaurant with Rooms	
Schiehallion Guest House	10 Glenshee Road, Braemar, Aberdeenshire, AB35 5YQ	013397 41679	★★★	Guest House	
The Invercauld Arms Hotel	Invercauld Road, Braemar, Aberdeenshire, AB35 5YR	01339 741605	★★★	Hotel	

Brechin

Northern Hotel	2 Clerk Street, Brechin, Angus, DD9 6AE	01356 625400	★★★	Small Hotel	♿

Bressay

Northern Lights Holistic Spa	Sound View Uphouse, Bressay, Shetland, ZE2 9ES	01595 820733	★★★★	Guest House	♿

Bridge of Allan

Knockhill Guest House	Bridge of Allan, Stirlingshire, FK9 4ND	01786 833123	★★★★	Guest House	⋀
Royal Hotel	55 Henderson Street, Bridge of Allan, Stirlingshire, FK9 4HG	01786 832284	★★★	Hotel	
The Queen's Hotel	24 Henderson Street, Bridge of Allan, Stirlingshire, FK9 4HP	01786 833268	★★★★	Small Hotel	♿

Bridge of Don

Premier Inn Aberdeen North (Murcar)	Mill Of Mundurno, Murcar, Bridge of Don, Aberdeenshire, AB23 8BP	08701 977012		Budget Hotel	

Bridge of Earn

The Last Cast	Main Street, Bridge of Earn, Perthshire, PH2 9PL	01738 812578	★★	Guest House	

Bridge of Orchy

Bridge of Orchy Hotel	Bridge of Orchy, Argyll, PA36 4AD	01838 400208	★★★★	Inn	

Bridgend, Isle of Islay

Bridgend Hotel	Bridgend, Isle of Islay, PA44 7PJ	01496 810212	★★★	Small Hotel	
The Meadows	Claggan Farm, Bridgend, Isle of Islay, PA44 7PZ	01496 810567	★★★★	Guest House	⋀

♿ Unassisted wheelchair access   ♿ Assisted wheelchair access   ⋀ Access for visitors with mobility difficulties
Ⓟ Bronze Green Tourism Award   ⒫⒫ Silver Green Tourism Award   ⒫⒫⒫ Gold Green Tourism Award
For further information on our Green Tourism Business Scheme please see page 9.

Awards correct as of mid August 2008

207

Broadford, Isle of Skye

Broadford Hotel	Broadford, Isle of Skye, IV49 9AB	01471 822414	★★★★	Hotel		
Seaview	Shore Road, Broadford, Isle of Skye, IV49 9AB	01471 820308	★★★	Guest House	朼	

Brodick, Isle of Arran

Auchrannie Country House Hotel	Brodick, Isle of Arran, KA27 8BZ	01770 302234	★★★★	Hotel	佳	𝒫𝒫
Auchrannie Spa Resort	Brodick, Isle of Arran, KA27 8BZ	01770 302234	★★★★	Hotel	𝒸	𝒫𝒫
Belvedere Guest House	Alma Road, Brodick, Isle of Arran, KA27 8AZ	01770 302397	★★★	Guest House	朼	
Carrick Lodge	Pier Lodge, Brodick, Isle of Arran, KA27 8BH	01770 302550	★★★	Guest House		
Dunvegan House	Shore Road, Brodick, Isle of Arran, KA27 8AJ	01770 302811	★★★★	Guest House		
Glenartney	Mayish Road, Brodick, Isle of Arran, KA27 8BX	01770 302220	★★★	Guest House		𝒫𝒫𝒫
Glencloy Farm Guest House	Glen Cloy, Brodick, Isle of Arran, KA27 8DA	01770 302351	★★★	Guest House		
Invercloy	Shore Road, Brodick, Isle of Arran, KA27 8AJ	01770 302225	★★★	Guest House		
Kilmichael Country House Hotel	Brodick, Isle of Arran, KA27 8BY	01770 302219	★★★★	Country House Hotel		
Ormidale Hotel	Brodick, Isle of Arran, KA27 8BY	01770 302293	★★	Small Hotel		
Strathwhillan House	Strathwhillan Road, Brodick, Isle of Arran, KA27 8BQ	01770 302331	★★★	Guest House	朼	

Brora

Royal Marine Hotel	Golf Road, Brora, Sutherland, KW9 6GS	01408 621252	★★★★	Hotel	

Broughty Ferry

Dundee East Premier Inn	Bell Tree,115-117 Lawers Drive, Broughty Ferry, Dundee DD5 3UP	0870 9906324		Budget Hotel	
Hotel Broughty Ferry	16 West Queen Street, Broughty Ferry, Dundee DD5 1AR	01382 480027	★★★★	Small Hotel	
Redwood Guest House	89 Monifieth Road, Broughty Ferry, Dundee DD5 2SB	01382 736550	★★★★	Guest House	
The Fisherman's Tavern Hotel	10-16 Fort Street, Broughty Ferry, Dundee DD5 2AD	01382 775941	★★	Small Hotel	𝒸
The Fort Hotel	58-60 Fort Street, Broughty Ferry, Dundee DD5 2AB	01382 737999	★★	Small Hotel	

Broxburn

Bankhead Farm	Dechmont, Broxburn, West Lothian, EH52 6NB	01506 811209	★★★★	Guest House	

Bruichladdich, Isle of Islay

An Taigh Odsa	Main Street, Bruichladdich, Isle of Islay, PA49 7UN	01496 850587	AWAITING GRADING

Buckie

Marine Hotel	Marine Place, Buckie, Banffshire, AB56 1UT	01542 832249	★★★	Small Hotel	
The Old Coach House Hotel	26 High Street, Buckie, Banffshire, AB56 1AR	01542 836266	★★★	Hotel	

𝒸 Unassisted wheelchair access   佳 Assisted wheelchair access   朼 Access for visitors with mobility difficulties
𝒫 Bronze Green Tourism Award   𝒫𝒫 Silver Green Tourism Award   𝒫𝒫𝒫 Gold Green Tourism Award
For further information on our Green Tourism Business Scheme please see page 9.

To find out more, call 0845 22 55 121 or go to visitscotland.com.

Bucksburn

Craibstone Estate	Scottish Agricultural College,Craibstone Estate, Bucksburn, Aberdeenshire, AB21	01224 711012	★★	Campus	
Travelodge Aberdeen Bucksburn	A96 Inverurie Road, Bucksburn, Aberdeen, Aberdeenshire, AB21 0HW	08719 846118	AWAITING GRADING		

Bunessan, Isle of Mull

Ardachy House Hotel	Uisken, Bunessan, Isle of Mull, PA67 6DS	01681 700505	★★★	Small Hotel	

Burntisland

Kingswood Hotel	Kinghorn Road, Burntisland, Fife, KY3 9LL	01592 872329	★★★	Small Hotel	♿

Burray, Orkney

Sands Hotel	Burray, Orkney, KW17 2SS	01856 731298	★★★★	Small Hotel	

Busta, Shetland

Busta House Hotel	Busta, North Mainland, Shetland, ZE2 9QN	01806 522506	★★★	Country House Hotel	

Cairndow

Cairndow Stagecoach Inn	Cairndow, Argyll, PA26 8BN	01499 600286	★★	Inn	

Cairnryan

Cairnryan House	Main Street, Cairnryan, Wigtownshire, DG9 8QX	01581 200624	★★★	Guest House	
Rhins of Galloway	A77 Coast Road, Cairnryan, Stranraer, Wigtownshire, DG9 8QU	01581 200294	★★★	Guest House	

Callander

Abbotsford Lodge Guest House	Stirling Road, Callander, Perthshire, FK17 8DA	0877 330066	★★★	Guest House	
Annfield House	18 North Church Street, Callander, Perthshire, FK17 8EG	01877 330204	★★★★	Guest House	
Arden House	Bracklinn Road, Callander, Perthshire, FK17 8EQ	01877 330235	★★★★	Guest House	
Brook Linn Country House	Leny Feus, Callander, Perthshire, FK17 8AU	01877 330103	★★★★	Guest House	
Dalgair House Hotel	115 Main Street, Callander, Perthshire, FK17 8BQ	01877 330283	★	Small Hotel	
Dunmor House	Leny Road, Callander, Perthshire, FK17 8AL	01877 330756	★★★★	Guest House	
Lubnaig House	Leny Feus, Callander, Perthshire, FK17 8AS	01877 330376	★★★★	Guest House	
Poppies Hotel and Restaurant	Leny Road, Callander, Perthshire, FK17 8AL	01877 330329	★★★	Small Hotel	
Riverview House	Leny Road, Callander, Perthshire, FK17 8AL	01877 330635	★★★	Guest House	
Roman Camp Hotel	Main Street, Callander, Perthshire, FK17 8BG	01877 330003	★★★★	Country House Hotel	🚶
Southfork Villa	25 Cross Street, Callander, Perthshire, FK17 8EA	01877 330831	★★★★	Guest House	
The Crags Hotel	101 Main Street, Callander, Perthshire, FK17 8BQ	01877 330257	★★★	Guest House	🚶
The Knowe	Ancaster Road, Callander, Perthshire, FK17 8EL	01877 330076	★★★★	Guest House	

♿ Unassisted wheelchair access ♿ Assisted wheelchair access 🚶 Access for visitors with mobility difficulties
Bronze Green Tourism Award Silver Green Tourism Award Gold Green Tourism Award
For further information on our Green Tourism Business Scheme please see page 9.

Awards correct as of mid August 2008

| The Old Rectory Guest House | Leny Road, Callander, Perthshire, FK17 8AL | 01877 339215 | ★★★ | Guest House | 🚶 |

by Callander

| Auchenlaich Farmhouse Guest House | Auchenlaich Farmhouse, Keltie Bridge, by Callander, Perthshire, FK17 8LQ | 01877 331683 | ★★★★ | Guest House | |
| Loch Achray Hotel | by Callander, Perthshire, FK17 8HZ | 01877 376229 | ★★★ | Hotel | 🏵🏵 |

Callanish, Isle of Lewis

Eshcol Guest House	21 Breasclete, Callanish, Isle of Lewis, HS2 9DY	01851 621357	★★★★	Guest House	
Leumadair Guest House	7 Callanish, Isle of Lewis, HS2 9DY	01857 621706	★★★★	Guest House	
Loch Roag Guest House	22A Breasclete, Callanish, Isle of Lewis, HS2 9EF	01851 621357	★★★★	Guest House	

Calvine

| The Struan Inn | Calvine, Perthshire, PH18 5UB | 01796 483208 | ★★ | Inn | |

Campbeltown

Craigard House	Low Askomil, Campbeltown, Argyll, PA28 6EP	01586 554242	★★★	Small Hotel	
Dellwood Hotel	Drumore, Campbeltown, Argyll, PA28 6HD	01586 552465	★★	Small Hotel	
Westbank Guest House	Dell Road, Campbeltown, Argyll, PA28 6JG	01586 553660	★★★	Guest House	

Canonbie

| Cross Keys Hotel | Main Road, Canonbie, Dumfries & Galloway, DG14 0SY | 013873 71205 | ★★★ | Inn | |

Carluke

| Wallace Hotel | 1 Yieldshields Road, Carluke, Lanarkshire, ML8 4QG | 01555 773 000 | ★★ | Restaurant with Rooms | |

Carnoustie

Aboukir Hotel	38 Ireland Street, Carnoustie, Angus, DD7 6AT	01241 852149	★★	Small Hotel	
Seaview Guest House	29 Ireland Street, Carnoustie, Angus, DD7 6AS	01241 851092	★★★★	Guest House	
Station Hotel	Station Road, Carnoustie, Angus, DD7 6AR	01241 852447	★★	Small Hotel	

Carradale Hotel	Carradale, Argyll, PA28 6RY	01583 431223	★★★	Small Hotel	
Dunvalanree	Portrigh Bay, Carradale, Argyll, PA28 6SE	01583 431226	★★★★	Restaurant with Rooms	♿ 🏵🏵
Kiloran Guest House	Carradale, Argyll, PA28 6QG	01583 431795	★★★	Guest House	

Carrbridge

Carrmoor Guest House	Carr Road, Carrbridge, Inverness-shire, PH23 3AD	01479 841244	★★★	Guest House	
Craigellachie House	Main Street, Carrbridge, Inverness-shire, PH23 3AS	01479 841641	★★★★	Guest House	
Dalrachney Lodge Hotel	Carrbridge, Inverness-shire, PH23 3AT	01479 841252	★★★	Country House Hotel	

♿ Unassisted wheelchair access   ♿ Assisted wheelchair access   🚶 Access for visitors with mobility difficulties
🏵 Bronze Green Tourism Award   🏵🏵 Silver Green Tourism Award   🏵🏵🏵 Gold Green Tourism Award
For further information on our Green Tourism Business Scheme please see page 9.
To find out more, call 0845 22 55 121 or go to visitscotland.com.

209

| Fairwinds Hotel | Carrbridge, Inverness-shire, PH23 3AA | 01479 841240 | ★★★ | Small Hotel | |
| The Cairn Hotel | Main Road, Carrbridge, Inverness-shire, PH23 3AS | 01479 841212 | ★★★ | Inn | *P* |

Carrutherstown

| Hetland Hall Hotel | Carrutherstown, Dumfries & Galloway, DG1 4JX | 01387 840201 | ★★★ | Hotel | ♿ |

Castle Douglas

Crown Hotel	King Street, Castle Douglas, Kirkcudbrightshire, DG7 1AA	01556 502031	★★	Inn	
Douglas Arms Hotel	200 - 206 King Street, Castle Douglas, Kirkcudbrightshie, DG7 1DB	01556 502231	★★★	Hotel	
Kings Arms Hotel	St Andrew Street, Castle Douglas, Kirkcudbrightshire, DG7 1EL	01556 502626	★★★	Inn	
Market Inn Hotel	6/7 Queen Street, Castle Douglas, Kirkcudbrightshire, DG7 1HX	01556 505070	★★★	Inn	
Station Hotel	1 Queen Street, Castle Douglas, Kirkcudbrightshire, DG7 1HX	01556 502152	★★	Small Hotel	
The Urr Valley Hotel	Ernespie Road, Castle Douglas, Kirkcudbrightshire, DG7 3JG	01556 502188	★★	Country House Hotel	

by Castle Douglas

| Balcary Bay Hotel | Auchencairn, by Castle Douglas, Kirkcudbrightshire, DG7 1QZ | 01556 640217 | ★★★ | Country House Hotel | ♿ |

Castle Kennedy

| Plantings Inn | Castle Kennedy, Wigtownshire, DG9 8SQ | 01581 400633 | ★★★ | Inn | |

Castlebay, Isle of Barra

| Castlebay Hotel | Castlebay, Isle of Barra, HS9 5XD | 01871 810223 | AWAITING GRADING | | |
| Craigard Hotel | Castlebay, Isle of Barra, HS9 5XD | 01871 810200 | ★★★ | Small Hotel | |

Castletown

| Greenland House | Main Street, Castletown, Caithness, KW14 8TU | 01847 821694 | ★★★ | Guest House | |

Ceres

| Meldrums Hotel | 56 Main Street, Ceres, Fife, KY15 5NA | 01334 828286 | ★★ | Inn | |

Clarencefield

| Farmers Inn | Main Street, Clarencefield, Dumfries & Galloway, DG1 4NF | 01387 870675 | ★★ | Inn | |

Clarkston

| Busby Hotel | Field Road, Clarkston, Glasgow, G76 8RX | 0141 644 2661 | ★★ | Hotel | |

Clydebank

| The Beardmore Hotel & Conference Centre | Beardmore Street, Clydebank, Greater Glasgow, G81 4SA | 0141 9516000 | ★★★★ | Hotel | ♿ *PP* |

Coldingham

| Dunlaverock | Coldingham Bay, Coldingham, Berwickshire, TD14 5PA | 01890 771450 | ★★★★ | Guest House | ♿ |

♿ Unassisted wheelchair access   ♿ Assisted wheelchair access   ♿ Access for visitors with mobility difficulties
P Bronze Green Tourism Award   *PP* Silver Green Tourism Award   *PPP* Gold Green Tourism Award
For further information on our Green Tourism Business Scheme please see page 9.

Awards correct as of mid August 2008

211

Priory View	Eyemouth Road, Coldingham, Eyemouth, Berwickshire, TD14 5NH	01890 771525	★★★	Guest House

Colintraive

Colintraive Hotel	Colintraive, Argyll, PA22 3AS	01700 841207	★★★	Small Hotel

Collin

Travelodge Dumfires	A75 Annan Road, Collin, Dumfries & Galloway, DG1 3SE	08719 846134	AWAITING GRADING	

Comrie

Royal Hotel	Melville Square, Comrie, Perthshire, PH6 2DN	01764 679200	★★★	Small Hotel

Connel

Grove House	Main Street, Connel, Argyll, PA37 1PA	01631 710599	AWAITING GRADING	
Lochnell Arms Hotel	Connel, Argyll, PA37 1RP	01631 710239	★★★	Inn
Ronebhal Guest House	Connel, Argyll, PA37 1PJ	01631 710310	★★★★	Guest House
Wide Mouthed Frog	Dunstaffnage Marina, Connel, Argyll, PA37 1PX	01631 567005	★★★	Restaurant with Rooms ♿

by Conon Bridge

Kinkell Country House	Easter Kinkell, by Conon Bridge, Ross-shire, IV7 8HY	01349 861270	★★★	Small Hotel ⟨person⟩

Corpach

Mansefield Guest House	Corpach, Inverness-shire, PH33 7LT	01397 772262	★★★★	Guest House

Coupar Angus

Red House Hotel	Station Road, Coupar Angus, Perthshire, PH13 9AL	01828 628500	★★★	Inn ⟨person⟩

Coylton

The Kyle Hotel	40-42 Main Street, Coylton, Ayrshire, KA6 6JW	01292 570312	★★★	Inn

Craigellachie

Highlander Inn	Victoria Street, Craigellachie, Speyside, AB38 9SR	01340 881446	★★★	Inn
Jura Hotel	Craighouse, Isle of Jura, PA60 7UX	01496 820243	★★	Small Hotel

Craignure, Isle of Mull

Isle of Mull Hotel	Craignure, Isle of Mull, PA65 6BB	08709 506267	★★★	Hotel
Pennygate Lodge	Craignure, Isle of Mull, PA65 6AY	01680 812333	★★★	Guest House

Crail

Balcomie Links Hotel	Balcomie Road, Crail, Fife, KY10 3TN	01333 450237	★★	Small Hotel
Caiplie Guest House	53 High Street, Crail, Fife, KY10 3RA	01333 450564	★★★	Guest House
Golf Hotel	4 High Street, Crail, Fife, KY10 3TD	01333 450206	★★★	Inn

♿ Unassisted wheelchair access   ♿ Assisted wheelchair access   ⟨person⟩ Access for visitors with mobility difficulties
Ⓟ Bronze Green Tourism Award   ⒫⒫ Silver Green Tourism Award   ⒫⒫⒫ Gold Green Tourism Award
For further information on our Green Tourism Business Scheme please see page 9.

     To find out more, call 0845 22 55 121 or go to visitscotland.com.

Marine Hotel	54 Nethergate, Crail, Fife, KY10 3TZ	01333 450207	★★★	Guest House	
The Hazelton	29 Marketgate, Crail, Fife, KY10 3TH	01333 450250	★★★	Guest House	
The Honeypot Guest House	6 High Street South, Crail, Fife, KY10 3TD	01333 450935	AWAITING GRADING		

Crianlarich

Ewich House	Strathfillan, Crianlarich, Perthshire, FK20 8RU	01838 300300	★★★★	Guest House	
Glenardran	Crianlarich, Perthshire, FK20 8QS	01838 300236	★★★	Guest House	
Highland Hotel	Crianlarich, Perthshire, FK20 8RW	01838 300272	★★★	Hotel	
Inverardran House	A85, Crianlarich, Perthshire, FK20 8QS	01838 300240	★★★	Guest House	
Riverside Guest House	Tigh Na Struith, Crianlarich, Perthshire, FK20 8RU	01838 300235	★★	Guest House	
Suie Lodge Hotel	Glendochart, Crianlarich, Perthshire, FK20 8QT	01567 820417	★★	Small Hotel	
The Lodge House	Crianlarich, Perthshire, FK20 8RU	01838 300276	★★★★	Guest House	
The Luib Hotel	Glendochart, Crianlarich, Perthshire, FK20 8QT	01567 820664	AWAITING GRADING		
West Highland Lodge	Crianlarich, Perthshire, FK20 8RU	01838 300283	★★★	Guest House	

by Crianlarich

Tyndrum Lodge	Tyndrum, by Crianlarich, Perthshire, FK20 8RY	01838 400219	★★	Inn	

Crieff

Achray House Hotel	St Fillans, Crieff, Perthshire, PH6 2NF	01764 685231	★★★	Small Hotel	⋏
Arduthie House	Perth Road, Crieff, Perthshire, PH7 3EQ	01764 653113	★★★★	Guest House	
Comely Bank Guest House	32 Burrell Street, Crieff, Perthshire, PH7 4DT	01764 653409	★★★	Guest House	♿
Crieff Hydro Hotel	Crieff, Perthshire, PH7 3LQ	01764 655555	★★★★	Hotel	⋏
Fendoch Guest House	Sma' Glen, Crieff, Perthshire, PH7 3LW	01764 655619	★★★	Guest House	⋏
Galvelbeg House	Perth Road, Crieff, Perthshire, PH7 3EQ	01764 655061	★★★	Guest House	
Kingarth	Perth Road, Crieff, Perthshire, PH7 3EQ	01764 652060	★★★	Guest House	
Leven House Hotel	Comrie Road, Crieff, Perthshire, PH7 4BA	01764 652529	★★	Small Hotel	
Murraypark Hotel	Connaught Terrace, Crieff, Perthshire, PH7 3DJ	01764 658000	★★★	Hotel	♿
The Crieff Hotel	45-47 East High Street, Crieff, Perthshire, PH7 3HY	01764 652632	★★	Inn	
The Knock Castle Hotel and Spa	Drummond Terrace, Crieff, Perthshire, PH7 4AN	01764 653806	AWAITING GRADING		
Yann's At Glenearn House	Perth Road, Crieff, Perthshire, PH7 3EQ	01764 650111	★★★★	Restaurant with Rooms	

by Crieff

Cultoquhey House	Gilmerton, by Crieff, Perthshire, PH7 3NE	01764 653253	★	Guest House	

♿ Unassisted wheelchair access   ♿ Assisted wheelchair access   ⋏ Access for visitors with mobility difficulties
🄿 Bronze Green Tourism Award   🄿🄿 Silver Green Tourism Award   🄿🄿🄿 Gold Green Tourism Award
For further information on our Green Tourism Business Scheme please see page 9.

Foulford Inn	Sma'Glen, by Crieff, Perthshire, PH7 3LN	01764 652407	★★	Inn	

Crinan

Crinan Hotel	Crinan, Argyll, PA31 8SR	01546 830261	★★★★	Small Hotel	

Crocketford, by Dumfries

Galloway Arms Hotel	Crocketford, by Dumfries, Dumfries & Galloway, DG2 8RA	01556 690248	★★	Small Hotel	
Lochview Motel & Restaurant	Crocketford, by Dumfries, Dumfries & Galloway, DG2 8RF	01556 690281	★	Lodge	

Cruden Bay

Kilmarnock Arms Hotel	Bridge Street, Cruden Bay AB42 0HD	01779 812213	★★★	Small Hotel	

Cullen

Crannoch Hotel	12 Blantyre Street, Cullen, Banffshire, AB56 4RQ	01542 840210	★★★	Inn	
Norwood House	11 Seafield Place, Cullen, Banffshire, AB56 4TE	01542 840314	★★★	Guest House	
Seafield Arms Hotel	19 Seafield Street, Cullen, Banffshire, AB56 4SG	01542 840791	★★★	Hotel	

Cumbernauld

Castlecary House Hotel	Castlecary Road,Castlecary, Cumbernauld, North Lanarkshire, G68	01324 840233	★★★	Hotel	♀
Glasgow Cumbernauld Premier Inn	4 South Muirhead Road, Cumbernauld, North Lanarkshire, G67 1AX	08701 977108		Budget Hotel	
Westerwood Hotel	1 St Andrews Drive, Cumbernauld, North Lanarkshire, G68 0EW	01236 457171	★★★★	Hotel	⌀

Cumnock

Lochside House Hotel	Cumnock, Ayrshire, KA18 4PN	01290 333000	★★★★	Hotel	♀
Royal Hotel	1 Glaisnock Street, Cumnock, Ayrshire, KA18 1BP	01290 420822	★★★	Small Hotel	

Cupar

Craigsanquhar Country House Hotel	Logie, Cupar, Fife, KY15 4PZ	01334 653426	★★★	Country House Hotel	

by Cupar

The Peat Inn	by Cupar, Fife, KY15 5LH	01334 840206	★★★★★	Restaurant with Rooms	

Dalbeattie

Rosemount	Kippford, Dalbeattie, Kirkcudbrightshire, DG5 4LN	01556 620214	★★★★	Guest House	

by Dalbeattie

Clonyard House Hotel	Colvend, by Dalbeattie, Kircudbrightshire, DG5 4QW	01556 630372	★★★	Country House Hotel	♀
Baron's Craig Hotel	Rockcliffe, by Dalbeattie, Kirkcudbrightshire, DG5 4QF	01556 630225	★★	Hotel	

Daliburgh, Isle of South Uist

Borrodale Hotel	Daliburgh, Isle of South Uist, HS8 5SS	01878 700400 [D [D4	★★★	Small Hotel	

⟨&⟩ Unassisted wheelchair access   ⟨&⟩ Assisted wheelchair access   ♀ Access for visitors with mobility difficulties
⟨P⟩ Bronze Green Tourism Award   ⟨PP⟩ Silver Green Tourism Award   ⟨PPP⟩ Gold Green Tourism Award
For further information on our Green Tourism Business Scheme please see page 9.

214   To find out more, call 0845 22 55 121 or go to visitscotland.com.

Dalkeith

The County Hotel	152 High Street, Dalkeith, Midlothian, EH22	0131 663 3495	★★★	Hotel
Newbattle Abbey College	Newbattle Road, Dalkeith, Midlothian, EH22 3LL	0131 663 1921	★★	Campus

Dalmally

Dalmally Hotel	Dalmally, Argyll, PA33 1AY	01838 200444	★★★	Hotel	
Glenorchy Lodge Hotel	Dalmally, Argyll, PA33 1AA	01838 200312	★★★	Small Hotel	人
Loch Awe Hotel	Loch Awe, Dalmally, Argyll, PA33 1AQ	01838 200261	★★★	Hotel	

Dalry

Blair House	Blair, Dalry, Ayrshire, KA24 4ER	01294 833100	★★★★★	Exclusive Use Venue

Dalrymple

Kirkton Inn	1-3 Main Street, Dalrymple, Ayrshire, KA6 6DF	01292 560241	★★	Inn

Dervaig, Isle of Mull

Bellachroy Hotel	Dervaig, Isle of Mull, PA75 6QW	01688 400314	★★★	Inn
Calgary Hotel	Dervaig, Isle of Mull, PA75 6QW	01688 400256	★★★	Restaurant with Rooms
Druimnacroish	Dervaig, Isle of Mull, PA75 6QW	01688 400274	★★★	Guest House

Dirleton

Open Arms Hotel	Dirleton, East Lothian, EH39 5EG	01620 850241	★★★	Small Hotel

Dollar

Castle Campbell Hotel	Bridge Street, Dollar, Clackmannanshire, FK14 7DE	01259 742519	★★★	Small Hotel	𝒫𝒫𝒫

Dornoch

Dornoch Castle Hotel	Castle Street, Dornoch, Sutherland, IV25 3SD	01862 810216	★★★	Hotel	人	𝒫
Dornoch Hotel	Dornoch, Sutherland, IV25 3LD	01862 810351	★★	Hotel		
Eagle Hotel	Dornoch, Sutherland, IV25 3SR	01862 810008	★★★	Small Hotel		

Dounby, Orkney

Smithfield Hotel	Dounby, Orkney, KW17 2HT	01856 771215	★★	Inn

Drumnadrochit

Benleva Hotel	Drumnadrochit, Inverness-shire, IV63 6UH	01456 450080	★★	Inn
Drumnadrochit Hotel	Drumnadrochit, Inverness-shire, IV63 6TU	01456 450218	★★★	Inn
Loch Ness Inn	Lewiston, Drumnadrochit, Inverness-shire, IV63 6UW	07889 496092	★★★	Inn
Loch Ness Lodge Hotel	Drumnadrochit, Inverness-shire, IV63 6TU	01456 450342	★★★	Hotel

♿ Unassisted wheelchair access   ♿ Assisted wheelchair access   人 Access for visitors with mobility difficulties
𝒫 Bronze Green Tourism Award   𝒫𝒫 Silver Green Tourism Award   𝒫𝒫𝒫 Gold Green Tourism Award
For further information on our Green Tourism Business Scheme please see page 9.

| Woodlands | East Lewiston, Drumnadrochit, Inverness-shire, IV63 6UJ | 01456 450356 | ★★★★ | Guest House | ⓙ |

Drymen

Buchanan Arms Hotel & Leisure Club	Main Street, Drymen, Stirlingshire, G63 0BQ	01360 660588	★★★	Hotel		ⓟ
Winnock Hotel	The Square, Drymen, Stirlingshire, G63 0BL	01360 660245	★★★	Hotel	ⓙ	ⓟⓟⓟ
Rowardennan Hotel	Rowardennan, Drymen, Stirlingshire, G63 0AR	01360 870273	★★★	Small Hotel	

Duchally, Auchterarder

| Duchally Country Estate | Duchally Country Estate, Duchally, Auchterarder, Perthshire, PH3 1PN | 01764 663071 | ★★★★ | Country House Hotel | | ⓟⓟ |

Dufftown

| Gowan Brae | 19 Church Street, Dufftown, Banffshire, AB55 4AR | 01340 821344 | ★★★ | Guest House |
| Tannochbrae Guest House & Scotts Restaurant | 22 Fife Street, Dufftown, Banffshire, AB55 4AL | 01340 820541 | ★★★ | Guest House |

Dulnain Bridge

| Rosegrove Guest House | Skye of Curr Road, Dulnain Bridge, Inverness-shire, PH26 3PA | 01479 851335 | ★★★ | Guest House |

Dumbarton

| The Abbotsford Hotel | Stirling Road, Dumbarton, Dunbartonshire, G82 2PJ | 01389 733304 | ★★★ | Hotel |

Dumfries

Aberdour Hotel	16-20 Newall Terrace, Dumfries, Dumfries & Galloway, DG1 1LW	01387 252060	★★	Small Hotel	
Aston Hotel	The Crichton, Bankend Road, Dumfries, Dumfries & Galloway, DG1 4ZZ	0845 6340205	★★★	Hotel	ⓙ
Cairndale Hotel & Leisure Club	English Street, Dumfries, Dumfries & Galloway, DG1 2DF	01387 254111	★★★	Hotel	
Dalston House Hotel	5 Laurieknowe, Dumfries, Dumfries & Galloway, DG2 7AH	01387 254422	★★★	Small Hotel	
Dumfries Premier Inn	Solway Gate, Annan Road, Collin, Dumfries, Dumfries & Galloway, DG1	08701 977078		Budget Hotel	
Edenbank Hotel	17 Laurieknowe, Dumfries, Dumfries & Galloway, DG2 7AH	01387 252759	★★	Small Hotel	
Hamilton House	12 Moffat Road, Dumfries, Dumfries & Galloway, DG1 1NJ	01387 266606	★★★★	Guest House	
Huntingdon House	18 St Marys Street, Dumfries, Dumfries & Galloway, DG1 1LZ	01387 254893	★★★★	Guest House	
Lochenlee Guest House	32 Ardwall Road, Dumfries, Dumfries & Galloway, DG1 3AQ	01387 265153	★★★	Guest House	
Moreig Hotel	67 Annan Road, Dumfries, Dumfries & Galloway, DG1 3EG	01387 255524	★★★	Small Hotel	
Queensberry Hotel	16 English Street, Dumfries, Dumfries & Galloway, DG1 2BT	01387 739913	★★	Small Hotel	
Rivendell	105 Edinburgh Road, Dumfries, Dumfries & Galloway, DG1 1JX	01387 252251	★★★★	Guest House	
Station Hotel	49 Lovers Walk, Dumfries, Dumfries & Galloway, DG1 1LT	01387 254316	★★★	Hotel	ⓟⓟⓟ
Torbay Lodge	31 Lovers Walk, Dumfries, Dumfries & Galloway, DG1 1LR	01387 253922	★★★★	Guest House	ⓚ
White Hart Hotel	Brewery Street, Dumfries, Dumfries & Galloway, DG1 2RP	01387 253337	★★	Inn	

⓰ Unassisted wheelchair access   ⓙ Assisted wheelchair access   ⓚ Access for visitors with mobility difficulties
ⓟ Bronze Green Tourism Award   ⓟⓟ Silver Green Tourism Award   ⓟⓟⓟ Gold Green Tourism Award
For further information on our Green Tourism Business Scheme please see page 9.

216   To find out more, call 0845 22 55 121 or go to visitscotland.com.

by Dumfries

Abbey Arms Hotel	1 The Square,New Abbey, by Dumfries, Dumfries & Galloway, DG2 8BX	01387 850489	★★	Inn	
Steamboat Inn	Carsethorn,Kirkbean, by Dumfries, Dumfries & Galloway, DG2 8DS	01387 880 631	★★★	Inn	
Cavens	Kirkbean, by Dumfries, Dumfries & Galloway, DG2 8AA	01387 880234	★★★★	Country House Hotel	

Dunbar

Barns Ness Hotel	Station Road, Dunbar, East Lothian, EH42 1JY	01368 863231	★★★	Small Hotel	
Springfield Guest House	Belhaven Road, Dunbar, East Lothian, EH42 1NH	01368 862502	★★★	Guest House	
The Rossborough Hotel	Queens Road, Dunbar, East Lothian, EH42 1LG	01368 862356	★★★	Small Hotel	

Dunblane

| Cromlix House | Kinbuck, Dunblane, Perthshire, FK15 9JT | 01786 822125 | ★★★★ | Country House Hotel | |
| Dunblane Hydro | Perth Road, Dunblane, Perthshire, FK15 0HG | 01786 822551 | AWAITING GRADING | | |

Dundee

Aberlaw Guest House	230 Broughty Ferry Road, Dundee DD4 7JP	01382 456929	★★★	Guest House	
Alcorn Guest House	5 Hyndford Street, Dundee DD2 1HQ	01382 668433	★★★	Guest House	
Anderson's Guest House	285 Perth Road, Dundee DD2 1JS	01382 668585	★★★	Guest House	
Apex City Quay Hotel & Spa	1 West Victoria Dock Road, Dundee DD1 3JP	01382 202402	★★★★	Hotel	🍃🍃🍃
Cullaig Guest House	1 Rosemount Terrace, Dundee DD3 6JQ	01382 322154	★★★	Guest House	
Dundee North Premier Inn	Outside Inn,Camperdown Leisure Park,Dayton Drive, Kingsway, Dundee	0870 9906420		Budget Hotel	
Dundee West Premier Inn	Gourdie House, Kingsway West, Dundee DD2 5JU	08701 977081		Budget Hotel	
Dunlaw House Hotel	10 Union Terrace, Dundee DD3 6JD	01382 221703	★★	Small Hotel	
Errolbank Guest House	9 Dalgleish Road, Dundee DD4 7JN	01382 462118	★★★	Guest House	
Grosvenor Hotel	1 Grosvenor Road, Dundee DD2 1LF	01382 642991	★★★	Guest House	
Hilton Dundee	Earl Grey Place, Dundee DD1 4DE	01382 229271	★★★★	Hotel	♟
Invercarse Hotel	371 Perth Road, Dundee DD2 1PG	01382 669231	★★★	Hotel	
Park House Hotel	40 Coupar Angus Road, Dundee DD2 3HY	01382 611151	★★★	Small Hotel	
Premier Inn Dundee Centre	Discovery Quay, Riverside Drive, Dundee DD1 4XA	08701 977079		Budget Hotel	
Queens Hotel	160 Nethergate, Dundee DD1 4DU	01382 322515	★★★	Hotel	
Shaftesbury Hotel	1 Hyndford Street, Dundee DD2 1HQ	01382 669216	★★★	Small Hotel	
St Leonard B&B	22 Albany Terrace, Dundee DD3 6HR	01382 227146/22746	★	Guest House	
Strathdon Guest House	277 Perth Road, Dundee DD2 1JS	01382 665648	★★★	Guest House	

     ♿ Unassisted wheelchair access   🦽 Assisted wheelchair access   ♟ Access for visitors with mobility difficulties
🍃 Bronze Green Tourism Award   🍃🍃 Silver Green Tourism Award   🍃🍃🍃 Gold Green Tourism Award
For further information on our Green Tourism Business Scheme please see page 9.

Swallow Hotel	Kingsway West,Invergowrie, Dundee DD2 5JT	01382 641122	AWAITING GRADING		
Taychreggan Hotel	4 Ellieslea Road, Broughty Ferry, Dundee DD5 1JG	01382 778626	★★★	Small Hotel	
The Craigtay Hotel	101 Broughty Ferry Road, Dundee DD4 6JE	01382 451142	★★	Small Hotel	
The Grampian	295 Perth Road, Dundee DD2 1JS	01382 667785	★★★	Guest House	
Travelodge Dundee	A90 Kingsway, Dundee DD2 4TD	08719 846135	AWAITING GRADING		
Travelodge Dundee Central	152-158 West Marketgait, Dundee DD1 1NJ	08719 846301	AWAITING GRADING		
West Park Centre	319 Perth Road, Dundee DD2 1NN	01382 647177	★★★	Campus	♿
Woodlands Hotel	13 Panmure Terrace, Barnhill, Dundee DD5 2QL	01382 480033	★★★	Hotel	
Your Hotel	296a Strathmore Avenue, Dundee DD3 6SP	01382 826000	★★	Lodge	♿

Dunfermline

Best Western Keavil House Hotel	Crossford, Dunfermline, Fife, KY12 8QW	01383 736258	★★★	Country House Hotel	🦽	🌿🌿
Clarke Cottage Guest House	139 Halbeath Road, Dunfermline, Fife, KY11 4LA	01383 735935	★★★	Guest House	🚶	
Davaar House Hotel	126 Grieve Street, Dunfermline, KY12 8DW	01383 721886	★★★	Small Hotel		
Express by Holiday Inn Dunfermline	Halbeath, Dunfermline, Fife, KY11 8DY	01383 748220	★★★	Metro Hotel	♿	
Garvock House Hotel	St John's Drive, Transy, Dunfermline, Fife, KY12 7TU	01383 621067	★★★★	Hotel	🦽	
King Malcolm Hotel	Queensferry Road, Dunfermline, KY11 8DS	01383 722611	★★★	Hotel		
Pitbauchlie House Hotel	Aberdour Road, Dunfermline, Fife, KY11 4PB	01383 722282	★★★	Hotel	🚶	
Pitreavie Guest House	3 Aberdour Road, Dunfermline, Fife, KY11 4PB	01383 724244	★★★	Guest House		
Premier Inn Dunfermline	Crooked Glen, Fife Leisure Park, Whimbrel Place, Dunfermline, Fife, KY11	0870 600 1486		Budget Hotel		
Rooms at 29 Bruce Street	29-35 Bruce Street, Dunfermline, Fife, KY12 7AG	01383 840041	AWAITING GRADING		

Dunkeld

Atholl Arms Hotel	Tay Street, Bridgehead, Dunkeld, Perthshire, PH8 OAQ	01350 727219	★★★	Small Hotel	
Hilton Dunkeld	Dunkeld, Perthshire, PH8 0HX	01350 727771	★★★★	Hotel	🌿🌿
Royal Dunkeld Hotel	Atholl Street, Dunkeld, Perthshire, PH8 0AR	01350 727322	★★★	Hotel	

by Dunkeld

| The Birnam Guest House | 4 Murthly Terrace,Birnam, by Dunkeld, Perthshire, PH8 0BG | 01350 727201 | ★★★ | Guest House |
| Kinnaird | Kinnaird Estate,Dalguise, by Dunkeld, Perthshire, PH8 0LB | 01796 482440 | ★★★★★ | Country House Hotel |

Dunoon

| Abbot's Brae Hotel | West Bay, Dunoon, Argyll, PA23 7QJ | 01369 705021 | ★★★★ | Small Hotel |
| Ardtully Guest House | 297 Marine Parade, Hunters Quay, Dunoon, Argyll, PA23 3HN | 01369 702478 | ★★★ | Guest House |

♿ Unassisted wheelchair access   🦽 Assisted wheelchair access   🚶 Access for visitors with mobility difficulties
🌿 Bronze Green Tourism Award   🌿🌿 Silver Green Tourism Award   🌿🌿🌿 Gold Green Tourism Award
For further information on our Green Tourism Business Scheme please see page 9.

Argyll Hotel	Argyll Street, Dunoon, Argyll, PA23 7NE	01369 702059	★★★	Hotel	
Bay House	West Bay Promenade, Dunoon, Argyll, PA23 7HU	01369 704832	★★★	Guest House	🍃
Craigen	85 Argyll Street, Dunoon, Argyll, PA23 7DH	01369 702307	★★	Guest House	
Craigieburn	Alexandra Parade, East Bay, Dunoon, Argyll, PA23 8AN	01369 702048	★★	Guest House	
Dhailling Lodge	155 Alexandra Parade, Dunoon, Argyll, PA23 8AW	07051 130655	★★★★	Guest House	
Enmore Hotel	111 Marine Parade, Dunoon, Argyll, PA23 8HH	01369 702230	★★★★	Small Hotel	
Esplanade Hotel	West Bay, Dunoon, Argyll, PA23 7HU	01369 704070	★★★	Hotel	
Hunters Quay Hotel	Marine Parade, Dunoon, Argyll, PA23 8HJ	01369 707070	★★★★	Small Hotel	🍃🍃
Mayfair Hotel	7 Clyde Street, Kirn, Dunoon, Argyll, PA23 8DX	01369 703803	★★★	Guest House	
Milton Tower Guest House	West Bay, Dunoon, Argyll, PA23 7LD	01369 705785	★★★	Guest House	
Park Hotel	3 Glenmorag Avenue, Dunoon, Argyll, PA23 7LG	01369 702383	★★★	Hotel	
Royal Marine Hotel	Hunter's Quay, Dunoon, Argyll, PA23 8HJ	01369 705810	★★★	Hotel	
Sebright	41A Alexandra Parade, Dunoon, Argyll, PA23 8AF	01369 702099	★★	Guest House	
St Ives Hotel	West Bay, Dunoon, Argyll, PA23 7HU	01369 702400	★★	Guest House	
The Cedars	51 Alexandra Parade, East Bay, Dunoon, Argyll, PA23 8AF	01369 702425	★★★★	Guest House	
West End Hotel	54 Victoria Parade, Dunoon, Argyll, PA23 7HU	01369 702907	★★	Small Hotel	

by Dunoon

The Osborne Hotel	44 Shore Road, Innellan, by Dunoon, Argyll, PA23 7TJ	01369 830445	★★	Small Hotel	
The Cot House Hotel	by Sandbank, Kilmun, by Dunoon, Argyll, PA23 8QS	01369 840260	★★	Inn	
Coylet Inn	Loch Eck, by Dunoon, Argyll, PA23 8SG	01369 840426	★★★	Inn	

Duns

Duns Castle	Duns, Berwickshire, TD11 3NW	01361 883211	★★★★	Exclusive Use Venue	

by Duns

Chirnside Hall Hotel	Chirnside, by Duns, Berwickshire, TD11 3LD	01890 818219	★★★★	Country House Hotel	

Duntocher

West Park Hotel	Great Western Road, Duntocher, Clydebank, G81 6DB	01389 872333	★★	Hotel	🚶

Dunure

The Dunure Inn	9-11 Harbour View, Dunure, Ayrshire, KA7 4LN	01292 500549	★★★	Inn	

Dunvegan, Isle of Skye

Dunorin House Hotel	2 Herebost, Dunvegan, Isle of Skye, IV55 8GZ	01470 521488	★★★	Small Hotel	

♿ Unassisted wheelchair access   ♿ Assisted wheelchair access   🚶 Access for visitors with mobility difficulties
🍃 Bronze Green Tourism Award   🍃🍃 Silver Green Tourism Award   🍃🍃🍃 Gold Green Tourism Award
For further information on our Green Tourism Business Scheme please see page 9.

Dunvegan Hotel	Main Street, Dunvegan, Isle of Skye, IV55 8WA	01470 521497	★★★	Small Hotel
Roskhill House	Roskhill, Dunvegan, Isle of Skye, IV55 8ZD	01470 521317	★★★	Guest House
The Tables	Main Street, Dunvegan, Isle of Skye, IV55 8WA	01470 521404	★★	Guest House

by Dunvegan, Isle of Skye

Three Chimneys	Colbost, by Dunvegan, Isle of Skye, IV55 8ZT	01470 511258	★★★★★	Restaurant with Rooms

Durness

Wild Orchid Guest House	Durine, Durness, Sutherland, IV27 4PN	01971 511280	★★★	Guest House

Dyce

Speedbird Inn	Argyll Road, Dyce, Aberdeen, Aberdeenshire, AB21 0AF	01224 772883	★★★	Hotel	♿
Travelodge Aberdeen Aiport	Burnside Drive Off Riverview Drive, Dyce, Aberdeen, Aberdeenshire, AB21	0871 984 6309	AWAITING GRADING		

Earlston

Broomfield House	10 Thorn Street, Earlston, Berwickshire, TD4 6DR	01896 848084	★★★	Guest House

East Calder

Ashcroft Farmhouse	7 Raw Holdings, East Calder, West Lothian, EH53 0ET	01506 881810	★★★★	Guest House

East Kilbride

Crutherland House Hotel	Strathaven Road, East Kilbride, Lanarkshire, G75 0QJ	01355 577000	★★★★	Hotel
Glasgow East Kilbride Central Premier Inn	Crooked Lum, Brunel Way, The Murray, East Kilbride G75 0JY	08701 977110		Budget Hotel
Glasgow East Kilbride Premier Inn	Kingway East, Meadow Place, Nerston, East Kilbride, Lanarkshire, G74 3AW	08708 506324		Budget Hotel
Glasgow East Kilbride Premier Inn	Eaglesham Road, East Kilbride, Glasgow, G75 8LW	0870 9906542		Budget Hotel
Torrance Hotel	135 Main Street, East Kilbride, Lanarkshire, G74 4LN	013552 25241	★★	Small Hotel

East Linton

Linton Hotel	3 Bridgend, East Linton, East Lothian, EH40 3AF	01620 860202	★★★	Restaurant with Rooms

Eastriggs

The Graham Arms Guest House	The Rand, Eastriggs, Dumfries & Galloway, DG12 6NL	01461 40031	★★★	Guest House	♟

Ecclefechan

Cressfield Country House Hotel	Townfoot, Ecclefechan, Dumfries & Galloway, DG11 3DR	01576 300281	★★★	Small Hotel

Eddleston

The Horseshoe Inn	Eddleston, Peeblshire, EH45 8QP	01721 730225	★★★★	Restaurant with Rooms

Edinburgh

A Haven Townhouse	180 Ferry Road, Edinburgh EH6 4NS	0131 554 6559	★★★	Metro Hotel

♿ Unassisted wheelchair access   ♿ Assisted wheelchair access   ♟ Access for visitors with mobility difficulties
🍁 Bronze Green Tourism Award   🍁🍁 Silver Green Tourism Award   🍁🍁🍁 Gold Green Tourism Award
For further information on our Green Tourism Business Scheme please see page 9.

220   To find out more, call 0845 22 55 121 or go to visitscotland.com.

Name	Address	Phone	Rating	Type	Access	Green
Aaran Lodge Guest House	30 Milton Road East, Edinburgh EH15 2NW	0131 657 5615	★★★★	Guest House		
Aaron Lodge	128 Old Dalkeith Road, Edinburgh EH16 4SD	0131 664 2755	★★★★	Guest House		
Abbey Lodge Hotel	137 Drum Street, Gilmerton, Edinburgh EH17 8RJ	0131 6649548	★★	Guest House	🕴	
Abbotsford Guest House	36 Pilrig Street, Edinburgh EH6 5AL	0131 554 2706	★★★	Guest House		
Abbotshead House	40 Minto Street, Edinburgh EH9 2BR	0131 668 1658	★★	Guest House		
Abcorn Guest House	4 Mayfield Gardens, Edinburgh EH9 2BU	0131 667 6548	★★★	Guest House		
Abercorn Guest House	1 Abercorn Terrace, Edinburgh EH15 2DD	0131 6696139	★★★★	Guest House		
Acer Lodge Guest House	425 Queensferry Road, Edinburgh EH4 7NB	0131 3362554	★★★★	Guest House		
Adria House	11-12 Royal Terrace, Edinburgh EH7 5AB	0131 556 7875	★★★	Guest House		
Afton Guest House	1 Hartington Gardens, Edinburgh EH10 4LD	0131 229 1019	★★★	Guest House		
Ailsa Craig Hotel	24 Royal Terrace, Edinburgh EH7 5AH	0131 556 1022	★★	Metro Hotel		
Airdenair Guest House	29 Kilmaurs Road, Edinburgh EH16 5DB	0131 668 2336	★★★	Guest House		
Airlie Guest House	29 Minto Street, Edinburgh EH9 1SB	0131 667 3562	★★★	Guest House		
Albyn Town House	16 Hartington Gardens, Edinburgh EH10 4LD	0131 229 6459	★★★	Guest House		
Allison House	17 Mayfield Gardens, Edinburgh EH9 2AX	0131 667 8049	★★★★	Guest House		
Alloway Guest House	96 Pilrig Street, Edinburgh EH6 5AY	0131 554 1786	★★★	Guest House		
Alness Guest House	27 Pilrig Street, Edinburgh EH6 5AN	0131 554 1187	★★	Guest House		
Amaragua Guest House	10 Kilmaurs Terrace, Edinburgh EH16 5DR	0131 667 6775	★★★★	Guest House		🍃🍃
Apex City	61 Grassmarket, Edinburgh EH1 2JF	0131 300 3456	★★★★	Hotel		🍃🍃🍃
Apex European Hotel	90 Haymarket Terrace, Edinburgh EH12 5LQ	0131 474 3400	★★★	Hotel		🍃🍃🍃
Apex International Hotel	31/35 Grassmarket, Edinburgh EH1 2HY	0131 300 3456	★★★★	Hotel		🍃🍃🍃
Appin House	4 Queens Crescent, Edinburgh EH9 2AZ	0131 668 2947	★★	Guest House		
Ardblair Guest House	1 Duddingston Crescent, Milton Road, Edinburgh EH15 3AS	0131 6203081	★★★	Guest House		
Ardenlee Guest House	9 Eyre Place, Edinburgh EH3 5ES	0131 5562838	★★★	Guest House		
Ardgarth Guest House	1 St Mary's Place, Portobello, Edinburgh EH15 2QF	0131 669 3021	★★★	Guest House	♿	
Ardleigh Guest House	260 Ferry Road, Edinburgh EH5 3AN	0131 552 1833	★★★	Guest House		
Ardmillan Hotel	9-10 Ardmillan Terrace, Edinburgh EH11 2JW	0131 337 9588	★★	Small Hotel		
Ardmor House	74 Pilrig Street, Edinburgh EH6 5AS	0131 554 4944	★★★★	Guest House		
Ard-Na-Said	5 Priestfield Road, Edinburgh EH16 5HH	0131 667 8754	★★★★	Guest House		
Arrandale Guest House	28 Mayfield Gardens, Edinburgh EH9 2BZ	0131 622 2232	★★★	Guest House		

♿ Unassisted wheelchair access   ♿ Assisted wheelchair access   🕴 Access for visitors with mobility difficulties
🍃 Bronze Green Tourism Award   🍃🍃 Silver Green Tourism Award   🍃🍃🍃 Gold Green Tourism Award
For further information on our Green Tourism Business Scheme please see page 9.

Name	Address	Phone	Rating	Type	Green
Ascot Guest House	98 Dalkeith Road, Edinburgh EH16 5AF	0131 667 1500	★	Guest House	
Ashdene House	23 Fountainhall Road, Edinburgh EH9 2LN	0131 6676026	★★★★	Guest House	୧୧୧
Ashgrove House	12 Osborne Terrace, Edinburgh EH12 5HG	0131 337 5014	★★★	Guest House	
Ashlyn Guest House	42 Inverleith Row, Edinburgh EH3 5PY	0131 552 2954	★★★	Guest House	
Auld Reekie Guest House	16 Mayfield Gardens, Edinburgh EH9 2BZ	0131 667 6177	★★★	Guest House	
Averon Guest House	44 Gilmore Place, Edinburgh EH3 9NQ	0131 229 9932	★★	Guest House	
Ayden Guest House	70 Pilrig Street, Edinburgh EH6 5AS	0131 554 2187	★★★★	Guest House	
Aynetree Guest House	12 Duddingston Crescent, Milton Road, Edinburgh EH15 3AS	0131 258 2821	★★★	Guest House	
Baird, Lee, Ewing and Turner House	18 Holyrood Park Road, Edinburgh EH16 5AY	0131 651 2011	★★	Campus	
Ballantrae Albany Hotel	39/43 Albany Street, Edinburgh EH1 3QY	0131 556 0397	AWAITING GRADING		
Ballantrae Hotel	8 York Place, Edinburgh EH1 3EP	0131 478 4748	★★★	Metro Hotel	
Ballantrae Hotel At The West End	6 Grosvenor Crescent, Edinburgh EH12 5EP	0131 225 7033	AWAITING GRADING		
Balmore House	34 Gilmore Place, Edinburgh EH3 9NQ	0131 2211331	★★★★	Guest House	
Barcelo Carlton Hotel	North Bridge, Edinburgh EH1 1SD	0131 472 3109	★★★★	Hotel	
Barrosa Guest House	21 Pilrig Street, Edinburgh EH6 5AN	0131 554 3700	★★	Guest House	
Ben Craig House	3 Craigmillar Park, Edinburgh EH16 5PG	0131 667 2593	★★★	Guest House	⃦
Ben Cruachan	17 McDonald Road, Edinburgh EH7 4LX	0131 556 3709	★★★★	Guest House	
Ben Doran	11 Mayfield Gardens, Edinburgh EH9 2AX	0131 667 8488	★★★★	Guest House	
Best Western Edinburgh City Hotel	79 Lauriston Place, Edinburgh EH3 9HZ	0131 622 7979	★★★	Hotel	
Bonnington Guest House	202 Ferry Road, Edinburgh EH6 4NW	0131 554 7610	★★★★	Guest House	
Brae Guest House	119 Willowbrae Road, Edinburgh EH8 7HN	0131 661 0170	★★★	Guest House	
Brae Lodge Guest House	30 Liberton Brae, Edinburgh EH16 6AF	0131 6722876	★★★	Guest House	⃦
Braid Hills Hotel	134 Braid Road, Edinburgh EH10 6JD	0131 447 8888	★★★	Hotel	
Brig O'Doon Guest House	262 Ferry Road, Edinburgh EH5 3AN	0131 552 3953	★★★	Guest House	
Briggend Guest House	19 Old Dalkeith Road, Edinburgh EH16 4TE	0131 258 0810	★★★	Guest House	
Brodie's Guest House	22 East Claremont Street, Edinburgh EH7 4JP	0131 556 4032	★★★	Guest House	
Brothaig House	18 Craigmillar Park, Edinburgh EH16 5PS	0131 667 2202	★★★	Guest House	
Bruntsfield Hotel	69-74 Bruntsfield Place, Edinburgh EH10 4HH	0131 229 1393	★★★★	Hotel	୧୧
Buchan & Haymarket Hotel	1-3 Coates Gardens, Edinburgh EH12 5LG	0131 337 1045	★★★	Metro Hotel	
Burns Guest House	67 Gilmore Place, Edinburgh EH3 9NU	0131 229 1669	★★★	Guest House	

  ♿ Unassisted wheelchair access   ♿ Assisted wheelchair access   ⃦ Access for visitors with mobility difficulties
  ୧ Bronze Green Tourism Award   ୧୧ Silver Green Tourism Award   ୧୧୧ Gold Green Tourism Award
For further information on our Green Tourism Business Scheme please see page 9.

Caledonian Hilton Hotel	Princes Street, Edinburgh EH1 2AB	0131 222 8888	★★★★★	Hotel	♿
Capital Guest House	7 Mayfield Road, Newington, Edinburgh EH9 2NG	0131 466 0717	★★★	Guest House	
Carrington	38 Pilrig Street, Edinburgh EH6 5AN	0131 554 4769	★★★	Guest House	
Casa Buzzo Guest House	8 Kilmaurs Road, Edinburgh EH16 5DA	0131 667 8998	★★★	Guest House	
Castle Park Guest House	75 Gilmore Place, Edinburgh EH3 9NU	0131 229 1215	★★	Guest House	
Castle View	30 Castle Street, Edinburgh EH2 3HT	0131 226 5784	★★★	Guest House	
Channings	South Learmonth Gardens, Edinburgh EH4 1EZ	0131 332 3232	★★★★	Hotel	🍃🍃
Charleston House Guest House	38 Minto Street, Edinburgh EH9 2BS	0131 667 6589	★★★	Guest House	🍃
Christopher North House Hotel	6 Gloucester Place, Edinburgh EH3 6EF	0131 225 2720	★★★★	Townhouse Hotel	
Clan Walker Guest House	96 Dalkeith Road, Edinburgh EH16 5AF	0131 667 1244	★★★	Guest House	
Claremont Hotel	14a/15 Claremont Crescent, Edinburgh EH7 4HX	0131 556 1487	★	Metro Hotel	
Classic Guest House	50 Mayfield Road, Edinburgh EH9 2NH	0131 6675847	★★★	Guest House	
Cluaran House	47 Leamington Terrace, Edinburgh EH10 4JS	0131 221 0047	★★★★	Guest House	
Craigellachie	21 Murrayfield Avenue, Edinburgh EH12 6AU	0131 337 4076	★★★★	Guest House	
Craigmoss Guest House	62 Pilrig Street, Edinburgh EH6 4HS	0131 554 3885	★★★★	Guest House	
Crioch Guest House	23 East Hermitage Place, Edinburgh EH6 8AD	0131 554 5494	★★★	Guest House	
Cruachan Guest House	53 Gilmore Place, Edinburgh EH3 9NT	0131 229 6219	★★★	Guest House	
Cumberland Hotel	1 West Coates, Edinburgh EH12 5JQ	0131 337 1198	★★★	Metro Hotel	
Davenport House	58 Great King Street, Edinburgh EH3 6QY	0131 558 8495	★★★★	Guest House	
Dene Guest House	7 Eyre Place, Edinburgh EH3 5ES	0131 556 2700	★★★	Guest House	
Dorstan House	7 Priestfield Road, Edinburgh EH16 5HJ	0131 667 6721	★★★	Guest House	
Dunedin Guest House	8 Priestfield Road, Edinburgh EH16 5HH	0131 6681949	★★★★	Guest House	
Dunstane City Hotel	5 Hampton Terrace, Edinburgh EH12 5JD	0131 337 6169	AWAITING GRADING		
Dunstane House Hotel	4 West Coates, Edinburgh EH12 5JQ	0131 337 6169	★★★★	Small Hotel	
Duthus Lodge	5 West Coates, Edinburgh EH12 5JG	0131 337 6876	★★★	Guest House	
Ecosse International	15 MacDonald Road, Edinburgh EH7 4LX	0131 556 4967	★★★	Guest House	
Edinburgh Agenda Hotel	92 St John's Road, Edinburgh EH12 8AT	0131 316 4466	★★	Hotel	
Edinburgh Brunswick	7 Brunswick Street, Edinburgh EH7 5JB	0131 556 1238	★★	Guest House	
Edinburgh Capital Hotel	187 Clermiston Road, Edinburgh EH12 6UG	0131 535 9988	★★★	Hotel	🍃
Edinburgh City Centre(Lauriston)Premier Inn	Laurison Place, Lady Lawson Street, Edinburgh EH3 9HZ	0870 990 6610		Budget Hotel	

♿ Unassisted wheelchair access   ♿ Assisted wheelchair access   🚶 Access for visitors with mobility difficulties
🍃 Bronze Green Tourism Award   🍃🍃 Silver Green Tourism Award   🍃🍃🍃 Gold Green Tourism Award
For further information on our Green Tourism Business Scheme please see page 9.

Awards correct as of mid August 2008

223

Name	Address	Phone	Rating	Type	Access
Edinburgh City Centre(Morrison St) Premier	1 Morrison Link, Edinburgh EH3 8DN	0870 238 3319		Budget Hotel	♿
Edinburgh East Premier Inn	Lady Nairne, 228 Willowbrae Road, Edinburgh EH8 7NG	08701 977091		Budget Hotel	
Edinburgh First	Chancellor Court, Pollock Halls,18 Holyrood Park Road, Edinburgh EH16	0131 651 2007	★★★	Campus	♿
Edinburgh House	11 Mcdonald Road, Edinburgh EH7 4LX	0131 556 3434	★★★	Guest House	
Edinburgh Marriott	111 Glasgow Road, Edinburgh EH12 8NF	0870 400 7293	★★★★	Hotel	♿
Edinburgh Minto Hotel	16-18 Minto Street, Edinburgh EH9 9RQ	0131 668 1234	★★★	Hotel	
Elas Guest House	10 Claremont Crescent, Edinburgh EH7 4HX	0131 556 1929	★	Guest House	
Elder York Guest House	38 Elder Street, Edinburgh EH1 3DX	0131 556 1926	★★★	Guest House	
Emerald House	3 Drum Street, Edinburgh EH17 8GG	0131 664 5918	AWAITING GRADING		
Express by Holiday Inn	16-22 Picardy Place, Edinburgh EH1 3JT	0131 5582300	★★★	Metro Hotel	♿
Express by Holiday Inn	Britannia Way, Ocean Drive, Edinburgh EH6 6LA	0131 555 4422	★★★	Metro Hotel	♿
Express by Holiday Inn (Edinburgh Royal Mile)	300 Cowgate, Edinburgh EH1 1NA	0131 524 8400	AWAITING GRADING		
Falcon Crest Guest House	70 South Trinity Road, Edinburgh EH5 3NX	0131 552 5294	★	Guest House	
Four Twenty Guest House	420 Ferry Road, Edinburgh EH5 2AD	0131 552 2167	★	Guest House	
Frederick House	42 Frederick Street, Edinburgh EH2 1EX	0131 226 1999	★★★	Lodge	
George Hotel	19 / 21 George St., Edinburgh EH2 2PB	0131 225 1251	★★★★	Hotel	
Gifford House	103 Dalkeith Road, Edinburgh EH16 5AJ	0131 667 4688	★★★★	Guest House	
Gil-Dun Guest House	9 Spence Street, Edinburgh EH16 5AG	0131 667 1368	★★★★	Guest House	
Gillis	100 Strathearn Road, Edinburgh EH9 1BB	0131 623 8933	★★★	Guest House	♿
Gladstone Guest House	90 Dalkeith Road, Edinburgh EH16 5AF	0131 6674708	★★★	Guest House	
Glenalmond Guest House	25 Mayfield Gardens, Edinburgh EH9 2BX	0131 668 2392	★★★★	Guest House	
Granville Guest House	13 Granville Terrace, Edinburgh EH10 4PQ	0131 229 1676	★★	Guest House	
Greenside Hotel	9 Royal Terrace, Edinburgh EH7 5AH	0131 557 0022	★★	Metro Hotel	
Grosvenor Gardens	The Grosvenor Gardens, Edinburgh EH12 5JU	0131 3133415	★★★	Guest House	
Halcyon Hotel	8 Royal Terrace, Edinburgh EH7 5AB	0131 556 1033	★★	Guest House	
Hampton Hotel	14 Corstorphine Road, Edinburgh EH12 6HN	0131 337 1130	★★★	Small Hotel	
Harvest Guest House	33, Straiton Place, Edinburgh EH15 2BA	0131 657 3160	★	Guest House	
Herald House Hotel	70/72 Grove Street, Edinburgh EH3 8AP	0131 228 2323	★★	Metro Hotel	
Heriott Park Guest House	254/256 Ferry Road, Edinburgh EH5 3AN	0131 552 3456	★★★	Guest House	
Highfield Guest House	83 Mayfield Road, Edinburgh EH9 3AE	0131 667 8717	★★★★	Guest House	

♿ Unassisted wheelchair access   ♿ Assisted wheelchair access   ♿ Access for visitors with mobility difficulties
ⓟ Bronze Green Tourism Award   ⓟⓟ Silver Green Tourism Award   ⓟⓟⓟ Gold Green Tourism Award
For further information on our Green Tourism Business Scheme please see page 9.

by Garve

Inchbae Lodge	by Garve, Ross-shire, IV23 2PH	01997 455269	★★	Guest House

Gatehouse of Fleet

Cally Palace Hotel	Gatehouse of Fleet, Kirkcudbrightshire, DG7 2DL	01557 814341	★★★★	Hotel
Murray Arms Hotel	Ann Street, Gatehouse of Fleet, Kirkcudbrightshire, DG7 2HY	01557 814207	★★★	Small Hotel
The Bank of Fleet Hotel	47 High Street, Gatehouse of Fleet, Kirkcudbrightshire, DG7 2HR	01557 814302	AWAITING GRADING	
The Bobbin Guest House	36 High Street, Gatehouse-of-Fleet, Kirkcudbrightshire, DG7 2HP	01557 814229	★★★	Guest House
The Ship Inn	1 Fleet Street, Gatehouse of Fleet, Kirkcudbrightshire, DG7 2JT	01557 814217	★★★★	Inn

Giffnock, Glasgow

Redhurst Hotel	27 Eastwoodmains Road, Giffnock, Glasgow G46 6QE	0141 6386465	★★	Small Hotel

Girvan

Southfield Hotel	The Avenue, Girvan, Ayrshire, KA26 9DS	01465 714222	★★	Small Hotel

Glamis

Castleton House Hotel	Glamis, Angus, DD8 1SJ	01307 840340	★★★	Country House Hotel

Glasgow

ABode Glasgow Ltd	129 Bath Street, Glasgow G2 2SZ	0141 2216789	★★★★	Hotel	
Acorn Hotel	140 Elderslie Street, Glasgow G3 7AW	0141 3326556	AWAITING GRADING		
Adelaide's Guest House	209 Bath Street, Glasgow G2 4HZ	0141 248 4970	★★	Guest House	
Albion Hotel	405-407 North Woodside Road, Glasgow G20 6NN	0141 339 8620	★★★	Metro Hotel	
Alison Guest House	26 Circus Drive, Glasgow G31 2JH	0141 556 1431	★★	Guest House	
Amadeus Guest House	411 North Woodside Road, Glasgow G20 6NN	0141 3398257	★★	Guest House	
Ambassador Hotel	7 Kelvin Drive, Glasgow G20 8QG	0141 946 1018	★★★	Metro Hotel	
Angus Hotel	966-970 Sauchiehall Street, Glasgow G3 7TH	0141 357 515	★★★	Lodge	
Argyll Hotel	973 Sauchiehall Street, Glasgow G3 7TQ	0141 337 3313	★★★	Hotel	
Belgrave Guest House	2 Belgrave Terrace, Glasgow G12 8JD	0141 337 1850	★★	Guest House	
Best Western Glasgow City Hotel	25/27 Elmbank Street, Glasgow G2 4PB	0141 227 2772	★★★	Metro Hotel	
Botanic Hotel	1 Alfred Terrace, Glasgow G12 8RF	01413 377007	★★★	Guest House	
Burnside Hotel	East Kilbride Road, Rutherglen, Glasgow G73 5EA	0141 634 1276	★★	Small Hotel	
Caledonian Court	Dobbies Loan, Glasgow G4 0JF	0141 3313980	★	Campus	
Campanile Glasgow	Tunnel Street, Glasgow G3 8HL	0141 287 7700	★★★	Hotel	♿

♿ Unassisted wheelchair access   ♿ Assisted wheelchair access   ♿ Access for visitors with mobility difficulties
P Bronze Green Tourism Award   PP Silver Green Tourism Award   PPP Gold Green Tourism Award
For further information on our Green Tourism Business Scheme please see page 9.

Name	Address	Phone	Rating	Type	Access
Carlton George Hotel	44 West George Street, Glasgow G2 1DH	0141 353 6373	★★★★	Hotel	♿
City Inn Glasgow	Finnieston Quay, Glasgow G3 8HN	0141 240 1002	★★★	Hotel	
Clifton Hotel	27 Buckingham Terrace, Glasgow G12 8ED	0141 3348080	★★	Guest House	
Craigpark Guest House	33 Circus Drive, Glasgow G31 2JG	0141 554 4160	★★	Guest House	
Crowne Plaza Hotel	Congress Road, Glasgow G3 8QT	0870 443 4691	★★★★	Hotel	♿ 🄿
Crowwood House Hotel	Cumbernauld Road, Muirhead, Glasgow G69 9BJ	0141 779 3861	★★★	Hotel	
Devoncove Hotel	931 Sauchiehall Street, Glasgow G3 7TQ	0141 334 4000	★★	Hotel	
Ewington Hotel	32 Balmoral Terrace, 132 Queen's Drive, Glasgow G42 8QW	0141 423 1152	AWAITING GRADING		
Express by Holiday Inn	Theatreland, 165 West Nile Street, Glasgow G1 2RL	0141 331 6800	★★★	Metro Hotel	
Express by Holiday Inn Glasgow	122 Stockwell Street, Glasgow G1 4LT	0141 548 5000	★★★	Metro Hotel	
Glasgow Bearsden Premier Inn	Milngavie Road, Glasgow G61 3TA	0870 9906532		Budget Hotel	
Glasgow Cambuslang Premier Inn	Orion Way, Cambuslang Investment Park, off London Road, Glasgow G32	0870 242 8000		Budget Hotel	
Glasgow City Centre George Square Premier Inn	Slice, 187 George Street, Glasgow G1 1YU	0870 2383320		Budget Hotel	
Glasgow City Centre Premier Inn (Argyle Street)	377 Argyle Street, Glasgow G2 4PP	0870 9906312		Budget Hotel	
Glasgow City Centre(Charing Cross)Premier Inn	10 Elmbank Gardens, Glasgow G2 4PP	0870 9906312		Budget Hotel	
Glasgow Hilton	1 William Street, Glasgow G3 8HT	0141 204 5555	★★★★★	Hotel	♿
Glasgow Marriott	500 Argyle Street, Glasgow G3 8RR	0141 226 5577	★★★★	Hotel	♿
Glasgow Pond Hotel	Great Western Road, Glasgow G12 0XP	0141 334 8161	★★★	Hotel	
Hampton Court Hotel	230 Renfrew Street, Glasgow G3 6TX	0141 332 6623	★★	Guest House	
Hilton Glasgow Grosvenor	Grosvenor Terrace, Glasgow G12 OTA	0141 339 8811	★★★★	Hotel	
Holiday Inn	161 West Nile Street, Glasgow G1 2RL	0141 352 8300	★★★★	Hotel	♿
Hotel Du Vin at One Devonshire Gardens	1 Devonshire Gardens, Glasgow G12 0UX	0141 339 2001	★★★★★	Townhouse Hotel	
Ibis Hotel Glasgow	220 West Regent Street, Glasgow G2 4DQ	0141 225 6000	★★	Hotel	♿
Ivory Hotel	2 Camphill Avenue, Glasgow G41 3AY	0141 636 0223	★★	Small Hotel	
Jurys Inn Glasgow	Jamaica Street, Glasgow G1 4QE	0141 314 4800	★★★	Hotel	♿ 🄿🄿🄿
Kelvingrove Hotel	944 Sauchiehall Street, Glasgow G3 7TH	0141 339 5011	★★★	Guest House	
Kincaid House Hotel	Milton of Campsie, Glasgow GG6 8BZ	0141 776 2226	★★★	Small Hotel	
Kings Park Hotel	250 Mill Street, Rutherglen, Glasgow G73 2LX	0141 647 5491	★★★	Hotel	
Lomond Hotel	6 Buckingham Terrace, Glasgow G12 8EB	0141 339 2339	★★	Guest House	
Manor Park Hotel	28 Balshagray Drive, Glasgow G11 7DD	0141 339 2143	★★★	Guest House	

♿ Unassisted wheelchair access ♿ Assisted wheelchair access 🚶 Access for visitors with mobility difficulties
🄿 Bronze Green Tourism Award 🄿🄿 Silver Green Tourism Award 🄿🄿🄿 Gold Green Tourism Award
For further information on our Green Tourism Business Scheme please see page 9.

To find out more, call 0845 22 55 121 or go to visitscotland.com.

Marks Hotel	110 Bath Street, Glasgow G2 2EN	0141 353 0800	★★★	Hotel		
McLays Guest House	268 Renfrew Street, Glasgow G3 6TT	0141 332 4796	★	Guest House		
Menzies Glasgow	27 Washington Street, Glasgow G3 8AZ	0141 2222929	★★★★	Hotel		
Murray Hall	Collins Street, Glasgow G4 0NG	0141 553 4148	★	Campus		
Newton House Hotel	248-252 Bath Street, Glasgow G2 4JW	0141 3321666	★★★	Guest House		
Novotel Glasgow Centre	181 Pitt Street, Glasgow G2 4DT	0141 222 2775	★★★	Hotel	🧏	
Oak Tree Inn	Balmaha, Glasgow G63 0JQ	01360 870357	★★★	Inn		
Park Inn Glasgow City Centre	2 Port Dundas Place, Glasgow G2 3LB	0141 333 1500	★★★★	Hotel		
Premier Inn Glasgow City Centre South	80 Ballater Street, Glasgow G5 0TW	0870 423 6452	★★★	Hotel	♿	
Quality Hotel Central	99 Gordon Street, Glasgow G1 3SF	0141 2219680	★★	Hotel		
Queen Margaret Hall	55 Bellshaugh Road, Glasgow G12 0SQ	0141 334 2192	★★	Campus	🧏	🄿
Rab Ha's	83 Hutcheson Street, Glasgow G1 1SH	0141 5720400	★★	Inn		
Radisson SAS Hotel Glasgow	301 Argyle Street, Glasgow G2 8DL	0141 204 3333	★★★★★	Hotel		🄿🄿🄿
Sherbrooke Castle Hotel	11 Sherbrooke Avenue, Glasgow G41 4PG	0141 427 4227	★★★	Hotel		
The Alamo Guest House Ltd	46 Gray Street, Glasgow G3 7SE	0141 339 2395	★★★	Guest House		
The Belhaven Hotel	15 Belhaven Terrace, Glasgow G12 OTG	0141 339 3222	★★★	Guest House		
The Fullarton Park Hotel	1230 Tollcross Road, Tollcross, Glasgow G32 8HH	0141 763 1027	AWAITING GRADING			
The Heritage	4-5 Alfred Terrace, Glasgow G12 8RF	07977 422428	AWAITING GRADING			
The Kelvin	15 Buckingham Terrace, Glasgow G12 8EB	0141 339 7143	★★	Guest House		
The Kirklee	11 Kensington Gate, Glasgow G12 9LG	0141 334 5555	★★★	Guest House		
The Malmaison	278 West George Street, Glasgow G2 4LL	0141 5721000	★★★★	Hotel		
The Merchant Lodge	52 Virginia Street, Glasgow G1 1TY	07779 299001	AWAITING GRADING			
The Millennium Glasgow Hotel	George Square, Glasgow G2 1DS	0141 332 6711	★★★★	Hotel		
The Piping Centre	30-34 McPhater Street, Glasgow G4 0HW	0141 353 0220	★★★	Restaurant with Rooms		
The Ramada Glasgow City	201 Ingram Street, Glasgow G1 1DQ	0141 248 4401	★★★	Hotel	🚶	🄿
The Sandyford	904 Sauchiehall Street, Glasgow G3 7TF	0141 334 0000	★★★	Lodge		
The Town House	4 Hughenden Terrace, Glasgow G12 9XR	0141 3570862	★★	Guest House		
The Townhouse Hotel	21 Royal Crescent, Glasgow G3 7SL	0141 332 9009	★★	Lodge		
The Victorian House Hotel	212 Renfrew Street, Glasgow G3 6TX	0141 332 0129	★★★	Lodge		
The Willow	228 Renfrew Street, Glasgow G3 6TX	0141 332 2332	★★	Guest House		

♿ Unassisted wheelchair access   🧏 Assisted wheelchair access   🚶 Access for visitors with mobility difficulties
🄿 Bronze Green Tourism Award   🄿🄿 Silver Green Tourism Award   🄿🄿🄿 Gold Green Tourism Award
For further information on our Green Tourism Business Scheme please see page 9.

Awards correct as of mid August 2008

Thistle Glasgow	36 Cambridge Street, Glasgow G2 3HN	0141 332 3311	★★★★	Hotel		
Travelodge Glasgow / Paisley Road	251 Paisley Road, Glasgow G5 8RA	08719 846142	AWAITING GRADING			
Travelodge Glasgow Central	5-11 Hill Street, Glasgow G3 6RP	08719 846335	AWAITING GRADING			
University of Strathclyde	Chancellors Hall, Rottenrow East, Glasgow G4 0NG	0141 553 4148	★	Campus		
Victoria Hall Limited	171 Kyle Street, Glasgow G4 0JQ	0141 3544100	★	Campus		
Wolfson Hall	Kelvin Campus,West Scotland Science Park,Maryhill Road, Glasgow G20 0TH	0141 3303773	★	Campus	♿	🍃

by Glasgow

Onslow Guest House	2 Onslow Drive,Dennistoun, by Glasgow G31 2LX	01415 546797	★★★	Guest House		
Seton Guest House	6 Seton Terrace,Dennistoun, by Glasgow G31 2HU	0141 556 7654	★★★	Guest House		
Glasgow Bellsill Premier Inn	Bellzielhill Farm, New Edinburgh Road,Bellshill, by Glasgow ML4 3HH	08701 977106		Budget Hotel		
Glasgow North East Stepps Premier Inn	Crowwood Roundabout, Cumbernauld Road,Stepps, by Glasgow G33 6HN	08701 977111		Budget Hotel		
Garfield House Hotel	Cumbernauld Road,Stepps, by Glasgow G33 6HW	0141 779 2111	★★★	Hotel		
Hilton Strathclyde	Pheonix Crescent,Bellshill, by Glasgow ML4 3JQ	01698 395500	★★★★	Hotel	♀	
Glasgow Milngavie Premier Inn	West Highland Gate, Main Street,Milngavie, by Glasgow G62 6JJ	08701 977112		Budget Hotel		

Glencaple

Nith Hotel	Glencaple, Dumfries & Galloway, DG1 4RE	01387 770213	★★	Small Hotel		

Glencoe

Clachaig Inn	Glencoe, Argyll, PH49 4HX	01855 811252	★★	Inn		🍃
Dorrington Lodge	6 Tigh Phuirst, Glencoe, Argyll, PH49 4HN	01855 811653	★★★	Guest House		
Dunire	Glencoe, Argyll, PH49 4HS	01855 811305	★★★	Guest House		
Kings House Hotel	Glencoe, Argyll, PH49 4HY	01855 851 259	★	Inn		
Scorry Breac Guest House	Hospital Drive, Glencoe, Argyll, PH49 4HT	01855 811354	★★★★	Guest House		

Glendale

Carter's Rest	8/9 Upper Milovaig, Glendale, Isle of Skye, IV55 8WY	01470 511272	★★★★	Guest House		

Glenfarg

The Famous Bein Inn	Glenfarg, Perthshire, PH2 9PY	01577 830216	★★★	Inn		

Glenfinnan

The Prince's House Hotel	Glenfinnan, Inverness-shire, PH37 4LT	01397 722246	★★★	Small Hotel		🍃🍃

Glenmoriston

Cluanie Inn	Glenmoriston, Inverness-shire, IV63 7YW	01320 340238	★★★	Inn		

♿ Unassisted wheelchair access   ♿ Assisted wheelchair access   ♀ Access for visitors with mobility difficulties
🍃 Bronze Green Tourism Award   🍃🍃 Silver Green Tourism Award   🍃🍃🍃 Gold Green Tourism Award
For further information on our Green Tourism Business Scheme please see page 9.

Glenrothes

Balgeddie House Hotel	Balgeddie Way, Glenrothes, Fife, KY6 3ET	01592 742511	★★★	Hotel	
Express by Holiday Inn	Leslie Road, Glenrothes, Fife, KY7 6XX	01592 745509	★★★	Metro Hotel	
Glenrothes Premier Inn	Bankhead Gate, Beaufort Drive, Bankhead Roundabout, Glenrothes, Fife,	08701 977114		Budget Hotel	
The Gilvenbank Hotel	Huntsman's Road, Glenrothes, Fife, KY7 6RA	01592 742077	★★★	Hotel	
Travelodge Glenrothes	Bank Head Park, Glenrothes, Fife, KY7 6GH	08719 846278	AWAITING GRADING		

Glenurquhart

Glenurquhart House	Marchfield, Glenurquhart, Inverness-shire, IV63 6TJ	01456 476234	★★★★	Restaurant with Rooms	

Golspie

The Golf Links Hotel	Church Street, Golspie, Sutherland, KW10 6TT	01408 633 408	★★	Small Hotel	

Gorebridge

Borthwick Castle	North Middleton, Gorebridge, Midlothian, EH23 4QY	01875 820514	★★★	Small Hotel	
Ivory House	14 Vogrie Road, Gorebridge, Midlothian, EH23 4HH	01875 820755	★★★★	Guest House	&#9855;

Gourock

Spinnaker Hotel	121 Albert Road, Gourock, Renfrewshire, PA19 1BU	01475 633107	★★	Small Hotel	&#128694;

Grangemouth

Grangeburn House	55 Bo'ness Road, Grangemouth, Stirlingshire, FK3 9BJ	01324 471301	★★★★	Guest House	
Leapark Hotel	130 Bo'ness Road, Grangemouth, Stirlingshire, FK3 9BX	01324 486733	★★★	Hotel	&#9855;
The Grange Manor	Glensburgh, Grangemouth, Stirlingshire, FK3 8XJ	01324 474836	★★★★	Hotel	

Grantown on Spey

An Cala Guest House	Woodlands Terrace, Grantown on Spey, Moray, PH26 3JU	01479 873 293	★★★★★	Guest House	🍃🍃
Ben Mhor Hotel	53-57 High Street, Grantown on Spey, Moray, PH26 3EG	01479 872056	★★★	Hotel	
Brooklynn	Grant Road, Grantown on Spey, Moray, PH26 3LA	01479 873113	★★★★	Guest House	🍃🍃
Craiglynne Hotel	Woodlands Terrace, Grantown-on-Spey, Moray, PH26 3JX	01479 872597	AWAITING GRADING		
Culdearn House	Woodland Terrace, Grantown-on-Spey, Moray, PH26 3JU	01479 872106	★★★★★	Small Hotel	
Dunallan House	Woodside Avenue, Grantown-on-Spey, Moray, PH26 3JN	01479 872140	★★★★	Guest House	
Garden Park Guest House	Woodside Avenue, Grantown-on-Spey, Moray, PH26 3JN	01479 873235	★★★	Guest House	
Garth Hotel	The Square, Grantown-on-Spey, Moray, PH26 3HN	01479 872836	★★★	Small Hotel	
Haugh Hotel	Cromdale, Grantown-on-Spey, Moray, PH26 3LW	01479 872583	★★	Inn	
Holmhill House	Woodside Avenue, Grantown on Spey, Moray, PH26 3JR	01479 873977	★★★★	Guest House	🍃

♿ Unassisted wheelchair access   ♿ Assisted wheelchair access   🚶 Access for visitors with mobility difficulties
🍃 Bronze Green Tourism Award   🍃🍃 Silver Green Tourism Award   🍃🍃🍃 Gold Green Tourism Award
For further information on our Green Tourism Business Scheme please see page 9.

Kinross Guest House	Woodside Avenue, Grantown-on-Spey, Moray, PH26 3JR	01479 872042	★★★★	Guest House		
Muckrach Lodge Hotel	Dulnain Bridge, Grantown-On-Spey, Moray, PH26 3LY	01479 851257	★★★	Country House Hotel		♿
Parkburn Guest House	High Street, Grantown-on-Spey, Moray, PH26 3EN	01479 873116	★★★	Guest House		
Ravenscourt House Hotel	Seafield Avenue, Grantown-on-Spey, Moray, PH26 3JG	01479 872286	★★★★	Small Hotel		
Rosehall Guest House	13 The Square, Grantown On Spey, Moray, PH26 3HG	01479 872721	★★★★	Guest House		
Rossmor Guest House	Woodlands Terrace, Grantown on Spey, Moray, PH26 3JU	01479 872201	★★★★	Guest House		
Seafield Lodge Hotel	Woodside Avenue, Grantown-on-Spey, Moray, PH26 3JN	01479 872152	★★★	Small Hotel		
The Pines	Woodside Avenue, Grantown-on-Spey, Moray, PH26 3JR	01479 872092	★★★★★	Guest Accommodation		
Willowbank	High Street, Grantown on Spey, Moray, PH26 3EN	01479 872089	★★★	Guest House		🚶

Greenock

Express by Holiday Inn	Cartsburn, Greenock, Renfrewshire, PA15 4RT	01475 786666	★★★	Metro Hotel	♿	
Greenock Premier Inn	Garvel Point, James Watt Way, Greenock, Renfrewshire, PA15 2AJ	08701 977 120		Budget Hotel		
James Watt College	Waterfront Campus, Customhouse Way, Greenock, Renfrewshire, PA15 1EN	01475 731360	★★	Campus	♿	
Tontine Hotel	6 Ardgowan Square, Greenock, Renfrewshire, PA16 8NG	01475 723316	★★★	Hotel	🚶	

Gretna

Alexander House	Glasgow road, Gretna, Dumfries & Galloway, DG16 5DU	01461 337056	★★★	Guest House		
Days Inn	Welcome Break Service Area, M74, Gretna, Dumfries & Galloway, DG16 5HQ	01461 337566	AWAITING GRADING		♿	
Gretna Hall Hotel	Gretna, Dumfries & Galloway, DG16 5DY	01461 338257	AWAITING GRADING			
Hunters Lodge Hotel	Annan Road, Gretna, Dumfries & Galloway, DG16 5DL	01461 338214	★★★	Small Hotel	♿	
Smiths @ Gretna Green	Gretna, Dumfries & Galloway, DG16 5EA	0845 3676768	★★★★	Hotel	♿	🏵🏵
Solway Lodge Hotel	97-99 Annan Road, Gretna, Dumfries & Galloway, DG16	01461 338266	★★★	Small Hotel		
The Garden House Hotel	Sarkfoot Road, Gretna, Dumfries & Galloway, DG16 5EP	01461 337621	★★★	Hotel	♿	

Gullane

Mallard Hotel	East Links Road, Gullane, East Lothian, EH31 2AF	01620 843288	★★	Small Hotel	

Haddington

Lennoxlove House	Lennoxlove Estate, Haddington, East Lothian, EH41 4NZ	01620 823720	★★★★★	Exclusive Use Venue	
Maitlandfield House Hotel	24 Sidegate, Haddington, East Lothian, EH41 4BZ	01620 826513	★★★★	Hotel	♿

Halbeath

Travelodge Dunfermline	Halbeath Junction, Halbeath, Fife, KY11 8PG	08719 846 287	AWAITING GRADING		

♿ Unassisted wheelchair access ♿ Assisted wheelchair access 🚶 Access for visitors with mobility difficulties
🏵 Bronze Green Tourism Award 🏵🏵 Silver Green Tourism Award 🏵🏵🏵 Gold Green Tourism Award
For further information on our Green Tourism Business Scheme please see page 9.

Hamilton

Avonbridge Hotel	Carlisle Road, Hamilton, Lanarkshire, ML3 7DG	01698 420525	★★★	Hotel		
Clydesdale Hotel	12 Clydesdale Street, Hamilton, Lanarkshire, ML3 0DP	01698 891897	★★★	Small Hotel		
Glasgow Hamilton Premier Inn	Hamilton Motorway Service(M74 N), Hamilton, Lanarkshire, ML3 6JW	08701 977124		Budget Hotel		
The Villa Hotel	49/51 Burnbank Road, Hamilton, Lanarkshire, ML3 9AQ	01698 891777	★★★	Small Hotel		

Harthill

Blairmains	Harthill, Lanarkshire, ML7 5TJ	01501 751278	★★	Guest House		

Hawick

Elm House Hotel	17 North Bridge Street, Hawick, Roxburghshire, TD9 9BD	01450 372866	★★★	Small Hotel	♿	
Hizzy's Guest House	23 B&C North Bridge Street, Hawick, Roxburghshire, TD9 9DB	01450 372101	★★	Guest House		
Mansfield House Hotel	Weensland Road, Hawick, Roxburghshire, TD9 8LB	01450 373988	★★★	Small Hotel		
Whitchester Guest House	Hawick, Roxburghshire, TD9 7LN	01450 377477	★★★	Guest House	♿	🍃🍃

Helensburgh

Knockderry Hotel	Shore Road, Cove, Helensburgh, Dunbartonshire, G84 0NX	01436 842283	★★★★	Country House Hotel		
RSR Braeholm	31 East Montrose Street, Helensburgh, Dunbartonshire, G84 7HR	01436 671880	★★	Lodge	♿	
Sinclair House	91/93 Sinclair Street, Helensburgh, Dunbartonshire, G84 8TR	01436 676301	★★★★	Guest House		🍃🍃
The County Lodge Hotel	Old Luss Road,Craigendoran, Helensburgh, Dunbartonshire, G84 7BH	01436 672034	AWAITING GRADING			

Helmsdale

Kindale House	5 Lillieshall Street, Helmsdale, Sutherland, KW8 6JF	01431 821415	★★★★	Guest House		

Holm, Orkney

Commodore Chalets	St Mary's, Holm, Orkney, KW17 2RU	01856 781319	★★★	Guest House		

Howwood

Bowfield Hotel & Country Club	Howwood, Renfrewshire, PA9 1DB	01505 705225	★★★	Hotel		🍃

Hoy, Orkney

Stromabank	Hoy, Orkney, KW16 3PA	01856 701494	★★★	Small Hotel	♿	

Huntly

Castle Hotel	Huntly, Aberdeenshire, AB54 4SH	01466 792696	★★★★	Country House Hotel		
Dunedin Guest House	17 Bogie Street, Huntly, Aberdeenshire, AB5 5DX	01466 794162	★★	Guest House		
Gordon Arms Hotel	The Square, Huntly, Aberdeenshire, AB54 8AF	01466 792288	★★	Small Hotel		
Greenmount Guest House	43 Gordon Street, Huntly, Aberdeenshire, AB54 8EQ	01466 792482	★★★	Guest House		

♿ Unassisted wheelchair access   ♿ Assisted wheelchair access   ♿ Access for visitors with mobility difficulties
🍃 Bronze Green Tourism Award   🍃🍃 Silver Green Tourism Award   🍃🍃🍃 Gold Green Tourism Award
For further information on our Green Tourism Business Scheme please see page 9.

Huntly Hotel	No 18, The Square, Huntly, Aberdeenshire, AB54 8BR	01466 792703	★★	Small Hotel		

Ingliston, by Edinburgh

The Quality Hotel Edinburgh Airport	Ingliston,by Edinburgh, Midlothian, EH28 8AU	0131 333 4331	★★★	Hotel		

Innerleithen

Caddon View	14 Pirn Road, Innerleithen, Peeblesshire, EH44 6HH	01896 830208	★★★★	Guest House		
Glede Knowe	16 St Ronan's Terrace, Innerleithen, Peeblesshire, EH44 6RB	0775 2294346	★★★★	Guest House		

Insch

The Lodge Hotel	Old Rayne, Insch, Aberdeenshire, AB52 6RY	01464 851205	★★	Small Hotel		

Inveraray

Creag Dhubh	Inveraray, Argyll, PA32 8XT	01499 302430	★★★★	Guest House		
Killean Farm House	Inveraray, Argyll, PA32 8XT	01499 302474	★★★	Guest House		
Loch Fyne Hotel	Newtown, Inveraray, Argyll, PA32 8XT	01499 302148	★★★	Hotel	♿	Ⓟ
Rudha-Na-Craige	Rudha-Na-Craige, Inveraray, Argyll, PA32 8YX	01499 302668	★★★★	Guest House		

Inverarnan

Beinglas Farm Campsite	Inverarnan, Ardlui, G83 7DX	01301 704281	★★★	Inn		

Invergarry

Forest Lodge	South Laggan, Invergarry, Inverness-shire, PH34 4EA	01809 501219	★★★	Guest House		
Craigard Guest House	Invergarry, Inverness-Shire, PH35 4HG	01809 501258	★★	Guest House		
Glengarry Castle Country House Hotel	Invergarry, Invernes-shire, PH35 4HW	01809 501254	★★★	Country House Hotel		

Invergordon

Kincraig House Hotel	Invergordon, Ross-shire, IV18 0LF	01349 852587	★★★★	Country House Hotel		

Inverkip

Inverkip Hotel	Main Street, Inverkip, Renfrewshire, PA16 OAS	01475 521478	★★★	Inn		ⓅⓅ

Inverness

Aberfeldy Lodge Guest House	11 Southside Road, Inverness IV2 3BG	01463 231120	★★★	Guest House		
Abermar Guest House	25 Fairfield Road, Inverness IV3 5QD	01463 239019	★★★	Guest House		
Ach Aluinn Guest House	27 Fairfield Road, Inverness IV3 5QD	01463 230127	★★★★	Guest House		
Acorn House	Bruce Gardens, Inverness IV3 5ED	01463 717021	★★★	Guest House		
Ardconnel House	21 Arconnel Street, Inverness IV2 3EU	01463 240455	★★★★	Guest House		
Avalon Guest House	79 Glenurquhart Road, Inverness IV3 5PB	01463 239075	★★★★	Guest House	♁	

♿ Unassisted wheelchair access ♿ Assisted wheelchair access ♁ Access for visitors with mobility difficulties
Ⓟ Bronze Green Tourism Award ⓅⓅ Silver Green Tourism Award ⓅⓅⓅ Gold Green Tourism Award
For further information on our Green Tourism Business Scheme please see page 9.

240   To find out more, call 0845 22 55 121 or go to visitscotland.com.

Ballifeary Guest House	10 Ballifeary Road, Inverness IV3 5PJ	01463 235572	★★★★	Guest House	
Beaufort Hotel	11 Culduthel Road, Inverness IV2 4AG	01463 222897	★★★	Hotel	
Castleview Guest House	2A Ness Walk, Inverness IV3 5NE	01463 241443	★★★	Guest House	
Craigmonie Hotel	9 Annfield Road, Inverness IV2 3HX	01463 231649	★★★	Hotel	
Craignay House	16 Ardross Street, Inverness IV3 5NS	01463 226563	★★★	Guest House	
Craigside Lodge	4 Gordon Terrace, Inverness IV2 3HD	01463 231576	★★★	Guest House	
Crown Guest House	19 Ardconnel Street, Inverness IV2 3EU	01463 231135	★★★	Guest House	
Dalmore Guest House	101 Kenneth Street, Inverness IV3 5QQ	01463 237224	★★★	Guest House	
Dunhallin House	164 Culduthel Road, Inverness IV2 4BH	01463 220824	★★★	Guest House	
Eden House	8 Ballifeary Road, Inverness IV3 5PJ	01463 230278	★★★★	Guest House	
Eildon Guest House	29 Old Edinburgh Road, Inverness IV2 3HJ	01463 231969	★★★	Guest House	
Express by Holiday Inn	Stoneyfield, Inverness IV2 7PA	01463 732700	★★★	Metro Hotel	⬆
Fraser House	49 Huntly Street, Inverness IV3 5HS	01463 716488	★★★	Guest House	
Furan Cottage	100 Old Edinburgh Road, Inverness IV2 3HT	01463 712094	★★★	Guest House	
Glen Mhor Hotel	9-12 Ness Bank, Inverness IV2 4SG	01463 234308	★★★	Hotel	
Glencairn and Ardross House	18-19 Ardross Street, Inverness IV3 5NS	01463 232965	★★★	Guest House	♿
Glenmoriston Town House	20 Ness Bank, Inverness IV2 4SF	01463 223777	★★★★	Hotel	
Heathmount Hotel	Kingsmills Road, Inverness IV2 3JU	01463 235877	★★★	Small Hotel	
Inverglen	7 Abertarff Road, Inverness IV2 3NW	01463 236281	★★★	Guest House	
Inverness Centre Premier Inn	Millburn Road, Inverness IV2 3QX	08701 977141		Budget Hotel	
Inverness East Premier Inn	Inshes Gate, Beechwood Business Park, Inverness IV2 3BW	08701 977142		Budget Hotel	
Ivanhoe Guest House	68 Lochalsh Road, Inverness IV3 8HW	01463 223020	★★	Guest House	
Kingsmills Hotel Inverness Ltd	Culcabock Road, Inverness IV2 3LP	01463 237166	★★★★	Hotel	♿
Loch Ness House Hotel	Glenurquhart Road, Inverness IV3 8JL	01463 231248	★★★	Hotel	
Lochardil House Hotel	Stratherrick Road, Inverness IV2 4LF	01463 235995	★★★★	Hotel	
MacDonald House	1 Ardross Terrace, Inverness IV3 5NQ	01463 232878	★★★	Guest House	
MacDougall Clansman Hotel	103 Church Street, Inverness IV1 1ES	01463 713702	★★	Metro Hotel	
Malvern	54 Kenneth Street, Inverness IV3 5PZ	01463 242251	★★★	Guest House	
Maple Court Hotel	Ness Walk, Inverness IV3 5SQ	01463 230330	★★★	Small Hotel	
Moray Park Guest House	1 Island Bank Road, Inverness IV2 4SX	01463 233528	★★★	Guest House	

♿ Unassisted wheelchair access   ♿ Assisted wheelchair access   ⬆ Access for visitors with mobility difficulties
🄿 Bronze Green Tourism Award   🄿🄿 Silver Green Tourism Award   🄿🄿🄿 Gold Green Tourism Award
For further information on our Green Tourism Business Scheme please see page 9.

Awards correct as of mid August 2008

Ness Bank Guest House	7 Ness Bank, Inverness IV2 4SF	01463 232939	★★★	Guest House		𝒫𝒫
New Drumossie Hotel	Perth Road, Inverness IV1 2BE	01463 236451	★★★★	Hotel	♿	
Palace Hotel	Ness Walk, Inverness IV3 5NG	01463 223243	★★★	Hotel		
Park Hill Guest House	17 Ardconnel Street, Inverness IV2 3EU	01463 223300	★★★	Guest House		
Ramada Jarvis Inverness	Church Street, Inverness IV1 1DX	01463 235181	★★★	Hotel	♿	𝒫𝒫
Redcliffe Hotel	1 Gordon Terrace, Inverness IV2 3HD	01463 232767	★★★	Small Hotel		
Riverview Guest House	2 Moray Park, Island Bank Road, Inverness IV2 4SX	01463 235557	★★★★	Guest House		
Rocpool Reserve Hotel	14 Culduthel Road, Inverness IV2 4AG	01463 240089	AWAITING GRADING			
Roseneath Guest House	39 Greig Street, Inverness IV3 5PX	01463 220201	★★★	Guest House		
Royston Guest House	16 Millburn Road, Inverness IV2 3PS	01463 231243	★★★	Guest House		
St Ann's House	37 Harrowden Road, Inverness IV3 5QN	01463 236157	★★★	Guest House		
Strathmhor Guest House	99 Kenneth Street, Inverness IV3 5QQ	01463 235397	★★★	Guest House		
Strathness House	4 Ardross Terrace, Inverness IV3 5NQ	01463 232765	★★★	Guest House		
Talisker House	25 Ness Bank, Inverness IV2 4SF	01463 236221	★★★	Guest House		
The Alexander	16 Ness Bank, Inverness IV2 4SF	01463 231151	★★★★	Guest House		
Thistle Inverness	Millburn Road, Inverness IV2 3TR	0870 333 9155	★★★	Hotel		
Travelodge Inverness	Stonyfield, A96 Inverness Road, Inverness IV2 7PA	08719 864 285	AWAITING GRADING			
Travelodge Inverness Fairways	Castle Heather, Inverness IV2 7PA	08719 846285	AWAITING GRADING			
Waterside Hotel	Ness Bank, Inverness IV2 4SF	01463 233065	★★★	Hotel		
Whinpark Guest House	17 Ardross Street, Inverness IV3 5NS	01463 232549	★★★	Guest House		
White Lodge	15 Bishops Road, Inverness IV3 5SB	01463 230693	★★★★	Guest House		
Winston Guest House	10 Ardross Terrace, Inverness IV3 5NQ	01463 234477	★★★	Guest House		

by Inverness

Bunchrew House Hotel	Bunchrew, by Inverness, Inverness-shire, IV3 6TA	01463 234917	★★★★	Country House Hotel	

Inverurie

Breaslann Guest House	Old Chapel Road, Inverurie, Aberdeenshire, AB51 4QN	01467 621608	★★★	Guest House	
Grant Arms Hotel	Monymusk, Inverurie, Aberdeenshire, AB51 7HJ	01467 651226	★★★	Inn	♿
Strathburn Hotel	Burghmuir Drive, Inverurie, Aberdeenshire, AB51 4GY	01467 624422	★★★	Hotel	✚
Thainstone House Hotel	Thainstone Estate, Inverurie Road, Inverurie, Aberdeenshire, AB51 5NT	01467 621643	AWAITING GRADING		

♿ Unassisted wheelchair access   ♿ Assisted wheelchair access   ✚ Access for visitors with mobility difficulties
𝒫 Bronze Green Tourism Award   𝒫𝒫 Silver Green Tourism Award   𝒫𝒫𝒫 Gold Green Tourism Award
For further information on our Green Tourism Business Scheme please see page 9.

242   To find out more, call 0845 22 55 121 or go to visitscotland.com.

Iochdar, Isle of South Uist

Anglers Retreat	1 Ardmore, Iochdar, Isle of South Uist, HS8 5QY	01870 610325	★★★	Guest House	

Irvine

The Gailes Lodge	Marine Drive, Gailes, Irvine, Ayrshire, KA11 5AE	01294 204040	★★★	Hotel	♿
Laurelbank Guest House	3 Kilwinning Road, Irvine, Ayrshire, KA12 8RR	01294 277153	★★★	Guest House	

Island of Bressay, Shetland

Maryfield House Hotel	Island of Bressay, Shetland, ZE2 9EL	01595 820207	★	Restaurant with Rooms	

Isle of Colonsay

The Colonsay	Isle of Colonsay, Argyll, PA61 7YP	01951 200316	★★	Small Hotel	

Isle of Eigg

Lageorna Guest House	Lageorna, Isle of Eigg, Inverness-shire, PH42 4RL	01687 482405	★★★★	Restaurant with Rooms	🍃🍃

Isle of Gigha

Gigha Hotel	Isle of Gigha, Argyll, PA41 7AA	01583 505254	★★★	Small Hotel	🍃

Isle of Iona

Argyll Hotel	Iona, Isle of Iona, Argyll, PA76 6SJ	01681 700334	★★★	Restaurant with Rooms	🍃🍃🍃
St Columba Hotel	Isle of Iona, Argyll, PA76 6SL	01681 700304	★★★	Hotel	🍃🍃

Isle of Whithorn

The Steam Packet Inn	Harbour Row, Isle of Whithorn, Wigtownshire, DG8 8LL	01988 500334	★★	Inn	

Jedburgh

Allerton House	Oxnam Road, Jedburgh, Roxburghshire, TD8 6QQ	01835 869633	★★★★	Guest House	🚶
Glenbank House Hotel	Castlegate, Jedburgh, Roxburghshire, TD8 6BD	01835 862258	★	Small Hotel	
Meadhon House	48 Castlegate, Jedburgh, Roxburghshire, TD8 6BB	01835 862504	★★★	Guest House	

John O'Groats

Seaview Hotel	John O'Groats, Caithness, KW1 4YR	01955 611220	★★	Small Hotel	🍃🍃

Johnstone

Lynnhurst Hotel	Park Road, Johnstone, Renfrewshire, PA5 8LS	01505 324331	★★★	Hotel	

Keiss

Sinclair Bay Hotel	Main Street, Keiss, Caithness, KW1 4UY	01955 631233	★★	Inn	

Kelso

Bellevue House	Bowmont Street, Kelso, Roxburghshire, TD5 7DZ	01573 224588	★★★	Guest House	

♿ Unassisted wheelchair access ♿ Assisted wheelchair access 🚶 Access for visitors with mobility difficulties
🍃 Bronze Green Tourism Award 🍃🍃 Silver Green Tourism Award 🍃🍃🍃 Gold Green Tourism Award
For further information on our Green Tourism Business Scheme please see page 9.

Cross Keys Hotel	36-37 The Square, Kelso, Roxburghshire, TD5 7HL	01573 223303	★★★	Hotel	⚡
Ednam House Hotel	Bridge Street, Kelso, Roxburghshire, TD5 7HT	01573 224168	★★★	Hotel	
Inglestone House	Abbey Row, Kelso, Roxburghshire, TD5 7HQ	01573 225800	★★★	Guest House	♿
Roxburghe Hotel and Golf Course	Heiton, Kelso, Roxburghshire, TD5 8JZ	01573 450331	★★★★	Country House Hotel	

Kemnay

| Bennachie Lodge Hotel | Victoria Terrace, Kemnay, Aberdeenshire, AB51 5RL | 01467 642789 | ★★ | Small Hotel | |

Kenmore

| Kenmore Hotel | The Square, Kenmore, Perthshire, PH15 2NU | 01887 830205 | ★★★ | Hotel | |

Kilbirnie

| Moorpark House Hotel | School Road, Kilbirnie, Ayrshire, KA25 7LD | 07767 324879 | ★★★★ | Country House Hotel | |

Kilbride, Isle of South Uist

| Polochar Inn | Polachar, Kilbride, Isle of South Uist, HS8 5TT | 01878 700215 | ★★★ | Inn | |

Kilchattan Bay, Isle of Bute

| St Blane's Hotel | Kilchattan Bay, Isle of Bute, PA20 9NW | 01700 831224 | ★★ | Small Hotel | |

Kildonan, Isle of Arran

| Kildonan Hotel | Kildonan, Isle of Arran, KA27 8SE | 01770 820207 | ★★★ | Small Hotel | ♿ |

Kilkenzie

| Dalnaspidal Guest House | Tangy, Kilkenzie, Argyll, PA28 6QD | 01586 820466 | ★★★★★ | Guest House | ♿ |

Killiecrankie

| Killiecrankie House Hotel | Killiecrankie, Perthshire, PH16 5LG | 01796 473220 | ★★★★ | Country House Hotel | |

Killin

Breadalbane House	Main Street, Killin, Perthshire, FK21 8UT	01567 820134	★★★	Guest House	🍃
Bridge of Lochay Hotel	Aberfeldy Road, Killin, Perthshire, FK21 8TS	01567 820272	★★★	Inn	
Craigbuie Guest House	Main Street, Killin, Perthshire, FK21 8UH	01567 820439	★★★	Guest House	
Dall Lodge Country House	Main Street, Killin, Perthshire, FK21 8TN	01567 820217	★★★★	Guest House	
Fairview House	Main Street, Killin, Perthshire, FK21 8UT	01567 820667	★★★	Guest House	
Killin Hotel	Main Street, Killin, Perthshire, FK21 8TP	01567 820296	★★	Hotel	
The Ardeonaig Hotel	South Loch Tay, Killin, Perthshire, FK21 8SU	01567 820400	★★★★	Small Hotel	
The Coach House Hotel	Lochay Road, Killin, Perthshire, FK21 8TN	01567 820349	★★	Inn	

♿ Unassisted wheelchair access   ♿ Assisted wheelchair access   ⚡ Access for visitors with mobility difficulties
🍃 Bronze Green Tourism Award   🍃🍃 Silver Green Tourism Award   🍃🍃🍃 Gold Green Tourism Award
For further information on our Green Tourism Business Scheme please see page 9.

To find out more, call 0845 22 55 121 or go to visitscotland.com.

Kilmarnock

Park Hotel	Rugby Park, Kilmarnock, Ayrshire, KA1 1UR	01563 545999	★★★★	Hotel		♿
Kilmarnock (Cotton Mills) Premier Inn	Moorfield Roundabout, Annadale, Kilmarnock, Ayrshire, KA1 2RS	08701 977148		Budget Hotel		
Howard Park Hotel	136 Glasgow Road, Kilmarnock, Ayrshire, KA3 1UT	01563 531211	★★	Hotel		
Dean Park Guest House	27 Wellington Street, Kilmarnock, Ayrshire, KA3 1DZ	01563 572794	★★★	Guest House		
Travelodge Kilmarnock	Junction A71/A76/A77 Kilmarnock bypass, Kilmarnock, Ayrshire, KA1 5LQ	08719 846149	AWAITING GRADING			

by Kilmarnock

Fenwick Hotel	Fenwick, by Kilmarnock, Ayrshire, KA3 6AU	01560 600478	★★★	Hotel		♟

Kilmory, Isle of Arran

Lagg Hotel	Lagg, Kilmory, Isle of Arran, KA27 8PQ	01770 870255	★★★	Small Hotel	

Kincraig

Braeriach Guest House	Braeriach Road, Kincraig, Inverness-shire, PH21 1NA	01540 651369	★★★★	Guest House		
Insh House Guest House	Kincraig, Inverness-shire, PH21 1NU	01540 651377	★★★	Guest House		🍃🍃
Suie Guest House	Kincraig, Inverness-shire, PH21 1NA	01540 651 344	★★★	Guest House		

Kinghorn

Bay Hotel	Burntisland Road, Kinghorn, Fife, KY3 9YE	01592 892222	★★★	Hotel		♿

Kingston

Fenton Tower	Kingston, North Berwick, East Lothian, EH39 5JH	01620 890089	★★★★★	Exclusive Use Venue	

Kingussie

Allt Gynack Guest House	Gynack Villa, 1 High Street, Kingussie, Inverness-shire, PH21 1HS	01540 661081	★★★	Guest House		
Arden House	Newtonmore Road, Kingussie, Inverness-shire, PH21 1HE	01540 661369	★★★★	Guest House		
Auld Alliance	East Terrace, Kingussie, Inverness-shire, PH21 1JS	01540 661506	★★★	Restaurant with Rooms		
Columba House Hotel & Garden Restaurant	Manse Road, Kingussie, Inverness-shire, PH21 1JF	01540 661402	★★★	Small Hotel	♿	
Duke of Gordon Hotel	Kingussie, Inverness-shire, PH21 1HE	01540 661302	★★★	Hotel		
The Cross at Kingussie	Tweed Mill Brae, Ardbroilach Road, Kingussie, Inverness-shire, PH21 1LB	01540 661166	★★★★	Restaurant with Rooms		🍃🍃
The Hermitage Guest House	Spey Street, Kingussie, Inverness-shire, PH21 1HN	01540 662137	★★★★	Guest House	♟	🍃🍃
The Scot House Hotel	Newtonmore Road, Kingussie, Inverness-shire, PH21 1HE	01540 661351	★★★	Small Hotel		

Kinloch Rannoch

Dunalastair Hotel	The Square, Kinloch Rannoch, Perthshire, PH16 5PW	01882 632323	★★★	Hotel	♿	🍃
Loch Rannoch Hotel	Kinloch Rannoch, Perthshire, PH16 5PS	01882 632201	★★★	Hotel		

♿ Unassisted wheelchair access ♿ Assisted wheelchair access ♟ Access for visitors with mobility difficulties
🍃 Bronze Green Tourism Award 🍃🍃 Silver Green Tourism Award 🍃🍃🍃 Gold Green Tourism Award
For further information on our Green Tourism Business Scheme please see page 9.

Kinlochbervie

Old School Restaurant & Rooms	Inshegra, Kinlochbervie, Sutherland, IV27 4RH	01971 521383	★★★	Restaurant with Rooms
The Kinlochbervie Hotel	Kinlochbervie, Sutherland, IV27 4RP	01971 521275	★★	Small Hotel

Kinlochleven

Edencoille	Garbhien Road, Kinlochleven, Argyll, PH50 4SE	01855 831358	★★★★	Guest House	
Highland Getaway	28 Leven Road, Kinlochleven, Argyll, PH50 4RP	01855 831506	★★★	Restaurant with Rooms	
MacDonald Hotel	Fort William Road, Kinlochleven, Argyll, PH50 4QR	01855 831539	AWAITING GRADING		
Mamore Lodge Hotel	Kinlochleven, Argyll, PH50 4QN	01855 831 213	★	Small Hotel	
Tailrace Inn	Riverside Road, Kinlochleven, Argyll, PH50 4QH	01855 831777	★★★	Inn	
Tigh-Na-Cheo	Garbien Road, Kinlochleven, Argyll, PH50 4SE	01855 831434	★★★★	Guest House	&#9855;

Kinross

Kirklands Hotel and Restaurant	20 High Street, Kinross, Perthshire, KY13 8AN	01577 863313	★★★	Small Hotel	
The Green Hotel	2 The Muirs, Kinross, Perthshire, KY13 8AS	01577 863467	★★★★	Hotel	🌿
The Grouse and Claret	Heatheryford, Kinross, Perthshire, KY13 0NQ	01577 864212	★★★	Restaurant with Rooms	
Travelodge Kinross M90	Turfhills Tourist Centre, Kinross, Perthshire, KY13 7NQ	08719 846151	AWAITING GRADING		&#9855;
Windlestrae Hotel	The Muirs, Kinross, Perthshire, KY13 8AS	01577 863217	★★★	Hotel	

Kintore

Torryburn Hotel	School Road, Kintore, Aberdeenshire, AB51 0XP	01467 632269	★★	Small Hotel

Kintyre

Ashbank Hotel	Carradale, Kintyre, Argyll, PA28 6RY	01583 431650	★★	Small Hotel	
Hunting Lodge Hotel	Bellochantuy, Kintyre, Argyll, PA28 6QE	01583 421323	★	Small Hotel	🚶

Kirk Yetholm

The Border Hotel	The Green, Kirk Yetholm, Scottish Borders, TD5 8PQ	01573 420237	★★★★	Inn

Kirkcaldy

Dean Park Hotel	Chapel Level, Kirkcaldy, Fife, KY2 6QW	01592 261635	★★★	Hotel
The Strathearn Hotel	2 Wishart Place, Kirkcaldy, Fife, KY1 2AS	01592 654731	★★	Small Hotel

Kirkcudbright

Fludha Guest House	Tongland Road, Kirkcudbright, Kirkcudbrightshire, DG6 4UU	01557 331443	★★★★★	Guest House	&#9855;
Gladstone House	48 High Street, Kirkcudbright, Kirkcudbrightshire, DG6 4JX	01557 331734	★★★★	Guest House	
Gordon House Hotel	116 High Street, Kirkcudbright, Kirkcudbrightshire, DG6 4JQ	01557 330670	★★★	Small Hotel	

♿ Unassisted wheelchair access ♿ Assisted wheelchair access 🚶 Access for visitors with mobility difficulties
🌿 Bronze Green Tourism Award 🌿🌿 Silver Green Tourism Award 🌿🌿🌿 Gold Green Tourism Award
For further information on our Green Tourism Business Scheme please see page 9.

| Royal Hotel | 50 St Cuthbert Street, Kirkcudbright, Kirkcudbrightshire, DG6 4DY | 01557 331213 | AWAITING GRADING | | | |
| Selkirk Arms Hotel | High Street, Kirkcudbright, Kirkcudbrightshire, DG6 4JG | 01557 330402 | ★★★ | Small Hotel | | |

Kirkhill

| Old North Inn | Kirkhill, Inverness, IV5 7PX | 01463 831296 | ★★ | Inn | | |

Kirkintilloch

| Smiths Hotel | 3 David Donnelly Place, Kirkintilloch, North Lanarkshire, G66 1DD | 0141 775 0398 | ★ | Hotel | | |

Kirknewton

| The Marriott Dalmahoy Hotel and Country Club | Kirknewton, Midlothian, EH27 8EP | 0131 3331845 | ★★★★ | Hotel | | |

Kirkwall, Orkney

Albert Hotel	Mounthoolie Lane, Kirkwall, Orkney, KW15 1JZ	01856 876000	★★★	Small Hotel		
Avalon House	Carness Road, Kirkwall, Orkney, KW15 1UE	01856 876665	★★★★	Guest House		
Ayre Hotel	Ayre Road, Kirkwall, Orkney, KW15 1QX	01856 873001	★★★	Hotel		
Bellavista	Carness Road, Kirkwall, Orkney, KW15 1UE	01856 872306	★★★	Guest House		
Brekkness Guest House	Muddisdale Road, Kirkwall, Orkney, KW15 1RS	01856 874317	★★★	Guest House		
Foveran Hotel	St Ola, Kirkwall, Orkney, KW15 1SF	01856 872389	★★★	Small Hotel		⌐⌐⌐
Kirkwall Hotel	Harbour Street, Kirkwall, Orkney, KW15 1LF	01856 872232	★★★	Hotel		
Lav'rockha Guest House	Inganess Road, Kirkwall, Orkney, KW15 1SP	01856 876103	★★★★	Guest House	♿	⌐⌐⌐
Lynnfield Hotel	Holm Road, Kirkwall, Orkney, KW15 1SU	01856 872505	★★★★	Small Hotel		
Orkney Hotel	Victoria Street, Kirkwall, Orkney, KW15	01856 873477	★★★	Hotel		⌐⌐
Polrudden Guest House	Peerie Sea Loan, Kirkwall, Orkney, KW15 1UH	01856 874761	★★★	Guest House		
Royal Oak Guest House	Holm Road, Kirkwall, Orkney, KW15 1PY	01856 873487	★★★	Guest House		
Sanderlay Guest House	2 Viewfield Drive, Kirkwall, Orkney, KW15 1RB	01856 875587	★★★	Guest House		
St Ola Hotel	Harbour Street, Kirkwall, Orkney, KW15 1LE	01856 875090	★★★	Guest House		
The Inn B&B	St Marys, Holm, Kirkwall, Orkney, KW17 2RU	01856 781786	★★★	Guest House		
The Shore, Rooms, Restaurant, Bar	Shore Street, Kirkwall, Orkney, KW15 1LG	01856 872200	★★★	Inn		
West End Hotel	14 Main Street, Kirkwall, Orkney, KW15 1BU	01856 872368	★★★	Small Hotel		

Kirriemuir

| Lochside Lodge & Roundhouse Restaurant | Bridgend of Lintrathen, Kirriemuir, Angus, DD8 5JJ | 01575 560340 | ★★★★ | Restaurant with Rooms | ♿ | |
| Thrums Hotel | 25 Bank Street, Kirriemuir, Angus, DD8 4BE | 01575 572758 | ★★★ | Small Hotel | | |

♿ Unassisted wheelchair access   ♿ Assisted wheelchair access   ♿ Access for visitors with mobility difficulties
⌐ Bronze Green Tourism Award   ⌐⌐ Silver Green Tourism Award   ⌐⌐⌐ Gold Green Tourism Award
For further information on our Green Tourism Business Scheme please see page 9.

by Kirriemuir

Glen Clova Hotel	Glen Clova, by Kirriemuir, Angus, DD8 4QS	01575 550350	★★★	Small Hotel	

Knipoch

Knipoch Hotel	Knipoch, Argyll, PA34 4QT	01852 316251	★★★	Small Hotel	

Knoydart, Mallaig

Doune Stone Lodges	Doune, Knoydart, Mallaig, Inverness-shire, PH41 4PU	01687 462667	★★★	Restaurant with Rooms	

Kyle of Lochalsh

Borodale House	Raasay, Kyle of Lochalsh, Ross-shire, IV40 8PB	01478 660222	★★★	Small Hotel	⸙

by Kyle of Lochalsh

Dornie Hotel	8-10 Francis Street,Dornie, by Kyle of Lochalsh, Ross-shire, IV40 8DT	01599 555205	★★★	Small Hotel	
Eilean A Cheo	Dornie, by Kyle of Lochalsh, Ross-shire, IV40 8DY	01599 555485	★★★	Guest House	
Tingle Creek Hotel	Erbusaig, by Kyle of Lochalsh, Ross-shire, IV40 8BB	01599 534430	★★★	Small Hotel	
Kintail Lodge Hotel	Glenshiel, by Kyle of Lochalsh, Ross-shire, IV40 8HL	01599 511275	★★★	Small Hotel	
Conchra House	Sallachy Road,Ardelve, by Kyle of Lochalsh, Ross-shire, IV40 8DZ	01599 555233	★★★	Guest House	
Caberfeidh Guest House	Upper Ardelve, by Kyle of Lochalsh, Ross-shire, IV40 8DY	01599 555293	★★★	Guest House	
Balmacara Mains Guest House	by Kyle of Lochalsh, Ross-Shire, IV40 8DN	01559 566242	★★★★	Guest House	

Kyleakin, Isle of Skye

Blairdhu House	Kyle Farm Road, Kyleakin, Isle of Skye, IV41 8PQ	01599 534760	★★★★	Guest House	
Corran Guest House	Kyleakin, Isle of Skye, IV41 8PL	01599 534859	★★★★	Guest House	
Glenarroch	Main Street, Kyleakin, Isle of Skye, IV41 8PH	01599 534845	★★★	Guest House	
Mackinnon Country House Hotel	Old Farm Road, Kyleakin, Isle of Skye, IV41 8PQ	01599 534180	★★★	Small Hotel	

Kylesku

Newton Lodge	Kylesku, Sutherland, IV27 4HW	01971 502070	★★★★	Guest House	

Laggan

The Rumblie	Gergask Avenue, Laggan, Inverness-shire, PH20 1AH	01528 544766	★★★★	Guest House	𝄯𝄯𝄯

Laggan Bridge

Monadhliath Hotel	Laggan Bridge, Inverness-shire, PH20 1BT	01528 544276	★★★	Small Hotel	

Lairg

Park House	Lairg, Sutherland, IV27 4AU	01549 402208	★★★★	Guest House	
The Nip Inn	Main Street, Lairg, Sutherland, IV27 4DB	01549 402243	★★★	Small Hotel	

♿ Unassisted wheelchair access   ♿ Assisted wheelchair access   ⸙ Access for visitors with mobility difficulties
🄿 Bronze Green Tourism Award   🄿🄿 Silver Green Tourism Award   🄿🄿🄿 Gold Green Tourism Award
For further information on our Green Tourism Business Scheme please see page 9.

248   To find out more, call 0845 22 55 121 or go to visitscotland.com.

by Lairg

Scourie Guest House	55 Scourie Village, by Lairg, Sutherland, IV27 4TE	01971 502001	★★★	Guest House
The Overscaig House Hotel	Loch Shin, by Lairg, Sutherland, IV27 4NY	01549 431203	★★★	Small Hotel
Tongue Hotel	Tongue, by Lairg, Sutherland, IV27 4XD	01847 611206	★★★★	Small Hotel

Lamlash

Glenisle Hotel	Shore Road, Lamlash, Isle of Arran, KA27 8LY	01770 600559	★★★	Small Hotel	
Lilybank	Shore Road, Lamlash, Isle of Arran, KA27 8LS	01770 600230	★★★★	Guest House	⋔

Lamlash Bay

Centre For The Earth Peace and Health	Holy Isle, Lamlash Bay, Isle of Arran, KA27 8GB	01770 601100	AWAITING GRADING	

Lanark

Cartland Bridge Country House Hotel	Glasgow Road, Lanark, Lanarkshire, ML11 9UE	01555 664426	★★★	Country House Hotel

Largs

Lilac Holm Guest House	14 Noddleburn Road, Largs, Ayrshire, KA30 8PY	01475 672020	★★★	Guest House
Tigh An Struan	29 Gogo Street, Largs, Ayrshire, KA30 8BU	01475 670668	★★★	Guest House
Tigh-Na-Ligh	104 Brisbane Road, Largs, Ayrshire, KA30 8NN	01475 673975	★★★	Guest House
Whin-Park Guest House	16 Douglas Street, Largs, Ayrshire, KA30 8PS	01475 673437	★★★★	Guest House
Willowbank Hotel	96 Greenock Road, Largs, Ayrshire, KA30 8PG	01475 672311	★★★	Hotel

by Larkhall

Shawlands Hotel	Ayr Road,Canderside Toll, by Larkhall, Lanarkshire, ML9 2TZ	01698 791111	★★★	Hotel	⋔

Lauder

Black Bull Hotel	9 Market Place, Lauder, Berwickshire, TD2 6SR	01578 722208	★★	Inn

by Lauder

The Lodge at Carfraemill	Carfraemill, by Lauder, Berwickshire, TD2 6RA	01578 750750	★★★★	Restaurant with Rooms

Lawers, Loch Tay

Ben Lawers Hotel	Lawers, Loch Tay, Perthshire, PH15 2PA	01567 820436	★★★	Inn

Lerwick, Shetland

Alderlodge Guest House	6 Clairmont Place, Lerwick, Shetland, ZE1 0BR	01595 695705	★★★	Guest House
Breiview	43 Kanterstead Road, Lerwick, Shetland, ZE1 0RJ	01595 695956	★★★	Guest House
Brentham House	7 Harbour Street, Lerwick, Shetland, ZE1 0LR	01950 460201	★★★★	Guest Accommodation
Eddlewood Guest House	8 Clairmont Place, Lerwick, Shetland, ZE1 0BR	01595 692772	★★★	Guest House

    ♿ Unassisted wheelchair access   ♿ Assisted wheelchair access   ⋔ Access for visitors with mobility difficulties
ᐰ Bronze Green Tourism Award   ᐰᐰ Silver Green Tourism Award   ᐰᐰᐰ Gold Green Tourism Award
For further information on our Green Tourism Business Scheme please see page 9.

Fort Charlotte Guest House	1 Charlotte Street, Lerwick, Shetland, ZE1 0JL	01595 692140	★★★	Guest House		
Glen Orchy Guest House	20 Knab Road, Lerwick, Shetland, ZE1 0AX	01595 692031	★★★	Guest House	⚡	🍃🍃
Grand Hotel	Commercial Street, Lerwick, Shetland, ZE1 0HX	01595 692826	★★★	Hotel		
Kveldsro House Hotel	Greenfield Place, Lerwick, Shetland, ZE1 0AN	01595 692195	★★★	Small Hotel		
Lerwick Hotel	15 South Road, Lerwick, Shetland, ZE1 0RB	01595 692166	★★★	Hotel		
Queen's Hotel	Commercial Street, Lerwick, Shetland, ZE1 0AB	01595 692826	★★	Hotel		
Shetland Hotel	Holmsgarth Road, Lerwick, Shetland, ZE1 0PW	01595 695515	★★★	Hotel	♿	
Solheim Guest House	34 King Harald Street, Lerwick, Shetland, ZE1 0EQ	01595 695275	★★★	Guest House		

Leslie

Rescobie House Hotel	6 Valley Drive, Leslie, Fife, KY6 3BQ	01592 749555	★★★	Small Hotel

Leven

Caledonian Hotel	81 High Street, Leven, Fife, KY8 4NG	01333 424101	★★★	Hotel
Dunclutha	16 Victoria Road, Leven, Fife, KY8 4EX	01333 425515	★★★★	Guest House
Lomond Guest House	6 Church Road, Leven, Fife, KY8 4JE	01333 300930	★★★	Guest House

Leverburgh, Isle of Harris

Grimisdale	Leverburgh, Isle of Harris, HS5 3TS	01859 520460	★★★★	Guest House

Linlithgow

The Star & Garter Hotel	1 High Street, Linlithgow, West Lothian, EH49 7AB	01506 846362	AWAITING GRADING	
West Port Hotel	West Port, Linlithgow, West Lothian, EH49 7AZ	01506 847456	★★	Small Hotel

by Linlithgow

The Bonsyde House Hotel	Bonsyde, by Linlithgow, West Lothian, EH49 7NU	01506 842229	★★★	Small Hotel

Livingston

Livingston Premier Inn	Deer Park Avenue, Deer Park, Livingston, West Lothian, EH54 8AD	0870 1977161		Budget Hotel		
Ramada Livingston	Almondview, Livingston, West Lothian, EH54 6QB	01506 431222	★★★	Hotel	⚡	🍃
Travelodge Livingston	The Hub, Almondvale Crescent, Livingston, West Lothian, EH54 6QX	08719 846288	AWAITING GRADING	

Loanhead

Aaron Glen Guest House	7 Nivensknowe Road, Loanhead, Midlothian, EH20 9AU	0131 440 1293	★★★	Guest House	⚡	

Loch Fyne

West Loch Hotel	Tarbert, Loch Fyne, Argyll, PA29 6YF	01880 820283	★★	Inn

& Unassisted wheelchair access   ♿ Assisted wheelchair access   ⚡ Access for visitors with mobility difficulties
🍃 Bronze Green Tourism Award   🍃🍃 Silver Green Tourism Award   🍃🍃🍃 Gold Green Tourism Award
For further information on our Green Tourism Business Scheme please see page 9.

To find out more, call 0845 22 55 121 or go to visitscotland.com.

Loch Harray, Orkney

| Merkister Hotel | Loch Harray, Orkney, KW17 2LF | 01856 771366 | ★★★ | Country House Hotel | 🅟 |

Loch Lomond

| Ardlui Hotel | Loch Lomond, Nr Arrocher, Dunbartonshire, G83 7EB | 01301 704243 | ★★★ | Small Hotel | |
| Culag Lochside Guest House | Luss, Loch Lomond, Argyll, G83 8PD | 01436 860248 | ★★★★ | Guest House | 🚶 |

Loch Ness-side

| Loch Ness Clansman Hotel | Brackla, Loch Ness Side, Inverness-shire, IV3 6LA | 01456 450326 | ★★★ | Hotel | |
| Loch Ness Lodge | Brachla, Loch Ness-side, Inverness-shire, IV3 8LA | 01456 459469 | ★★★★★ | Exclusive Use Venue | |

Lochboisdale, Isle of South Uist

| Brae Lea House | Lasgair, Lochboisdale, Isle of South Uist, HS8 5TH | 01878 700497 | ★★★ | Guest House | |
| Lochboisdale Hotel | Lochboisdale, Isle of South Uist, HS8 5TH | 01878 700332 | ★★ | Small Hotel | |

Lochcarnan, Isle of South Uist

| Orasay Inn | Lochcarnan, Isle of South Uist, HS8 5PD | 01870 610298 | ★★★ | Small Hotel | ♿ |

Lochcarron

| Rockvilla Hotel | Main Street, Lochcarron, Ross-shire, IV54 8YB | 01520 722379 | ★★★ | Inn | |

Lochearnhead

Lochearn House	Lochearnhead, Perthshire, FK19 8NR	01567 830380	★★★★	Guest House	
Lochearnhead Hotel	Lochside, Lochearnhead, Perthshire, FK19 8PU	01567 830229	★★	Small Hotel	
Mansewood Country House	Lochearnhead, Stirlingshire, FK19 8NS	01567 830213	★★★★	Guest House	
Monachyle Mhor	Balquhidder, Lochearnhead, Perthshire, FK19 8PQ	0877 384622	★★★★	Small Hotel	

Locheport, Isle of North Uist

| Langass Lodge | Locheport, Isle of North Uist, HS6 5EX | 01876 580285 | ★★★ | Restaurant with Rooms | 🅟🅟🅟 |

Lochgilphead

| Empire Travel Lodge | Union Street, Lochgilphead, Argyll, PA31 8JS | 01546 602381 | ★★★ | Lodge | ♿ |

by Lochgilphead

| Cairnbaan Hotel | Cairnbaan, by Lochgilphead, Argyll, PA31 8SJ | 01546 603668 | ★★★ | Small Hotel | |
| Ford House | Ford, by Lochgilphead, Argyll, PA31 8RH | 01546 810273 | ★★★ | Guest House | |

Lochgoilhead

| Drimsynie House Hotel | Lochgoilhead, Argyll, PA24 8AD | 01301 703247 | ★★★ | Small Hotel | |
| Lochgoilhead Hotel | Lochgoilhead, Argyll, PA24 8AA | 01301 703 247 | ★★ | Small Hotel | |

♿ Unassisted wheelchair access   ♿ Assisted wheelchair access   🚶 Access for visitors with mobility difficulties
🅟 Bronze Green Tourism Award   🅟🅟 Silver Green Tourism Award   🅟🅟🅟 Gold Green Tourism Award
For further information on our Green Tourism Business Scheme please see page 9.

The Lodge	Lochgoilhead, Argyll, PA24 8AE	01301 703193	★★★★★	Exclusive Use Venue	🍃🍃
The Shore House Inn	Lochgoilhead, Argyll, PA24 8AA	01301 703340	★★★	Inn	

Lochinver

Inver Lodge Hotel	Lochinver, Lairg, Sutherland, IV27 4LU	01571 844496	★★★★	Hotel	
The Albannach	Baddidarroch, Lochinver, Sutherland, IV27 4LP	01571 844407	★★★★	Small Hotel	
Polcraig Guest House	Cruamer, Lochinver, Sutherland, IV27 4LD	01571 844429	★★★★	Guest House	

by Lochinver

Cruachan Guest House	Stoer, by Lochinver, Sutherland, IV27 4JE	01571 855303	★★★★	Guest House	

Lochmaben

The Crown Hotel	8 Bruce Street, Lochmaben, Dumfries & Galloway, DG11 1PD	01387 811750	★★	Inn	♿

Lochmaddy, Isle of North Uist

Carinish Inn	Carinish, Lochmaddy, Isle of North Uist, HS6 5EJ	01876 580673	★★★	Inn	
Temple View Hotel	Carinish, Lochmaddy, Isle of North Uist, HS6 5EJ	01876 580676	★★★★	Small Hotel	
Tigh Dearg Hotel	Lochmaddy, Isle of North Uist, HS6 5AE	01876 500700	★★★★	Small Hotel	🦽 🍃

Lochranza, Isle of Arran

Apple Lodge	Lochranza, Isle of Arran, KA27 8HJ	01770 830229	★★★★	Guest House	
Lochranza Hotel	Shore Road, Lochranza, Isle of Arran, KA27 8HL	01770 830223	★★★	Inn	

Lochwinnoch

The Hungry Monk	Largs Road, Lochwinnoch, Renfrewshire, PA12 4JF	01505 843848	★★★★	Inn	

Lockerbie

Dryfesdale Country House Hotel	Dryfebridge, Lockerbie, Dumfries & Galloway, DG11 2SF	01576 202427	★★★★	Hotel	🦽
Kings Arms Hotel	29 High Street, Lockerbie, Dumfries & Galloway, DG11 2JL	01576 202410	★★★	Small Hotel	
Lockerbie Premier Inn (Annandale Water)	Annandale Water Motorway Services,J16 M74, Johnstonebridge, Lockerbie,	8701977163		Budget Hotel	
Queens Hotel	Annan Road, Lockerbie, Dumfries & Galloway, DG11 2RB	01576 202415	★★★	Hotel	
Ravenshill House Hotel	12 Dumfries Road, Lockerbie, Dumfries & Galloway, DG11 2EF	01576 202882	★★	Small Hotel	
Somerton House Hotel	35 Carlisle Road, Lockerbie, Dumfries & Galloway, DG11 2DR	01576 202583	★★★	Small Hotel	

by Lockerbie

Dinwoodie Lodge Hotel	Johnstone Bridge, by Lockerbie, Dumfries & Galloway, DG11 2SL	01576 470289	★★	Small Hotel	

Lossiemouth

Links Lodge	Stotfield Road, Lossiemouth, Moray, IV31 6QS	01343 813815	★★★★	Guest House	🚶

♿ Unassisted wheelchair access   🦽 Assisted wheelchair access   🚶 Access for visitors with mobility difficulties
🍃 Bronze Green Tourism Award   🍃🍃 Silver Green Tourism Award   🍃🍃🍃 Gold Green Tourism Award
For further information on our Green Tourism Business Scheme please see page 9.

| The Skerry Brae Hotel | Stotfield Road, Lossiemouth, Moray, IV31 6QS | 01343 812040 | ★★★ | Small Hotel | |

Lundin Links

| Old Manor Hotel | 55 Leven Road, Lundin Links, Fife, KY8 6AJ | 01333 320368 | ★★ | Hotel | |

Luss

| The Lodge on Loch Lomond | Luss, Dunbartonshire, G83 8NT | 01436 860201 | ★★★★ | Hotel | 𝒫𝒫 |

Macduff

| Knowes Hotel | 78 Market Street, Macduff, Banffshire, AB44 1LL | 01261 832229 | ★★ | Small Hotel | |
| The Park Hotel | Fife Street, Macduff, Banffshire, AB44 1YA | 01261 832265 | ★★★ | Guest House | |

Macmerry

| Adniston Manor | West Adniston Farm, Macmerry, East Lothian, EH33 1EA | 01875 611190 | ★★★★ | Guest House | ♀ |

Mallaig

Garramore House	South Morar, Mallaig, Inverness-shire, PH40 4PD	01687 450268	★★	Guest House	
Seaview	Main Street, Mallaig, Inverness-shire, PH41 4QS	01687 462059	★★★	Guest House	
The Moorings	East Bay, Mallaig, Inverness-shire, PH41 4PQ	01687 462225	★★★	Guest House	
West Highland Hotel	Mallaig, Inverness-shire, PH41 4QZ	01687 462210	★★★	Hotel	
Western Isles Guest House	East Bay, Mallaig, Inverness-shire, PH41 4QG	01687 462320	★★★	Guest House	

Markinch, by Glenrothes

Balbirnie House Hotel	Balbirnie Park, Markinch, by Glenrothes, Fife, KY7 6NE	01592 610066	★★★★	Hotel	♿
Laurel Bank Hotel	1 Balbirnie Street, Markinch, by Glenrothes, Fife, KY7 6DB	01592 611205	★★	Small Hotel	
Town House Hotel	1 High Street, Markinch, by Glenrothes, Fife, KY7 6DQ	01592 758459	★★★★	Restaurant with Rooms	

Maryculter

| Maryculter Country House Hotel | Maryculter, Kincardineshire, AB12 5GB | 01224 732124 | ★★★★ | Country House Hotel | 𝒫𝒫 |
| Old Mill Inn | South Deeside Road, Maryculter, by Aberdeen, Kincardineshire, AB12 5FX | 01224 733212 | ★★★ | Inn | |

Meikleour

| Meikleour Hotel | Meikleour, Perthshire, PH2 6EB | 01250 883206 | ★★★★ | Inn | |

Melrose

Braidwood	Buccleuch Street, Melrose, Roxburghshire, TD6 9LD	01896 822488	★★★★	Guest House	
Burts Hotel	Market Square, Melrose, Roxburghshire, TD6 9PL	01896 822285	★★★	Small Hotel	
Dryburgh Abbey Hotel	St Boswells, Melrose, Roxburghshire, TD6 0RQ	01835 822261	★★★★	Country House Hotel	
Dunfermline House	Buccleuch Street, Melrose, Roxburghshire, TD6 9LB	01896 822411	★★★	Guest House	

♿ Unassisted wheelchair access ♿ Assisted wheelchair access ♀ Access for visitors with mobility difficulties
𝒫 Bronze Green Tourism Award 𝒫𝒫 Silver Green Tourism Award 𝒫𝒫𝒫 Gold Green Tourism Award
For further information on our Green Tourism Business Scheme please see page 9.

George & Abbotsford Hotel	High Street, Melrose, Roxburghshire, TD6 9PD	01896 822308	★★	Hotel	
The Town House Hotel	3 Market Square, Melrose, Roxburghshire, TD6 9PQ	01896 822645	★★★	Townhouse Hotel	
Waverley Castle Hotel	Melrose, Roxburghshire, TD6 9AA	01896 436600	★★★	Hotel	

Melvich

| Bighouse Lodge | Melvich, Sutherland, KW14 7YJ | 01641 531207 | ★★★★ | Country House Hotel | |
| Melvich Hotel | Melvich, Sutherland, KW14 7YJ | 01641 531206 | ★★★ | Small Hotel | |

Menstrie

| Broomhall Castle | Long Row, Menstrie, Clackmannanshire, FK11 7EA | 01259 763360 | ★★ | Hotel | |

Millport, Isle of Cumbrae

| The Cathedral of the Isles | The College, Millport, Isle of Cumbrae, KA28 0HE | 01475 530353 | ★★★ | Guest House | ♿ |

Milton

| Milton Inn | Dumbarton Road, Milton, Dunbartonshire, G82 2DT | 01389 761401 | ★★★ | Inn | ⚗ |

Milton of Culloden

| Culloden House Hotel | Milton of Culloden, Inverness, IV1 2NZ | 01463 792181 | ★★★★ | Hotel | |

Minnigaff

| Flowerbank Guest House | Millcroft Road, Minnigaff, Wigtownshire, DG8 6PJ | 01671 402629 | ★★★ | Guest House | |

Mintlaw

| Saplinbrae House Hotel | Old Deer, Mintlaw, Aberdeenshire, AB42 4LP | 01771 623 515 | ★★ | Small Hotel | |

Moffat

Annandale Arms Hotel	High Street, Moffat, Dumfries & Galloway, DG10 9HF	01683 220013	★★★	Small Hotel	
Auchen Castle Hotel	Beattock, Moffat, Dumfries & Galloway, DG10 9SH	01683 300407	★★★★	Country House Hotel	
Balmoral Hotel	High Street, Moffat, Dumfries & Galloway, DG10 9DL	01683 20288	★★★	Inn	
Bridge House	Well Road, Moffat, Dumfries & Galloway, DG10 9JT	01683 220558	★★★★	Guest House	
Buccleuch Arms Hotel	High Street, Moffat, Dumfries & Galloway, DG10 9ET	01683 220003	★★★	Small Hotel	⟨PPP⟩
Buchan Guest House	Beechgrove, Moffat, Dumfries & Galloway, DG10 9RS	01683 220378	★★★	Guest House	
Hartfell House	Hartfell Crescent, Moffat, Dumfries & Galloway, DG10 9AL	01683 220153	★★★★	Guest House	
Limetree House	Eastgate, Moffat, Dumfries & Galloway, DG10 9AE	01683 220001	★★★★	Guest House	⚗
Marchbankwood House	Beattock, Moffat, Dumfries & Galloway, DG10 9RG	01683 300118	★★★★	Guest House	
Moffat House Hotel	High Street, Moffat, Dumfries & Galloway, DG10 9HL	01683 220039	★★★	Hotel	
Rockhill Guest House	14 Beechgrove, Moffat, Dumfries & Galloway, DG10 9RS	01683 220283	★★★	Guest House	

♿ Unassisted wheelchair access ♿ Assisted wheelchair access ⚗ Access for visitors with mobility difficulties
⟨P⟩ Bronze Green Tourism Award   ⟨PP⟩ Silver Green Tourism Award   ⟨PPP⟩ Gold Green Tourism Award
For further information on our Green Tourism Business Scheme please see page 9.

Seamore House	Academy Road, Moffat, Dumfries & Galloway, DG10 9HW	01683 220404	★★★	Guest House	
Stag Hotel	22 High Street, Moffat, Dumfries & Galloway, DG10 9HL	01683 220343	★★	Inn	
Star Hotel	44 High Street, Moffat, Dumfries & Galloway, DG10 9EF	01683 220156	★★	Small Hotel	
Well View Hotel	Ballplay Road, Moffat, Dumfries & Galloway, DG10 9JU	01683 220184	★★★★	Restaurant with Rooms	

Monifieth, Dundee

Milton Hotel	Grange Road, Monifieth, Dundee DD5 4LU	01382 539016	★★★	Small Hotel	
Premier Inn Dundee Monifeith	Monifeith Farm, Ethiebeaton Park, Monifieth, Dundee DD5 4HB	08701 977080		Budget Hotel	

Monkton

Ayr Premier Inn	Monkton Lodge, Kilmarnock Road, Monkton, Ayrshire, KA9 2RJ	08701 977020		Budget Hotel	

Montrose

Best Western Links Hotel	Mid Links, Montrose, Angus, DD10 8RL	01674 671000	★★★★	Hotel	☥
Oaklands	10 Rossie Island Road, Montrose, Angus, DD10 9NN	01674 672018	★★★	Guest House	
Park Hotel	61 John Street, Montrose, Angus, DD10	01674 663400	★★★	Hotel	

Morar, by Mallaig

Morar Hotel	Morar, by Mallaig, Inverness-shire, PH40 4PA	01687 462346	★★	Hotel	

Motherwell

Dakota Hotel	Eurocentral Business Park, Motherwell, North Lanarkshire, ML1 4UD	01698 835444	★★★	Hotel	
Express by Holiday Inn	Strathclyde Park M74 Jct 5, Motherwell, Lanarkshire, ML1 3RB	01698 852375	★★★	Metro Hotel	♿
Moorings Hotel	114 Hamilton Road, Motherwell, Lanarkshire, ML1 3DG	01698 258131	★★★	Hotel	♿
Motherwell College Stewart Hall	Dalzell Drive, Motherwell, Lanarkshire, ML1 2DD	01698 261890	★	Campus	♿
The Alona Hotel	Strathclyde Country Park, Motherwell, North Lanarkshire, ML1 3RT	0870 112 3888	★★★★	Hotel	♿

by Motherwell

Glasgow Motherwell Premier Inn	Edinburgh Road,Newhouse, by Motherwell, Lanarkshire, ML1 5SY	08701 977164		Budget Hotel	

Muir of Ord

Fairburn Lodge & Activity Centre	Urray, Muir of Ord, Ross-shire, IV6 7UT	01997 433397	★★	Lodge	
Ord House Hotel	Muir of Ord, Ross-shire, IV6 7UH	01463 870492	★★	Country House Hotel	

Musselburgh

Arden House	26 Linkfield Road, Musselburgh, East Lothian, EH21 7LL	0131 665 0663	★★★★	Guest House	
Carberry Tower	Musselburgh, East Lothian, EH21 8PY	0131 665 3135	AWAITING GRADING		☥
Edinburgh Inveresk Premier Inn	Craig House,Carberry Road, Musselburgh, East Lothian, EH21 8PT	08701 977092		Budget Hotel	

♿ Unassisted wheelchair access   ♿ Assisted wheelchair access   ☥ Access for visitors with mobility difficulties
🅿 Bronze Green Tourism Award   🅿🅿 Silver Green Tourism Award   🅿🅿🅿 Gold Green Tourism Award
For further information on our Green Tourism Business Scheme please see page 9.

Travelodge Edinburgh Musselburgh	Service Area, A1 Old Craighall, Musselburgh, East Lothian, EH21 8RE	08719 846138	AWAITING GRADING			

Nairn

Aurora Hotel	2 Academy Street, Nairn, Nairn-shire, IV12 4RJ	01667 453551	★★	Small Hotel		
Bracadale House	Albert Street, Nairn, Inverness-shire, IV12 4HF	01667 452547	★★★★	Guest House		
Braeval Hotel	Crescent Road, Nairn, Inverness-shire, IV12 4NB	01667 452341	★★★	Small Hotel		
Cawdor House	7 Cawdor Street, Nairn, Inverness-shire, IV12 4QD	01667 455855	★★★★	Guest House		
Claymore House Hotel	45 Seabank Road, Nairn, Inverness-shire, IV12 4EY	01667 453731	★★★★	Small Hotel		
Golf View Hotel	Seabank Road, Nairn, Inverness-shire, IV12 4HD	01667 452301	AWAITING GRADING			
Invernairne Guest House	Thurlow Road, Nairn, Inverness-shire, IV12 4EZ	01667 452039	★★★	Guest House		
Sunny Brae Hotel	Marine Road, Nairn, Inverness-shire, IV12 4AE	01667 452309	★★★★	Small Hotel		PPP
Windsor Hotel	16 Albert Street, Nairn, Inverness-shire, IV12 4HP	01667 453108	AWAITING GRADING		♿	

Ness, Isle of Lewis

The Cross Inn	Cross Ness, Ness, Isle of Lewis, HS2 0SN	01851 810152	★★★	Inn	♿	

Nethybridge

Mountview Hotel	Nethybridge, Inverness-shire, PH25 3EB	01479 821 248	★★★	Small Hotel		PP
Nethybridge Hotel	Nethybridge, Inverness-shire, PH25 3DP	01479 821203	★★★	Hotel	♿	

New Lanark

New Lanark Mill Hotel	New Lanark, Lanarkshire, ML11 9DB	01555 667200	★★★	Hotel	♿	PPP

Newburgh

Mosspaul	Teviothead, Hawick, Newburgh, Roxburghshire, TD9 0LP	01450 850245	★★★	Restaurant with Rooms	♿	

Newcastleton

Liddesdale Hotel	17 Douglas Square, Newcastleton, Roxburghshire, TD9 0QD	01387 375255	★★★	Inn		

Newcraighall

Edinburgh (Newcraighall) Premier Inn	Cuddie Brae, 91 Newcraighall Road, Newcraighall, Edinburgh, EH21 8RX	0870 990 6336		Budget Hotel		

Newton Stewart

Bladnoch Inn	Main Street,Bladnoch, Newton Stewart, Wigtownshire, DG8 9AB	01988 402200	★★	Inn		
Creebridge House Hotel	Minnigaff, Newton Stewart, Wigtownshire, DG8 6NP	01671 402121	★★★	Small Hotel		
Galloway Arms Hotel	Victoria Street, Newton Stewart, Wigtownshire, DG8 6DB	01671 402653	★★★	Inn		
Kirroughtree House	Newton Stewart, Wigtownshire, DG8 6AN	01671 402141	★★★★	Country House Hotel		
Rowallan	Corsbie Road, Newton Stewart, Wigtownshire, DG8 6JB	01671 402520	★★★	Guest House		

♿ Unassisted wheelchair access   ♿ Assisted wheelchair access   ♿ Access for visitors with mobility difficulties
P Bronze Green Tourism Award   PP Silver Green Tourism Award   PPP Gold Green Tourism Award
For further information on our Green Tourism Business Scheme please see page 9.

Stables Guest House	Corsbie Road, Newton Stewart, Wigtownshire, DG8 6JB	01671 402157	★★★	Guest House
The Bruce Hotel	88 Queen Street, Newton Stewart, Wigtownshire, DG8 6JL	01671 402294	★★★	Hotel

by Newton Stewart

Ellangowan Hotel	St John Street,Creetown, by Newton Stewart, Wigtownshire, DG8 7JF	01671 820201	★★	Small Hotel

Newtonmore

Alvey House	Golf Course Road, Newtonmore, Inverness-shire, PH20 1AT	01540 673260	★★★	Guest House
Ard-Na-Coille	Kingussie Road, Newtonmore, Inverness-shire, PH20 1AY	01450 673214	★★★★★	Guest House
Balavil Sport Hotel	Main Street, Newtonmore, Inverness-shire, PH20 1DL	01540 673220	★★	Hotel
Coig Na Shee	Fort William Road, Newtonmore, Inverness-shire, PH20 1DG	01540 670109	★★★★	Guest House

North Ballachulish

Creag Mhor Lodge	Onich, North Ballachulish, Inverness-shire, PH33 6RY	01855 821379	★★★★	Guest House
The Lodge on the Loch Hotel	Onich, North Ballachulish, Fort William, PH33 6RY	01855 821237	★★★	Small Hotel

North Berwick

12 Quality Street	North Berwick, East Lothian, EH39 4HP	01620 892529	★★★	Restaurant with Rooms
MacDonald Marine Hotel & Spa	Cromwell Road, North Berwick, East Lothian, EH39 4LZ	0870 400 8129	★★★★	Hotel
Nether Abbey Hotel	Dirleton Avenue, North Berwick, East Lothian, EH39 4BQ	01620 892802	★★★	Small Hotel

North Kessock

Kessock Hotel	North Kessock, Inverness-shire, IV1 1XN	01463 731208	★★★	Small Hotel
Anchor and Chain	Coulmore Bay, North Kessock, Inverness-shire, IV1 3XB	01463 731313	★★★	Restaurant with Rooms

North Queensferry

Queensferry Hotel	St Margarets Head, North Queensferry, Fife, KY11 1HP	01383 410000	★★★	Hotel

North Ronaldsay, Orkney

Observatory Guest House	North Ronaldsay, Orkney, KW17 2BE	01857 633200	★★★	Guest House	♿

Oban

Alexandra Hotel	The Esplanade, Oban, Argyll, PA34 5AA	1838200444	★★★	Hotel
Alltavona	Corran Esplanade, Oban, Argyll, PA34 5AQ	01631 565067	★★★★	Guest House
Alt Na Craig	Glenmore Road, Oban, Argyll, PA34 4PG	01631 563637	★★★★	Guest House
Ards House	Connel, Oban, Argyll, PA37 1PT	01631 710255	★★★★	Guest House
Ayres Guest House	3 Victoria Crescent,Corran Esplanade, Oban, Argyll, PA34 5JL	01631 562 260	★★	Guest House
Beech Grove Guest House	Croft Road, Oban, Argyll, PA34 5JL	0163166111	★★★★	Guest House

♿ Unassisted wheelchair access   ♿ Assisted wheelchair access   ♿ Access for visitors with mobility difficulties
🌿 Bronze Green Tourism Award   🌿🌿 Silver Green Tourism Award   🌿🌿🌿 Gold Green Tourism Award
For further information on our Green Tourism Business Scheme please see page 9.

Awards correct as of mid August 2008   257

Columba Hotel	North Pier, Oban, Argyll, PA34 5QD	01631 562183	★★	Hotel	
Corriemar	6 Esplanade, Oban, Argyll, PA34 5AQ	01631 562476	★★★★	Guest House	
Dungallan Country House	Gallanach Road, Oban, Argyll, PA34 4PD	01631 563799	★★★★★	Guest House	
Dunheanish Guest House	Ardconnel Road, Oban, Argyll, PA34 5DW	01631 566556	★★★	Guest House	
Glenbervie Guest House	Dalriach Road, Oban, Argyll, PA34	01631 564770	★★★★	Guest House	
Glenburnie	Esplanade, Oban, Argyll, PA34 5AQ	01631 562089	★★★★	Guest House	
Glengorm	Dunollie Road, Oban, Argyll, PA34 5PH	01631 564386	★★★	Guest House	
Glenrigh Guest House	The Esplanade, Oban, Argyll, PA34 5AQ	01631 562991	★★★★	Guest House	
Glenroy Guest House	Rockfield Road, Oban, Argyll, PA34 5DQ	01631 562 585	★★★	Guest House	
Gramarvin Guest House	Breadalbane Street, Oban, Argyll, PA34 5PE	01631 564622	★★★	Guest House	
Great Western Hotel	Corran Esplanade, Oban, Argyll, PA34 5PP	01631 563101	★★★	Hotel	
Greencourt Guest House	Benvoullin Road, Oban, Argyll, PA34 5EF	01631 563987	★★★★	Guest House	
Hawthornbank Guest House	Dalriach Road, Oban, Argyll, PA34 5JE	01631 562041	★★★★	Guest House	
Heatherfield House	Albert Road, Oban, Argyll, PA34 5EY	01631 562806	★★★★	Guest House	
High Cliff	35 Glencruitten Road, Oban, Argyll, PA34 4EW	01631 564134	★★★★	Guest House	
Kathmore Guest House	Soroba Road, Oban, Argyll, PA34 4JF	01631 562104	★★★	Guest House	
Kelvin Hotel	Shore Street, Oban, Argyll, PA34 4LQ	01631 562150	★	Guest House	
Kilchrenan House	Corran Esplanade, Oban, Argyll, PA34 5AQ	01631 562663	★★★★	Guest House	
Kings Knoll Hotel	Dunollie Road, Oban, Argyll, PA34 5JH	01631 562536	★★★	Small Hotel	
Lagganbeg Guest House	Dunollie Road, Oban, Argyll, PA34 5PH	01631 563151	★★★	Guest House	
Maridon House	Dunuaran Road, Oban, Argyll, PA34 4NE	01631 562670	★★★	Guest House	
Oban Bay Hotel	Esplanade, Oban, Argyll, PA34 5AE	0870 950 6273	★★★	Hotel	⌐P
Queens Hotel	Esplanade, Oban, Argyll, PA34 5AG	01631 562505	AWAITING GRADING		
Roseneath Guest House	Dalriach Road, Oban, Argyll, PA34 5EQ	01631 562929	★★★	Guest House	
Royal Hotel	Argyll Square, Oban, Argyll, PA34 4BE	01631 563021	★★★	Hotel	
Sgeir Mhaol Guest House	Soroba Road, Oban, Argyll, PA34 4JF	01631 562650	★★★	Guest House	
St Anne's Guest House	Dunollie Road, Oban, Argyll, PA34 5PH	01631 562743	★★	Guest House	
Strathnaver Guest House	Dunollie Road, Oban, Argyll, PA34 5JQ	01631 63305	★★★	Guest House	
Sutherland Guest House	Corran Esplanade, Oban, Argyll, PA34 5PN	01631 562539	★★	Guest House	
The Barriemore	Corran Esplanade, Oban, Argyll, PA34 5AQ	01631 566356	★★★★	Guest House	

♿ Unassisted wheelchair access   ♿ Assisted wheelchair access   ♟ Access for visitors with mobility difficulties
P Bronze Green Tourism Award   PP Silver Green Tourism Award   PPP Gold Green Tourism Award
For further information on our Green Tourism Business Scheme please see page 9.

The Caledonian Hotel	Station Square, Oban, Argyll, PA34 5RT	01631 563133	★★★★	Hotel	↑
The Kimberley Hotel	Dalriach Road, Oban, Argyll, PA34 5EQ	01631 571115	AWAITING GRADING		
The Manor House	Gallanoch Road, Oban, Argyll, PA34 4LS	01631 562087	★★★★	Restaurant with Rooms	
The Old Manse	Dalriach Road, Oban, Argyll, PA34 5JE	01631 564886	★★★★	Guest House	
Thornloe Guest House	Albert Road, Oban, Argyll, PA34 5EJ	01631 562879	★★★★	Guest House	⌐⌐
Ulva Villa	Soroba Road, Oban, Argyll, PA34 4JF	01631 563042	★★★	Guest House	
Wellpark House	Esplanade, Oban, Argyll, PA34 5AQ	01631 562948	★★★	Guest House	
Woodside Hotel	Tweeddale Street, Oban, Argyll, PA34 4DD	01631 562184	★	Inn	

by Oban

Willowburn Hotel	Clachan Seil, by Oban, Argyll, PA34 4TS	01852 300276	★★	Small Hotel	⌐⌐⌐
Greenacre	Connel, by Oban, Argyll, PA31 1PJ	01631 710756	★★★	Guest House	
Mactalla	Connel, by Oban, Argyll, PA37 1PJ	01631 710465	AWAITING GRADING		
The Oyster Inn	Connel, by Oban, Argyll, PA37 1PJ	01631 710666	★★★★	Inn	
Falls of Lora Hotel	Connel Ferry, by Oban, Argyll, PA37 1PB	01631 710483	★★★	Hotel	
Braeside Guest House	Kilmore, by Oban, Argyll, PA34 4QR	01631 770243	★★★★	Guest House	

Old Deer, Peterhead

| Aden House | 19 Abbey Street, Old Deer, Peterhead, Aberdeenshire, AB42 5LN | 01771 622573 | ★★★ | Guest House | |

Old Meldrum

| Meldrum House Hotel Golf Country Estate | Old Meldrum, Aberdeenshire, AB51 0AE | 01651 872294 | ★★★ | Country House Hotel | |
| The Redgarth | Kirkbrae, Oldmeldrum, Aberdeenshire, AB51 0DJ | 01651 872353 | ★★★★ | Inn | |

Onich

| Camus House | Lochside Lodge, Onich, Inverness-shire, PH33 6RY | 01855 821200 | ★★★ | Guest House | |

Orphir, Scapa Flow, Orkney

| Houton Bay Lodge | Houton Bay, Orphir, Scapa Flow, Orkney, KW17 2RD | 01856 811320 | ★★★★ | Inn | ↑ |

Paisley

Ardgowan Town House Hotel	92 Renfrew Road, Paisley, Renfrewshire, PA3 4BJ	0141 889 4763	★★★	Guest House	↑
Ashtree House	9 Orr Square, Paisley, Renfrewshire, PA1 2DL	0141 8486411	★★★★	Guest House	
Dryesdale	37 Inchinnan Road, Paisley, Renfrewshire, PA3 2PR	0141 889 7178	★★	Guest House	
Express by Holiday Inn Glasgow Airport	St Andrews Drive, Paisley, Renfrewshire, PA3 2TJ	0141 842 1100	★★★	Metro Hotel	♿
Glasgow Airport Premier Inn	Whitecart Road, Glasgow Airport, Paisley, Renfrewshire, PA3 2TH	0870 2383321		Budget Hotel	

♿ Unassisted wheelchair access   ♿ Assisted wheelchair access   ↑ Access for visitors with mobility difficulties
⌐ Bronze Green Tourism Award   ⌐⌐ Silver Green Tourism Award   ⌐⌐⌐ Gold Green Tourism Award
For further information on our Green Tourism Business Scheme please see page 9.

Awards correct as of mid August 2008

Glasgow Paisley Premier Inn	Phoenix Retail Park, Paisley, Renfrewshire, PA1 2BH	08701 97713		Budget Hotel		
Holiday Inn Glasgow Airport	Abbotsinch, Paisley, Renfrewshire, PA3 2TR	0870 4009031	★★★	Hotel		PP
Ramada Glasgow Airport	Marchburn Drive, Abbotsinch, Paisley, Renfrewshire, PA3 2SJ	0141 840 2200	★★★	Hotel	﴾ᕕ	P
Travelodge Glasgow Airport	Marchburn Drive, Paisley, Renfrewshire, PA3 2SJ	08719 846335	★★★	Lodge	﴿	
Watermill Hotel	1 Lonend, Paisley, Renfrewshire, PA1 1SR	0141 889 3201	AWAITING GRADING			

Papa Westray, Orkney

Beltane House	Papay Community Cooperative Ltd, Papa Westray, Orkney, KW17 2BU	01857 644321	★★	Guest House	

Pathhead

The Stair Arms Hotel	Ford, Patthead, Midlothian, EH37 5TX	01875 320277	★★	Inn	

Peebles

Castle Venlaw Hotel	Edinburgh Road, Peebles, Peeblesshire, EH45 8QG	01721 720384	★★★★	Country House Hotel	
Cringletie House Hotel	Edinburgh Road, Peebles, Peeblesshire, EH45 8PL	01721 725750	★★★★	Country House Hotel	﴿
Glentress Hotel	Innerleithen Road, Peebles, Peeblesshire, EH45 8NB	01721 720100	★★	Small Hotel	
Lindores	60 Old Town, Peebles, Peeblesshire, EH45 8JE	01721 722072	★★★	Guest House	
Peebles Hotel Hydro	Innerleithen Road, Peebles, Peeblesshire, EH45 8LX	01721 720602	★★★★	Hotel	
The Park Hotel	Innerleithen Road, Peebles, Peeblesshire, EH45 8BA	01721 720451	★★★	Hotel	
Tontine Hotel	High Street, Peebles, Peeblesshire, EH45 8AJ	01721 720892	★★★	Hotel	

by Peebles

Cardrona Hotel Golf & Country Club	Cardrona, by Peebles, Peeblesshire, EH45 6LZ	01896 831144	★★★★	Hotel	﴾ᕕ

Penicuik

Peggyslea Farm	Nine Mile Burn, Penicuik, Midlothian, EH26 9LX	01968 660930	★★★★	Guest House	

Pennyghael, Isle of Mull

Pennyghael Hotel	Pennyghael, Isle of Mull, PA70 6HB	01681 704288	AWAITING GRADING		

Perth

Aaron	85 Glasgow Road, Perth PH2 OPQ	01738 444728	★★★	Guest House	
Achnacarry Guest House	3 Pitcullen Crescent, Perth PH2 7HT	01738 621421	★★★★	Guest House	
Ackinnoull Guest House	5 Pitcullen Crescent, Perth PH2 7HT	01738 634165	★★★★	Guest House	
Adam Guest House	6 Pitcullen Crescent, Perth PH2 7HT	01738 627179	★★★	Guest House	
Albert Villa Guest House	63 Dunkeld Road, Perth PH1 5RP	01738 622730	★★★	Guest House	
Almond Villa Guest House	51 Dunkeld Road, Perth PH1 5RP	01738 629356	★★★★	Guest House	

﴿ Unassisted wheelchair access   ﴾ᕕ Assisted wheelchair access   ↑ Access for visitors with mobility difficulties
P Bronze Green Tourism Award   PP Silver Green Tourism Award   PPP Gold Green Tourism Award
For further information on our Green Tourism Business Scheme please see page 9.

To find out more, call 0845 22 55 121 or go to visitscotland.com.

Ardfern House	15 Pitcullen Crescent, Perth PH2 7HT	01738 637031	★★★★	Guest House		
Arisaig Guest House	4 Pitcullen Crescent, Perth PH2 7HT	01738 628240	★★★★	Guest House	♀	*PPP*
Beechgrove Guest House	Dundee Road, Perth PH2 7AQ	01738 636147	★★★★	Guest House		
Cherrybank B&B	217 Glasgow Road, Perth PH2 0NB	01738 451982	★★★★	Guest House		
Cherrybank Inn	210 Glasgow Road, Perth PH2 0NA	01738 624349	★★★	Inn	♀	
Clifton House	36 Glasgow Road, Perth PH2 0PB	01738 621997	★★★★	Guest House		
Clunie Guest House	12 Pitcullen Crescent, Perth PH2 7HT	01738 623625	★★★★	Guest House		
Dunallan Guest House	10 Pitcullen Crescent, Perth PH2 7TH	01738 622551	★★★★	Guest House		
Express by Holiday Inn	200 Dunkeld Road,Inveralmond, Perth PH1 3AQ	01738 636666	★★★	Metro Hotel		
Grampian Hotel	37 York Place, Perth PH2 8EH	01738 621057	★★★	Small Hotel		
Hazeldene Guest House	Strathmore Street, Perth PH2 7HP	01738 623550	★★★★	Guest House		
Heidl Guest House	43 York Place, Perth PH2 8EH	01738 635031	★★★	Guest House		
Huntingtower Hotel	Crieff Road, Perth PH1 3JT	01738 583771	★★★	Hotel	♿	
Lovat Hotel	Glasgow Road, Perth PH2 0LT	01738 636555	★★★	Hotel		*P*
New County Hotel	26 County Place, Perth PH2 8EE	0738 623355	★★★	Hotel		
Parklands Hotel	2 St Leonards Bank, Perth PH2 8EB	01738 622451	★★★★	Small Hotel		*P*
Pitcullen Guest House	17 Pitcullen Crescent, Perth PH2 7HT	01738 626506	★★★	Guest House		
Quality Hotel Perth	Leonard Street, Perth PH2 8HE	01738 624141	AWAITING GRADING			
Queens Hotel	105 Leonard Street, Perth PH2 8HB	01738 442222	★★★	Hotel		*PP*
Ramada Hotel	West Mill Street, Perth PH1 5QP	01738 628281	★★★	Hotel		*P*
Rowanlea	87 Glasgow Road, Perth PH2 0PQ	01738 621922	★★★★	Guest House		
Salutation Hotel	34 South Street, Perth PH2 8PH	01738 630066	★★	Hotel		*PP*
Sunbank House	50 Dundee Road, Perth PH2 7BA	01738 624882	★★★★	Guest House	♀	
The Gables Guest House	24 Dunkeld Road, Perth PH1 5RW	01738 624717	★★★	Guest House		
The Royal George	Tay Street, Perth PH1 5LD	01738 624455	★★★	Hotel		
The Townhouse	17 Marshall Place, Perth PH2 8AG	01738 446179	★★★	Guest House		
Travelodge Perth Broxden Junction	Broxden Trunk Road Service Area, Perth PH2 0PL	08719 846250	AWAITING GRADING			
WoodLea Hotel	23 York Place, Perth PH2 8EP	01738 621744	★★★	Small Hotel		

by Perth

| Glencarse Hotel | Glencarse, by Perth, Perthshire, PH2 7LX | 01738 860206 | AWAITING GRADING | | ♿ | |

♿ Unassisted wheelchair access   ♿ Assisted wheelchair access   ♀ Access for visitors with mobility difficulties
P Bronze Green Tourism Award   *PP* Silver Green Tourism Award   *PPP* Gold Green Tourism Award
For further information on our Green Tourism Business Scheme please see page 9.

Peterhead

Carrick Guest House	16 Merchant Street, Peterhead, Aberdeenshire, AB42 1DU	01779 470610	★★	Guest House	
Invernettie Guest House	South Road, Burnhaven, Peterhead, Aberdeenshire, AB42 0YX	01779 473530	★★★	Guest House	♿
Palace Hotel	Prince Street, Peterhead, Aberdeenshire, AB42 6PL	01779 474821	★★★	Hotel	

Pitcaple

Pittodrie House Hotel	Pitcaple, Aberdeenshire, AB51 5HS	08701 942111	★★★	Country House Hotel	

Pitfodels, Aberdeen

The Marcliffe Hotel and Spa	North Deeside Road, Pitfodels, Aberdeen AB15 9YA	01224 861000	★★★★★	Hotel	♿

Pitlochry

Acarsaid Hotel and Lodge	8 Atholl Road, Pitlochry, Perthshire, PH16 5BX	01796 472389	★★★	Hotel	
Almond Lee	East Moulin Road, Pitlochry, Perthshire, PH16 5HU	01796 474048	★★★	Guest House	
Annslea Guest House	164 Atholl Road, Pitlochry, Perthshire, PH16 5AR	01796 472430	★★★	Guest House	
Atholl Villa Guest House	29/31 Atholl Road, Pitlochry, Perthshire, PH16 5BX	01796 473820	★★★	Guest House	
Beinn Bhracaigh	Higher Oakfield, Pitlochry, Perthshire, PH16 5HT	01796 470355	★★★★	Guest House	
Birchwood Hotel	2 East Moulin Road, Pitlochry, Perthshire, PH16 5DW	01796 472477	★★★	Small Hotel	
Buttonboss Lodge	27 Atholl Road, Pitlochry, Perthshire, PH16 5BX	01796 472065	★★★	Guest House	
Carra Beag Guest House	16 Toberargan Road, Pitlochry, Perthshire, PH16 5HG	01796 472835	★★★	Guest House	
Claymore Hotel	162 Atholl Road, Pitlochry, Perthshire, PH16 5AR	01796 472888	★★★	Small Hotel	
Craigatin House & Courtyard	165 Atholl Road, Pitlochry, Perthshire, PH16 5QL	01796 472478	★★★★	Guest House	⚡
Craigmhor Lodge	27 West Moulin Road, Pitlochry, Perthshire, PH16 5EF	01796 472123	★★★★	Guest House	
Craigroyston Guest House	2 Lower Oakfield, Pitlochry, Perthshire, PH16 5HQ	01796 472053	★★★★	Guest House	
Craigvrack Hotel	38 West Moulin Road, Pitlochry, Perthshire, PH16 5EQ	01796 472399	★★★	Small Hotel	⚡
Cuil -an- Daraich Guest House	2 Cuil -an- Daraich, Logierait, Pitlochry, Perthshire, PH9 0LH	01796 482750	★★★	Guest House	♿
Dalshian House	Old Perth Road, Pitlochry, Perthshire, PH16 5TD	01796 472173	★★★	Guest House	
Derrybeg Guest House	18 Lower Oakfield, Pitlochry, Perthshire, PH16 5DS	01796 472070	★★★★	Guest House	
Dundarach Hotel	Perth Road, Pitlochry, Perthshire, PH16 5DJ	01796 472862	★★★	Hotel	
Dunmurray Lodge Guest House	72 Bonnethill Road, Pitlochry, Perthshire, PH16 5ED	01796 473624	★★★★	Guest House	
Easter Croftinloan Farmhouse	Croftloan Farm, Pitlochry, Perthshire, PH16 5TA	01796 473454	★★★★	Guest House	
Fasganeoin Country House	Perth Road, Pitlochry, Perthshire, PH16 5DJ	01796 472387	★★★	Guest House	
Green Park Hotel	Clunie Bridge Road, Pitlochry, Perthshire, PH16 5JY	01796 473248	★★★★	Country House Hotel	⚡

♿ Unassisted wheelchair access   ♿ Assisted wheelchair access   ⚡ Access for visitors with mobility difficulties

🍃 Bronze Green Tourism Award   🍃🍃 Silver Green Tourism Award   🍃🍃🍃 Gold Green Tourism Award

For further information on our Green Tourism Business Scheme please see page 9.

Knockendarroch	Higher Oakfield, Pitlochry, Perthshire, PH16 5HT	01796 473473	★★★★	Small Hotel		
Macdonalds Restaurant & Guest House	140 Atholl Road, Pitlochry, Perthshire, PH16 5AG	01796 472170	★★★	Guest House		
Moulin Hotel	Moulin Hotel, 11-13 Kirkmichael Road, Pitlochry, Perthshire, PH16 5EW	0796 47 2196	★★★	Hotel		
Pine Trees Country House Hotel	Strathview Terrace, Pitlochry, Perthshire, PH16 5QR	01796 472121	★★★★	Country House Hotel		
Pitlochry Hydro Hotel	Knockard Road, Pitlochry, Perthshire, PH16 5JH	01796 472666	★★★	Hotel		
Rosehill	47 Atholl Road, Pitlochry, Perthshire, PH16 5BX	01796 472958	★★★	Guest House		
Rosemount Hotel	12 Higher Oakfield, Pitlochry, Perthshire, PH16 5HT	01796 472302	★★★	Small Hotel		
Scotlands Hotel	40 Bonnethill Road, Pitlochry, Perthshire, PH16 5BT	01796 472292	★★★	Hotel		
Strathgarry Hotel	113 Atholl Road, Pitlochry, Perthshire, PH16 5AG	01796 472469	★★★	Restaurant with Rooms		
The Atholl Palace	Atholl Road, Pitlochry, Perthshire, PH16 5LY	01796 472400	★★★	Hotel	⋏	◫
The Poplars	27 Lower Oakfield, Pitlochry, Perthshire, PH16 5DS	01796 472911	★★★	Guest House	⋏	
The Well House	11 Toberargan Road, Pitlochry, Perthshire, PH16 5HG	01796 472239	★★★★	Guest House	⋏	
Tigh Na Cloich Hotel	Larchwood Road, Pitlochry, Perthshire, PH16 5AS	01796 472216	★★★	Small Hotel		◫◫
Tir Aluinn	10 Higher Oakfield, Pitlochry, Perthshire, PH16 5HT	01796 473811	★★★	Guest House		
Torrdarach House	Golf Course Road, Pitlochry, Perthshire, PH16 5AU	01796 472136	★★★★	Guest House		
Wellwood House	13 West Moulin Road, Pitlochry, Perthshire, PH16 5EA	01796 474288	★★★★	Guest House		
Westlands Hotel	160 Atholl Road, Pitlochry, Perthshire, PH16 5AR	01796 472266	★★★	Small Hotel		

by Pitlochry

East Haugh House Country Hotel & Res	East Haugh, by Pitlochry, Perthshire, PH16 5TE	01796 473121	★★★★	Small Hotel	⋏	
Talladh-a-Bheithe Lodge	Loch Rannoch, by Pitlochry, Perthshire, PH17 2QW	01882 633203	★★★	Guest House		

Plockton

Plockton Inn	Plockton, Ross-shire, IV52 8TW	01599 544222	★★★	Inn		
The Haven Hotel	3 Innes Street, Plockton, Ross-shire, IV52 8TW	01599 544223	★★	Small Hotel		

Polmont, Falkirk

Beancross	West Beancross Farm, Polmont, Falkirk, Stirlingshire, FK2 0XS	01324 718333	★★★	Restaurant with Rooms		
Falkirk East Premier Inn	Cadger's Brae, Beancross Road, Polmont, Falkirk, Stirlingshire, FK2 0YS	08701 977098		Budget Hotel		
Inchyra Grange Hotel	Grange Road, Polmont, Stirlingshire, FK2 0YB	01324 711911	★★★★	Hotel	♿	

Poolewe

Corriness House	Poolewe, Ross-shire, IV22 2JU	01445 781785	★★★★	Guest House		
Pool House	Poolewe, Rosshire, IV22 2LD	01445 781272	★★★★	Small Hotel		◫◫◫

& Unassisted wheelchair access   ♿ Assisted wheelchair access   ⋏ Access for visitors with mobility difficulties
◫ Bronze Green Tourism Award   ◫◫ Silver Green Tourism Award   ◫◫◫ Gold Green Tourism Award
For further information on our Green Tourism Business Scheme please see page 9.

Awards correct as of mid August 2008   263

Port Charlotte, Isle of Islay

Port Charlotte Hotel	Main Street, Port Charlotte, Isle of Islay, PA48 7TU	01496 850360	★★★★	Small Hotel

Port Ellen, Isle of Islay

Glenegedale House	Glenegedale, Port Ellen, Isle of Islay, PA42 7AS	01496 300400	★★★★★	Guest House
Machrie Hotel	Port Ellen, Isle of Islay, PA42 7AN	01496 302310	★★★	Small Hotel

Port Elphinstone, Inverurie

Ardennan House Hotel	Kemnay Road, Port Elphinstone, Inverurie, Aberdeenshire, AB51 3XD	01467 621502	★★	Small Hotel

Port William

Monreith Arms Hotel	The Square, Port William, Wigtownshire, DG8 9SE	01988 700232	★★	Inn

Portlethen

Aberdeen South Premier Inn	Mains of Balquham, Portlethen, Aberdeenshire, AB12 4QS	08701 977013		Budget Hotel

Portpatrick

Braefield Guest House	Braefield Road, Portpatrick, Wigtownshire, DG9 8TA	01776 810255	★★★	Guest House	⚡
Dunskey Guest House	Heugh Road, Portpatrick, Wigtownshire, DG9 8TD	01776 810241	★★	Guest House	
Knockinaam Lodge	Portpatrick, Wigtownshire, DG9 9AD	01776 810471	★★★★	Small Hotel	
Portpatrick Hotel	Heugh Road, Portpatrick, Wigtownshire, DG9 8TQ	01776 810333	★★	Hotel	⚡
Rickwood House Hotel	Heugh Road, Portpatrick, Wigtownshire, DG9 8TD	01776 810270	★★★	Guest House	
The Fernhill Hotel	Heugh Road, Portpatrick, Wigtownshire, DG9 8TD	01776 810220	★★★	Hotel	⚡
The Waterfront Hotel	7 North Crescent, Portpatrick, Wigtownshire, DG9 8SX	01776 810800	★★★	Small Hotel	

Portree, Isle of Skye

Almondbank	Viewfield Road, Portree, Isle of Skye, IV51 9EU	01478 612696	★★★★	Guest House	
An Airidh	6 Fisherfield, Portree, Isle of Skye, IV51 9EU	01478 612250	★★★	Guest House	
Auchendinny	Treaslane, Portree, Isle of Skye, IV51 9NX	01470 532470	★★★	Guest House	♿
Balloch	Viewfield Road, Portree, Isle of Skye, IV51 9ES	01478 612093	★★★★	Guest House	
Coolin View Guest House	Bosville Terrace, Portree, Isle of Skye, IV51 9DG	01478 611280	★★★	Guest House	
Corran Guest House	Eyre,Kensaleyre, Portree, Isle of Skye, IV51 9XE	01470 532311	★★★★	Guest House	
Cuillin Hills Hotel	Portree, Isle of Skye, IV51 9QU	01478 612003	★★★★	Country House Hotel	♿
Dalriada	Achachork, Portree, Isle of Skye, IV51 9HT	01478 612397	★★★	Guest House	
Givendale Guest House	Heron Place, Portree, Isle of Skye, IV51 9GU	01478 612183	★★★	Guest House	
Green Acres Guest House	Viewfield Road, Portree, Isle of Skye, IV51 9EU	01478 613175	★★★★	Guest House	

♿ Unassisted wheelchair access   ♿ Assisted wheelchair access   ⚡ Access for visitors with mobility difficulties
𝒫 Bronze Green Tourism Award   𝒫𝒫 Silver Green Tourism Award   𝒫𝒫𝒫 Gold Green Tourism Award
For further information on our Green Tourism Business Scheme please see page 9.

264   To find out more, call 0845 22 55 121 or go to visitscotland.com.

Marmalade	Home Farm Road, Portree, Isle of Skye, IV51 9LX	01478 611711	★★★	Small Hotel	
Meadowbank House	Seafield Place, Portree, Isle of Skye, IV51 9ES	01478 612059	★★★	Guest House	
Quiraing Guest House	Viewfield Road, Portree, Isle of Skye, IV51 9ES	01478 612870	★★★★	Guest House	
Rosebank House	Springfield Road, Portree, Isle of Skye, IV51 9QX	01478 612282	★★★	Guest House	
Rosedale Hotel	Beaumont Crescent, Portree, Isle of Skye, IV51 9DF	01478 613131	★★★	Hotel	
Royal Hotel	Bank Street, Portree, Isle of Skye, IV51 9BU	01478 61 2525	★★★	Hotel	
The Bosville Hotel	10 Bosville Terrace, Portree, Isle of Skye, IV51 9DG	01478 612846	★★★★	Hotel	
Viewfield House Hotel	Portree, Isle of Skye, IV51 9EU	01478 612217	★★★★	Guest House	♁

by Portree, Isle of Skye

| Greshornish House Hotel | Edinbane, by Portree, Isle of Skye, IV51 9PN | 01470 582266 | ★★★★ | Country House Hotel | |
| Peinmore House | by Portree, Isle of Skye, IV51 9LG | 01478 612 574 | ★★★★ | Guest House | |

Portsoy

| Station Hotel | Seafield Street, Portsoy, Aberdeenshire, AB45 2QT | 01261 842327 | ★★ | Small Hotel | |

Prestwick

Fernbank Guest House	213 Main Street, Prestwick, Ayrshire, KA9 1LH	01292 475027	★★★	Guest House	🄿
Golf View	17 Links Road, Prestwick, Ayrshire, KA9 1QG	01292 671234	★★★★	Guest House	
Kincraig Guest House	39 Ayr Road, Prestwick, Ayrshire, KA9 1SY	01292 479480	★★★	Guest House	
North Beach Hotel	5-7 Link's Road, Prestwick, Ayrshire, KA9 1QG	01292 479069	★★	Small Hotel	
Parkstone Hotel	Esplanade, Prestwick, Ayrshire, KA9 1QN	01292 477286	★★★	Hotel	♿
Prestwick Old Course Hotel	13 Links Road, Prestwick, Ayrshire, KA9 1QG	01292 477446	★★	Small Hotel	

Renfrew

| The Normandy Hotel | Inchinnan Road, Renfrew, Renfrewshire, PA4 5EJ | 0141 886 4100 | ★★★ | Hotel | 🄿🄿 |
| Glynhill Hotel | 169 Paisley Road, Renfrew, Near Glasgow Airport, Renfrewshire, PA4 8XB | 0141 886 5555 | ★★★ | Hotel | |

Reston

| The Craw Inn | Auchencrow, Reston, Berwickshire, TD14 5LS | 01890 761293 | ★★★ | Inn | |

Rhu

| Rosslea Hall Hotel | Ferry Road, Rhu, Dunbartonshire, G84 8NF | 01436 439955 | ★★★ | Hotel | ♿ |

Roslin

| Original Rosslyn Inn | Main Street, Roslin, Midlothian, EH25 9LE | 0131 440 2384 | ★★ | Inn | |

♿ Unassisted wheelchair access   🦽 Assisted wheelchair access   ♁ Access for visitors with mobility difficulties
🄿 Bronze Green Tourism Award   🄿🄿 Silver Green Tourism Award   🄿🄿🄿 Gold Green Tourism Award
For further information on our Green Tourism Business Scheme please see page 9.

Awards correct as of mid August 2008

265

Rosneath

Easter Garth	The Clachan, Rosneath, Argyll & Bute, G84 0RF	01436 831007	★★★	Guest House

Rosyth

Cochranes Hotel	Hilton Road, Rosyth, Fife, KY11 2BA	01383 420101	AWAITING GRADING	

Rothesay, Isle of Bute

Argyle House	3 Argyle Place, Rothesay, Isle of Bute, PA20 0AZ	01700 502424	★★	Guest House
Bayview Hotel	21-22 Mountstuart Road, Rothesay, Isle of Bute, PA20 9EB	01700 505411	★★★★	Guest House
Bute House	4 West Princess Street, Rothesay, Isle of Bute, PA20 9AF	01700 502481	★★★	Guest House
Glenburn Hotel	Mount Stewart Road, Rothesay, Isle of Bute, PA20 9JB	01700 502500	★★★	Hotel
Glendale Guest House	20 Battery Place, Rothesay, Isle of Bute, PA20 9DU	01700 502329	★★★★	Guest House
The Ardyne	37-38 Mountstuart Road, Rothesay, Isle of Bute, PA20 9EB	01700 502052	★★★	Small Hotel
The Commodore	12 Battery Place, Rothesay, Isle of Bute, PA20 9DP	01700 502178	★★★	Guest House
The Victoria Hotel	55 Victoria Street, Rothesay, Isle of Bute, PA20 0AP	01700 500016	★★★	Small Hotel

Rothienorman

Rothie Inn	Main Street, Rothienorman, Aberdeenshire, AB51 8UD	01651 821206	★★★	Inn

Rousay, Orkney

The Taversoe	Frotoft, Rousay, Orkney, KW17 2PT	01856 821325	★★★	Inn

Roy Bridge

Roy Bridge Hotel	Roy Bridge, Inverness-shire, PH31 4AN	01397 712236	★★	Inn	
The Stronlossit Inn	Roy Bridge, Inverness-shire, PH31 4AG	01397 712253	★★★	Small Hotel	🏃♿

Salen, Isle of Mull

Ard Mhor House	Pier Road, Salen, Isle of Mull, PA72 6JL	01680 300255	★★★	Guest House	♿
Salen Hotel	Salen, Isle of Mull, PA72 6JE	01680 300324	AWAITING GRADING		

Sandhead

Tigh-Na-Mara Hotel & Restaurant	Main Street, Sandhead, Dumfries & Galloway, DG9 9JF	01776 830210	★★★	Inn

Sandwick, Shetland

Orca Country Inn	Hoswick, Sandwick, Shetland, ZE2 9HL	01950 431226	★★★	Inn

Sanquhar

Blackaddie House Hotel	Blackaddie Road, Sanquhar, Dumfries & Galloway, DG4 6JJ	01659 50270	★★★	Country House Hotel

♿ Unassisted wheelchair access 🏃♿ Assisted wheelchair access 🏃 Access for visitors with mobility difficulties
℗ Bronze Green Tourism Award ℗℗ Silver Green Tourism Award ℗℗℗ Gold Green Tourism Award
For further information on our Green Tourism Business Scheme please see page 9.

266   To find out more, call 0845 22 55 121 or go to visitscotland.com.

Scalloway, Shetland

Scalloway Hotel	Main Street, Scalloway, Shetland, ZE1 0RT	01595 880444	★★	Small Hotel

Scarinish, Isle of Tiree

Tiree Scarinish Hotel	Scarinish, Isle of Tiree, PA77 6UH	01879 220308	★★	Inn

Scarista, Isle of Harris

Scarista House	Scarista, Isle of Harris, HS3 3HX	01859 550238	★★★★	Guest House	ⓟ

Scone, Perth

Murrayshall Hotel	Scone, Perth, Perthshire, PH2 7PH	01738 551171	★★★★	Country House Hotel	
Perth Airport Skylodge	Norwell Drive, Perth Airport, Scone, Perthshire, PH2 6PL	01738 555700	★★★	Lodge	✦

Scourie

Eddrachilles Hotel	Badcall Bay, Scourie, Sutherland, IV27 4TH	01971 502080	★★★	Small Hotel
Scourie Hotel	Scourie, Sutherland, IV27 4SX	01971 502396	★★★	Small Hotel

Scouseburgh, Shetland

Spiggie Hotel	Scouseburgh, Shetland, ZE2 9JE	01950 460409	★★★	Small Hotel

Seamill

Seamill Hydro	39 Ardrossan Road, Seamill, Ayrshire, KA23 9NB	01294 822217	★★★	Hotel	ⓟⓟ

Selkirk

Heatherlie House Hotel	Heatherlie Park, Selkirk, Selkirkshire, TD7 5AL	01750 721200	★★★	Small Hotel
The County Hotel	Market Square, 3-5 High Street, Selkirk, Selkirkshire, TD7 4BZ	01750 721233	★★★	Small Hotel
The Glen Hotel	Yarrow Terrace, Selkirk, Selkirkshire, TD7 5AS	01750 20259	★★★	Small Hotel
The Philipburn Country House Hotel	Linglie Road, Selkirk, Selkirkshire, TD7 5LS	01750 20747	★★★★	Country House Hotel
Tower Street Guest House	29 Tower Street, Selkirk, Selkirkshire, TD7 4LR	01750 23222	★★★	Guest House

by Selkirk

Cross Keys Inn	Main Street, Ettrickbridge, by Selkirk, Scottish Borders, TD7 5JN	01750 52224	★★★	Inn
Tushielaw Inn	Ettrick Valley, Selkirkshire, TD7 5HT	0750 62205	★★	Inn

Shapinsay, Orkney

Balfour Castle	Balfour Village, Shapinsay, Orkney, KW17 2DY	01856 711282	★★★	Country House Hotel

Shieldaig

Tigh-an-Eilean Hotel	Shieldaig, Ross-shire, IV54 8XN	01520 755251	AWAITING GRADING	

& Unassisted wheelchair access &Є Assisted wheelchair access ✦ Access for visitors with mobility difficulties
ⓟ Bronze Green Tourism Award ⓟⓟ Silver Green Tourism Award ⓟⓟⓟ Gold Green Tourism Award
For further information on our Green Tourism Business Scheme please see page 9.

Shieldinish, Isle of Lewis

The Loch Erisort Inn	Shieldinish, Isle of Lewis, HS2 9RA	01851 830473	AWAITING GRADING	

Sleat, Isle of Skye

Duisdale Hotel	Isle Ornsay, Sleat, Isle of Skye, IV43 8QW	01471 833202	★★★★	Country House Hotel
Hotel Eilean Iarmain	Camus Cross, Sleat, Isle of Skye, IV43 8QR	01471 833332	★★★	Small Hotel
Kinloch Lodge	Sleat, Isle of Skye, IV43 8QY	01471 833214	★★★★	Country House Hotel

Sorn

The Sorn Inn	Main Street, Sorn, Ayrshire, KA5 6HU	01290 551305	★★★★	Restaurant with Rooms

South Queensferry

Dakota Forth Bridge	Ferry Muir Retail Park, South Queensferry, West Lothian, EH30 9QZ	08704 234293	AWAITING GRADING	
Dundas Castle	South Queensferry, West Lothian, EH30 9SP	0131 3192039	★★★★★	Exclusive Use Venue
Edinburgh South Queensferry Premier Inn	Queens Crossing, Builyeon Road, South Queensferry, Edinburgh, West Lothian,	08701 977		Budget Hotel
Priory Lodge	8 The Loan, South Queensferry, West Lothian, EH30 9NS	0131 331 4345	★★★★	Guest House ♀

South Ronaldsay

The Creel Restaurant & Rooms	Front Road, St Margaret's Hope, South Ronaldsay, Orkney, KW17 2SL	01856 831311	★★★★	Restaurant with Rooms

Spean Bridge

Coire Glas Guest House	Roybridge Road, Spean Bridge, Inverness-shire, PH34 4EU	01397 712272	★★★	Guest House
Distant Hills Guest House	Roybridge Road, Spean Bridge, Inverness-shire, PH34 4EU	01397 712452	★★★★	Guest House
Inverour Guest House	Roy Bridge Road, Spean Bridge, Inverness-shire, PH34 4EU	01397 712218	★★★	Guest House
Old Pines Hotel and Restaurant	Gairlochy Road, Spean Bridge, Inverness-shire, PH34 4EG	01397 712324	★★★	Small Hotel ♿
Old Smiddy Restaurant with Rooms	Roy Bridge Road, Spean Bridge, Inverness-shire, PH34 4EU	01397 712335	★★★★	Restaurant with Rooms
Spean Bridge Hotel	Main Road, Spean Bridge, Inverness-shire, PH34 4ES	01397 712250	★★	Hotel
The Braes Guest House	Spean Bridge, Inverness-shire, PH34 4EU	01397 71243	★★★	Guest House 🍃🍃
The Heathers	Invergloy Halt, Spean Bridge, Inverness-shire, PH34 4DY	01397 712077	★★★★	Guest House ♀

by Spean Bridge

Corriegour Lodge Hotel	Loch Lochy, by Spean Bridge, Inverness-shire, PH34 4EA	01397 712685	★★★	Small Hotel

St Andrews

11 Queens Gardens	St Andrews, Fife, KY16 9TA	01334 478751	★★★★	Guest House
Albany Hotel	56-58 North Street, St Andrews, Fife, KY16 9AH	01334 477737	★★★	Metro Hotel
Amberside	4 Murray Park, St Andrews, Fife, KY16 9AW	01334 474644	★★★	Guest House

♿ Unassisted wheelchair access   ♿ Assisted wheelchair access   ♀ Access for visitors with mobility difficulties
🍃 Bronze Green Tourism Award   🍃🍃 Silver Green Tourism Award   🍃🍃🍃 Gold Green Tourism Award
For further information on our Green Tourism Business Scheme please see page 9.

Directory of all VisitScotland Assured Serviced Establishments, ordered by location.

Establishments highlighted have an advertisement in this guide.

Annandale Guest House	23 Murray Park, St Andrews, Fife, KY16 9AW	01334 475310	★★★★	Guest House		
Ardgowan Hotel	2 Playfair Terrace, St Andrews, Fife, KY16 9HX	01334 472970	★★★	Small Hotel		
Arran House	5 Murray Park, St Andrews, Fife, KY16 9AW	01334 474 724	★★★	Guest House		
Aslar House	120 North Street, St Andrews, Fife, KY16 9AF	01334 473460	★★★★	Guest House		
Bell Craig	8 Murray Park, St Andrews, Fife, KY16 9AW	01334 472962	★★★	Guest House		
Brooksby House	Queens Terrace, St Andrews, Fife, KY16 9ER	01334 470723	★★★★★	Guest House		
Brownlees	7 Murray Place, St Andrews, Fife, KY16 9AP	01334 473868	★★★★	Guest House		
Burness House	1 Murray Park, St Andrews, Fife, KY16 9AW	01334 474314	★★★★	Guest House		
Cameron House	11 Murray Park, St Andrews, Fife, KY16 9AW	01334 72306	★★★★	Guest House		
Charlesworth House	9 Murray Place, St Andrews, Fife, KY16 9AP	01334 476528	★★★★	Guest House		
Cleveden Guest House	3 Murray Place, St Andrews, Fife, KY16 9AP	01334 474212	★★★★	Guest House		
Craigmore Guest House	3 Murray Park, St Andrews, Fife, KY16 9AW	01334 472142	★★★★	Guest House		
Deveron House	64 North Street, St Andrews, Fife, KY16 9AH	01334 473513	★★★	Guest House		
Doune House	5 Murray Place, St Andrews, Fife, KY16 9AP	01334 475195	★★★★	Guest House		
Dunvegan Hotel	7 Pilmour Place, North Street, St Andrews, Fife, KY16 9HZ	01334 473105	★★★	Small Hotel		
Fairmont St Andrews	St Andrews, Fife, KY16 8PN	01334 837000	★★★★★	Hotel		🍃🍃🍃
Five Pilmour Place	North Street, St Andrews, Fife, KY16 9HZ	01334 478665	★★★★	Guest House		
Glenderran Guest House	9 Murray Park, St Andrews, Fife, KY16 9AW	01334 477951	★★★★	Guest House		
Greyfriars Hotel	129 North Street, St Andrews, Fife, KY16 9AG	01334 474906	★★★	Small Hotel		
Hazelbank Hotel	28 The Scores, St Andrews, Fife, KY16 9AS	01334 472466	★★★	Metro Hotel		
Lorimer House	19 Murray Park, St Andrews, Fife, KY16 9AW	01334 476599	★★★★	Guest House		
Macdonald Rusacks Hotel	Pilmour Links, St Andrews, Fife, KY16 9JQ	01334 474321	★★★★	Hotel		
McIntosh Hall	Abbotsford Crescent, St Andrews, Fife, KY16 9HT	01334 467000	★★	Campus		
Montague House	21 Murray Park, St Andrews, Fife, KY16 9AW	01334 479 287	★★★	Guest House		
Nethan House	17 Murray Park, St Andrews, Fife, KY16 9AW	01334 472104	★★★★	Guest House		🍃🍃
New Hall, University of St Andrews	North Haugh, St Andrews, Fife, KY16 9XW	01334 467000	★★★	Hotel		🍃🍃🍃
Ogstons on North Street	127 North Street, St Andrews, Fife, KY16 9AG	01334 473387	★★★	Inn		
Old Course Hotel, Golf Resort & Spa	St Andrews, Fife, KY16 9SP	01334 474371	★★★★★	Hotel		
Rufflets Country House Hotel	Strathkinness Low Road, St Andrews, Fife, KY16 9TX	01334 472594	★★★★	Country House Hotel	♿	🍃🍃🍃
Scores Hotel	76 The Scores, St Andrews, Fife, KY16 9BB	01334 472451	★★★	Hotel		

♿ Unassisted wheelchair access ♿ Assisted wheelchair access ↟ Access for visitors with mobility difficulties
🍃 Bronze Green Tourism Award 🍃🍃 Silver Green Tourism Award 🍃🍃🍃 Gold Green Tourism Award
For further information on our Green Tourism Business Scheme please see page 9.

Awards correct as of mid August 2008

Shandon House	10 Murray Place, St Andrews, Fife, KY16 9AP	01334 472412	★★★	Guest House
St Andrews Golf Hotel	40 The Scores, St Andrews, Fife, KY16 9AS	01334 472611	★★★★	Hotel
The Grange Inn	Grange Road, St Andrews, Fife, KY16 8LJ	01334 472670	★★★	Restaurant with Rooms
The Inn At Lathones	by Largoward, St Andrews, Fife, KY9 1JE	01334 840494	★★★★	Inn
The New Inn	21 - 23 St Marys Street, St Andrews, Fife, KY16 8AZ	01334 461333	★★★	Inn
The Old Station, Country Guest House	Stratvithie Bridge, St Andrews, Fife, KY16 8LR	01334 880505	★★★★	Guest House ♿
The Russell Hotel	26 The Scores, St Andrews, Fife, KY16 9AS	01334 473447	★★★	Small Hotel
The West Port	170 South Street, St Andrews, Fife, KY16 9EG	01334 473186	★★★	Inn
Yorkston House	68-70 Argyle Street, St Andrews, Fife, KY16 9BU	01334 472019	★★★	Guest House

by St Andrews

Edenside House	Edenside, by St Andrews, Fife, KY16 9QS	0133483 8108	★★★	Guest House
St Michaels Inn	St Michaels,Leuchars, by St Andrews, Fife, KY16 0DU	01334 839220	★★★	Inn
Pinewood Country House	Tayport Road,ST Michaels, by St Andrews, Fife, KY16 0DU	01334 839860	★★★★	Guest House

St Boswells

Buccleuch Arms Hotel	The Green, St Boswells, Roxburghshire, TD6 OEW	01835 822243	★★★	Small Hotel
Clint Lodge Country House	Clinthill, St Boswells, Melrose, Roxburghshire, TD6 0DZ	01835 822027	★★★★	Guest House

St Catherines

Thistle House	St Catherines, Argyll, PA25 8AZ	01499 302209	AWAITING GRADING	

St Combs, Fraserburgh

The Tufted Duck Hotel	Corsekelly Place, St Combs, Fraserburgh, Aberdeenshire, AB43 8ZS	01346 582481	★★★	Small Hotel

St Fillans

The Four Seasons Hotel	St Fillans, Perthshire, PH6 2NF	01764 685333	★★★	Small Hotel

Staffin, Isle of Skye

Flodigarry Country House Hotel	Flodigarry, Staffin, Isle of Skye, IV51 9HZ	01470 552203	★★★	Country House Hotel
Glenview	Culnacnoc, Staffin, Isle of Skye, IV51 9JH	01470 562248	★★	Restaurant with Rooms

Stanley

Ballathie House Sportsman's Lodge	Kinclaven, Stanley, Perthshire, PH1 4QN	01250 883268	★★★	Lodge
Tayside Hotel	51 Mill Street, Stanley, Perth, Perthshire, PH1 4NL	01738 828249	★★★	Small Hotel

by Stanley

Ballathie House Hotel	Kinclaven, by Stanley, Perthshire, PH1 4QN	01250 883268	★★★★	Country House Hotel ♟

♿ Unassisted wheelchair access   ♿ Assisted wheelchair access   ♟ Access for visitors with mobility difficulties
🄿 Bronze Green Tourism Award   🄿🄿 Silver Green Tourism Award   🄿🄿🄿 Gold Green Tourism Award
For further information on our Green Tourism Business Scheme please see page 9.

270   To find out more, call 0845 22 55 121 or go to visitscotland.com.

Stein, Waternish, Isle of Skye

Stein Inn	MacLeods Terrace, Stein, Waternish, Isle of Skye, IV55 8GA	01470 592362	★★★	Inn	𝓟𝓟𝓟

Stirling

Allan Park Hotel	20 Allan Park, Stirling FK8 2QG	01786 473598	★	Metro Hotel		
Barcelo Stirling Highland Hotel	Spittal Street, Stirling FK8 1DU	01786 272727	★★★★	Hotel		
Burns View	1 Albert Place, Stirling FK8 2QL	01786 451002	★★★	Guest House		
Castlecroft Guest House	Ballengiech Road, Stirling FK8 1TN	01786 474933	★★★	Guest House		
Express by Holiday Inn - Stirling	Springkerse Business Park, Stirling FK7 7XH	01786 449922	★★★	Metro Hotel	♿	
Forth Guest House	23 Forth Place, Riverside, Stirling FK8 1UD	01786 471020	★★★★	Guest House		
Garfield Guest House	12 Victoria Square, Stirling FK8 2QZ	01786 473730	★★★	Guest House		
Linden Guest House	22 Linden Avenue, Stirling FK7 7PQ	01786 448850	★★★★	Guest House		
Munro Guest House	14 Princes Street, Stirling FK8 1HQ	01786 472685	★★★	Guest House		
OSTA	78 Upper Craigs, Stirling FK8 2DT	01786 430890	★★★★	Restaurant with Rooms		
Park Lodge Hotel	32 Park Terrace, Stirling FK8 2JS	01786 474862	AWAITING GRADING			
St Alma	37 Causewayhead Road, Stirling FK9 5EG	01786 465795	★★	Guest House		
Stirling Management Centre	University of Stirling, Stirling FK9 4LA	01786 451666	★★★	Hotel	♿	𝓟𝓟
Stirling Premier Inn	Pirnhall Inn, Whins of Milton, Glasgow Road, Stirling FK7 8EX	08701 977241		Budget Hotel		
The Golden Lion Hotel	8-10 King Street, Stirling FK8 1BD	01786 475351	★★★	Hotel		
The Portcullis	Castle Wynd, Stirling FK8 1AG	01786 472290	★★★	Inn		
The Whitehouse	13 Glasgow Road, Stirling FK7 0PA	01786 462636	★★★	Guest House		

by Stirling

Travelodge Stirling	Service Area, Pirnhall, by Stirling FK7 8EU	08719 846178	AWAITING GRADING		♿

Stonehaven

Heugh Hotel	Westfield Road, Stonehaven, Kincardineshire, AB39 2EE	01569 762379	★★★	Small Hotel	
Station Hotel	Arduthie Road, Stonehaven, Kincardineshire, AB39 2NE	01569 762277	★★	Inn	
The Belvedere Hotel	41 Evan Street, Stonehaven, Kincardineshire, AB39 2ET	01569 762672	★★	Small Hotel	
The Ship Inn	5 Shore Head, Stonehaven, Kincardineshire, AB39 2JY	01569 762 617	★★	Inn	
Woodside of Glasslaw	Stonehaven, Kincardineshire, AB39 3XQ	01569 763799	★★★	Guest House	

Stornoway, Isle of Lewis

Braighe House	20 Braighe Road, Stornoway, Isle Of Lewis, HS2 0BQ	01851 705287	★★★★★	Guest House	

♿ Unassisted wheelchair access   ♿ Assisted wheelchair access   🚶 Access for visitors with mobility difficulties
𝓟 Bronze Green Tourism Award   𝓟𝓟 Silver Green Tourism Award   𝓟𝓟𝓟 Gold Green Tourism Award
For further information on our Green Tourism Business Scheme please see page 9.

Cabarfeidh Hotel	Manor Park, Stornoway, Isle of Lewis, HS1 2EU	01851 702604	★★★	Hotel	
Caladh Inn	9 James Street, Stornoway, Isle of Lewis, HS1 2QN	01851 702740	★★	Hotel	
Hal-O The Wynd	2 Newton Street, Stornoway, Isle of Lewis, HS1 2RE	01851 706073	★★★	Guest House	
Hebridean Guest House	61 Bayhead, Stornoway, Isle of Lewis, HS1 2DZ	01851 702268	★★★	Guest House	
Holm View Guest House	18 Bhraighe Road,Branahuie, Stornoway, Isle of Lewis, HS2 0BQ	01851 706826	★★★★	Guest House	
Number Six	Memorial Avenue, Stornoway, Isle of Lewis, HS1 2QR	01851 703014	★★★★	Guest House	
Park Guest House	30 James Street, Stornoway, Isle of Lewis, HS1 2QN	01851 702485	AWAITING GRADING		
Royal Hotel	Cromwell Street, Stornoway, Isle of Lewis, HS1 2DG	01851 702109	★★	Hotel	

by Stornoway, Isle of Lewis

Galson Farm Guest House	South Galson, by Stornoway, Isle of Lewis, HS2 0SH	01851 850492	★★★★	Guest House	

Strachur

The Creggans Inn	Strachur, Argyll, PA27 8BX	01369 860279	★★★	Small Hotel	

Stranraer

Harbour Guest House	11 Market Street, Stranraer, Wigtownshire, DG9 7RF	01776 704626	★★★	Guest House	
Harbour Lights Guest House	7 Agnew Crescent, Stranraer, Wigtownshire, DG9 7JY	01776 706261	★★★	Guest House	
Ivy House & Ferry Link	London Road, Stranraer, Wigtownshire, DG9 8ER	01776 704176	★★★	Guest House	
North West Castle Hotel	Royal Crescent, Stranraer, Wigtownshire, DG9 8EH	01776 704413	★★★★	Hotel	
Torrs Warren Hotel	Stoneykirk, Stranraer, Dumfries & Galloway, DG9 9DH	01776 830204	★★★	Small Hotel	

Strathaven

Rissons at Springvale	18 Lethame Road, Strathaven, Lanarkshire, ML10 6AD	01357 521131	★★★	Restaurant with Rooms	↟
Strathaven Hotel	Hamilton Road, Strathaven, Lanarkshire, ML10 6SZ	01357 521778	★★★	Hotel	⌀

Strathdon

The Colquhonnie House Hotel	Strathdon, Aberdeenshire, AB36 8UN	01975 651210	★★★	Inn	⌀

Strathpeffer

Ben Wyvis Hotel	Strathpeffer, Ross-shire, IV14 9DN	01997 421323	★★★	Hotel	⌀
Garden House	Garden House Brae, Strathpeffer, Ross-shire, IV14 9BJ	01997 421242	★★★	Guest House	
Highland Hotel	Strathpeffer, Ross-shire, IV14 9AS	01997 421457	★★	Hotel	

by Strathpeffer

Coul House Hotel	Contin, by Strathpeffer, Ross-shire, IV14 9ES	01997 421487	★★★	Country House Hotel	

♿ Unassisted wheelchair access   ♿ Assisted wheelchair access   ↟ Access for visitors with mobility difficulties
⌀ Bronze Green Tourism Award   ⌀⌀ Silver Green Tourism Award   ⌀⌀⌀ Gold Green Tourism Award
For further information on our Green Tourism Business Scheme please see page 9.

Dromnan Guest House	Garve Road, Ullapool, Ross-shire, IV26 2SX	01854 612333	★★★★	Guest House	🚶
Eilean Donan Guest House	14 Market Street, Ullapool, Ross-shire, IV26 2XE	01854 612524	★★★	Guest House	
Point Cottage	22 West Shore Street, Ullapool, Ross-shire, IV26 2UR	01854 612494	★★★★	Guest House	
Riverside	Quay Street, Ullapool, Ross-shire, IV26 2UE	01854 612239	★★★	Guest House	
Strathmore Guest House	Morefield, Ullapool, Ross-shire, IV26 2TH	01854 612423	★★★	Guest House	
The Argyll Hotel	18 Argyll Street, Ullapool, Ross-shire, IV26 2UB	01854 612422	★★	Small Hotel	
The Ferry Boat Inn	Shore Street, Ullapool, Ross-Shire, IV26 2UJ	01854 612366	AWAITING GRADING		
Westlea Guest House	2 Market Street, Ullapool, Ross-shire, IV26 2XE	01854 612594	★★★★	Guest House	

Unst, Shetland

Buness House	Balta Sound, Unst, Shetland, ZE2 9DS	01957 711315	★★★★	Guest House

Uphall

Houstoun House Hotel	Uphall, West Lothian, EH52 6JS	01506 853831	★★★	Country House Hotel
Oatridge Hotel	2-4 Main Street, Uphall, Broxburn, West Lothian, EH52 5DA	01506 856 465	★★	Inn

Uplawmoor

Uplawmoor Hotel	66 Neilston Road, Uplawmoor, Renfrewshire, G78 4AF	01505 850565	★★★	Small Hotel	🍃🍃

Upper Largo

Monturpie Guest House	Monturpie, Upper Largo, Fife, KY8 5QS	01333 360254	★★★	Guest House

Virkie, Shetland

Sumburgh Hotel	Sumburgh, Virkie, Shetland, ZE3 9JN	01950 60201	★★★	Hotel

Walkerburn

The George Hotel	29 Galashiels Road, Walkerburn, Peeblesshire, EH43 6AF	01896 870336	★★	Inn
Windlestraw Lodge	Tweed Valley, Walkerburn, Peeblesshire, EH43 6AA	01896 870636	AWAITING GRADING	

Walls, Shetland

Burrastow House	Walls, Shetland, ZE2 9PD	01595 809307	★★★★	Guest House	♿

West Calder

Limefield House	West Calder, West Lothian, EH55 8QL	01506 871237	★★★	Guest Accommodation

West Wemyss

The Belvedere Hotel	Coxstool, West Wemyss, Fife, KY1 4SL	01592 654167	★★★	Small Hotel

Westhill

Aberdeen Westhill Premier Inn	Shepherds Rest, Stakis Road, Westhill, Aberdeenshire, AB32 6HF	0870 9906348		Budget Hotel

♿ Unassisted wheelchair access   ♿ Assisted wheelchair access   🚶 Access for visitors with mobility difficulties
🍃 Bronze Green Tourism Award   🍃🍃 Silver Green Tourism Award   🍃🍃🍃 Gold Green Tourism Award
For further information on our Green Tourism Business Scheme please see page 9.

| Holiday Inn Aberdeen West | Westhill Drive, Westhill, Aberdeen, Aberdeenshire, AB32 6TT | 01224 270300 | ★★★★ | Hotel | ♿ |
| Kilnhall | Strawberry Field Road, Westhill, Aberdeenshire, AB32 6TB | 01224 279640 | ★★★★ | Guest House | |

Westray, Orkney

| Cleaton House | Cleaton, Westray, Orkney, KW17 2DB | 01857 677508 | ★★★★ | Small Hotel | |

Whitburn

| Best Western Hilcroft Hotel | East Main Street, Whitburn, West Lothian, EH47 0JU | 01501 740818 | ★★★ | Hotel | ♿ |

Whitebridge

| Whitebridge Hotel | Whitebridge, Inverness-shire, IV2 6UN | 01456 486226 | ★★ | Small Hotel | |

Whiting Bay, Isle of Arran

Eden Lodge	Whiting Bay, Isle of Arran, KA27 8QH	01770 700357	★★	Inn	
Invermay	Shore Road, Whiting Bay, Isle of Arran, KA27 8PZ	01770 700431	★★	Guest House	
The Burlington	Shore Road, Whiting Bay, Isle of Arran, KA27 8PZ	01770 700255	★★★	Guest House	
Viewbank House	Golf Course Road, Whiting Bay, Isle of Arran, KA27 8QT	01770 700326	★★★	Guest House	

Wick

Mackays Hotel	46 Union Street, Wick, Caithness, KW1 5ED	01955 602323	★★★	Hotel	
Nethercliffe Hotel	Louisburgh Street, Wick, Caithness, KW1 4NS	01955 602044	★★★	Small Hotel	
Queens Hotel	16 Francis Street, Wick, Caithness, KW1 5PZ	01955 602992	★★	Small Hotel	

Wigtown

| Hillcrest House | Maidland Place, Station Road, Wigtown, Wigtownshire, DG8 9EU | 01988 402018 | ★★★ | Guest House | |
| Wigtown House | 19 Bank Street, Wigtown, Wigtownshire, DG8 9HR | 01988 402391 | ★★ | Guest House | |

Wishaw

| Herdshill Guest House | 224 Main Street, Bogside, Wishaw, Lanarkshire, ML2 8HA | 01698 381579 | ★★★ | Guest House | |

♿ Unassisted wheelchair access   ♿ Assisted wheelchair access   ⇡ Access for visitors with mobility difficulties
P Bronze Green Tourism Award   *PP* Silver Green Tourism Award   *PPP* Gold Green Tourism Award
For further information on our Green Tourism Business Scheme please see page 9.

278   To find out more, call 0845 22 55 121 or go to visitscotland.com

To find out more, call 0845 22 55 121 or go to visitscotland.com